The Price

The Price

R.S. Brown

ISBN-13: 9781537395159
ISBN-10: 1537395157

Preface

Four young children and their protective father try to endure and survive the mother's post-partum depression and anger until one fateful night. Everything changes when the mother is arrested for domestic violence after attacking the father in their home. Afterwards, the father says to their kids, "All I want for you is a happy mom," but he doesn't know that a happy mother will come at a cost.

This is a story of how a community, counselors, and courts have failed this family and how one father fights to stay connected to the only things that really matter...

...His children.

Introduction

For two years, I thought the concept of this book would be to act as a guide for others on how to emotionally survive divorcing someone with Borderline Personality Disorder, who's also obsessed with distortion campaigns and parental alienation campaigns. Once I started writing it, however, it became much more than that. Writing forced me to look back at who I used to be, and although I hardly recognize the person I was five years ago, I know I have to own up to those haunting choices for the rest of my life. At times during my failed marriage, I also took the wrong path, and though I have taken great strides to face those decisions head on, there is no doubt that I still have to put forth a considerable amount of time and effort to repair myself and the relationships with my four children. During these last three years, I have realized who my true friends are, those that sometimes surprised me with their trust, and a few more that I met and uncovered along the way. Conversely, I am grateful for the sifted out "friends" who weren't there for me when they heard of my troubles, both real and fabricated, and in the end, I am blessed with a small core of true friends I know I can rely on.

If I may ask one thing of the reader as they go through the chapters — please keep in mind that the nature of this book is to provide a sense of community and support for others divorcing someone who vilifies their name throughout their community and is obsessed in their determination to ruin their relationship with their children. Hopefully, hearing some of my experiences will provide others going through similar situations with a little comfort, knowing my family and I survived, and that ultimately, you are not alone. Most importantly to me, it may also serve as a guide on what to expect in the future, helping to lessen the blow if something similar to the recounts put forth here happen to you.

Acknowledgements

The last several years have been an almost impossible journey for everyone close to me. The seemingly constant barrage of lies, hate, and manipulations that my family and I have had to defend against, explain, and process has been all-consuming and has put us under an amount of stress and internal strife that is beyond my capability to put into words. To keep my sanity, and to reassure myself I wasn't the evil person I was made out to be, I had to study psychological disorders and learn terms and concepts most family counselors know little about.

I have a few friends — and only a few — who believe me, who believe in me, and most importantly, who have cared enough about me to hear my side and see through the torrent of propaganda. I am eternally grateful to those who have stood by me and offered their support, their words, and especially their ear as I tried to wade through all of the sadness and loss:

My friends, who were always there, never wavering.

My parents, who have provided their support in every way imaginable and have been a rock – a constant that I can always rely on.

My sister, with her incredible insight and ability to summarize complex ideas into the most focused of thoughts.

And to the most beautiful person — inside and out — I have ever met, my girlfriend, "Bobbie." She is a friend and lifelong partner who has had to endure everything along with me and she gladly chose to stand beside me and hold my hand through it all. Our respect and love for each other has grown exponentially through the strife and sorrow that's contained here — the mark of a true lady and confidant. She came into my life at the perfect time and in the perfect way and rescued me from despair and hopelessness. There isn't any way I can ever repay her, though I vow to always try.

I would also like to thank the authors of the two books I read that provided great insight and understanding into Borderline Personality Disorder and Parental Alienation. Paul T. Mason and Randi Kreger's book, *Stop Walking On Eggshells*, was so powerful and moving that often I could only read it in bits and pieces as I was nearly overcome with emotions from their profoundly accurate description of the woman I knew for 15 years. It was an invaluable resource to explain what my ex-wife was going through. *Divorce Casualties*, the definitive book on parental alienation, was exact in its description of the obsessed alienator. I give Dr. Darnall the highest compliment when I say that it has greatly changed how

I understand my children and how I parent them. It was an indispensable resource explaining what my children were going through. With these two books, I have gained what was once an unthinkable level of compassion and comprehension.

Explanation of Terms

To help clarify some of the terms in this book, here are a few that I have learned over the last three years.

Parental Alienation: When a parent says or does things to get their children to dislike or even hate the other parent.

"Obsessed alienators have a fervent cause: to destroy the targeted parent. They align the children to his or her side and together, with the children, campaign to destroy their relationship with the targeted parent. For the campaign to work, the obsessed alienator enmeshes the children's personalities and beliefs into their own. This is a process that takes time, but it is one that the children, especially the young, are completely helpless to combat. It usually begins well before the divorce is final. The obsessed parent is angry, bitter, or feels betrayed by the other parent." — Douglas Darnall, *Divorce Casualties*.

"The psychological manipulation of a child into showing unwarranted fear, disrespect or hostility towards a parent and/or other family members. It is a distinctive and widespread form of psychological abuse - towards both the child and the rejected family members - that occurs almost exclusively in association with family separation or divorce. Most commonly, the primary cause is a parent wishing to exclude another parent from the life of their child, but other family members or friends, as well as professionals involved with the family (including psychologists, lawyers and judges), may contribute significantly to the process. It often leads to the long-term, or even permanent, estrangement of a child from one parent and other family members and, as a particularly adverse childhood experience, results in significantly increased risks of both mental and physical illness for children." — Wikipedia.

<u>Borderline Personality Disorder:</u> Think of Mommy Dearest. People with this disorder are sometimes referred to as Borderlines.

"Borderline personality disorder (BPD) is a serious mental illness that centers on the inability to manage emotions effectively. Sometimes all relationships are affected, sometimes only one." — Borderlinepersonalitydisorder.com

"Characterized by inappropriate and intense rages and extreme difficulty controlling their anger. They frequently start physical fights and they are extremely quick to feel abandonment, even if it's only imagined. 'High-functioning' Borderlines are often described as charismatic, nice, and sociable outside their home and family members often think of Jekyll and Hyde when trying to describe their behaviors." — Psychcentral.com

"Because some people with severe BPD have brief psychotic episodes, experts originally thought of this illness as atypical, or borderline, versions of other mental disorders. While mental health experts now generally agree that the name 'borderline personality disorder' is misleading, a more accurate term does not exist yet." — ncbi.nlm.nih.gov

Distortion Campaigns: To drag a person's name through the mud in a series of lies and manipulations that have little, if any, truth to them. A staple of Borderlines.

"The intent is to destroy the target's reputation and thereby destroy the target's relationships with family and friends, employers, co-workers, doctors, teachers, therapists, and others. The intent may even be to force the target to leave the community, put the target in prison, or even kill the target. As with so many things involving Borderlines and their typical inability to understand or respect boundaries, there really are no limits. They will use basically any means available to them to cause damage to their target, including denigration, endless disparaging remarks, fabrication, false accusations, and even teaching others (including their children!) to lie on their behalf as part of their vilification campaign." — BPDFamily.com

Gaslighting: The attempt of one person to overwrite another person's reality. Another hallmark of Borderlines.

"A form of psychological abuse or brainwashing in which a victim is manipulated into doubting their own memory, perception and sanity. Instances may range from the denial by an abuser that previous abusive incidents ever occurred, up to the staging of bizarre events by the abuser with the intention of disorienting the victim." — Wikipedia.

"The gaslighter will most likely be highly skilled at covering their tracks and being a skilled master or mistress of deception." — Elephantjournal. com

<u>Psychological Projection:</u> Someone does something inconsiderate, malicious, or even evil and fiercely claims the targeted person did or said it. They back it up with manipulations (gaslighting and distortion campaigns) and occasionally flat-out lies.

"Attributing your own repressed thoughts or actions onto someone else." — Wikipedia.

Contents

Informational

All of the stories in The Price are true, though people's real names have been changed to protect their identity.

For further information, please visit RSBrownThePrice.com

A New Beginning

The first time I saw Betty in 1997, she was walking towards me in a stream of people at the military base we both worked at. I was talking to a friend of mine in the hall, and though it is very uncharacteristic of me to just gawk, I told Ron to stop talking so I could just watch this incredibly beautiful girl walk by — and though I tried not to stare or get caught looking, I couldn't help but to adore her. I said to Ron, "Did you see that face?! Who is that?!" Ron laughed and said, "That's the new optometry tech, everyone is talking about her." I could only blurt, "Jeeezuuus."

In the weeks leading up to seeing Betty walk down the hall, I was asked by my dad to sell a small private plane for his good friend Jack, who worked at the base and whose office was right across from the optometry room, where presumably Betty worked. Between my two jobs of flying and landscaping, and a slew of half-finished projects to finish, I'd procrastinated getting Jack's plane listed. But when I realized Jack's office was across from Betty's, I got cracking on selling Jack's plane. It worked just as I had wanted it to, as it seemed every time I went to Jack's office to update him on the status of the plane and if it had any offers, I saw Betty. We started to talk more and more and it was pretty clear she enjoyed talking to me, even seeming to flirt a little.

When Jack's plane sold, I went to his office one last time under the auspices of leaving him a note, but I was really hoping to see Betty — and I did. I asked her why she wasn't wearing a coat in the near-freezing weather and she responded that she didn't have a winter coat. I was wearing my leather flight jacket that she had previously said she liked a lot, so I offered it to her with the caveat that I would get it back in the spring. There, I had just insured she had to talk to me at some point in the future, as I knew that, without a reason, hanging around her office in that distant part of the base would be awkward. I could hardly wait.

A few months went by and it was time to go and reclaim my coat. When I did, we got to talking about her 21st birthday, which had just passed, and she said that her boyfriend had left her at home and went out with his friends till three in the morning. This was about the biggest open door I had ever seen, so I responded with, "Well, if you ever want to go out and celebrate, just let me know — I'll take you." She smiled and said she would like that. I called her a few days later and arranged to go out with a friend of mine so it seemed like less of a date to keep her conscious off any moral obligation to her boyfriend. The three of us had a great night and within a couple of days she had a new boyfriend.

Almost right away, we started spending all of our free time together, and because both of us had been quite lonely in the year before we started dating, we developed a close bond very quickly. I think it's fairly safe to say that in our first year, she fell completely in love with me, and though I cared about her — and loved her — I was not in love. In that first year, I drove her back and forth to her college when she had a foot surgery, I helped her buy her first car, I taught her how to ride a motorcycle, and we went on several trips. I tried to get that deep, in-love feeling, but it was fleeting. The last two long-term relationships I'd had were with extremely smart and intellectually challenging women — maybe too much so. Betty had great qualities, but a strong intellect was not one of them, and I made a mistake not uncommon to other couples — I stayed in the relationship because I was comfortable with her and uncomfortable with being single for a prolonged time again.

With the gift of hindsight, I now realize that I place a very high emphasis on time in a relationship, and the longer I am in one, the more value I put on staying in it. Most people can say that about themselves, but I seem to take it to an extreme. During the first year with Betty, I occasionally started to see a different side of her. She would get extremely angry and even go into a rage at issues I thought were very minor. Though I can't remember anything specific within our first year, I vividly remember in the Summer of 2000, I took her to a park about an hour away to have a romantic lunch and walk through the woods. Within minutes of getting there, I became quite sick and I told her I thought we should leave because I wasn't feeling well. She was disappointed and accused me of not wanting to be intimate with her. I repeatedly reassured her that I wanted to spend the afternoon with her in the park, but my stomach was turning and I just couldn't. We left, and as we started driving, she went from accusing me of not caring about our time together to full-blown yelling, "You don't love me!" Within minutes, and without any provocation, it escalated even further to Betty becoming so irate that she punched me in the eye as I was merging onto the interstate at 70 miles per hour. I stopped the car in the berm and yelled, "What the hell is wrong with you!? I am sick and don't feel I can go ten minutes without having to go to the bathroom, and you punch me in the face?!" Betty said, "You don't love me, you have never loved me, and you're always just making excuses to get out of doing things with me!"

I remember not believing what I had just heard and didn't even want to dignify it with a response. I just got back on the highway and, as would become common for us, we sat in complete silence for the rest of the drive home.

After we separated, I did some reading on personality disorders. From what I read in the book *Stop Walking on Eggshells*, Betty exhibits many of the traits of someone who is a "high functioning" person with border-line personality disorder. One of the traits of a high functioning border-line is to take very small slights against them and stew over them until they eventually explode. To quote *Stop Walking on Eggshells*: "They take meaningless little things and turn them into mountains of criticism, interrogation, and pain. They look for any cues that might reveal that the person they care about doesn't really love them and is about to desert them. Their rage is usually intense, unpredictable, and is unaffected by logical argument." Looking back on our time together, it becomes clear that this happened more than I cared to admit. My parents remind me of an incident in their driveway shortly after we became engaged, if I claim I didn't see how volatile she was before I married her. It was Christmas Eve in 2001, and I wanted to stay at my parents' house with my family and guests while Betty went to church with her family. There was no discus-sion or compromise with Betty — she would go straight to accusing and yelling to try to get her way. We were outside my parents' house with Betty screaming that I didn't love her and that I hated her family. These incidents were common enough that I had to be reminded of this spe-cific one by my mom some twelve years later. I only vaguely remember the screaming as this episode was drowned out by so many other con-tentious arguments. My mom said she could hear Betty from inside her house, and friends of my parents just getting out of their car obviously heard her. This couple in particular strongly questioned my parents about the viability of our upcoming marriage. My parents, no doubt, had their own concerns. Betty and I had our good times of course, or I wouldn't have stayed, but if I was ever going to be in a close relationship with her, these inexplicable outbursts would have to stop.

Rewinding just a few months, in the Fall of 2001, I was getting some pressure from Betty's mom and some light-hearted questioning from my parents about marriage and grandkids. I was 32 and I knew I wanted a son. It's not that I didn't want a daughter, but I knew I had to have a boy. Ideally, I would have a daughter second as that was the way I grew up with my younger sister. I guess I thought this had the benefit of the boy protecting the girl, though I should have known better; as kids, I teased and taunted my sister with a fervor very few people can relate to. The fact that Betty and I had been dating three and a half years made the decision of who to marry and have kids with obvious. I committed myself to the classic delusion of marrying someone whom I wasn't head-over-heels in love with — hoping that we would grow closer, that it would be good enough, or that they would change into the person that I could feel that way about.

We married in May of 2002, just three weeks after I had been furloughed as a pilot from Delta Air Lines and gone back to being on call for my military unit to fly post-911 support missions from home. These 45-day military assignments came and went, and to find more a more steady paycheck, Betty and I both picked up temporary assignments at Andrews Air Force Base in Washington D.C. It was an unstable time and we didn't know how long the military work would last, but we decided in mid-October to start a family anyway. She was pregnant within a week.

THE RISE AND FALL

It was obvious almost right away that Betty was very different when she was pregnant. She was happy, content, and far more sensual than she was while we were dating. When I was going to be deployed for an indefinite time at the start of Gulf War II, she was five months pregnant and took it all in stride, which was very uncharacteristic of her before she became pregnant. She had our parents and supportive neighbors to help her get the house ready and who could be there within minutes if anything urgent came about before I returned home, but she was confident and just had a reassurance about her that I wasn't used to. I ended up returning home from the deployment in mid-May, about six weeks before our first child would be born. In late June, Betty had a bad rash from the pregnancy and the doctors were concerned enough to talk about inducing her. She was at peace with whatever the doctors wanted to do and seemed to accept that mother nature was in charge and everything would turn out fine. She was a happy, young, and beautiful pregnant woman. In hindsight, I wish I would have done more to let her know I felt that way. Though not cold and distant, I was not the warm, romantic type — I didn't buy flowers or always tell her the things I should have.

Stephen was born with much fanfare, as he was the very first grandchild on my family's side. I had my boy, my parents had a grandson, my sister had a nephew, and my grandparents had a great-grandson. It was an incredibly joyous time — for two days. When I brought Betty and Stephen home, I carried Stephen in his car seat and helped Betty up the sidewalk. We got settled in and, as is natural with any newborn, people wanted to come over and see our new addition. But Betty was tired and wasn't up for it for the first few days, and any visitors from my family clearly stressed her out. After my mom came over the evening Stephen came home, she told me not to let anyone else in the house. Over the next several weeks, I tried to be understanding, but what I couldn't understand was why her family had an open door and my family didn't. It became increasingly harder to tell my family, including my aunts and uncles, that Betty was still tired and any visits would have to wait.

Around a week after Stephen was born, I told my aunt and cousin they could come over to see the baby, but their visit distressed Betty and we had a big argument about it immediately after they left. Frustrated, I asked her, "Why can't my family come over and see Stephen?" Betty shot back, "I'm tired and I don't feel like having visitors! Why don't you try having a f---ing baby!" I asked, "How long do I have to keep telling people they can't see Stephen? It's getting weird!" Betty didn't say anything, she just went back downstairs and sat on the couch, which she hardly moved from except to go to bed at night. I tried my best to take into consideration that she was the one getting up to breast-feed Stephen and that I got to sleep through most of the night — she needed the downtime and naps. The evening we had this argument, my parents came over to see Stephen and I remember taking a picture of my mom holding Stephen as she said, "He is just the sweetest baby!" Stephen looked up at her with his big blue eyes and I looked over at Betty, standing at the top of the game room stairs, glaring at me as if I had better do something about my parents being there. It was frustrating that her family, but not mine, was welcome to come and go as they pleased.

I wish I could say that we found a routine that worked for us, that Betty became comfortable and happy in motherhood, that we could proudly show off our beautiful boy, but I was concerned that Betty would embarrass me as she seemed to stop caring what my parents thought about her demeanor and her growing depression. I have to admit that I was not adjusting well to this new dynamic of the near-constant needs of an infant combined with Betty's anger and depression. One night I blurted, "I want my life back." I quickly realized it was just extreme frustration, making it sound like I would trade our beautiful baby boy for our simpler life of just three weeks prior. Of course I wouldn't, but Betty heard those words and it drove an even bigger wedge between us that only seemed to grow with every passing day. For the next five months, the only time we had any sense of normalcy is when we stepped out of the house and into the public eye, when Betty would seem to put it all behind her — she'd smile and laugh, and proudly show off Stephen like we were a normal family. I knew we weren't normal — still, I gladly took the breather from the contentious relations at home. I tried to enjoy the countless people who admired our son and his eyes — eyes that were so incredibly big and blue that, during a walk, a lady on the other side of the street said to her friend, "Oh my God, look at that baby's eyes!" It was a common reaction, and Betty enjoyed the accolades as much as I did. I had hoped that her big smiles and laughs would continue once we'd returned to the house and I could stop walking on eggshells around her, but she would revert to the person I didn't know nor cared to be around as soon as we walked through the door. I didn't fully realize this until nine years later, but the house was a prison to her, and if I could do a few things over again, one would be to get her out of it a lot more.

Six months after Stephen was born, Betty was not only hostile, but aggressive and looked to pick fights with me. I still vividly remember coming home one night with Betty screaming at the top of her lungs at me as I took Stephen, bundled in his little car-carrier, from the cold garage into our game room. He was crying and I raised my voice at her and said, "Stop! Just stop! You are scaring him; he knows something is very wrong!" I had hoped she would realize that she was upsetting our helpless baby, but it just made things worse and she continued to yell even louder. I called my mom to the house that night, hoping that my mom's presence and help would calm Betty. After months of seeing us grow apart, and seeing the tension when she walked in, she said, "Well, isn't this a happy home." She wasn't being snide — she said it with a tone of disappointment that I knew was about the environment in which we were raising Stephen in his most formative time and his welfare was already becoming a concern of hers.

It was also around this time that I first started seeing scratches and redness across Stephen's face when I came home from work — some of which I still have pictures of as a grim reminder. They weren't deep or frequent, but I was, of course, concerned. Betty would blame Stephen's two-and-a-half-year-old cousin, whom he was around quite a bit at Betty's parents' house. I believed it because it seemed plausible at the time. I was trying not to upset Betty even more, and I probably didn't want to face the truth, but I had my suspicions. I now know that it was in fear of Betty's outbursts that I choose to not confront her more and I look back with extreme regret and a realization that I was a coward for not being more proactive and intervening.

Betty's mother was a huge influence in her life — far more so than in your typical mother-daughter relationship. The problem with that is that Pat is a very angry person, but she hides it well. It was clear, even then, that I could never live up to her expectations and Pat looked at me much like she looked at Betty's father — no matter what I did, it wouldn't be good enough. When Betty and Pat took Stephen to Branson, Missouri, and I chose to stay home and work at the base and on our house, which had every piece of drywall off the game room walls, Pat came back and, without even saying as much as hello, yelled at my mom. "When is your son going to take some responsibility for this baby!" she said. My mom didn't say anything, she just thought, "He's working on their house and he's making money working at the base, he never sits! What more do you want him to do?" Pat fostered much of the hostility in our house, whether directly or indirectly, and if Betty was ever going to accept me as a husband and father, Pat would have to be on board with it.

By February of 2004, Betty was pregnant again. It was a bit of a surprise to me; to say we weren't close anymore would be a gross understatement as lack of intimacy wasn't measured in days or even weeks, but months. I remember her standing at the top of the half-flight of stairs telling me the news after coming out of the bathroom, and she was smiling ear-to-ear. I guess I thought a second child, possibly a baby girl, could be what she was missing because she seemed, in that moment, to be genuinely happy again. At the ultrasound, when we learned that it would be a girl, she laughed and looked at me, clapping her hands as she literally bounced up and down in her chair and said, "Yay." There was still a little bit of tension and stress during her second pregnancy, but that was to be expected, seeing as how we had one infant, another on the way, and a bunch of big unfinished house projects — not to mention that I still hadn't been called back to my full time job at Delta. But things now seemed back to normal for a young, growing family and I was optimistic for our future.

Betty delivered Julie on a crisp and beautiful fall morning. After all the admiration and ogeling over our first daughter, she was tired from being up most of the night and wanted to get a nap. I guess I thought that having babies was now just a walk in the park for us, because while Betty and Julie napped, I actually went to the base for a couple of hours to spread the news (and cigars) and get a few things done. When I returned a few hours later, the scene at the hospital was a repeat of fifteen months earlier when Stephen was born — our families laughing and talking loudly and wearing huge smiles as they stared at our new baby girl. One of my favorite things about being in the hospital quickly became watching everyone press their faces up against the glass to admire Julie, wondering just what lie ahead for her over the next ninety years, and waiting so patiently for her to move just the slightest amount to show that she was alive and well. Two days later, I brought Julie and Betty home from the hospital in our new made-for-a-growing-family minivan. Seeing Julie and Stephen in their car seats side-by-side in the middle of the van hit me funny and I remember telling myself, "I hope you're ready for this level of responsibility. They are yours — completely helpless and dependent on you and they deserve the very best you can provide." I was up to the task, but as parents we want to be our very best every minute for our children.

Within a day of coming home, the cycle of postpartum anger and depression started to repeat itself and we picked up right where we had left off just nine months before. Betty was sad, angry, lonely, and depressed. I started to vigorously defend myself now and tried to stop any escalation or future aggression by becoming as loud and angry as she was. I strongly identify with numbers, and to put it in that context, if she came at me at a level of four, I would give her the same attitude or tone of disrespect at a four. Betty then would make it an eight and I would too. She would then come at me at a sixteen, at which point I would usually just remove myself from the house, doing yard work or running errands until we both cooled off. Again, outside the house, we appeared normal and happy, though we were both extremely unhappy and miserable inside our house and inside ourselves almost all of the time.

This went on for nine months until she became pregnant again in late July of 2005. During those nine months, I had decided, against my dad's suggestion and against Betty's repeated requests, to leave Delta for Southern Airlines. It was far more than just switching companies though, as I had to go to Dallas for three weeks and pay for the 737 qualification myself before I could even be considered for an interview. Between that cost and lost work, it added up to at least two months of military pay at a time where finances were tight due to Betty being a stay-at-home mom and only able to work at the base one weekend a month, my projects renovating our 45-year-old home, and the fact that I had been furloughed from Delta and hadn't had a full time job in over two years.

By August of 2005, the happy hormones generated by her pregnancy were clearly flowing through her and all was well, though this time I knew the clock on Mr. Hyde turning into Dr. Jekyll was ticking down and her due date, in late March of 2006, was not something I looked forward to.

The emotional and apparent hormonal cycle repeated, just like after the first two kids, and again, it got even worse. The fighting reached levels of 32 and even 64 with her now punching me and throwing things at me. I wish I could remember how the argument started, but late one night she threw her wedding rings across our bedroom and immediately tried to scratch me with both of her hands. When I grabbed her upper arms to stop her, she started screaming and yelled, "Let go of me!" like I was the aggressor. "Only if you don't scratch me!" I yelled as I tightened my grip on her arms and glared into her eyes. She glared back at me, but then relaxed her arms, which I took as "Okay," so I let go.

Now the phone was ringing, which was odd at midnight. It was from a blocked number and no one answered it when I tried to pick up. I figured the call was from our next door neighbors, whom I had known for fifteen years, and it was probably their way of getting us to stop screaming. Betty and I were still on the upstairs landing when I hung up and started walking down the stairs. I heard a rattle and her grunt and when I turned around, the office chair had just started coming down the stairs at me. I still remember the sound of the chair's wheels clanking as it tumbled and I jumped to the side. The chair glanced off of me and hit the wall between the kids' rooms. Pointing at the gouges in the wall, I sarcastically asked her, "Are you going to fix that, or am I going to have to do it?" I, of course, would be the one that had to fix the wall, but the question really meant, "How long do I have to cover up for you inside and outside of our house?"

After she turned around and went back into our room, I took my dad's advice of just leaving the house to temporarily get away from her. When I told her I was leaving and spending the night at a hotel, she said, "Go ahead, I'll call the cops and tell them someone stole my car!" In light of that threat, I walked around our street a few times to allow both of us to calm down and I then slept on the game room couch. It wouldn't dawn on me until years after we separated, but threatening to call the police if I left highlights the fact that Betty didn't want me to be able to get away from her — I was the outlet for her anger and it was now my role in life to just take it. To this day, she still feels that way.

Just a few days after this incident, it was drill weekend at the base and I saw Betty's immediate supervisor, Marylee. When she saw me, she said, "Oh my God! Betty brought your kids out here again a few days ago and you two make the most beautiful children! And you are so happy! You are like the model family, perfect! Are you going to have any more of those beautiful babies?! You'd better, because the world needs more of those!" What was I to say? Everyone at the base, without exception, really liked Betty and if I did try to let the cat out of the bag, I would've been dismissed as a lunatic. Of course, I also protected Betty's image because she was my wife and it would have been inappropriate and extremely embarrassing to tell her supervisor, but it was also a bit self-serving too. I always thought Betty could use her widespread popularity at the base to eventually get a full-time job when the kids were in grade school. I don't remember what I said to Marylee, but I know from the countless times she had nothing but praise for our "perfect family" that it would've been hard for me to respond — I couldn't say anything truthful about our family's happiness, and I didn't like bragging about how beautiful my kids were.

Still in the Summer of 2006, I was driving all of us to our community drive-in movie theater and Betty punched me in the eye right in front of our three kids during a senseless argument; a hammer-fist just like she had done six years prior. Another note-worthy argument weeks later ended abruptly and left me stunned — not an easy task anymore.

There was a well-publicized story about Andrea Yates, who had just been found innocent in the murder of her five kids (by reason of insanity) after drowning them in a bathtub in her Houston home in 2001. Betty watched the news of it in the game room that evening while I came in and out from working on the deck just outside the sliding glass door. We got into an argument that night and it ended when she walked halfway up the game room steps, turned around, and in a cold, reassured tone said, "I'm just going to kill us all." Knowing what she had just watched and realizing that she probably thought she could get away with it like Andrea Yates did, I asked, "Do you know what you just said?!" It has been ten years since this happened, but Betty's look of determination is burned into my mind forever as she responded, "We'd all be better off." She then turned and walked up the steps and I was left to wonder what would happen the rest of the night while we slept.

One of the more regretful consequences of all the stress I was under was that I wasn't emotionally available for anyone who may have needed me. Normally, I am extremely compassionate, yet when one of my best friends, Norm, was going through a divorce that left him in shambles during this time, I didn't make an effort to meet up with him or even call just to get his mind off of his very obvious pain — only seeing him when he made the effort. He is one of just a few life-long friends who is incredibly forgiving and understanding, but I felt it was very selfish of me regardless of my circumstances and years later I would feel a strong compulsion to apologize and make amends to him.

It's important to note, in the midst of all this darkness, that it wasn't all doom and gloom within our family. We went on the occasional trip, including going to the beach once a year, and again, the time outside our home was usually pleasant, or at least looked normal. At home, we ate out a lot and that became almost a staple — Betty was pleasant in public, I got to talk and interact with our captive kids at the table, and there wasn't a stress-inducing mess to clean up. I also started to develop a very close bond with our baby, Noel, who I would call "crazy baby" because of her very funny personality and the fact that she always seemed so excited to see me. I enjoyed our three kids immensely, playing with them and getting as much video of their time as babies and toddlers as my schedule would allow. When I watch the videos of this time now, I am reminded of these fleeting moments of normalcy and I wish beyond words that I would have done more to try to find ways to give them a normal childhood.

The arguing was taking a big toll on me. One of the ways the stress manifested itself was an inability to sleep. In what has to be the most unpredictable thing I could have chosen to do, I started drinking to escape and to help me sleep. Unpredictable because I could count on two hands the number of times I drank alcohol before I was in my thirties, always having had a great respect for how society looked down on heavy drinkers (I didn't drink often, but when I did, I liked the "buzzed" feeling). In 2001, I read three reports within weeks of each other on how one or two glasses of red wine a day was found to have health benefits. The last report was from Princeton, and I thought that fact alone lent the findings enough credibility to believe in it. At the time, I took three or four different supplements as I have always wanted to stay healthy as I aged, and red wine seemed to be a supplement whose benefits outweighed the fact that I dreaded the taste of it. I had to choke down one glass of Franzia boxed wine each night, but I stuck with it — and it would eventually stick to me.

Now immersed back in the arguing after Noel was born in 2006, I still remember the first time I went downstairs to have a second glass to fall asleep. I laid in the spare room bed, as sleeping in different rooms became routine after our frequent arguments. I was stewing over that night's argument when I started thinking about alcohol as a sedative, instead of a supplement, and I was desperate to fall asleep. I viewed my restlessness as another victory for her in this escalating power struggle between us, and damn it, I would show her she couldn't get to me like that. The problem was the alcohol worked, and the well-known fact that the body builds up an alcohol tolerance happened to me as I resorted to the wine more and more to fall asleep. Within months, that second glass became four or five to put me to sleep. It didn't help matters that I had acquired a taste for red wine over those five years and now I was actually quite fond of the distinctive tastes and aromas of inexpensive, but clearly better, bottled wines.

There was one other escape for me besides alcohol: photography. It served the purpose of capturing my kids' childhood, something of utmost importance to me to preserve since early on in Betty's first pregnancy. Now late 2006, Stephen was in preschool and doing things, such as a Christmas concert, that I videoed and played over and over again for him in the hopes of convincing him — and myself — that we were a normal family just going through some growing pains. Looking back, I really knew better, but I didn't know what else to do at the time.

Now 2007, it was more of the same contentious pins-and-needles living inside our home and a happy facade on the outside. The most memorable issue that year was our trip to Disney World. I first told Betty early that year that I wanted to take the kids to Disney World in the fall, when the weather was cooler, and it wasn't as crowded. Right away, she got her mother, Pat, involved and within a week, her whole family and some of mine were going. Parents, brothers, sisters, cousins, grandparents, aunts and uncles — around twenty-five people in all. And it was going to be over the summer, not the fall. When Betty invited my parents and my sister and her boyfriend Mark, she said, "You should go with us, it will be fun!" Because of some of the things that had happened, my parents hesitated, not wanting to add to Betty's stress, but she insisted that it would be a great time. I strongly disagreed with these new plans because of the heat and having three very young kids with us, but the more I tried to convince her, the more she dug in. Despite the trip being my idea, which I reminded her of, she became extremely angry if I said one word about the timing of it and she accused me of not wanting to be around her family — an accusation I heard anytime I declined to do anything with her family regardless of why. She would repeatedly say to me, "Well, the kids and I are going over the summer whether you go or not!" At this point, I gave up, hoping I would be wrong about the weather and lines. In a prelude for what was to come on the vacation, she had been incredibly volatile, even by her standards, for the week or two before we left.

As we toured the park the first day, I first heard the phrase "walking on eggshells" from my mother, who had decided to come down with my dad when I gave up all hope for a trip with just Betty and the kids. This trip was significant for my parents because, for the first time, they saw how Betty showed little regard for our kids' welfare — she wasn't just a young mother who was angry with her husband. Problems surfaced over the first few days when she became so caught up with seeing as much of the park as possible that our kids were beyond exhausted, and their behavior and actions showed it. Early mornings and late nights with very little stopping during the day and very little time to eat was the only schedule she knew.

On the third day, we went to a show that turned out to be very loud and there were large, scary characters that, as we sat in the front row, seemed to come out at us from the stage. Stephen started screaming at the top of his lungs and my dad and I wanted to take him out, but Betty said, "No! He'll be fine!" and her face told both of us there would be a heavy price to pay if we did. My dad became more insistent and Betty became furious. After the show, she said to him some of the worst things you can say to someone — things he still won't tell me to this day, even for the purposes of writing this book. I wasn't there, but his mother was, and my parents had to convince my grandmother to stay in Orlando instead of going back home to Pittsburgh afterwards. In the afternoon that day, I remember laying fifteen-month-old Noel in her stroller and she actually appeared to fall asleep before her head was on the backrest. My aunt Audrey and her husband Frank, who have a house in Orlando, decided to join us for the day. Frank noticed Noel falling asleep and said, "Did you see that? I've never seen anything like that! She was asleep before she was even laying down!" Eventually, I lashed out at Betty, telling her how ridiculous she was being and that our kids were miserable and exhausted. She became enraged, yelling at me in the very crowded park for trying to budget time for our kids to get a nap. People all around us were staring. I thought, "We could be on a Jerry Springer episode." Determined to do what was right for our kids, I picked up Stephen, who seemed the most tired, and told her, "I am taking Stephen back for a nap and we will come back when I think you have settled down." About fifteen minutes later, while Stephen and I were walking towards our rental car after getting off of the monorail, I noticed a policeman running towards me, motioning and yelling for me to stop. He was speaking into a walkie-talkie and he looked very concerned as he pointed at Stephen and, when he approached us, asked, "A boy who fits his description was reported missing; do you know this child?!" Completely taken aback, I said, "Yes, he is my son." The officer looked confused and skeptical when he continued, "Is his name Stephen?" I said "Yes." He continued, "And what is your name?" I said, "Rob. He and I have the same name — his first name is Rob, but he goes by his middle name of Stephen." His glare became a look of perplexion and he said in a more calm tone, "And he is your son? Do you have any ID?" I said "Sure," and I produced my driver's license. He looked at it very closely before declaring, "Looks legitimate to me." During the inspection, Stephen reached up and grabbed my hand, which the officer quickly took note of. After I was handed my license back, he looked at Stephen and asked, "So this is your dad?" and Stephen looked at him and vigorously nodded his head while squeezing my hand. We just stood there for a couple of seconds in awkward silence before I tried to offer an explanation, "I'm sorry, but my wife is absolutely crazy sometimes; I don't know what is wrong with her. She has been in a rage and I told her he was exhausted and I was going to take him back to the room to get a nap." The officer looked at me in disbelief, most likely because

Betty had called and reported her son missing when she knew he was with me. He finally said, "Okay, you can go," and I took Stephen to the hotel for a nap as I intended. I met back up with my parents a bit later, wanting their help if she decided to do or say anything hostile. My mom then told me about a call she had just gotten from Betty, where she said, "You will never see your grandkids ever again!"

When we eventually met up with Betty, she looked at me with a face that said it all: "Don't even think of confronting me, or you will regret it for the rest of your life!" — and, in weighing how much my kids, my parents, and I were already enduring, I wisely elected to move on and battle another day.

When I look at the pictures taken that morning of us at the Mickey Mouse breakfast, just hours before I would be stopped for abducting my own son, the kids look tired, but we look genuinely happy — what a farce, nothing could be further from the truth. It disgusted me. The rest of our trip wore on, almost as miserable as that day. My parents and I went home shell-shocked, trying to figure out what happened and what went wrong.

There was one bright spot in our trip; in what has to be the closest thing to a miracle I will ever be a part of, we conceived Christian the night I supposedly abducted Stephen. I remember Betty initiated the intimacy that night, which was extremely rare for her during our entire time together and never happened after Stephen was born, so I thought it must have been her way of trying to get me to forget about the call to the police. This, and the fact that our intimacy was rare, made the date of conception easy to figure out.

Now pregnant again, her good hormones were flowing, but not like the previous three times. She wasn't happy so much as she was less-angry. We tried some counseling, but it was doomed to fail when I pleaded with the mid-50's woman to address my biggest issue with Betty, and that was her lying and variations of lying — manipulating, in other words. The counselor's disappointing response was, "That is not important," and it ended after three appointments.

One thing I started to notice more of was Betty's resentment of any of my achievements and a jealousy towards both my mother and I that I couldn't explain. For instance, I had worked hard for five years to get my black belt in a very disciplined martial art, and her response was always, "That is a complete waste of time." She wouldn't even entertain the thought of going to my test. Big renovation projects around the house that turned out better than expected were never good enough for her or done fast enough. I believe Betty was jealous of my mom because my mom is attractive, has a good job, excels at her sport of tennis, has a lot of friends, is extremely well respected, is a good cook, and most divergent from Betty, is a great mother (and grandmother). Betty was, and still is, very attractive, but she doesn't have any of the other attributes my mother has. Out of pure jealousy, Betty would often lash out at my mom, even when it was completely unjustified. One night while I was on a trip, my mom cooked dinner for Betty and the kids. My mom started talking about how grateful she was for all of the good things in her life, especially our kids. Even though Betty was about to eat a dinner that my mom had prepared, she became confrontational and said in a barbed, raised voice, "My mom and I think you're a phony; nobody can be that happy and nice!" My mom let it slide and realized that was just Betty. It didn't bother her much as long as she got to see her grandkids. A couple of days later, Betty then said to her, "My mom and I are extremely jealous people," as if this was supposed to be a satisfactory explanation for her hostile remarks. True to Betty's behavior of the last ten years, she rarely said she was sorry for her frequent outbursts.

This is the Betty we lived with though; never happy for the gifts of our beautiful, healthy children, and incredibly unappreciative of what was provided for her by both my parents and me. My mom and dad note that Betty never once in our fifteen years together asked how they were or if there was anything she could do to help them, since they helped her so much. It was all about Betty and what she needed and getting away from the kids, while she got to vent about how hard her life was, or who was doing her wrong. Unbeknownst to me until we separated, many of my parents' friends and neighbors referred to her as "The Princess" because they saw this and her sense of entitlement. My mom's friends would tell her, "She's using you," and my mom had a great response: "I like being used like that because I get to spend time with the kids." It didn't help that Betty wasn't very involved with our kids, only begrudgingly shuffling them to their activities and complaining about what an effort it was to do so, while being very vocal about all of the better things she could do with her time. My parents' friends knew she worked only two days a month at the base, and that she viewed the time there as more of a weekend getaway with friends and a getaway from her kids, than as a job. I had hoped during all of this time that it was just a phase and she would eventually return to the person that I had married — content and wanting to contribute to our family's finances. I knew it had to still be in her somewhere.

Christian was born in the spring of 2008. Less than five minutes after he came into the world, I asked the doctor, whom we knew fairly well, to join me in an empty room just across the hall. I pleaded with her to talk to Betty about going on medication for what I believed to be, "moderate to severe postpartum depression." The doctor sensed my great concern and fear when I said, "Doc you MUST talk to Betty. In thirty-six hours, I am going to have a monster on my hands!" Dr. Cirrilli asked, "She's that bad?" I said, "Really bad, and she won't listen to me — she's likely to do the opposite of anything I suggest to fix it. Can you please talk to her, but be very careful in how you word it? Don't sound like it is her fault at all, make it sound like her depression is normal or even expected or she won't go for any of it." Dr. Cirrilli looked concerned and said, "Sure, let me see what I can do and I will be very careful." I tried to convey the seriousness of the situation one more time by saying, "Please, we can't live like this anymore." I saw this as a chance to get Betty some help from a professional, and in hindsight, it was really the first time I had disclosed to anyone that Betty wasn't the person she pretended to be while outside our home. To keep any embarrassment to a bare minimum, Betty went on, in her words, "a very low dose" of an anti-depressant.

Despite the anti-depressant, after Christian was born, Betty picked right back up from where she'd been nine months ago. I was also seeing more bruises and scratches on Stephen and sometimes Julie too. In one of the more egregious times of seeing the signs of physical abuse, I came home from a trip in late June and Stephen had deep bruises and some scratches over most of the left side of his face and neck. I asked Betty what happened, and I got the usual, "He was playing with his cousins." But his face didn't look like it had been caused by careless play — a lot of the deeper bruising and scratches were in the shape of a hand with its fingers spread slightly apart, so I skeptically asked, "I don't think any kid did that, what is going on?!" She got defensive and angrily repeated the cousin excuse and walked away. My parents' neighbor, Christine, questioned me days later, asking me if I knew how Stephen got them. By this time, it had occurred to me what was really happening. I repeated the lie that a cousin did it to Christine to protect Betty, something I regretfully would start doing more and more to avoid the embarrassment of owning up to a secretly angry, depressed wife.

One of the ways I was starting to avoid Betty was to work overtime and I relied on my mom more and more to make sure the kids were okay. I have the perfect job to use to get away, and I started taking advantage of it by picking up extra trips on top of my regular schedule. Instead of working the normal twelve or thirteen days a month, I was now working eighteen to twenty. The local newspaper wrote an article on me, featuring people with interesting jobs. I guess being a pilot in the military and with an airline fulfilled that requirement. In the article, I'm quoted as saying that I miss my family, but once I'm off to work, it's "Woohoo!" What is buried in that remark is how happy I was to get away from Betty. I was so intent on getting away from our caustic atmosphere at home, that 45 minutes after my vasectomy, I was on an airplane going to work.

I greatly missed the kids, but I also missed adult interaction and any interaction with Betty was risking too much. Our overnights at work are fun and there is a lot of socializing amongst the crews that filled a big, gaping hole in my life. The party atmosphere prevalent on overnights at this time only exasperated my addiction to drinking though, as I could drink almost as much as I wanted (up to the FAA mandated eight hours before reporting to the airplane) without Betty knowing. This atmosphere also led to two affairs in 2006 and 2007, each lasting around six months — something I never thought I'd be capable of. The two coworkers had similar situations at home where they couldn't talk to their spouses for fear of being ignored, belittled, or yelled at, despite their husbands being nice to everyone else around them. We talked, vented, and bonded over our similarities and sought the human interaction and respect we all crave. I remember on the flight home, after I met the first one, thinking that I'd walk in the door and it would be written all over my face, or that the guilt would be too much for me and I would confess my indiscretion. When I walked through the front door after being gone for four days, Betty was standing right there in the kitchen and she immediately turned her back to me without saying a word. I coldly thought, "Oh well, you deserve it." This was significant to me because I have always, to a fault even, been a one-woman man. "Is this how bad it is? I can cheat and not have any remorse?!" I thought. The answer was a pensive "Yes." Both affairs ended mutually and respectfully when the obstacle of living on near opposite ends of the country became too much.

In the fall of 2008, Betty started talking about needing a bigger house. I had just spent the last seven years rebuilding and remodeling our current 1,900 sq/ft house to exactly the way we wanted it and moving was the last thing I wanted to, so I questioned why, after all this work, was this a good time to upsize. She would say that she needed more space to "get away from the kids" and it was hard not to think that this might be what she needed. I knew being stuck in that house with no real play area for the kids was a big part of the problem and it was hard not to think more space was the way out of our unhappiness. After all, it was only at home that she was angry and depressed. I tried to postpone the decision to look for a bigger house for as long as possible because I knew leaving that house after I had just remodeled it myself from top to bottom would be very hard for me. But the question of "What is best for our kids and family in the long term?" flew through my head every time I gave it any thought and we started looking for houses in my parents' neighborhood.

In late 2008, the stress in my life became too much for me and I started drinking significantly more. The withdrawal symptoms and yearning for a drink was almost as impairing as having several glasses of wine in me now. In desperation to save my family and get Betty the help she needed, I tried to reduce our marital discord (and my stress-caused drinking) by appealing to Pat about her daughter's postpartum depression one night. The possibility of Betty's vaunted role model helping me to get her to finally admit she at least didn't feel right seemed very unlikely, but it was my last resort. We drove over under the pretense of just visiting, but when we got there, I had the kids go upstairs while Pat, Betty, and I stood in the laundry room. Pat refused to believe what I had to say about Betty and it became heated when I said, "Pat! She is out of control! She attacks me, she attacks the kids — both verbally and physically! I know you've seen the kids' bruises and scratches, those are hers!" Pat shot back, "Rob! You are the problem! You drink and don't help her with the kids at all! She does all the work; everything for the kids, while you just do whatever the hell you want!"

With that, I knew three things: 1. Pat believed Betty's version that she's the care-taker for the kids and I didn't care one bit about them. 2. Pat looked at me the way she looked at her husband Dale; only good for making money and nothing I did would ever be good enough for her daughter or grandkids. 3. I was not going to be able to recruit Pat no matter what, and, without Betty's admission to a problem, our future was very, very bleak. In a laughable end to the discussion, as we were leaving, Pat had the audacity to say to me, "If you ever need anything, I mean anything, you just come and talk to me. Okay?"

My downward spiral did not go unnoticed by my superiors in the military, as they saw me arriving late to work for a few ground-based tasks and I once slept in on an overnight assignment when I was supposed to greet a General at his airplane. Right after that, a colleague of mine, Steve, took me into a room and said with great disappointment, "Unbelievable Rob, what the hell is going on with you?" I just looked at him, not knowing what to say as I didn't want to lie. How could I tell him that I had become addicted to alcohol and that Betty was extremely angry and depressed when all he knew was that I didn't drink and that Betty was very well liked on the base?! His anger and frustration turned to compassion and he asked me, "Are you okay?" I responded that my life was too hectic be-tween both flying jobs and four young kids at home and that I should think about getting a minimum time Cat E job in the military until I reached my twenty years for retirement. He liked that I recognized my perceived prob-lem, and agreed that some big changes needed to be made.

Though Steve was an indirect supervisor, he was not in my direct chain-of-command and I felt the weight of my two direct commanders' eyes upon me. I preempted a discussion about my performance with them by requesting separate meetings, and I repeated the excuse that I had given to Steve. Both were extremely supportive and encouraged me to do what was right for Betty, my kids, and myself and I fondly reflect on those talks with nothing but respect for their tone, words, and compas-sion. In the end, it took me almost a year to finally get out of the flying aspect of the military, a year that wasn't much better, but my commanders knew I was taking strides to get out and that must have appeased them enough to let the smaller infractions slide.

In an odd contrast to others with alcohol problems, I was working out harder than ever to try and dampen the increasingly powerful and debilitating withdrawal symptoms. Because of my busy work schedule, my karate instructor gave me the key to his Do Jung and I would go there after hours and punch and kick the wood plank mounted on the wall and the heavy punching bag with a vigor and determination few have ever had. As I hit them, I would yell, "Take that alcohol!! Leave me the f--k alone!!" along with other gasps of desperation as I viewed the bag as my addiction that I so, so desperately wanted to be stronger than — to beat it in a fight. But I couldn't beat my addiction and I knew it. I would leave time after time with tears running down my face and with my hands and feet swollen and bruised. On trips, I would go to the hotel gym and lift weights and run on the treadmill in an extreme effort that would either end this battle with a heart attack or, at the very least, calm my nerves and desire to drink that night. As I ran faster and faster, I could feel my heart trying to pound through my ribs, my chest getting tighter, and I would become extremely weak. I wanted as much of that pain as possible, as that was exactly what the withdrawal symptoms were like. I wanted to burn the all-consuming cravings out of me — to give myself a fighting chance during the night, but it never worked; my addiction had grown too big, too powerful, and it swam through my veins in complete control of my mind and body.

In early 2009, we found a house in my parents' neighborhood and it was perfect for us. And that was my problem with it; I didn't think we would find a house I couldn't find fault with and I really wasn't ready to move out of our original home. To add to the new house's appeal, the sister of my life-long friend Jay lived across the cul-de-sac. Helena had two kids a few years older than ours who were great role models, and my kids really looked up to them (Helena's daughter, Annie, was a gymnast, just like my two daughters). When I talked to Helena about the house, looking for some problem that would be unknown to the casual observer, she had only praise for the neighbors and said the house seemed perfect for us. Eventually, I became pressured by Betty and my agent to put an offer in, so I put in a low-ball offer, which aggravated Betty and the agent, with the agent saying "That's almost insulting." What a great surprise, then, to get a voicemail when I landed in Phoenix that night that said they had countered just above my offer. My next move of countering in the middle was quickly and emphatically shot down by the agent, with her saying, "Come on Rob, they came all the way down to $460,000 and you want to squabble over $2,500?! You're going to ruin any trust with them when it comes time to negotiate the inspection findings!" I almost couldn't bring myself to say it, to accept the offer, but what choice did I have? I went through with it, asking myself, "What are the chances the house burns to the ground before we actually move in?" All went according to plan (not my plan), and I found myself selling things and borrowing money from my parents and grandparents to be able to afford the steep closing costs because we hadn't sold the original house yet.

Dealing with Betty's anger, my spiraling alcoholism, paying two mortgages (the original home wouldn't sell for over a year, and selling the home I thought I would live in for the rest of my life became too much for me and it became impossible to keep my urges to drink at bay. The month before we were to move, I made a call to the head of an FAA program called HIMS, short for Human Intervention Motivation Study, to see about getting some professional help for a problem I no longer had any control over. The doctor told me if I were to enroll in HIMS, I would be required to stay in a rehab for a minimum of 28 days and I would be off work for "about a year." I was stunned to hear there wasn't an intermediate program for someone who just wanted some help and education to regain control over their life and the all-or-nothing view of alcoholism the FAA had was a complete turn off. I certainly wasn't going to choose go to a rehab and take a year off of work when I still wasn't sure I had an alcohol problem, not to mention the new financial obligation of two mortgages. My supervisors at Southern were always very supportive of me, and they knew something wasn't right with my increasing number of sick calls, but they couldn't know what I was too proud to tell them.

That year, I went into my early morning simulator intoxicated. If I was seen as suspicious and got caught, I was going to have to face the music and fess up to my growing problem — and there was a part of me that wished to be caught, to end the hopeless charade. I certainly wasn't going to end it on my own volition; I was too ashamed to turn to friends, too proud to turn to professionals, too afraid to turn to my bosses, and too above AA. In the end, I was so afraid of tripping up on the simulator tests that I summoned all of the mental energy I had and, with an internal awareness bordering on paranoia, forced myself to stay ahead of the plane for the entire morning and did what just hours before I had believed would be nearly impossible — I passed both tests with hardly any issues. Looking back on it, that day was a failure because I really had the perfect opportunity to arrest the free-fall my health, mental state, and entire life were in by declaring I had an alcohol problem and insurmountable family problems, but the sad fact is, I would never admit to such weaknesses on my own.

When we moved in May, Betty was excited, but the newness of the bigger home quickly faded and gave way to a new set of issues not uncommon to home buyers: the house needed new carpet, refinished wood floors, and paint in some of the rooms. With the financial stretch and new house projects added to our normal stress, we resumed fighting and sleeping in separate rooms within weeks. I was stressed beyond words and went back and forth trying to decide if I should tell my bosses that I needed a month or two off. But between not knowing how exactly to word it and thinking I could keep on keeping on, I tried to endure. How long could I keep up the hoax was the question, but I always foolishly thought some solution was right around the corner. Without that big consequence that pressured me to disclose that my life was a sham, I was committed to the status quo of maintaining both houses, including finishing a massive deck I had started five years before on the original house, working two jobs, trying to survive Betty's light-switch moods, and desperately trying to cure myself of my addiction — all while trying to carry on as if we were the perfect family to the rest of the world.

I look back on the last half of 2009 with a big, black vignetting around any scene I picture. It seemed at least one of the kids had some scratches and bruises almost every time I came home from a trip and I have to admit I stopped questioning Betty for the most part as I knew she would become defensive and I would get her standard response. I regrettably started to pick my battles — though that is one I should have always picked. My drinking kept lock-step with her anger and I was now having to call off of work from both of my jobs as the increasing severity of the fog, and other crippling symptoms of withdrawal, were as debilitating as actually drinking.

Our relationship was becoming more physical too, and not in the way most couples desire. I have a picture of Betty and I in October where I have a black eye and Betty has bruises on her upper arms from me trying to restrain her slaps and punches. We went to a neighborhood Halloween party together with these marks; Betty wore a short-sleeved shirt that showed her bruises and there wasn't any hiding my eye. I knew everyone there was looking at us, aghast, wondering what in the hell was going on with the new neighbors, but we carried on as if nothing was wrong, just like we always had.

A few nights later, I got so drunk that Betty called the police. The police questioned me and I admitted to being drunk when I said, "You would drink too if you were married to her." As I stood up in handcuffs, I looked behind me at Betty upstairs on the landing and I saw Julie standing there. My five-year-old daughter watched the police escort me out of the house. I was always determined to keep any evidence of my drinking away from my kids, but my determination wasn't good enough anymore and I failed my family, and especially my daughter in a big, big way. This was the first, but would not be the last time one of my kids would see me drunk. My determination to keep my drinking hidden from them was falling further behind my physical need for alcohol. Of all of the wrong choices I have made in my life, this will always be far and away my biggest, most painful, most searing regret. To add salt to the wound, I saw Helena's husband Tom at his front door and he watched me get into the back of the police car that night. So desperate to keep my reputation clean, two days later I made that night even worse by insulting his intelligence with a crazy story about a guy who was arrested in front of my house for roaming the neighborhood, as if Tom couldn't make out it was me from only a hundred feet away.

The night I was escorted out of my house (I wasn't officially arrested), my dad told the police that I could just stay at his house. I had to wake up four hours later for an interview to get the Cat E position with the Colonel who would be my boss. Proof that I had become a functioning alcoholic, he commented that I was well put-together and would be a great asset to the position of monitoring the Civil Air Patrol. It was also this night that caused my parents to look into getting me into a rehab as I was now hopelessly addicted. Betty agreed that rehab was in our best interest and, though there was probably some compassion, she most likely thought that this was a great way to show her family that our problems were my fault. After all, Betty's stance was that she didn't have a problem — I was the problem, which she said any time I asked her to see a counselor or look into increasing or switching her low-dose antidepressant to a stronger or different one.

I remember the great shame, embarrassment and regret of my choices on the hour drive to my first rehab. How did I — the one with enough will power to run eight marathons starting when I was fifteen, to endure military survival school, to be the most fit in every physical way possible — lose this battle of will?! It didn't matter now, and I was faced with being admitted into a facility for four weeks that didn't look particularly clean or house people that I would normally associate with. The few patients I could see from the admissions desk looked like mostly drug addicts and were just kids to me. Regardless, I wasn't getting a ride home from my parents and I went into the bathroom to make the tearful call to scheduling to call off sick for my trip the next day.

After I checked in and said goodbye to my parents and Betty, I walked into the cafeteria and looked at the other patients — or, to me, inmates. This was a jail sentence and I wanted out ASAP and I plotted my release from the very first minute. The few adults there looked disheveled and I thought, "I can't be an alcoholic, I don't look anything like these people. I just need to get some medicine to overcome the painful withdrawal symptoms and I'll be fine." I went on two medications immediately and I felt great as I sobered up with absolutely zero symptoms of withdrawal. The next day was New Year's Eve and I missed my kids so much, it hurt. My resolve to get out of the cold, damp, confined prison became absolutely steadfast and after only five days there I told my counselor that I would be leaving the next day. She had me come into her rather large office and I met her and another woman. Both had probably seen the likes of me a thousand times and they tried to talk me out of leaving "AMA" — against medical advice. Their determination was almost as strong as mine; my counselor literally threw a large book at me when she realized I could not be swayed. I used this as more confirmation that I wasn't like any of these people and I believed I was justified in my departure, twenty-two days early.

When Betty came to get me, she was elated that I seemed healthy, happy, and I didn't look like death anymore. I was beyond elated that she came to get me out of that hell and get me back to the kids. It was as if we had breathed a second life into our marriage — for thirty-six hours. The next night, the medication I was given had worn off and my mind wouldn't stop pounding with thoughts of the wine rack in our basement that was still stocked with dozens of bottles of addiction. I waited for Betty to fall asleep and I tried so quietly to make my way down the stairs to quench my insatiable need for alcohol. In one of the more embarrassing moments of my life, Betty rounded the corner into the storage room where I kept the wine and I literally had the bottle straight up, trying to get it into me as fast as possible. She was justifiably furious and immediately called my parents, and now I was having to explain to the three of them why the six days spent at a rehab were a complete waste of time and money. I tried to downplay my actions by saying, "I just wanted to be able to sleep," but the look on my parents' faces told me there was grave concern and I wasn't fooling anyone but myself.

After the humiliating and humbling realization that I might really have a problem, I did most of my drinking in 2010 on the road to try to conceal my addiction from Betty. There were exceptions where I did drink at home, and one was in the Summer of 2010 when I showed Stephen a wrestling hold after sneaking a few glasses of wine. Stephen wasn't interested, but I made him watch and try a few other holds on me when he got upset. I raised my voice and told him he had to at least try and he smelled the alcohol on my breath. He cried and said, "You've been drinking!" I was completely taken aback by the fact that he knew what that meant, the embarrassment of my seven-year-old son catching me with alcohol on my breath in the middle of the afternoon, and especially that Betty looked at me with a piercing glare as she hurried over to me to smell my breath. When she got to me, I said, "What?!" "You've been drinking!!" Betty said. "I only had a few and I'm not drunk — so what?!" and that was it, the cat was out and she was furious.

She took the kids up to my parents' and told me my dad would be down to talk some sense into me. True to the trait of addicts being faced with having their addiction suddenly taken from them, I guzzled as much vodka as I could without vomiting before he got there. By now, my addiction had grown too powerful, and I was too weak, afraid, and dependent to live without my drug of choice. I screamed at him to get out of my house and I grabbed him and forced him out. The shame I felt as soon as I slammed the door was indescribable, and I punched the corner of a wall with all the force my years of karate had taught me. Already in an oblivious state, I finished myself off by drinking more vodka and I drifted off into another blackout.

When I came to the next morning, I went up to my parents' house to apologize to my dad, my mom and Betty, where she and the kids spent the night. My dad was sitting in his office when I walked through the door, and before I could say anything, he said, "I love you." What was I to say? Sorry had become worn out and meaningless and sorry, to me, means I won't do it again. We all knew I would do it again and we all knew my problem was growing. I said it anyway, feeling as pathetic and worthless as a grateful-yet-desperate son could be. He gave me a hug and said, "It's going to be okay." After I went into the kitchen to see the others, I saw the kids were eating waffles. They didn't know what had happened, as my mom acted as if it was another ordinary sleepover. I acted as normal as possible and gave the kids a kiss on top of the head and I went over to my mom and Betty. Hoping to get the same warm, understanding hug that my dad had given me, I whispered, "I'm sorry." My mom started crying, and said, "We can't do this anymore." She was right and I had a new determination right then and there to not drink at home no matter how desperate I felt. It was no secret to my mom that, despite the fact that I only drank a few times in the first half of 2010 — a big improvement from 2009 — when I did drink, I was blacking out.

Still in the kitchen, Betty asked, "What happened to your hand?!" (We would find out later that morning that I had broken a small bone in my wrist.) Then I went into the office and sat down at the computer my dad had been sitting at when I first got there, and the webpage on alcoholism he must have been reading was open. In bold letters, it said, "An alcoholic has difficulty abstaining from alcohol and once he or she starts drinking, they cannot stop." I had just broken Betty's and my parents' trust for the countless time, and my dad was reading about how to understand my addiction — I was filled with unspeakable shame.

Though I managed to greatly slow down my drinking after breaking my hand, mostly because I couldn't get away on my trips with my wrist in a cast for six weeks, I was still able to drink on two short military trips I took during that time. A good friend of mine, Ken, worked with me and saw me get so drunk the last night that he knew he couldn't take me to the airport because he knew I would never be let on the plane, even as a passenger. He also knew I had been struggling with alcoholism and tried to talk to me and tell me that his dad was a life-long active alcoholic. "My dad was never there for me; he was always drinking. Do you believe his alcohol was more important to him than his kids?! You really should look into AA, I always wished he cared enough to do at least that. What could it hurt?" My external answer was "Nothing," but my internal answer was "My pride." I was still in denial as to being a true alcoholic and I didn't feel I needed AA or professional help. Because I didn't have a program to help me in recovery, have a sponsor, or have big enough consequences for my drinking yet — a rock bottom — I was destined to "cave to the crave" more and more often.

A very persistent rift between Betty, Pat, and I concerned putting sunblock on the kids. I was very vigilant — they would say obsessive — about applying it, and Pat and Betty wouldn't put any sunblock on the kids. I would go over to Pat and Dale's, where the kids would often go in the summer, to apply it before the sun became intense and apply it again every ninety minutes. I would then play with the kids in the pool, or out in the yard, and I would usually go home around 4:00 to work around the house. One day, I had a lot of yardwork to do at the house and, after I went to Pat and Dale's to put sunblock on the kids, I asked Pat to ensure that Betty reapplied it throughout the day so I didn't have to make the ten-mile drive back to do it. Pat said her standard response, "All those chemicals in sunblock are worse than just getting sunburned." I said, "Please, just this once?" She agreed and I went back home. But when Betty came home that evening, the kids' faces were very red, especially Stephen's and Noel's. I was frustrated and confronted Betty and an argument ensued. It wasn't to the level that I thought Betty was going to hit me, but she took full advantage of my hand being in a cast and, without being able to grab her arms, she hit and scratched me on the right side of my face. Now, with a cast and three scratches just below my eye, I was hesitant to go out in public. But, in the days ahead, we carried on as we usually had, going out to dinner and acting like this was all normal — because, for us, it was.

After my hand healed in the fall, I went back to work and quickly got back into drinking every night. I started wearing my alcohol problem on my face in the form of wrinkles and baggy, droopy eyes. I knew I couldn't hide it anymore when Betty said one afternoon, after I woke up at 2:00 pm from the night before, "Look at you, you've gone and wrinkled up your face! You're so ugly now, that I have to think of other men just to have sex with you!" It hurt to hear and her lack of physical attraction wasn't going to help our already extremely distant marriage.

It left me with a helpless, empty feeling that, despite Betty's obvious disdain for our kids, was a powerful reminder that I was failing our family as egregiously as she was.

From this, I knew my appearance was deteriorating and when I went to Julie's sixth birthday party with my mom there, I looked so bad I had to admit that I had started drinking again. I told her, "Don't worry Mom, it will be okay." How many times had I told her I could control my drinking and that it would be okay? I don't know, but the look of concern on her face told me that by now she knew otherwise.

My dad knew otherwise too, because after Betty and I got into an argument late one night, she called him down to the house because I had been drinking. He brought a good friend of his who is in excellent shape and was an accomplished boxer years before. Jack's demeanor is very calm and he is as nice and friendly as they come, but I know from the stories of their military days that he is quite capable of defending himself and anyone on his side if they are threatened — and that's exactly what he was there for, to physically defend my dad if needed. He is well respected and because he had also recently flown at the base, he still knew a lot of the people I worked with in the military — people I was desperately trying to keep from hearing news of my drinking and it was one more leak I had to worry about. Because of their friendship (and his restrained temperament), Jack never said anything about it, and once again I didn't have any real consequences for my drinking besides some contained embarrassment. It was another wakeup call that I didn't heed.

For Christmas in 2010, I did my best to act like everything was fine and to make the kids feel special and loved. We gave them a lot of presents and I acted excited for them with the video camera running continuously and my digital SLR snapping countless pictures. When the kids finished, I made sure they knew that Mom had gotten lots of presents too, which I had spent considerable effort, time, and money getting that year. It all seemed normal as we watched her open them up. Betty tried to look happy, but I caught her looking out the window a lot. She looked at me with a blank expression several times as she probably wondered why I would try so hard to give her and the kids a nice Christmas, but I wouldn't stop drinking. As it turned out, she didn't get me any presents, and she didn't have any shame or sorrow for it. Days later, she would say I didn't deserve to have a Christmas — and I didn't disagree.

By early January, my addiction had consumed every part of me again and I stopped caring what Betty thought or knew about my drinking. Her brother Robby was an on-again, off-again recovering alcoholic and she had always defended him to others when he acted out, saying things like, "It's a disease, just like cancer. You wouldn't blame someone with cancer, would you?" and, "He was born with it, he can't help it," but I didn't get any of those considerations. When I questioned her about this, she said, "He's trying to get better, you aren't," and, highlighting the insular atmosphere of her family, "He's part of my family, you never will be!" I said, "I'm not?!" to the family comment. "No!" she said, "It's just me and my family, and you are not part of it!" Hearing it just confirmed what I already knew, and I had an odd thought of the day I would one day die: I might have to lay next to her and "her family" forever — which didn't sit well with me.

The second week of January was my vacation and I couldn't wait to be able to drink and not worry about how much my job limited me. I didn't waste any time either — I stopped at the liquor store on the way home from my last trip and took the six five-liter boxes of wine into the shed before walking through the front door. The kids were at school, and I drank an entire box and put a noticeable dent in a second box in just a few hours. Betty knew I was going to the shed too often over the last couple of weeks, this day especially, and she went down there as I cut the grass with the tractor in the front yard. When I saw her walking towards me, glaring and holding the empty box of wine in one hand and the receipt stamped hours before in the other, I knew I was in big trouble. She yelled, "You just bought these this morning, and one whole box is gone and you've started on another!" She wasn't asking, she knew. At first, I denied I could drink that much, but her glare said she knew otherwise. I had been caught and I offered a weak and empty, "Sorry."

For the rest of the week, I drank just enough during the day to keep my shaking down and my heart from exploding while drinking inconceivable amounts of alcohol after the kids went to sleep. I would sleep till the early afternoon and then walk to the bus stop to get the kids, trying so hard to keep up the appearances of an upper middle class father of four for the neighbors and for my young, impressionable kids. It worked for a few days, but one night I started an argument with Betty.

Our frequent fights were all the same in that Betty would verbally or physically attack me, usually about mundane things such as "piles" of stuff around the house, and I would assertively defend myself. But this night I drank too much and I layed into her. I was so drunk, I don't even remember what instigated me or even most of what I said, but I do remember a few seconds when Julie laid next to Betty in the bed just staring at me. Throughout our marriage, there are a few memories so bad and so traumatic for my kids that they are seared into my mind forever, and the memory of Julie's face this horrible night is certainly one of them.

The next day, I woke up and went straight to Julie and then Betty and apologized as best as I could, over and over. I was full of regret and I was truly sorry for this unprecedented behavior. I was baffled as to what had gotten into me that had caused me to berate my 115-pound wife like that, but I didn't like myself anymore and I said to Betty, "If I ever do that again, you have absolute and complete control over what happens next." My intent was that she could take me back to rehab or drive me hundreds of miles away and kick me out of the car, and I would honor my word — and twenty-four hours later, I was faced with exactly that.

The next night was a repeat and when I woke up the following day, she coldly reminded me of my promise. I just pensively said, "Okay." I didn't know what she was planning to do, but I knew I would be without alcohol for a while at least. So while she coordinated for my mom to watch the kids, I snuck to the basement where I had stashed some bottom shelf vodka and guzzled as much as my throat and reflexes could tolerate. I went upstairs and laid on the couch, basking in the feeling of the cheap vodka running through my veins and taking in its effect when Betty realized, by the smell, that I had just drank again. She told me to get into the car, and I did so obediently, without any fuss or questioning. She had decided to take me to the local hospital, the one I was born at forty-one years before. I was admitted there, a drunken disgrace, for possible alcohol poisoning, though I had been much more inebriated in other binges.

I was coherent and alert, as much as I could be considering how much alcohol I had in me. Much to my surprise then, and certainly to the young nurse who did the breathalyzer, my BAC was .68. Proof that I really didn't have my priorities straight, I remember thinking, "That is Jamoir Jagr's number," and I told the nurse, "By my calculation, you will have to release me around 11:00 tonight." She said, "You will get released when we feel it is safe for you to be out." I shot back, "You can't keep me here if I'm sober, and I should be at .08 in thirteen or fourteen hours!" After a few more rounds with the young nurse, she said to me in a calm, matter of fact tone, "You're a d---head." I apologized and I thought of what I must have been like to incite this young girl to say something that she knew could result in her termination.

From then on, I stayed in my room trying to keep my heart rate up in any way possible to metabolize the alcohol faster. Running in place and the hundreds of push-ups must have worked, because by 9 p.m. I was at .08 and the hospital had to release me. Now I had the problem of getting to my home seven miles away, in a snow storm, so I called my sister. She rejected my first call, but answered the second one I made a minute later. "Sandi, I need you to come and pick me up from the Sewickley hospital," I tried to say as normal as possible. Sandi has zero tolerance for BS and lies, and I got a taste of that when she said, "No way Rob, no way! You are out of control! Do you hear me?! Out. Of. Control!" I said, "But I don't have a way home and I'll have to walk if you don't pick me up." She said, "That's your problem; maybe you should just stay there and get some help, but I don't want you around Betty or the kids right now." In one of the dumbest questions I have ever blurted, I asked, "Why?" Sandi said, "Rob! Mom said Betty is ready to kill you and we all know she is fully capable of actually doing it, not to mention you have managed to mostly keep your drinking from your kids and you need to get some professional help, maybe back to rehab, before you run out of luck with that. Come on, think of your kids for God's sake!" I started crying, half sincerely and half to get her sympathy and get the ride, when she solemnly said, "I'm not doing it Rob, I just can't," and hung up the phone. I had to go back into the hospital and ask the staff, whom I had disgraced myself with all day and night, for the phone number for a cab. I called the cab and had him drop me off at the top of my neighborhood so my neighbors wouldn't suspect anything.

I walked down our street with my tail between my legs and filled with guilt, but I had my priorities and I went straight to the shed to get my fill so I could fall asleep. I sat on the dust covered floor and drank enough to get me through the night as I didn't have any in the house; I had drunk almost everything from my hidden stashes inside the house that morning. I got the garage door open with the keypad, but when I got to the door that led into the house, it was locked. I tried all of the other outside doors, but they were locked too. I viewed the locked door from the garage into the house as a slap in the face from Betty, that I wasn't welcome in my own home because we had never locked that door. As the alcohol took effect, I vaguely remember grabbing the sledge hammer and hitting the wooden door trying to open it. When I did, I heard Betty, just on the other side of it, scream, "Go away Rob, I am calling the police!" I heard her start to talk to the police dispatcher and I tore out of there and through the snow-covered back yard to my parents' in a complete panic. By then, I was so drunk that I had blacked out, remembering only a half second of the spree when I almost tripped and fell.

The next morning, and against my parents' firm request, I had the gall to retrace my strides through the foot of snow and go back to the house.

When I got home, Betty's mom was there and she screamed, "Rob! What are you doing?! You have a family to take care of and provide for and you're scaring the hell out of them!" Another weak, empty, and pathetic apology from me. I stood there in foggy thought; I didn't know what was happening to me. I would drink with the intention of just calming my nerves and to sedate me for bed, but once I started, I couldn't stop drinking everything I could find until I blacked out. I used to be such a happy and fun moderate drinker in my twenties; who was this angry, threatening drunk?! I didn't know him, nor did I want to, but I would reintroduce myself every night given any chance to drink. Pat then said, "You're going to lose your job if you keep this up and we're taking you to a rehab right now!" Scared of being a prisoner again, I yelled, "No! I'm not going no matter what!" "What do you want to do then? You can't stay here anymore until you get help!" she said. We went round and round and afterwards I looked at Betty and thought of the four kids upstairs and acquiesced. "Okay. Fair enough, but no rehabs."

I was now at a point that some small part of me wanted professional help. I felt hopeless and my intellect or willpower was 100% powerless against this strengthening monster. I thought of our four absolutely beautiful and truly wonderful kids, who deserved so much better than a drunk dad who tried to hide it, or worse, a dad who was drunk in front of them. Not to mention I wouldn't be able to care or provide for them much longer in this condition and they deserved the best life I could provide. Pat then said, "We will take you to the Butler VA hospital." Distrusting, I asked, "Is it a rehab?" She said, "No, it is a detox." I didn't ask what a detox was, but it didn't sound too invasive so, not having any other palatable options, I agreed to go. During the hour long drive, I sat in the back of the van and thought of how it had come to this, and I pounded on the seat with my fist, just muttering, "No, no, no," over and over. Pat realized I wasn't disappointed or mad at anyone but myself, and tried to reassure me that everything would be okay if I just listened and cooperated with the staff, which I agreed to do.

When we got there, the lady asked me a series of questions about how much and how often I was drinking. I was embarrassed, in large part, because I really didn't know. I didn't know because I was drinking wine out of a 44-ounce Big Gulp cup, not a glass, and guzzling vodka straight from the bottle. If I took a guess, it would be an incomprehensible and shameful number that I didn't want to face. With Betty and her mom sitting behind me, I just said, "A lot." Unsurprisingly, I was admitted for detox, which I would soon come to learn meant days, not hours, confined to a small, dark part of the old hospital while I was fed anti-withdrawal drugs and occasionally allowed to interact with other alcoholics and drug addicts who weren't any happier about being there than I was. I had a small room that I shared with a twenty-one-year-old heroin addict who didn't talk, which was fine by me. There was an odd mix of strong smells in the dimly lit part of the hospital, best described as stench trying, and largely succeeding, to overcome Clorox and floral spray.

About eight of us would meet after lunch to discuss why we were there and how we would handle our addiction when we were free to go back to our rooms, but the rest of the time was spent doing nothing but staring at four walls. This is the part I hated, seemingly wasting time doing absolutely nothing and held captive by over-scheduled, understaffed, and largely compassion-less nurses. I was caged again; a prisoner lumped with others that I had nothing in common with — or so I thought at the time.

I've always been, what I would call, resourceful — Betty would say sneaky — and I snuck my cell-phone into the detox center so I could alleviate one of the worst parts of confinement and that is little-to-no contact with the outside world. She wasn't happy about it when I first contacted her, but calling on my resourcefulness, I told her that I knew I would miss her and the kids and I would want to leave early if I couldn't talk to them. The first two nights, I went into the community shower and ran the water to drown out my short conversations with Betty and the kids, who just thought I was on a trip. The third night, of what would turn out to be four total, Betty informed me that she found the Southern brochure for the HIMS program that I had in a compartment of my suitcase. It had been sitting in there for the twenty-one months since I called in April of 2009 and decided I wanted no part of its unreasonable and lengthy requirements. She then told me the news that left me stunned and in complete bewilderment, "I called the 800 number and talked with Dan Lipper. He and Dr. Lambeau [the doctor I get my FAA medical from] arranged for you to go straight to rehab from detox tomorrow." Shocked, I forgot I wasn't allowed to have a phone and in a raised voice I said, "What?!" She repeated herself and added "It's in a place called Father Martin's Ashley and it's near Baltimore." Quieter, but still reeling from the news, I said, "What? No! Please, please tell me you didn't do that!?" "I did and Southern is behind you 100%; they want you to get help," she said. "Gaaaaawd. How long is the rehab? And please don't tell me four weeks." I said. She said, "Yes, it is four weeks and you don't have a choice now." I missed the kids so bad it hurt. I said to her, "The only way I'm going is if I can come home and see the kids — spend the night at home with them tomorrow and I'll go Tuesday. That is the only way I am agreeing to it, and you can tell my boss I said so." Betty said, "I don't want you at home, I don't trust that you won't drink." I said, "I know my promises in regards to drinking are nearly worthless, but I will do anything, I mean anything, to see the kids before I have to spend a month away from them." Betty heard the sincerity, desperation, and determination in my voice and must have realized the potential benefit outweighed the risk and agreed to at least ask Dr. Lambeau. I was ecstatic when Betty texted me the news that I could spend the night at home the next day, but I would be on an airplane for Baltimore first thing Tuesday. Overcome with excitement, I snuck back into the shower with my phone, and trying to show my appreciation, I called Betty and told her where all of my hiding spots for the wine and vodka were throughout the house, garage, and shed. "Get it out, get all of it out," I pleaded. I didn't trust myself at all and this was as much of a reassurance for me as it was for her. I could just go home and not have to worry about my addiction calling my name, its close proximity haunting me all night. Knowing it was gone, I could enjoy the precious little time with my kids before I was off to my next sentence.

On the drive home from the VA hospital, Betty and I stopped to see Dr. Lambeau, who wanted to talk with us before I left for Baltimore. When we walked in, he welcomed us and said, "Rob, I'm proud of you and I believe in you." Feeling ashamed and dejected, I said, "You do?!" He continued, "We're going to get you the best help the medical field has to offer and you're going to come back a sober man and a sober pilot." I was overwhelmed with emotion as I looked at him, his words sinking in, and I put my face in my hands and started crying uncontrollably. "I don't know what is wrong with me," was all I could say. "Look, you have a lot to live for! You have four young kids who count on you and your beautiful wife here loves you and cares enough for you that she made this happen," he said. When he said that about Betty loving and caring for me, I snapped out of it because I knew that wasn't true. I looked over at Betty, her arms crossed and looking distant and for the first time I realized that she was just afraid I would lose my job. This wasn't about concern for me or our marriage, this was about protecting what I called the money stream — my job. My concern for the kids' welfare around Betty weighed heavily on me and I was hesitant to leave them alone with her for a prolonged amount of time. After all of the rah-rah talk from Dr. Lambeau though, I knew that now was not the time to question her motives.

The four weeks at Father Martin's went by very slowly, though it is an extremely nice facility and it was well staffed with knowledgeable and caring counselors who had to be in recovery themselves. In a repeat of the hospital, I cut a hole in the side of my bag and snuck my phone in so I could maintain contact with the kids, as the thought of the once-a-week, five-minute ration on calls was heart wrenching for me. Betty didn't like that I already wasn't following the rules and she went through the HIMS director to get me to turn it in — she meant business on my recovery. At least one of us did — I was just doing and saying what I had to to get the hell out of there.

After four long weeks, Betty, her mom, and my parents came to my "Graduation." As most people know, any alcoholic introduces them-selves to groups of other alcoholics by saying, "I'm so-and-so and I'm an alcoholic." I couldn't muster the courage to say that when addressing the other graduates and students for my thank you speech. Instead, I said, "I'm Rob. Alcoholic." I couldn't say, "I am," because I only be-lieved with about 90% probability that I was an alcoholic, even after twenty-eight days of meetings, classes, and studying the so-called dis-ease. All of these should have told me I was, but I was still embarrassed by the term "alcoholic" and I still had my job and family — I hadn't hit a big low point like almost everyone else in there. $35,000 later, I was still in denial.

The $35,000 Smoke Screen

The FAA wants pilots with alcohol abuse problems to have about one year off of work and to attend ninety AA meetings within the first ninety days out of rehab — "90 in 90" in AA parlance. I wanted to show my level of cooperation and get back to work in the bare-minimum six months, so I went to as many as five meetings a day and kept an impeccable log of them. The problem being, I was too fixated on getting back to work and I didn't try to understand the steps of AA. I was just mindlessly regurgitating what I needed and wanted to hear myself say. Also thrown into the mix was the fact that, when I wasn't at meetings, I was home, and I took full advantage by spending my time with the kids. I walked them to and from the bus stop, helped them with their homework, took them to their activities and out to eat, laid in bed and read to them, and gladly cleaned up after them at the end of the day.

In first week that I was home, I was looking at the pictures and videos my mom had taken of the kids while I was in Father Martin's, and I noticed that Julie and Noel had bruises and scratches on their faces in the videos from early February. I asked my mom, though I already knew the answer, what had happened. She said, "I don't know what happened to the girls, but something happened with Stephen when you first left. He had some deep scratches all along his arm and neck and the school called her about it." Feeling so bad for the kids, I just hung my head. My mom continued, "And she was indignant about it! She said to me, 'Do you believe the school called me about his scratches?' and I just thought, 'Well of course they're going to call when he has scratches all over him!'" I never asked my mom why she didn't tell me that it happened on her own — Betty, my mom, and I had grown so used to protecting what we wanted protected within our dysfunctional family that she didn't say anything to me until I asked. My protection priorities were shielding Betty's anger from the rest of the world and making sure the kids were okay (not working on and protecting my sobriety). Betty's highest priority was keeping her anger hidden from the rest of the world — being extremely nice and sociable while outside the home (only me, my parents, and the kids would know her other side). My mom's priorities were to protect everyone, and in this case, she didn't want me to have to worry about anything more than staying sober.

Being home all of the time was not as much fun with Betty though. She and I had endured as long as we had because I spent most of my time on the road. Now we were around each other almost all day and night and our interactions were often tense. Though we did try to occasionally go to the gym together (in different parts of the gym), or to lunch together, we mostly avoided each other during the day and, at night, we went to sleep at different times on the edge of our respective sides of the bed. And because my relationship with the kids was better than ever, the happiness and commotion of playing with them every chance I could get would quickly bring out Betty's jealousy. She had an extremely low tolerance for laughter, and generally the sound of fun, and she would frequently yell at us to be quiet. To avoid her, we started playing more and more outside as the winter turned into spring, something the neighbors, and especially Helena and Tom, must have been happy to see after the last eighteen months of dysfunction.

Something I had noticed since roughly 2005, and had just now gotten the gumption to ask Betty about after I came home from Father Martin's, was the van's persistently low gas mileage history. It was rated for 16/25, and I could consistently get 17-18 in mostly city driving, but over time it would drop to around 13 if I didn't reset the trip computer. I suspected that she was letting it run with the kids in it, but she just said she'd let it run if "the kids wanted to finish watching a movie." I was skeptical because we put over 1,000 miles a month on the van and my quick math told me that equated to a lot idling. I had nothing more to go on, and so I dropped it.

Throughout our marriage, Betty struggled to have fun and enjoy the kids while we were in our home, only pretending to be happy with them when we were in front of others. She appeared to resent their very existence and the work of transporting, feeding, and cleaning up after them was not something she embraced in parenthood. It was made worse by my constant presence at home now, even though I was doing almost all of those chores. I enjoy cleaning and home projects, as it lets me shut my brain off, and to lessen her stress, I also started doing the majority of the house work when the kids and I weren't playing. And, unwilling to work or play, I think Betty started to wonder where she fit in within our family. Her routine became one of sleeping in, reading the newspaper, going to the gym, getting naps, and wiping down the kitchen counter tops seemingly thirty times a day, even if no one had sat there in the twenty minutes since she'd last cleaned them.

When the kids got home from school, she would avoid them by calling her mom and sister and talking for an inordinate amount of time. My repaired relationship and closeness with the kids only caused her to become even more distant with all of us and our marriage became one of see-and-avoid.

Though the time with the kids was wonderful, I really missed the camaraderie and adult interaction the airline overnights provided. Just a month after finishing my second rehab, I put the kids to sleep and I was back at the local dive bar shortly thereafter. I went under the auspices of loneliness and needing some me-time, but really, I craved a drink and I succumbed to my addiction again, just one month out of rehab. I had only three drinks over two hours, but that did more to solidify in my mind that I could control my drinking than to make me realize that I have a dyed-in-the-wool problem — a common experience amongst alcoholics before they become sober for life. In a truly pathetic decision, I actually had the audacity to get my two-month coin at my favorite AA meeting the very next morning. Getting coins for longevity in sobriety is one of the better reinforcements and is something I really respect in the program. You will occasionally see someone with years of sobriety go up and get the 24 hour coin because they had a week moment and drank, a very humbling step that is usually followed by a short speech on where they went wrong and what they will try and do better so the rest of us can learn from those mistakes. And here I was, disgracing the program, trying to fool everyone (including myself) so I could keep up the charade with my sponsor and go back to work ASAP. It was a house of cards though, and I started "controlled drinking" most nights. Some nights I controlled it, and some nights it controlled me, not a game of chance I had any possibility of winning in the long run.

Part of the HIMS program mandates that I must see a counselor who specializes in addiction periodically. Dr. Lambeau's go to was Francine, and to her credit, it was apparent she didn't trust what I was saying to her from the start. She wasn't brash with her doubt, she would just look at me with her head turned sideways and make a lot of notes, seemingly only when I lied to her about where I was on my recovery.

On my third visit to her, Betty came with me under the auspices of wanting to know how I was doing in my recovery, but I think she really went to have a counseling session of her own. I welcomed Betty's attendance as it was difficult to find relevant things to talk about for an hour every other week and maybe Betty and I could use a mediator to find some common ground and better our distant marriage. We talked about how I had done wrong with my alcoholism, and touched on the surface of Betty's "lack of patience" with the kids and me, but her big abuses of punching me and bruising and scratching the kids were left out. That was fine with me. After all, I had to convince this woman that I wasn't going to drink anymore if I wanted to go back to work and if she knew that kind of stress was part of almost everyday life for me, then I might never get back. As intended by Betty, she got to vent a little about me and the frustration of raising four kids, but with what she said and how she said it, it sounded like we were just a normal growing family when the truth was much, much darker than her portrayal.

A few days before Noel's Pre-kindergarten "graduation," where the kids sing in front of their parents, I came in from doing some yard work late one night. I went into the kids' rooms to check on them as they slept, and I saw a deep bruise that covered most of Noel's temple and cheek. Betty's trademark three fingers were also left imprinted just below Noel's right eye. Seeing marks on the kids' faces was nothing new, but Noel's face was worse than usual and we were going to be in front of a hundred kids and parents that week. I crawled into bed and wondered. I wondered if we were going to be questioned by any of the dozens of parents at the graduation. I wondered if someone was going to notice and call the police. I wondered what Noel had done. I wondered if she was okay. And I wondered just who it was that slept two feet away from me.

By late-May, in the effort to get back to work, I was taking the hardest aptitude tests I could ever imagine and interviewing with two psychiatrists, experts in the field of addiction, as part of the standard FAA requirements to determine if I had done any damage to my memory while drinking. This was all in an effort to obtain the FAA's clearance to reapply for my First Class medical license — a license as crucial as my Airline Transport Pilot license as both are needed to fly commercially. One glaring problem that came out of the tests was the disparity I have always had between verbal and mathematical aptitude, and I went as far as to take Dr. Lambeau my high school SAT results, showing that my math scores had been double that of my verbal before I had ever had my first drink. The two psychs had some normal hesitation in their reports, consistent with other alcoholic pilots' similar reports, but based on their recommendation that I could return to work, I must have been fairly convincing in my assertions that I had my life together, understood my addiction, and realized I could never drink again — even though I had just drunk the night before both interviews and the day-long memory tests. Dr. Lambeau wasn't as convinced and, unbeknownst to me, he intentionally dragged out the application for reinstatement with the FAA by several months. By late October, I finally got the FAA's letter stating that I could reapply for my medical license with the stipulations that I had to be monitored by Dr. Lambeau and his appointed psychiatrist, Dr. Thompson, for five years.

As I was getting ready, in the hours before I left for the week of retraining in Dallas, I wondered how things would be between Betty and the kids in my absence. In my nine months off, I had tried to get her to positively interact with the kids at home with absolutely no success, a big concern of mine as I was going to be gone a lot from now on. It was also time to readdress two other concerns with her — she was very reluctant to feed the kids and she would not walk them to or from the bus stop. In my nine months off, I would feed the kids right after school (to be fair, she would feed them on occasion too), but Betty would yell at them when they wanted fed again in the six hours before bed, and get mad at me too for feeding them that second time. Preparing food, even if it's just a bowl of cereal, leaves a mess, and any mess or disorder, no matter how small, was the bane of Betty's sanity. The bus stop issue went back to 2009 when my mom (and our next door neighbor) told me that Stephen, just in first grade at that time, was walking alone to and from the bus stop and in the morning "waiting for the bus all by himself." (Her house had a view of the stop from about 700 feet away.) I had addressed this concern with Betty quite a few times over the last two years, but now Julie was out of preschool and riding the same bus and the thought of our kids ending up missing made me sick. I couldn't leave for work wondering how things were going to be; I had to know and I would have to tell her how I wanted the kids treated if I didn't like what she initially had to say. Nervous of her reaction, I started with, "Are you going to be okay with the kids while I'm gone?" Already sounding defensive, she said, "What do you mean?!" and I quickly dug in to let her know I was not going to be blown off or placated. I raised my voice and said, "What do you mean, 'What do I mean?!' For nine months, you haven't wanted anything to do with the kids and now I'm going back to work and I have to wonder what kind of mom you're going to be to them!" Betty started to talk over me, but I was not having any part of it — it was time to get my kids a mom that appreciated them. I yelled, "Stop!! I've watched you for nine months, ignoring and completely resenting our kids and now I have to leave them with you for up to a week at a time! My mom is not their mom, YOU need to be their mom!" A full blown argument ensued and I continued yelling, "You need to start going to the bus stop, doing their homework with them, feeding them, and taking them where they need to go without bitching about it right in front of them! I'm a pilot, THAT is YOUR job, THAT is what YOU do!" I was so scared of getting a call while on a trip that one of our kids was missing, that I accepted the growing risk of Betty becoming physical and drove home the point of the bus stop over and over. She screamed, "Thank God you're going back to work, you're a f---ing drunk and no one wants you at home anyway!" In the end, Betty took on the part of the kids' homework with a level of organization and detail I didn't expect, but she hardly ever went to the bus stop, so my mom continued to watch the kids from her bedroom window.

Now that I felt no one was watching me while I was in Dallas for a week, I started drinking heavily again. I started flying trips just days later, and my three-year tradition of ramping up the drinking to truly alarming levels during the latter part of the year was not going to be broken. Only my bosses, my company monitor, and Chicago based instructor pilots knew I was in the HIMS program, and before I flew a trip, I would check the schedule of each one of them to make sure they were not going to be overnighting where I was — not quick or easy with about twenty-five pilots total to look up. Though they likely didn't know I wasn't allowed to drink, I was blatantly risking my job by drinking in front of the other pilots, but I was too brazen to care.

Now in early 2012, I was home one night and Betty and I had just had another big argument, which were quite frequent if I haven't conveyed that clearly enough. During the argument, she had said, "You're so ugly, I have to think of other men to have sex with you!" twice. Though this wasn't the first time I had heard this, it hurt and caught my attention again. Recently I'd noticed she had been texting a lot (which she didn't normally do, she always talked to her mom and sister), so I looked at her phone once she fell asleep. I found it open to her Facebook page, and as she had recently "defriended" me, I felt Facebook was a good place to start. I looked at her messages and there was a thread with one of our local policemen, whom we knew from our kids being in some of the same sports as his. Within the messages, Betty had told him how angry I was and that I was always drunk and she didn't have anyone to talk to. I thought, "If he only knew that she was the angry, violent one. I'm just an alcoholic." They had carried on for quite a while over a couple of weeks and the last message from him said, "We should just talk on the phone, here is my number." I then looked at our cell phone bill online and saw that he and Betty had been talking while I was on my trips and it was usually late at night when, I would guess, he was on patrol. I didn't question Betty about the calls or any concerns of an affair — instead I kept it to myself, thinking that if she was going to engage in that, then she would eventually do something that unequivocally gave it away as I didn't have enough evidence to confront her with just yet. Not to mention it was hard to fault her, seeing as how I'd had two secret affairs and the alcohol was taking a toll on my appearance and in more ways than just my attractiveness. This probable affair didn't do anything to help stem my urge to drink, and I, for the third time, stayed on the path of a nearly hopeless alcoholic.

One night at the bar on a layover in Buffalo, a young male flight attendant started talking to me about my day and we had a nice conversation for a few minutes, but when he realized I was more interested in the Super Bowl preview on ESPN, he quickly got combative and accused me of hating gays. I took offense at his audacity to stereotype me (a colleague had just made national news when he didn't know his microphone was stuck on and was heard bashing gays over the radio) and I glared at him and said, "My brother-in-law is gay, and he and I are pretty good friends." Though I thought this would end the issue, he came back with, "Well, you had better get used to us, because there are a lot of us and we're growing!" I became more frustrated that he had continued along the lines that I was a hater, and I responded, "I don't have to get used to it, I don't have a problem with it! Now my problem is with you." He looked at me and rolled his eyes and I said, "Your behavior is embarrassing. Do you think your parents would be proud of you?" A few more things were said by both of us, but I noticed he was tuning me out and had turned his stool away from me. I paid for my wine and went to the elevator, but I knew I needed to be the bigger person and apologize to him, so I went back to the bar. He refused to acknowledge me when I said, "Hey, I'm sorry. I shouldn't have said that and again, I'm very sorry." He sat there, looking away from me without saying a word. Seeing this, the bartender kindly motioned for me to leave, so I gave up and went to my room.

A few days later, I got a call from HR and the pleasant-sounding lady said that I had a sexual harassment claim filed against me and there would be an investigation. Apparently (I never got confirmation), he took the question of his parents being proud of him to mean that they don't approve of his sexuality, not me being condescending of his age and immature behavior as I meant it. I knew this had a lot of potential to blow up in my face, and though I knew I hadn't said anything to the flight attendant that I couldn't defend, I was surely going to have to defend my presence at the bar to my boss. He was already leery of my sobriety after a foolish stunt I'd pulled just two months before where I was caught by a fellow employee throwing out beer cans while in uniform. I preempted any request for an explanation from my boss by requesting to meet with him first. That would go a long way towards keeping him off my trail, or so I thought. When we met, we said hello and his opening question was, "So, what were you doing at a bar?" Struggling to remain calm and confident, I said, "Well, it is a restaurant too," trying to imply that I was merely eating, not drinking. A funny line from a former commander came to mind after he looked at me for a few seconds, his eyes studying my face and body language — "When you're explaining, you're losing" — and I was certainly doing both. Along the lines of "trust, but verify," he said "Okay, that's fine," but I could tell he didn't fully believe me and he was going to do a little research. His words rang in my head for the next few days because on everyone's first day at Southern, we are told that the only thing that will definitely get you fired, no questions asked, is if you lie. I was probably going to be caught violating the terms of my reinstatement AND I had lied — it was hard not to think I was going to be terminated and Southern would have two very good reasons to do so.

I had a strong notion that my boss was going to contact the hotel and ask the bartender if I'd had anything to drink or not, so in complete desperation (an alcoholic mindset was also a strong contributing factor), I took $5,000 in cash out of my bank and the next day, I flew to Buffalo to offer it to the bartender. When I walked into the empty bar — I mean restaurant — he saw me and I gingerly asked if he could sit at one of the remote tables. He obliged and I proceeded to tell him about the harassment claim and made up a story about how the flight attendant accused me of having too much to drink and my boss would be calling him to find out if I did or not. He was nice, but questioned why having just a few drinks was so wrong. "Do you know how many of your crew come in here and drink three or four drinks? I can't take your money," he said. Desperate, I then explained that I was in a program where I couldn't drink at all, but he had the same polite, admirable response, "I'm not going to lie and I can't take your money." I thanked him for his time and I left knowing I was in big trouble.

Knowing I was now unable to contain the damage, when I got home, I explained to Betty about the on-going investigation. But I still didn't tell her that I had drunk, I only told her about the confrontation with the coworker. She questioned why I was concerned, saying, "He came after you, and you didn't say anything bad, so what is the big deal? This will probably just blow over. HE is the one that should be in trouble!" I couldn't remember the last time I'd heard her defend or advocate for me, and her words hit me. I didn't want to disappoint her after she showed some trust in me, and I thought, "I need a miracle."

During the last few days of the investigation (it took four weeks because the flight attendant kept changing his story and the lady from HR told me they wanted to see how many times he would change it and contradict the bartender's and my story, which were almost exactly the same), I was drinking so much at night that I didn't think I was going to live much longer. The night after what I figured would be my last flight at Southern, and maybe my last commercial flight ever, I drank so much that I was in a complete blackout the next morning. I was only commuting home, not working, but I vaguely remember getting ready to walk through the TSA scanner when I looked up at the agent. He immediately knew that something was wrong with me, so I turned and sprinted down the long hall, past other crew members and hundreds of passengers, and out of the airport. I remember thinking there had to be a video camera on me and I was done for — now my boss and maybe the whole country would know how low I had sunk. I woke up later that evening in the room of the empty row house several of us rented, wondering who had seen what and what had been caught on camera.

That night, I looked at my schedule and saw that all of my future trips had been pulled and my qualification was "inactive." Knowing the game was up, I called my company sponsor and tearfully disclosed I had drunk again. He responded, "Well, that changes things," but vowed to advocate for me to keep my job and go back to rehab, which I never thought I'd be so glad to hear. The next day, while at home playing baseball with the three older kids in the cul-de-sac (trying to be a part of their life while they still thought I deserved to be), I got the call from my boss that he'd found out from the bartender that I had drunk and that I should contact my doctor about what to do next. "Are you saying…I'm not terminated?" I asked. He said, "That's right Rob, we just want to see you get better and have a good long career here, but you're going to be out quite a while." I said, "Thank you so very much, I can't find the words to express my gratitude. And when I come back, you will get twenty good years from me — I guarantee it." "I look forward to that. Have a good day Rob, we'll be here when you come back," was all he said. Oddly, it generated a new low; now I felt that, not only did I not deserve my kids, but I didn't deserve my company.

The next day, Betty and I went to Dr. Lambeau's office and he already had a place in mind that had a tough, no nonsense counselor. "Rob, you're going to go to Marworth up in Scranton this weekend after I make the call, and I have news for you, this isn't a twenty-eight-day program. They can keep you as long as it takes, and I will tell them you are not to come home one minute earlier than they think is in your long-term best interest — until you have this f---ing disease under control," he said. "What?! How long are we talking?!" I said. "I don't know. Right now your life is out of control and I have to tell you, you just made me look like a f---ing idiot to the FAA and everyone who runs the HIMS program nationwide. Now look, I believe in you, I think your heart is in the right place, but this addiction has absolutely ruined your life and it will kill you if you keep it up. I will not let you go back to work until I am 100% confident you will never drink again, do you understand me?!" His voice and tone were now elevated, and I just hung my head, knowing how hard I had let him down when he took a chance on me less than a year ago, sending me back too early the first time because of my false promises to him. "I understand. I am so sorry, so very sorry." I just kept repeating that knowing that this addiction was far, far too strong, too powerful, too big, too ingrained in every cell of my body as I now could not live, could not survive without alcohol.

I was certain I couldn't live without alcohol ever again, but I didn't have the courage to tell him that and I agreed to go because I didn't know how to tell him or Betty that I was hopeless. I was also very concerned for our kids' welfare as I knew being gone for an extended time would stress Betty out and I didn't trust her alone with no one to hold her accountable, but I was out of options. Dr. Lambeau went on about how I had a great future in front of me, but I rewound to the part where he said Marworth could keep me as long as they wanted and I had to have a time frame or I would go crazy. "How long can they keep me, doc?" I asked. He said, "I told you as long as I feel is necessary, and I know the guy who runs the place. We went to medical school together and he trusts me, so it's up to me and it won't be quick. If you're looking for an answer, it could be up to six months, ten months, I don't know." I gasped, "Ten months?! I can't do it! Please, I can't do that!" He said, "Well, the people who treat you and I will decide how long you stay and I'm telling you, it's open ended. Look, you are actually going to be in treatment with people who are professionals, just like you. These are doctors, physicians, lawyers, psychiatrists, professors, other pilots. Trust me, you won't be the smartest one there!" he said, laughing and trying to get me to accept the thing I had grown to hate more than anything in life — being a prisoner in rehab. I just said, "What choice do I have." It wasn't a question, but an acquiescence to my fate and I thanked him.

That was Friday, but I wasn't leaving for Scranton until Sunday, so I called Marworth as instructed by Dr. Lambeau. They told me the best thing an alcoholic of my depth could hear — keep drinking. If one has become dependent enough on alcohol, you could die from the withdrawal, so rehabs and detoxification facilities actually want you to wait until you're under their doctoral supervision and on anti-withdrawal drugs before you stop. I drank moderately Friday night, and Saturday all of us spent the night at Betty's parents so she could go to the base Sunday morning and I would drive myself to Scranton while the kids stayed there. That was the intended plan, but I was faced with leaving for an extremely long time and not being able to drink for months or maybe, if a miracle occurred and I actually came home from Marworth dedicated to staying sober, the rest of my life.

Saturday night and almost all of Sunday were a blur; I had followed the instructions to drink very well. I woke up Sunday afternoon to "Get up, we're going to drive you to Scranton." Betty was standing over me after coming home from her day working at the base — I, obviously, wasn't about to make it out of even the driveway on my own. It was time for me carry out my sentence and a panic set in that I wouldn't see my kids for six months. I remember asking for a minute to say bye to Stephen, who was watching TV on the other side of the house. It's fuzzy, but I apologized to him and told him I was going away for a while and I would explain all of it when he got older. I remember him smiling somewhat uncomfortably and giving me a hug. And I still wonder just what he saw in me that day.

Betty and her mom apparently took me to our house to get some clothes and toiletries for my incarceration — I don't remember anything until the next morning except a fuzzy memory of the nurse waiting for me outside as we pulled up to Marworth early the next morning. I woke up in the hospital-type bed around noon, quite alert and aware due to the drugs I was administered. Like all rehabs, phone calls to the outside are a privilege and only allowed during a narrow window of time once or twice a week, but I pleaded with the head nurse there to allow me to call and thank Betty for driving me. I said hello and Betty, probably caught a bit off guard and wondering if I had escaped, just said a cautious "Hi."

I said, "I am so very sorry for what I did yesterday, and I thank you for bringing me here." Betty said, "I came straight to the base, so I can't talk long." I said, "Okay, and please tell your mom I said thank you too. I would like to call her, but I was lucky to just be able to call you." She said, "Okay, I'll tell her." Feeling pensive and trapped, I ended with, "Before you go, I want you to know I'm going to get better and we are going to live the life we deserve — I promise." My promises meant absolutely nothing at this point, but she said, "I want to believe you."

GRATEFUL FOR NEW HOPE

Rehabs are filled with people who don't want to be there, usually forced by family and/or employers and I certainly fit that description. It may have been obvious to everyone else, but when I hung up the phone with Betty, it hit me that this was my home, like it or not, until I got sober or fooled the doctors into thinking I was going to stay sober — neither of which looked quick or easy with Dr. Lambeau to appease. Not long after I hung up with Betty, I was greeted by Phil, who was about as happy as I was being there — Phil "jumped the wall" the very next day. He told me we were in the same group — "The Professionals" as we were known. I laughed and asked, "Professional what? Druggies and drinkers?!" Phil said, "No, we're a small group of doctors, lawyers, professors, and, well, you're the pilot right?" I said, "Yeah, if the FAA ever lets me even near a plane again I am." "Well, look around. This place is filled with loser kids with rich parents. Don't listen to them, they'll just bring you down," he said. I thought, "I have a wife and four kids I can't provide for because I can't stay away from the bottle, and they're going to bring me down?!" Phil then said, "Look, we have Tony as our counselor and he is one tough son of a bitch. He won't like you and he won't believe anything you say even if it is the truth and he's been doing this longer than you and I have been alive, and it's his recommendation to Dr. Withers when we get out, so you might want to just get used to those facts right now." Hearing that made me realize, within twenty minutes of being conscious in Marworth, that if I wanted to get out of there in a reasonable amount of time, I had best get down to the business of getting sober, as fooling this Tony guy sounded like too tall of an order. The drinking (the buying, hiding, and disposing of the boxes and bottles too), lies, manipulations, stress, physical and mental decay all left me defeated and for the first time I felt I had surrendered to my vastly superior adversary. There was a calm that came over me in realizing that I had to surrender to beat it. And if I figured out why I drank and how to get sober in there, and I drank on the very drive home, I'd deal with it then, but God damn it, I saw my first glimpse of light at the end of the tunnel and for the first time in three years I had a glimpse of long-term hope against this nasty addiction.

As I walked into the small room where "The Professionals" met for ninety minutes every day, I got my first glimpse of Tony — and he of me. He was mid-fifties with a distinguished salt and pepper beard and an expressionless face. He looked at me for only a second, but as we arranged the couches and chairs into a circle, his look told me he was analyzing if I was going to lie to him about getting sober or not. His only words were, "We're wasting too much time," as we slid the furniture around. When we sat down, everyone introduced themselves to me. One thing stood out as I heard about their families and careers and a brief synopsis of what landed them in the room, and that was how accomplished everyone was. Over the last four years I couldn't figure out how I, a person who prided himself on above average intellect and willpower, couldn't outsmart my addiction — and neither could these gents who were far, far smarter than I. I thought The Professionals was just a feel-good label to get me to buy into this and give the group and the whole thing a chance. But as my peers went around the room, I heard from a psychiatrist, an anesthetist, a radiologist, a doctor of internal medicine (Phil), a highly renowned lawyer from NYC, and two professors from Ivy League schools — both, coincidentally, the head of their departments of Urology and Dentistry. I've always felt a sense of pride in being an airline pilot, but my first thought was I am clearly on the low end of the totem pole in this group. They all had an addiction to alcohol (with two also addicted to pain medications), so my second thought was, "If I they couldn't outsmart alcohol, I sure the hell wasn't going to."

At the end of that first session, I met Tony in his office and then Dr. Withers in his. It was a day with some big first impressions and I had to leave these two, in essence my parole officers, with the feeling that I was sincere in trying to understand my addiction and embrace a sober life. The meeting with Tony was short and I was brutally honest with him when he asked for me to assess myself. "I don't know why I drink, and I don't know if I can stay sober for the rest of my life, but I guess that's why I'm here and not out there," I said, as I pointed out his window. He appreciated my candor and said, "That's refreshing." Looking back on it, it's clear Tony was only assessing my level of honesty, both with him and with myself, and to see if I was going embrace the learning process or just say what I had to get the hell out — which described almost all of his patients he would later disclose to me in my final days there.

The meeting with Dr. Withers was almost an hour; quite a long assessment, considering that the facility had almost a hundred patients and dozens of employees that he oversaw. Dr. Lambeau probably had a hand in that, and during that session, Dr. Withers made it well known that he was "under very strict guidance" from Dr. Lambeau that I was not to be released until he was reasonably sure I would never drink again. I explained to Dr. Withers how hopeless of an alcoholic I was just days before and, though I thought of my kids and its impact on them, I accepted that I would die soon. "I essentially chose death over my family and future. In fact, I welcomed death. For the last month, I just wanted to be left alone, to go somewhere private and just drink until I quietly disappeared. It would have been better than living in that hell," I said trying to describe how gripping my addiction had become. My most powerful moment in my time at Marworth came when Dr. Withers then asked, "Have you ever heard of a wet house?" I responded, "No." "Well, maybe it's a good thing you hadn't. They are facilities for the truly hopeless alcoholics and they let you drink yourself to death." Pensive, I thought, "That sounds too good to be true, I could have drunk and died with people who understood me." Then, as the reality of never seeing my kids again set in, being only with strangers who didn't care about me, I thought, "I might be there now if Southern had fired me." I also wanted to say that a part of that hell I mentioned was living with Betty, but I had learned at Father Martin's the year before that if you're serious about your recovery, you don't blame anyone but yourself for picking up the bottle — and I absolutely had to carry on the perception of dedication to the tenets of recovery at all cost, even if it meant I had to hide a significant piece of the puzzle.

Just three days after landing myself in there, Betty told me a distant friend of mine, who prides himself on his immense willpower and the fact he has never drunk, stopped by our house. He's never done that and we hadn't talked for a couple of years, so I would guess he heard about my latest incarceration through Betty's brother. He asked a lot of questions about where I was, and when Betty told him I was on a trip, he asked when I would be back, saying, "We all need to catch up." He and his wife don't live that close to us, so dropping in under the auspices of just saying hi was not very believable. This was just confirmation that the whole world was going to know I was in rehab again and I was powerless to stop the word from spreading. Doing an assessment of the situation I put myself in, I knew I had a few true friends, my family, and, in due course, my job. I thought, "The rest of the world can think what it wants, I still have everything I'll ever need." This incident, and the lifting of the internal fog over those first few days, made that sliver of light from the first day much brighter and I started to accept my situation.

After a week, I had settled into the routine of the day and took advantage of the new gym by working out as hard as ever. I tend to do things to an extreme, hence why I was there, and the way I exercise is also subject to that trait. Intense workouts really clear my mind and focus me on what's important and it helped me to concentrate on getting my life back on track. During one of my workouts, I thought of channeling that trait of extremism in a positive way. It wasn't some pipe dream or fleeting flight of fancy; I asked for time out of the large groups and classes I wasn't getting much out of and I got to work intently on writing about how I was going to be good employee, a good husband, a good son, and far and away most importantly, a good father to my four children. Page after page of reflection, thoughts, planning, and hope, and every last word was contingent on staying sober — without that, there was nothing to fight for, it would all be gone. Those notes came home with me and, coupled with a sketchy journal I kept on my computer and the audio recordings of Betty's rages from years before (recorded in the hope that she would realize what she was doing to our family if I could get her to listen to them), became the not-known-at-the-time basis for this book.

My weeks there were starting to pass and one of the more helpful things for me came in the form of the mutual trust, respect, and friendships our group was forming. To hear them talk about their addiction, how they had made a mess of their professional and personal lives, and how they couldn't beat it in the face of the destruction of trust and respect, helped me to dismiss the thought that addiction is just a lack of wanting or willpower and the shame that came with it. Members of the group started to be released around the ten-week point if they instilled confidence in Tony, and, as I had a good patient-counselor relationship with him and Dr. Withers, I started to think my stay would be closer to that amount of time, not most of a year like Dr. Lambeau had previously alluded to.

A month into it, I had another one-on-one meeting with Tony. I was nervous, as I felt like he analyzed every word and its inflection when I spoke, and I looked at it as more of an interview than anything else. He started the session with, "Why did you drink?" I mostly dismissed it, saying, "I don't know." He asked it again, "Why did you drink?" Thinking he didn't hear me, I just repeated, "I don't know," with a little more emphasis. He looked at me intently, asking again louder and slower, and I muttered a much less confident, "I don't know." He asked a fourth time and I looked at him for what seemed like minutes, knowing I had to come up with the real answer. "I'm lonely," I blurted, almost turning the answer into a question. He just looked at me, patiently waiting for more. "I'm lonely," I said again to him with more reassurance. Then, dumbfounded at the obviousness of it, I said it again so I could hear myself saying it — saying the elusive answer to why I chose to destroy my career, my finances, my family, my reputation, and my mind and body — everything I valued. It was too much to take in all at once and I burst out crying and buried my face in my hands from the shame of its simplicity. I left his office shortly thereafter and asked him if I could have an hour to myself to try and absorb what I had just learned, to look back at the last four years to see just how much of the drinking the loneliness had caused. With everyone in class, I went into the empty workout room and, in a daze, tried to think it over while sitting on a weight bench. It hit me why I didn't think of it before. "I'm married. I'm married AND lonely," I thought, almost as baffled as I had been in Tony's office. And this is the moment I finally understood my addiction.

Phone calls were only allowed twice a week, but in my first week, I negotiated with Dr. Withers to call every other day at a minimum because it would be difficult to learn anything and clear my mind if I was worried about how Betty was doing with the kids for up to four days at a time. He hesitated, worried that the other patients would see the preferential treatment, so I pleaded with him by disclosing that she was easily overwhelmed and had been physically abusive to the kids many times. With that, he agreed and added, "You can call as many times as circumstances warrant if you feel things aren't going well at home." Most of the time, I only called every other day from his assistant's office, as I didn't want the other patients knowing I was getting special treatment. The need to make the extra calls also helped get the point across to Dr. Withers that my home life was less than ideal without directly indicting Betty as one of the reasons for my drinking.

Over the years when I was working, I would typically ask Betty how the kids were if I couldn't talk to them myself. They were always "fine" or she might vent about their misbehaviors or having to run them around, but she is never, and I do mean never, one to admit any chance of wrongdoing on her part. Yet I would come home from my trips and see scratches and bruises on the kids' faces. So it was very noteworthy when I called her one evening and she said, "Stephen and I didn't have a very good day." It struck me as unusual and I can still vividly remember her saying it four years later. I asked her, "What happened," and she said, "Nothing, he's just being Stephen," which is family vernacular for him moping, refusing to do things, or picking on his siblings. I didn't want to stress her out by pressing the issue and I was powerless to do anything about it, so I just let it go with, "Okay," but I laid in bed that night wondering if everything, especially Stephen, was truly okay.

I had now been in Marworth for five weeks. Over that time, my honesty and dedication to truly getting sober earned me some respect from Tony, Dr. Withers, and my group. I knew my place amongst my group peers, in that I realized they were much smarter than me, but my confidence in knowing I had to admit defeat to win wasn't something their personalities easily led them to embrace. They were as successful as they were because of their intellect and determination, but, like me just five weeks before, that same intellect and determination is what kept them from admitting they couldn't beat their addiction — always fighting an adversary that rapidly got stronger the more you fought it.

I could sense that I wasn't going to be at Marworth for any longer than the rest of the professionals and that became a reality when my insurance said they would not be paying for any more than forty-five days. The problem was, Dr. Withers, Dr. Lambeau, and Tony had to be confident that I understood my addiction enough not to drink again — a tall order to fill in half the time the program was designed for. I couldn't afford the near $1,000 a day price tag, but I also knew too much pressure to leave from me would alarm them. Again, I called on my affinity for graphs and charts, bypassing much of my inability to put things clearly into words. Tony and Dr. Withers liked the chart I made it because it showed a typical alcoholic's ability to stay sober over their life and where my plots were, past, present, and future. Not that dots on a chart can convince doctors and counselors exclusively that I would stay sober, but the very fact that I could come up with the idea, was able to talk about where my plots fell, and most importantly, why, was enough to impress them and get me into the final part of the program a month early. In the two weeks before we are released, The Professionals get to go to AA meetings in the town of Scranton and actually get to go home for forty-eight hours. Though I still felt like I was under a microscope, it was nice to feel that little bit of trust. In the two trips home, the program required quite a bit of time at AA meetings, but seeing my family again, and them seeing me in a happy, healthy state, was one of the greatest moments of my life.

THE LONG ROAD BACK

I drove home from Marworth hooting and hollering like someone who had just pulled off an impossible victory over the most formidable opponent, because that is exactly what happened between me and my nemesis of alcohol. Living with an addiction is just that, you have to live with it — as in the rest of your life. One never wins or "beats it" as I've heard talk-show hosts say about celebrities on TV, but I knew I had it this time and I also knew that I would be reunited with my kids as fast as I could get home. I was so excited that I made the five-hour trip in four, not even stopping to go to the bathroom on the drive home — instead, going in the plastic coke bottles I brought as I passed cars and eighteen-wheelers as I drove down I-80.

When I returned from Marworth, I couldn't wait to spend every minute possible with the kids. I tried to reestablish a closeness with Betty, and it was a nice reunion with her, but her biggest problem with me, that I wasn't working, still existed. We were back to avoiding each other in just a few days, and I settled into a mostly single dad role. Just like my last return from rehab fourteen months before, it served both purposes of keeping Betty's stress down and I got to interact with the kids as much as possible. We had our first week of fairly low-conflict family life since Betty was last pregnant (and I wasn't consumed with consuming alcohol), which had been over four years ago. But the normalcy gave way when we got into another argument, about what I don't know, but it was noteworthy because she said, "You're exactly the same as when you left two months ago! You're not any different, you just don't drink!" I looked at her and wondered, "What in the hell did you expect, for me to come home a world-class chef who buys you flowers every day? It wasn't a magic school; it was a rehab." When school let out for the summer and the kids were home all day, her depression turned to anger, which turned to rage. Physical fights and screaming became part of our everyday life again.

One of the more persistent disagreements Betty and I had over the years came to a head in June one morning. Our disagreements centered around the time she insisted we attend the church service — 8:00 a.m. Saturday nights were a time I wanted to have fun with the kids, watching a movie or doing something like bowling or miniature golf, but the church was twenty-five minutes away and getting the kids out of bed at 7:15 meant an early bedtime the night before. I would periodically ask Betty to go to the 10:00 service, or preferably, the 9:00 service, at the church we'd been married at, just five minutes away, but her "real family" went to the distant, early service and it simply was not up for discussion. I once asked her, "If Sunday is a day of rest, why are we setting our alarm for 6:45?" If looks could kill... This particular Sunday, with about fifteen minutes to go in the service, I was sneezing a lot and I excused myself to go to the bathroom to avoid any further embarrassment. As Betty and her family sit in the first row, I didn't want to walk in front of everyone for the last ten minutes, so I waited in the back until the service was over. After chatting with a few of the people we regularly saw there, we got into our van. As soon as the door shut, she yelled,

"You never want to be with my family! You hate my family!" and a litany of other accusations, with the kids sitting right behind us. People were still walking out of church and, judging by their stares, they could easily hear her. I let her go, knowing that I would only prolong the episode by defending myself, and when she was done, I said to her, "Don't you ever ask me to go to church with you ever again," — and she didn't. A couple of years later, my absence at church had turned into things like I never cared about raising the kids and that I was atheist. The eight-year-old disagreement over the time she went and why was conveniently left out.

One of the ways I tried to keep Betty calm was by not changing our spending habits. We still ate out a lot with the kids, we went on occasional trips, and did some home improvements. Contradicting the strategy of living like we always had though, one morning I had the audacity to ask her to look into finding work as a teacher or getting a full-time job at the base when the kids went back to school that fall. Substitute teaching just a day or two a week would have sufficed. She glared at me and said, "You put us in this f---king position, not me! It's not my responsibility to get us out of it!" And that was just the start of a verbal offensive that ended in her saying, "I'll just kill you, problem solved!" Betty couldn't shock me anymore; I had heard it all. But the problem was, I believed her when she threatened to kill me and I started to put my shoes on to go somewhere — anywhere but there. When Betty saw me leaving, she yelled throughout the house, "Kids, come here! Come see this! Your dad doesn't want to be with you, so he's leaving! Kids, now!" I glared at Betty and whispered, "What the hell are you doing?!" As the kids started to appear from their rooms and the basement, they stopped and looked at her with fear of what might happen next all over their faces. To get them to come to her, she then sounded nicer and softer, "Come here, I want to tell you something." They gathered around her as I stood there wondering what she was doing and ready to intervene. "Your dad is an alcoholic and he has been in and out of three rehabs." Now I was in shock — and unable to say anything that wouldn't incite her even more. After she repeated herself, I knew she wanted me to become angry in front of the kids so they would have a reason to hate me like she did. When I sneered at her, she upped the ante, "He doesn't even have a job anymore, and we'll probably have to move. You won't have a home and you won't even be able to eat." Our four kids were all under eight years old, completely lost and afraid. I started to lose my composure, and yelled, "Betty! Stop!" She cruelly smiled, knowing I couldn't stop her, and she knelt down to their level and said, "It's true," as I walked out the door. I left hoping that would get her to stop by removing at least one of her motivations, that of the kids seeing me disgraced. But as I left, I turned around to look through the glass storm door and she was still kneeling and talking to them, their scared faces telling me the end was nowhere near. When I got in my car, she came out and stood in the driveway behind me for a couple of minutes so that I couldn't leave. I knew this was just a game to her, but I was losing my patience and I rolled down the window and said in a calm, but stern tone, "Please move, Betty." She said "No!" After we went back and forth a few more times, she finally said, "We didn't need you for two months, and we don't need you now, and if you come back here I WILL kill you."

This argument, and the thought that she might try to kill me in my sleep, led to the first of our two short separations. I drove around our town looking at apartments, but I quickly learned that they needed far more time to do credit and background checks than I had. In complete desperation, I drove to my parents' house (but parked on a different street in case Betty drove by), and I looked on Craigslist. I thought if someone was looking to rent their house, perhaps they'd sympathize with my plight and let me in that very night. I called a lady who lived five miles from our neighborhood and she told me she was looking to rent the upstairs of her new home. When I went over that evening to look around she was a bit distant with me at first as she was probably leery of renting to a man fifteen years younger than she was. But when she showed me her kitchen she said, "You can put beer or whatever in the fridge, but I don't drink, so I don't keep any in the house." My curiosity was piqued and I asked her the coded question for AA, "Are you a friend of Bill?" She turned her head, almost like a curious dog, and said, "Yes. Yes I am! Are you?!" I said I most definitely was and from there on we had a mutual bond and trust. I gave her my check and spent that night, and the next seven, there.

My separation, if eight days even counts as a separation, was so short because Betty knew how to get to me — by withholding the kids. I would call Betty to talk to the kids, but she wouldn't let me unless I told her where I was. But I refused; the need to protect my safe-house was paramount. I never told anyone, including my parents, of its location as I didn't want them to either have to lie or cave to Betty's pressure. After a couple of days at Andrea's house, I couldn't stand knowing the kids were so close but I could not see or talk to them, so I started going to the girls' gym practices. Betty quickly caught on and stopped taking them until I either told her where I was staying or I came home. This was my first realization that she would be extremely controlling with the kids if I were to divorce her. After a week, I was weary of being without the kids and Betty knew she was wearing me down. She called me one night and asked me to look at the master bath sink, which was leaking onto the floor. I knew I'd be able to see the kids, even though they were sleeping, and the thought of water running down to the lower floor concerned me, so I went to the house. When I walked in, Betty was standing at the top of the steps in the Victoria's Secret underwear that I had bought her a couple of years before and she'd never worn. She knew I wouldn't be able to resist, and as much of an embarrassment as it is to admit, the leaking sink was a ruse and my separation was over as fast as it started.

Just like the summer before, the six of us went on a few weekend trips. One was a trip to Lake Erie, where we rented a boat. I had always wondered if I would enjoy boating and I knew that Betty loved pools; this was the perfect time to find out if we had a mutual interest. We rented a small, under-powered boat and we instantly fell in love with it. I watched Betty during the three-hour trip on the lake and she looked happy just sitting and laying there as we bobbed over the small waves, and I knew any time spent on a boat was time she and I could be content. We also tried tubing and I took some of pictures of the kids and her on it, and if one didn't know any better, we looked as happy and healthy as families could be.

We came home and Betty and I scoured every possible outlet for a fixer-upper boat that was both affordable and yet big enough to fit our family of six plus a few friends — the fact that I didn't know how to trailer a boat, or much about operating one, didn't matter. I actually had to tell Betty to give the search a rest after a few days because she was searching incessantly. We found one after six days and it was perfect; it was big enough to hold nine and it was in marginal shape, keeping the cost down. From then on, time on the boat became one of my highest priorities. Yes, it was fun and yes the kids liked tubing off the back of it, and yes, the prepping and towing was a lot of work, but seeing her happy gave me hope — hope for her to be happy and rejoin our family. The boat seemed to have an after-effect on Betty that nothing else was able to do, and she carried that happiness for hours afterwards.

We were spending the same amount of money as if I was working, maybe more with the boat, and I was getting about half of my normal paycheck in the form of disability, so I decided to ramp up the camera rental business I had started a year before to see if I could fill the financial hole. Originally, I rented to only a few select photographers, but I needed to expand the business to bridge the gap until I went back to Southern. I started by joining forces with my cross-town competitor, Ben. We were busy as Ben and I took on more clients, but I needed a lot more equipment if we were going to make the fledgling company a reliable resource for photographers throughout the city. I knew it was going to take at least $50,000 to buy all of the cameras and lenses and that is almost exactly what I had in an online investment account. As I figured this out, I asked Betty to come into the room and I told her, "I want to grow the camera business — a lot. I think it can make us enough money until I get back to work, but I have to buy quite a bit more on the Canon side and everything for Nikon." She looked at me intently and asked, "Where are you getting the money from?" I said, "From our Ameritrade account and home equity loan. Our Ameritrade is worth less than what we have put into it over the ten years, so that money can actually work for us in the form of rentals instead of going down." After giving it a few seconds, she said, "I trust you." With her approval, I liquidated the account and I was shopping online within minutes for used, but good condition cameras and lenses. Ben got to work revising the website, creating spreadsheets, making client lists and newsletters, and suddenly we found ourselves entrepreneurs.

One night I was downstairs reading about a potential new camera for the business when I heard Betty yell, "You're a little f---ing witch!" I yelled, "Betty!" and I went up into the girls' room where Betty was picking up clothes and Julie was sitting on the floor, crying. Betty said, "I told her to put these clothes away and she said no!" Still crying, Julie became emphatic, "But I'm wearing them tomorrow!" Betty yelled, "I don't care!" in an extremely angry and condescending tone that told me this could get a lot worse. I don't remember much else, besides just kneeling down to Julie and telling her, "It's okay," as Betty left the room, with the shock of hearing her say that to our seven-year-old daughter settling into my mind.

This highlighted Betty's mindset of, "Do what I tell you, or I will make you regret it," and she was not open to any contradiction or negotiating. At a very young age, Julie had developed an adept ability to negotiate while also knowing when it was futile and time to back down — so I knew Julie was most likely a hundred percent in the right before I even went upstairs. But Julie's young mind was already starting to out-wit Betty's limited reasoning ability and this was not the first — nor would it be the last — time Betty would perceive her authority as threatened and lash out. Most differences ended with Betty having nothing left to say except an angry, "Because I said so!" Betty's need for a perfectly organized and clean house with four kids, and her fierce enforcement methods, were growing problems within our troubled family and her expectation that the kids, and me to some extent, become subservient was neither realistic nor healthy.

On Julie's eighth birthday, I was cleaning the house when two women knocked on the door. I initially thought they were camera clients there for a pickup that I must have forgotten about, but seeing their messenger bags and clipboards through the glass told me otherwise. "Hi, I'm Sheila from Child Youth and Family, are you Rob?" one asked when I opened the door. "Yes, I am," I said as a huge chill came over me. "We're here to investigate an allegation that your son Stephen has had some bruises on his neck; may we come in?" Absolutely in shock, I stared and muttered, "Sure." We sat down at the kitchen table (Betty stood off to the side) and I called my mom to bring Stephen down to our house. I hung up and asked, "Who called you and what did they say?" They, of course, could not disclose that, but I wasn't thinking clearly yet. They asked me some questions about my relationship with Stephen and the other three kids, questions that are now lost in the fog of it all. What woke me up was Stephen walking through the door and saying "Hi" as he came over to me. I introduced him to the ladies and, probably thinking they were just camera clients like I initially did, he sat on my lap. I saw Sheila sit up a little and look over at the other lady, who went from looking at us to annotating something on her clipboard. Sheila's tone changed from business-like to cheery and excited to talk to a nine-year-old when she said, "I see you like being with your dad, Stephen. What are some of the things you like to do with him?" Stephen, happy but embarrassed at the thought of suddenly getting to talk about himself, said, "Well...we play baseball and build Thomas the Train track and build Lincoln Log houses and...build Legos, annnd... ride bicycles...and do lots of other things." Sheila said, "That's a lot!" After a little more chit-chat, she said, "Okay Stephen, it was very nice meeting you, but may I have a few minutes to talk to your mom and dad alone?" As he got up, I noticed the women focused on the back and sides of his neck, but he didn't have any visible marks. I then asked him to play outside so there wasn't any chance he could hear us.

Sheila's continued smile gave me some reassurance that she knew I had not abused Stephen and she asked Betty to sit down to ask both of us some questions. As we were finishing, it hit me like a ton of bricks — that Betty was probably the one who left bruises on Stephen's neck and she may have even been the one who called CYF — on me! The bruises on Stephen were healed and mostly gone now, but her history of scratching and bruising the kids around their necks and faces was well known to the school, my family, and our neighbors. In the days before the CYF visit, I told her I was going to separate again or even divorce her if she didn't get some professional help or go on stronger medication for her anger. She knew I was serious too, because she had found a brochure in my car just a few days before for a nice apartment complex that had a pool and other things for the kids to do. Was this allegation intended to give her a leg up, or give me pause if I decided to divorce her? I looked up at Betty, just sitting there all proper with her hands folded, chatting with the agents. I started to ask some questions of my own, most of which the two women weren't allowed to answer. "When did this person call you? Where did it happen? Did they identify themself?" The questions were, of course, all met with protection for the caller's identity. I then asked, "What is stopping this person from calling CYF again with the same allegation against me?!" The other lady said, "Nothing, they can call every day until your kids are eighteen and we would have to come here and check on them every time." Sheila chimed in, "And there is a family we do that with. Someone calls every day and every day we have to go — no exceptions." I said, "Well, I guess you can't take any chances." When they left, I just wanted to enjoy Julie's party, which would begin in less than an hour, not confront Betty. The following day, I almost asked her if she was the one who called CYF, but I knew it would instigate a huge fight. I thought, "What is she going to say, actually admit she did it?!" and I just became more resolved to separate again.

Later that week, I answered our house phone and it was Betty's sister, Peg. She was crying, which is very unlike her as she is strong-willed and somewhat mean. She said, "Rob, can you get Betty?" I said, "Sure Peg, hold on." I knew something was very wrong, and as I walked up to Betty in the entryway, I told her, "It's Peg. This isn't going to be a very good conversation." I stood there as Betty said, "Hello?...What?...What Peg? Peg?!" and she dropped the phone and literally ran around the house screaming "No!" at the top of her lungs over and over. Her brother, Robby, had just killed himself and it came without any warning — easily the biggest shock I have ever had. The mother of Stephen's best friend had just pulled into our driveway to drop off Stephen when we got the call. I met Paige out in the driveway and we could hear Betty screaming inside the house. I told her what had just happened and asked her if she could take Stephen back up to her house. She agreed, of course, and offered to tell my parents what had happened so we could go and meet Betty's family, who were gathering at Betty's oldest brother's house. Paige was my parents' next-door neighbor (to the downhill side), so her arrival could not have been better timed. When we got to Daniel's, the sadness and despair was beyond my ability to put into words — and it still is. The family was torn apart and there wasn't anything we could do or say; he was gone forever. We knew he suffered from depression, but there wasn't any foreshadowing nor a note to make sense of it, his conflict almost all internal.

The next day we went to Betty's parents' house and Betty's mom Pat asked me to be in charge of the pictures for his viewing. I felt honored to be trusted again by the family that had had to witness my last drinking binge just seven months before and I took to the task with a determination and fervor that showed I wanted nothing more than to make amends. I asked the whole family to get as many pictures as they could find and I got started on putting together a slide show set to his favorite music that showed his very outgoing, fun-loving personality and life as he would want those who knew him to remember him. It was a huge responsibility and I wanted to capture it in the very best way possible.

Pat and Dale also entrusted me to be the one to tell the kids and Pat wanted me to tell them as we sat on their bed. When we had all gathered in their bedroom and were sitting, I told them that Uncle Robby had been in an accident and, "He is in heaven now." Julie immediately erupted in tears and repeated "No!" just like Betty the night before. I looked at Stephen and he had a blank stare and I asked him if he was okay. He just stared, still processing what he had just heard. All of us were huddled on the bed crying, the adults trying to be strong for the kids, but the pain was far too much to be kept in and those ten minutes were some of the most powerful moments and memories in my life.

In Betty's defense, she didn't initially take her brother's suicide out on me like I had braced for. In the week after, our lives were actually quite normal, if you can call a broke, unemployed, alcoholic father and an angry, abusive mother who resented her four kids' existence normal. But after that first week, Betty was done with the self-reflection and prayer and we returned to our paradigm of the last nine years. Our opposition resumed with one of our more persistent arguments, her low tolerance for things left out by the kids and me. I would defend us if the things were often used, further inciting her need for the perfectly organized house. My stance was that we were a busy house with four little kids and there were going to be temporary messes, but the inside of our house had to look like she wanted the outside world to perceive us — perfect. This, despite the fact that our family was so broken and her anger and depression so great that I had begun keeping a journal of her behavior, now on my computer titled WSHD, for What She Has Done.

A couple of weeks after Robby's suicide, we had two issues in one day. In the morning, I was trying to give her some sense of purpose, so I asked if she would hand out cameras and lenses when I went back to work. "I set this up so you can run it from home and still make some money," I told her. I also told her she could keep most of the money and do whatever she wanted with it; it would be hers. She became dis-tressed and said, "I don't want to do that." I asked, "Why not?" and she said, "I don't know, I guess I don't like cameras." But the stage was set, and she knew I was frustrated, even though I was trying so hard not to show it. Just a little bit later, she blew up because I had a small stack of papers on the kitchen table and I tried to explain why I wanted them there. But after doing so, I quickly tried to placate her by taking the papers, mostly mail, and putting them in the library. Probably sensing that her tirade got her what she wanted, for me to move the papers, she then said, "And what about all of the other f---ing piles of crap you have all over the house, like in the dining room?!" We didn't use the dining room and, with the kids and their schoolwork overtaking the small study, I had made the dining room table my office. "That's my office, that's all pertaining to the camera business," I said.

I was now applying a new tactic to counteract Betty's hostility. Instead of repeatedly defending and explaining myself, which only incited her, I started saying my piece and then I would leave the house for an hour or two. This didn't work for her though because it didn't fit the family model she grew up with. After having kids, Pat used Dale as her punching bag, figuratively speaking. Betty's sister had been doing the same thing to her once strong, independent husband over the last several years too. The men were expected to just stand there and take it as the women vented their anger. In the fifteen years I've known Betty and her family, I've never once heard Pat say anything nice about Dale. Dale is a hard worker too, both at home and at work, but Pat would yell at him because he wasn't working on whatever she wanted — demands which almost always seemed to me to be unreasonable. Every time, he would just stand there and take it, never once defending himself. No doubt, Betty was very frustrated that I didn't fall in line with the family dynamic and she had recently started making me pay for leaving the house after arguments by throwing things I valued into the garbage. They may have only been toiletries or camera magazines, hardly anything of significant value, but it was spiteful because she knew I wanted or needed them. Of more concern though, I knew if throwing out the little things didn't work to keep me from leaving, she would move on to bigger, more valuable things and I had to weigh the pros and cons of leaving very carefully.

When I came home after the mail incident, Betty was sitting at my laptop in my makeshift dining room office. She had never shown an interest in my computer before and when she looked up at me, she looked vindicated. Skeptical, I asked her, "What are you doing?" She didn't say a word, she just got up and walked away with a smirk. When I sat down, I saw that she had deleted a folder I had on the desktop simply labeled

"Kids," which were the pictures I had started taking of the kids' bruises and scratches right before my first separation just months before. My screen had dozens of folders, mostly of various pictures, and coupled with the fact she had never bothered to look at my computer before and that my covert folder was a nondescript name, made me too complacent. The Kids folder was right next to the Excel spreadsheet WSHD, and I am lucky she didn't see and delete that too. Betty was clearly jealous of my growing relationship with the kids, so I guess she was looking for pictures my mom had taken of me playing with them when she came across this folder. It did occur to me to have the hard drive recovered, but it was prohibitively expensive. A year and a half later, I would do just that, but they were not recoverable.

The very next day, we had another fight when I confronted her about not meeting the kids at the bus stop. I couldn't be there because I had to meet Ben to exchange a few lenses for the upcoming weekend and again, our disagreement went south and ended with her rounding up the kids and saying all of the same scarring things she had said to them several times before. I left the house and when I pulled out of the driveway, Betty was standing on the sidewalk and, reminiscent of four months before, said, "If you come back, I will kill you." I said, "You can't kill what you can't find," and I left. I called Andrea as I was pulling away, and for the second time that year, I briefly separated.

About a week into the separation, I was curious about the possibility of being single again and I made an account on a free dating site, Plenty of Fish, that Andrea had just told me about. Although I only looked at some of the online profiles, I began to wonder what life would be like with a couple of the women I seemed to have a lot in common with and whose natural demeanor appeared to be of happiness and affection. My stance within our marriage had become one of tolerating Betty's volatility and hostility towards me and the kids and, if she didn't get help for her anger, I was eventually going to look elsewhere for long-term companionship. I looked, wanting a glimpse into the future I suppose. The problem with divorcing her now was that I didn't trust her living alone with the kids and I wanted her accountable to me for their well-being and upbringing. This need for accountability and protection for the kids prevented me from thinking seriously about divorce until all of the kids were old enough to defend themselves, get themselves to their activities, and have more of my influence on ideas of what is right and wrong — at least another ten years away from this point considering Christian was only five.

I managed to stay separated for two weeks this time, until the pain of not getting to talk to the kids wore me down and broke me again. Although mostly a bluff, I was quick to tell Betty during my negotiations with her to come home of my window shopping on the dating site and that I would be happy with or without her. Even considering the broken state of our marriage, I was still surprised when she said, "I've been on there too," in reference to Plenty of Fish, though it could have been a lie as she tried to regain some of her lost control in our marriage.

At my next counseling session with Francine, I was back to living at home and Betty came with me. The session was, of course, consumed by Robby's death and Betty told Francine I separated just weeks afterwards. Francine looked at me and said, "What?! Her brother dies and you leave her?!" Not being sure how to respond to such an uninformed accusation, and starting to waver on shielding Francine from the worst of our marriage, I told her, "There's so much you don't know! Some of it might be life or death!" Betty just sat there, completely silent. Francine, shaking her head and holding her hands out, said, "There has already been a death, and that was her brother! What were you thinking? What were you thinking?! She needed you and you abandoned her!" I said, "Francine, that's not the way it was, I didn't abandon her." Francine was still shaking her head and I decided to cut my losses and move on with the discussion by just listening to Betty talk, but it caused a rift between Francine and I for months.

Now December, our disability was set to run out in six months on May 9th. It was apparent that my camera business was not going to cut it as our only income and my respectful but persistent requests for Betty to find work fell on deaf ears. I wanted to ask Dr. Lambeau about starting the long process of going back to work in light of the fact it had taken six months from when we started last time, but I knew he would probably balk at the prospect until I had been sober a year. Regardless, the day our disability was to run out was a big looming black cloud to Betty and she wanted answers about what we (really only me) were going to do for money if I wasn't back to flying by then. I knew the process of interviews, tests, and the FAA's review would be lengthy seeing as how I'd lied to everyone about my (lack of) sobriety the first time, and the process of determining if I was drinking or not would be longer due to the lost trust with everyone involved. So one evening, I waited until Dr. Lambeau's last patient was gone to appeal to him. I told him my disability was running out and I reminded him of his words before I left for Marworth when he was still trying to sell me on it: "We'll get you back to work ASAP." — and he blew up. "I have Dr. Withers and Francine telling me you are 'The Master Manipulator' and God damn it, you embarrassed the f---ing hell out of me and Dr. Thompson last time! You don't f---ing come in here and tell me how it's"— I leaned forward in my chair and loudly interrupted, "Hey! I've done everything you've asked me to do and I'm sober and you know it, God damn it! If you think you're going to make me pay for embarrassing you last time by bringing up the past, I won't have it! Who are WE, who are YOU talking about?! The Rob Black, the drunk, or the Rob Black of the last nine months who has legitimately worked his ass off and completely turned his life around?!" With Betty and her ever escalating anger to go home and answer to, I took a huge, uncalculated gamble; he would either get my application going, or his massive ego would cause him to explode and abandon me as his patient, completely ruining any chance of going back to work in the next three years. I sat back and prepared for his reaction. He looked at me intently with his furrowed brow telling me that he didn't immediately know which way he was going to react — processing the surprise of someone who he was supposed to have complete control over challenging his mindset. We sat there in silence for an uncomfortably long time just looking at each other. My unyielding stare must have told him I was serious and the situation was dire because he finally relaxed and said, "Okay Rob, I'll look at getting you back. We'll start by scheduling the interview and tests with Dr. Becker." "Thank you," I simply said. He must have regretted his words somewhat, and looking to take his authority back, his voice became deep and loud again as I stood up to leave, "And don't you f--k it up this time, I've had it dealing with all your shit!" I smiled at him and said, "Thanks doc."

Unbeknownst to me, although Dr. Lambeau said he would start the process, he didn't say when, and his intention to drag it out as long as possible became clearer with each week that passed without an appointment to see Dr. Becker. When I would call his office to see if the interview and the day-long aptitude tests that follow it were scheduled, I got, "Dr. Becker is backed up for weeks," and, "He is on vacation." Breaking the news to Betty left her visibly unsettled each time and her disdain for the kids and me got significantly worse. From January of 2013 on, she belittled the three older kids countless times, calling Stephen "Stupid" and the girls "Little f---ing witches" or "Little f---ing bitches" more often. And, through her "meetings" with the kids, she outlined how and why our family was in financial ruin time and time again.

In late February, Julie had a gym meet in Morgantown, West Virginia and all six of us drove down the day before. Betty hardly ever drove (she significantly pulses, or jabs, the gas pedal, which my mentioning had caused more than one heated argument), but I asked her to drive this time because it was an easy route (I-79 runs from Pittsburgh to Morgantown) and I could work on editing some pictures of the kids and Julie's last gym meet until I fell asleep, as I was tired from working on them the night before. When I looked up from my computer, I saw us about to cross a bridge that I knew wasn't on I-79. I asked her, "Where are we?" and she said, "On 79." I said, "I don't think so." I spoke with a bit of uncertainty, wondering if I could be wrong, but when I put the course in my phone, it confirmed that we were heading east on I-70, not south on I-79, twenty-two miles off course. There is a small section where the two highways are one, and she must have stayed on 70 despite the marked interchange when they split again. When I realized this, I knew if I said anything she would blow up, so I just put my face in my hands trying hard to keep my mouth shut. When she saw me and sensed my frustration, she yelled, "Well, you're over there working on those God damned pictures!" like they were some frivolous pursuit.

Putting my face back into my hands, I said as calmly as I could, "Betty, all you had to do was stay on I-79," and with that she'd had it.

Now speeding so she could get to the next exit and turn around, she called her dad and said, "Dad, Rob doesn't know how to get there, can you tell me?" I said, "What? I do too." Betty ignored me, getting directions from her dad instead of admitting I knew the way. Now turned around and heading in the right direction, and with Betty off the phone, I asked, "Why did you call your dad? I know exactly where we are." She didn't say a word, she just stared straight ahead. I was determined to get an answer, so I asked again. Betty abruptly sped up again, passing an 18-wheeler. After passing the truck, she pulled back over into the right lane and hit the brakes. I screamed, "No!" and jerked the steering wheel, pulling the car onto the shoulder of the road. The trucked passed us halfway into the left lane with its horn blowing as it tried to avoid hitting us. I yelled, "What are you doing?!" She didn't say a word, she just accelerated normally and got back on the road like it never happened. I was shaking, but I had to keep her from trying it again, so I tried to say in a calmer tone, "What are you doing?" She stared out the window and pulled off the exit in front of us and onto a nearby side street. She stopped the van under a bridge and got out of the van, and I did too. "What are you doing?" I asked. "I'm walking home! I can't f---ing stand to be around you anymore!" she yelled. "You are not walking home; we are 60 miles away, Betty. Please, can we just get back in the van and go to the hotel?" I said, now in a very calm, reassuring voice to get her to get back into the van. She kept walking away, and I wondered what effect this was having on the kids and I became determined to get her into the car. The only way I knew to get Betty to do what I wanted was to appeal to her fragile ego, so I said, "Look Betty, I'm sorry if I acted frustrated, I'm just so tired and I have so much work to do. It's not your fault; let's just get back in and go." She was still walking away, but her glances back at me told me she was on the cusp of cooperating. "Look, we have all day and night to get there and it only cost us forty-five minutes, so who cares? Come on, please? I'll drive the rest of the way." With that, she turned around and glared at me, as if to say, "I'll get in, but if you ever bring this up again, I will kill you." She got in the passenger seat and, as I drove away, I turned on a movie and chatted with the kids to put them at ease. Unbeknownst to me, Betty was in the passenger seat stewing. I should have known because of what I had previously identified as her "anger profile," where she'd get madder and madder at whatever provoked her, regardless of what I said or did, including apologizing, and then she would explode in an uncontrollable rage. Normally, if that is the right word, this would be followed by two to three days of avoiding me (and me her) and after that she acted like nothing ever happened. A day or two later, it would be time to fight again. A story in the book *Stop Walking On Eggshells* says it a different way: "My wife threw the car keys at my head and accused me of hating her when I took the kids to the movies. When we got back, she acted like nothing had happened. She wondered why I was still upset and told me that I have problems letting go of my anger." Now back on the highway and after a few minutes of stewing, it was time to explode and she did that by punching me with a hammer fist square in the eye as I looked in the side view mirror to move into the left lane. I knew by now that when she got to this stage it was best to become passive, to let her do what she wanted. And what she wanted was for me to fight back in front of the kids, but I just looked at her in disgust and drove in silence, bracing for her to hit me again. When I didn't engage, she yelled, "You're a f---ing asshole!" and climbed into the back seat between Christian and Stephen, where she opened my overnight bag. Then she opened Christian's window and threw out my socks and underwear. Again, this was just to provoke me into battling her, but I didn't, and she finally gave up and stayed back there for the rest of the drive, pretending to watch the movie.

When we got to the hotel, I went into the bathroom and put makeup concealer around my red eye. I got the idea years before, when I had to fly to Chicago to start work with a slightly bruised eye. By now I had gotten pretty good at applying it and making my marks and bruises mostly go away (scratches, when they happened, were much more diffi-cult to hide). Once again, by covering my eye, I protected Betty's image in front of the other gym parents because I was too ashamed to admit how dysfunctional our family had become. Besides, who would believe it anyway? Betty was sure to be her smiling, soft-spoken, chatty self and the kids were so used to the fighting that this was somewhat normal to them. Though I'm sure they were very scared, none of the kids did or said anything when Betty slammed on the brakes, when she got out of the van, when she punched me, or when she threw my stuff out the window — that was just Mom and she would be fine as soon as we were around other adults.

Monday morning, I called Francine and told her what had happened. I sensed an air of skepticism from her that I was making it up or greatly exaggerating my recount of the drive. She said she would call Betty right away and I asked for her to call me as soon as they finished talk-ing. Just fifteen minutes later, Francine called me back. "Rob, I talked to Betty," she said. "Oh really, what did she say?" I asked, expecting Francine to tell me Betty's side of the story — that I instigated the whole thing and I was the one being combative. "She admitted to hitting you while you were driving and throwing your things out the window and said she didn't know what came over her — like she stepped outside of herself," Francine said. Completely taken aback that Betty would admit any fault, I had to clarify. "Those were her words?! The stepping outside of herself?!" "All of it," Francine said. I chuckled with relief that finally someone other than myself was learning who the real Betty was and that maybe, together, we could start to figure out what was going on inside Betty's head. It was not the first time, but after Betty admitted this to Francine, I pressed Francine to get Betty on some very serious medication — not the typical Zanex, Zoloft, and whatever else was out there for people with run-of-the-mill depression. I didn't want to act like a doctor of internal medicine, but I'd asked Francine about lithium for Betty many times. The problem was, Betty refused to admit she had a problem and wouldn't see a psychiatrist, who would be the one to prescribe her such a drug.

After this, I started trying to recruit a few of the neighborhood women to take Betty to lunch or dinner, or anything to get her out of the house. I perceived the house was the problem as that was, despite the recent incident in the car, where Betty was most consistently angry. One lady in particular, whom Betty identified with because her younger brother had recently died too, walked her dog every morning around 9:00. After I got the kids off to school, I walked up to her house and, when I saw her about to walk her dog, I asked her if she could talk for a bit. "Sure Rob, what's going on?" she said as she put Stadler back inside. "Here, let's sit down and talk," she said and we sat at the end of her driveway by the street. I said, "I just want to see if you can get Betty out of the house once in a while. You know, take her to lunch or something like that. Tea even." "Sure. Is everything okay?" "No," I said, trying to gauge the interest in her eyes. "I know your brother's passing was very hard on you, and again, I am so sorry Jeanne — I just don't know what to say. I know you were close with him." "I was very close with him, and people don't understand that. They think because he wasn't my husband or child that I shouldn't be so upset. They just don't understand. How is Betty doing with her brother's suicide? Is she getting help with that?" "Well, she and her mom go to support groups once in a while, but I think she has some long-term postpartum depression that runs far deeper than her brother's death. That certainly didn't help, mind you, but this has been going on for ten years." "Ten years?" Jeanne said, a bit surprised. Though I was embarrassed, I felt a weight lifting off my chest as she came to grips with the amount of time Betty had been suffering from depression. "Yeah, ten years. She was fine when she was pregnant. In fact, better than fine, she was great! Always happy. But now, Christian is five you know, and she thinks there isn't any way she can have postpartum depression because it's been so long. She is in complete denial," I said. "I had some with Allie. It's normal, but you have to be able to talk about it or it just gets worse," she said. "I know, and that's why I need you, Paige, and anyone else we can think of to take her out; she needs to get out of that house and just talk — talk about anything." "Wow Rob, that is so nice of you to care about her like that." "Thank you Jeanne. And we've had our differences — far, far more than most couples and I don't know what is going to happen to us in the end, but I will always care for her." "Sure Rob, I'll talk with her and see if she wants to go to lunch or something like that." I felt that this had some potential to work and I also felt a little relief at being able to talk about Betty's depression and I had to fight back the tears as I said, "Thank you Jeanne. I can't thank you enough." For almost an hour, we talked about the many things in life that pertain to being parents and we ended our conversation laughing. Jeanne tried several times to meet with Betty, and Betty would agree to go to lunch, but she would always cancel just before they were supposed to meet.

One of the things I was trying to do for the kids to give them an escape and give them a sense of identity was to encourage them in sports. I took pictures of my girls in gymnastics and printed off their pictures for them to display in their rooms and put in their backpacks and school notebooks. I played soccer with Noel and soccer and baseball with the boys in the cul-de-sac. Stephen played Little League baseball, but he was just going through the motions and it showed. At the start of the spring in 2013, he was quite frankly one of, if not the, worst players in the league. Determined to get him to a point where the coaches and other parents didn't consider him an automatic strikeout or an automatic error in the field, I practiced with him every day for at least ninety minutes. Our routine became one of getting him off the school bus and, after a snack, heading to the nearby baseball field. My arm was only accurate for roughly thirty pitches, so I bought a pitching machine and fired ball after ball at him. I slowly turned up the speed until he could barely get the bat around in time, and then back the speed back down to a normal speed. We would then work on his catching and throwing and his improvement was so rapid, that with every game, he was noticeably better and his coaches started to move him up in the batting order and into the infield as the season progressed.

By the playoffs, his attitude on and off the field was remarkably different; a complete transformation from the shy loner, lacking confidence and maturity and never having his head in the game to a boy who stood taller and looked outward instead of down. Without sounding bossy, he was cheering his team on and telling other players how many outs there were, where the play would be, and where to stand. He would look around and make sure his teammates had their head in the game, something the better players did with him before. He was hitting the ball hard and taking full advantage of the speed he was born with. A complete surprise to me, he brought the same confidence home, going from picking on his siblings and always complaining about any work asked of him to acting like the eldest sibling, a leader, correcting them on behavior and comments he used to make, and doing the things we asked of him without hardly any fuss. Before the game that determined if his team would play for the championship, he and I spent over an hour in the batting cages and I slowly ramped up the machine to eighty-five miles per hour, getting him ready to face the fastest pitcher in the league. This boy was accurate and could throw an estimated fifty-five mph and I knew this was the opportunity for Stephen to shine and show everyone, especially himself, just how far he'd come. Near the end of the game, he connected with a fastball and hit a line drive down the right field line to the fence. His speed got him home just before the throw — a home run that was the key play in his team advancing to the finals. I was so excited when I heard the crack of the bat that I unknowingly put my video camera down to watch the ball and Stephen round the bases instead of looking through the viewfinder, only realizing my gaffe as he rounded third. I then picked up my camera and snapped a few slightly out of focus pictures as he left a trail of dust and crossed home plate. How I so wish I could have that moment back and have gotten it on video, but he was the hero regardless. We had gotten to know some of the parents on the other team, and over the season, they witnessed his unbelievable improvement, and in an extraordinary display of goodwill and sportsmanship, even they were cheering for him.

His team barely lost the championship game against the same team just two days later, but over the course of the season, he helped bring his whole team from looking a bit like the Bad News Bears, just two months before, to a team that was exciting and fun to watch. In a moment that still brings me to tears when I look at the picture I took, his coach, whose own son was one of the most determined athletes I've ever seen, handed him his trophy with a look of complete respect and admiration. He knew Stephen's vast improvement and leadership had been instrumental in getting them to the championship and he leaned over to look Stephen in the eye as he shook Stephen's other hand, still baffled by the young man he didn't recognize from eight weeks before.

I gave my first "lead," a speech in AA parlance, at a meeting just days after the season ended and I told the story of Stephen from the standpoint of how grateful I was for my recovery giving me the opportunity to do that with my son. "Just fifteen months before, I was losing my life to alcohol and I wouldn't have been around to coach him. He wouldn't have ever been able to accomplish what he did — or that would have been some other dad that would have had to teach him," I said. Several of the women there were crying and I struggled to hold back the tears, proud of both myself and especially of my son.

The baseball and soccer seasons ended as my disability insurance ended and Betty's escalating anger made the good times limited to the fields, where she was in her element, socializing with the other parents and carrying out her perception of a normal family. In sharp contrast, at home her demeanor kept lock step with my prospects for returning to work, and the letter Dr. Lambeau just received from the FAA said that wasn't happening any time soon. When my aptitude scores came back, just like the first time, my math results were extremely high and my verbal scores were inversely low. Whomever reviews these tests at the FAA didn't buy that this was a life-long trait and thought that the extreme disparity in scores could mean that I'd done some damage to my memory during my drinking days, so they demanded CAT scans, MRIs, and more psychiatric interviews. Once these were complete, it would take the FAA the standard ten weeks just to respond to any new findings or requests. Scheduling these took a few weeks, then Dr. Lambeau had to read the results, and then write why he thought I deserved the FAA's consideration. So each time the FAA turned me down and wanted more tests, it cost me a minimum of three months in returning to work — if they approved.

One of the things that Betty started doing more of, as the uncertainty of returning to work wore on, was damaging or destroying things I valued. In May, I did some laundry one night, but when I didn't know where Betty would want me to put two of the girls' sweatshirts, I hung them right outside the laundry room on the kitchen island chairs. Instead of being grateful I did the laundry, or just putting the girls' sweatshirts away herself, she became irate. With the kids probably about to fall asleep, she yelled, "You can't do anything! You can't even put away a f---ing shirt!" She kept yelling, but there was nothing I could do or say to calm her down, I just had to let her get it out. When she couldn't invoke a reaction out of me, she screamed "You're a f---ing idiot!" She went out into the garage and I heard a thud. When she came back inside, she walked by me with a diabolical grin and went upstairs. When I went out to inspect the garage, I saw one of my dress shoes laying beside our sports car.

This wasn't just any sports car though, as it represented just about all we had left in sellable assets if we needed six months worth of money for living expenses and the mortgage until I got back to work. On the rear fender, there was a dent and as I walked around the front of the car, there was a wide scratch that was probably from the toe of the same shoe. She knew from conversations I'd had with my dad that I was probably going to sell it soon. I bought it in 2006 (at the time, she wanted me to) because I knew it had a good chance of appreciating and it was one of the few investments I made that I had been right about. The day I got it, I told her that it needed to stay all original and any body or paint work would devalue it significantly. That made it a perfect target for her scorched earth mentality. I would only be guessing as to why she threw the shoe at it and my best guess is that, simply, I liked it and we were close to needing its equity.

As I began to look back on the many things I'd missed in my alcohol induced fog over the previous years, one was my lack of compassion for Norm when he and his wife suddenly divorced seven years before. I went over to his house, and after I said "Hi" to his second wife Miesha and two young kids, I asked him for a word in private. "Norm, you're not going to believe this, but my life has been completely upside down for ten years and I came here to apologize for not being there for you when Marla left," I said. "What are you talking about?" he said, trying to ease my obvious pain as he saw the tears start to run down my face. "Betty isn't who you think she is — she isn't who anyone thinks she is. She is the most angry, depressed woman you've never met and, except for her pregnancy with Julie, she has been ever since Stephen was born," I said. He sat there, trying to think of something to say, but words escaped him. I continued, "She was, and is, out of control and I just want to apologize for not helping you through that time, but I was consumed with my own problems. I am so sorry; I should have been there for you. I don't know, maybe it would've led to me telling you about Betty then and things would be different now — she respects you and maybe we could've gotten her some help." Norm said, "Hey! I'm not judging you or Betty. We all have our issues and you know I'm always here for you. Why didn't you tell me about Betty before though? I mean, how bad could it be?" "I've always just protected her, I'm not even sure why. Embarrassment? But it's bad. If I told you how bad you wouldn't believe it. I mean, if I told you that the Betty you knew punched and scratched me and bruised and scratched our kids regularly, what would you say?" Norm said, "I wouldn't believe it. I mean I would believe you, but I wouldn't believe it." I said, "I know what you're trying to say, no one would believe it. She's so good at just walking out the door, smiling and making chit-chat — putting on a front. But that's all it is, a front for her inner hell." Norm said, "Well, let me tell you there's more people going through that than you know." I didn't know it at the time, but he was alluding to the fact that he'd heard a good friend of mine was going through the same issue where his wife was angry, depressed, and occasionally violent in their home but put on a happy face when she left the house.

Days later, on Stephen's tenth birthday, we had a pool party for him at Pat and Dale's. Ten was so monumental for me when I was kid. "Double digits!" I remember thinking thirty-plus years before. So I got Stephen out of the pool at 2:30 and went to the side of the house to be alone with him. He asked, "What are we doing, Dad?" I said, "You were born at 2:33 and 40 seconds Stephen, and I just want to hold you as that time passes." He kept his eyes slightly down as we walked, but I saw him smile. We had a couple of more minutes when we got there, and I took the that time to get on my knee to look him in the eye and say, "I want you to know how much I love you, Stephen. You're everything to me and you are so incredibly special. This is a big moment for me because when you were born exactly ten years ago, I became a dad for the first time." He smiled and gave me a hug. I picked him up and held him for the next minute as 2:33:40 p.m. passed, trying to keep my head beside his so he wouldn't see me crying. I had planned this all week, but when the moment came, I realized it was as much about sorrow as it was about joy or celebration — his life, and that of his siblings, being scarred so frequently now.

One example of how we lived like I had never lost the income from flying was Betty would still get her nails and hair done regularly. Her haircuts were $200 plus tip — a "Brazilian blowout" I was told. She came home from one of these appointments in mid-July and, after one of the most vivid memories of our struggles, I had to give up on trusting Betty to be around our kids alone. She had gone to one of the hair or nail appointments (I didn't note which) in the late morning and was supposed to return around two o'clock. Julie was at Dani's house and the other three played downstairs in our finished basement. I told them not to take out many toys, knowing how mad Betty got at the slightest bit of clutter around the house, which I was now calling "The Museum" whenever I would confront Betty about her unrealistic need for a perfectly tidy house.

When she got home, I was cleaning up from the kids' lunch and she didn't say one word as she walked right past me. Her face was that of someone on a life-or-death mission and she got down to the business of inspecting the house for anything left out, as she did any time after she came back from somewhere alone. When she got to the basement, she yelled, "Stephen, Noel, Christian! Get down here, now!" I said "Now what?" But she didn't answer, and the kids slowly went downstairs as I cautiously continued with the dishes. Then I heard a cacophony of nois-es, and I ran down the steps to see Betty kicking and throwing the toys at the kids. I yelled, "What are you doing?!" Betty screamed, "You're all a bunch of f---ing slobs!" I tried to out scream her with, "Leave them alone!" but she was furious and she was going to get it out. "I can't leave you alone with these f---ing slobs – and you're a f---ing slob too! I f---ing hate all of you! Do you hear me?! F---ing HATE all of you!" she screamed as she pointed at us. I looked at my kids, their incredible fear and sadness showing in their eyes, and I said to Betty in a more calm, but disappointed, tone, "Just go upstairs, we will put away the toys."

The kids were so scared and shaken that I started crying. I didn't want them to see me, so I turned around and went into the bathroom for a minute, softly asking them to clean up the toys from behind the closed door. Betty went upstairs to the kitchen and I heard her finishing the dishes. I came out of the bathroom and huddled up the kids and I hugged each one of them and said, "I'm sorry, I don't know what is wrong with Mom." I didn't say it in a mean way, I just knew something was clinically wrong with their mom and I felt powerless to do anything about it. As we stood there, the kids started crying and I felt deeply obligated and compelled to try and fix it somehow. I looked into their big blue eyes and said, "I've never tried this before, but I don't know what else to do. We're all going to go upstairs and stand around your mom and give her a hug at the same time and tell her, 'We love you, Mommy.' Okay?" All of us were scared and apprehensive of what she might do, but I was hopeful it would calm her down and get her to make amends with them. When we got up there, we surrounded her as she stood at the counter and, just like we planned, all of us gave her a hug as we said, "We love you, Mommy." She reacted by shoving the kids away and screaming at them like she had a few minutes before in the basement, saying, "I hate you! Get away from me, I hate all of you! You're a bunch of f---ing slobs!" She then walked a few feet over and stood by the knife set. She was almost smiling as she put her hand on the counter just beside the knives. I looked at her in disbelief and when I saw her reach for one of the knives, I screamed at the kids, who were still standing near her, "Get out of the house, get out now! Get out now! I'll get your shoes, just get out now! Run!" I then repeated, "Get out of the house now!" until I saw the last one, Christian, run out the front door. I was right behind them grabbing their shoes and shuffling them into the car. I fully expected Betty to run into the driveway, blocking me, but she never came outside and we left as fast as we could. As we drove away, my heart pounded from the incredible amount of adrenaline. The kids were scared but also a bit confused as to why I had them run out of the house because they couldn't see Betty reaching for the knives from where they were behind the stove. We left the house, and to keep Betty from withholding Julie and making us return before we wanted, we went to go get her at Dani's house. When Sadie answered, I tried not to give it away that my whole life was upside down so I only said, "Hi Sadie, I'm sorry, but I need to get Julie a bit early." She said, "Sure, I'll go get her." When Julie came to the door, she asked, "I'm supposed to stay till five o'clock, why do I have to go now?" To keep her inquisitive mind at bay in front of Sadie, I just said, "Well, I need to talk to you about something." As we walked away, Julie was already asking what I had to say that was so important to take her away from her best friend. "Mom got really mad and I'm not sure what we are going to do. We may spend the night in a hotel, but I don't know yet," is all I said. Julie had to know by now that "really mad" relative to her mom was very serious and she didn't question me after that.

We drove around for a while as I tried to make conversation to get their minds on happier things, and we ended up at Chick-Fil-A so the kids could go in the play area while I figured out what to do. While we were there, I called Francine and told her what had happened. Furious, she said, "You need to have Betty restrained under a 302!" "I don't know what that is Francine," I said. She explained, "It's an involuntary admission to a psychiatric hospital!" "Francine! She will never go for that! She'll claw my eyes out waaay before that happens!" I said, still trying to get her to understand how physical Betty could be. Francine continued to say that I needed to 302 her, "Or call the police." My mind started to drift after I heard the "involuntary admission" part because it's not hard to think of how violent Betty would become if I tried anything of the sort — I was scared of a 115-pound woman and it simply wasn't an option to even try. I felt all alone and without any answers as to how to protect my kids from their own mother.

After I hung up with Francine, I connected to the internet to see if Betty had made any calls to the police, possibly reporting the kids as missing like she had at Disney World six years before. She made one five-minute call to her mom and sent a text to her sister and that was it. I went back and forth on getting a hotel room for the night, but after eight hours of internal debate, I decided we should try to go back home. I told the kids to stay in the car while I went in and made sure Betty had calmed down. She was upstairs, sitting in bed watching TV and she didn't even acknowledge that I was there when I walked through the room and into the bathroom to test her demeanor. When she just sat there on the bed as if nothing had happened, I went back out to the car and got the kids and quietly got them into bed. I wanted to sleep in the spare room with the door locked so the sound of her trying to get in would wake me, but

I knew I had to sleep next to her in case she went after the kids in the middle of the night and I found myself laying there most of the night, regretting my decision to not get a hotel.

Though I still had a sliver of hope that Betty would be an integral part of our family at some point in the future, I did give in a little on protecting her reputation after this incident. It only took a few weeks after I disclosed Betty's anger to Norm to say a little of the same to another friend. When Lori saw me at her sister's annual July party, she sent me a message saying, "Once again, really good seeing you. Married life is treating you great. You always look so damn happy." I responded, that our married life was "rough" and it was "too much for a Facebook message." I was sorry to have to tell her that, but I just couldn't hide it anymore if I was confronted. Lori responded that she had no idea we weren't happy.

Around this time, I also disclosed to Betty's sister-in-law, Kerry, when we found ourselves alone at Pat and Dale's pool and the kids had gone inside after swimming, that I thought Betty was suffering from severe postpartum depression. I remember Kerry being very receptive to me and comparing Betty to Betty's sister and husband when she said, "And Peg wants another baby now! That's the last thing they need; she's miserable now too! And she thinks another kid will just take that away?! It doesn't work that way and they're headed for trouble too!" Kerry knew I wasn't bashing Betty, I was only looking out for her and our family. She said it was entirely believable that Betty suffered from postpartum depression after having four kids in under five years (she should know, she also had four kids in a short amount of time).

Maybe I was both giving up on protecting Betty and deciding to do what was right for our children. After all, without Betty taking the first step of admitting she needed help, there would be no hope of a resolution, and who better to recruit than her family and her all-important mother. If I could enlist them and turn them, especially Pat, from her enablers into my supporters, the kids and I might actually have a way out of our unseen hell. I didn't pursue it any further, because I needed Kerry to take it from there, but I was too soft when I said to her, "Maybe you could talk to Pat, she won't listen to me." I should have been more firm and more directive, telling Kerry that I needed her help and I that I needed her to talk to Pat to advocate for our family. Restoring my family had to start with the ring-leader, Pat, but she would never listen to me — the memory of my rejected plea for help with her daughter's depression four and a half years before was still in the forefront of my mind.

I hadn't completely given up on Betty though; after all, she was still our kids' mother and my wife. A few days later, I tried to bring Betty back into our family by joking with her a little. The door was open as she sat on the toilet by the front entrance when I walked by, and I used a joke that I'd made up for our kids. "What are you doing?" I asked. She looked up at me and said matter of factly, "I'm going to the bathroom." I smiled and said, "How can you go to the bathroom, you're already there?" Her reaction surprised me; she didn't laugh or get mad, but instead she looked at me with a distant and hurting expression like, "What are you doing? Don't you know how much I hate myself?"

When this didn't work, I set out to clean her van, as she had recently said she wanted it detailed. I spent one whole day on the outside and two days on the inside, taking to the van like the extreme perfectionist I tend to be. I stripped the interior by taking out everything that could be removed. All of the van's guts sat in our garage overnight as I cleaned everything that had a surface on the inside and got to the parts in the driveway the next day. Betty would come out and occasionally look to see what I was doing, but she didn't say anything except to ask on updates for when it would be done. She asked in a nice tone, so I thought that we were making progress, but when I finished, she didn't thank me. I had become too sensitive to the idea that I was tuning into her inert dad and, when she came at me the next day for another one of my "piles," I sternly questioned her. "I worked for three days cleaning your van and you didn't even thank me! You just expect everything to be done for you while you take naps and do nothing!" I said. She shot back, "You did that on your own, I didn't ask you! So don't hold that over my head!" I said, "It isn't about whether you asked me or not, it's about showing appreciation! Do you think I want to do anything for you if you have zero of that?!" She yelled, "I don't expect you to do anything for me, you'll just f--k it up anyway!" as she walked away. This was one of the many things that happened in 2013 that would steer me towards divorce, which I would start looking into a month later.

Now in August, we went to the Outer Banks with Betty's entire family for our annual vacation. Though a lot of fun most of the time, these trips are a vivid reminder of how dysfunctional her immediate family tends to be and why I did my best to limit the kids' exposure to them. Both on the way down and back from the beach for the last four years, I'd found places for just the six of us to stop and see, to give me a chance to influence the kids more and lessen the damage of seeing how Betty's family interacted. The fighting and bashing for the most petty of things, or of anyone who was more successful than they were, wasn't how I wanted to raise my kids. A lot of times, Betty's family would blame entire races or whole groups of people for their (or the country's) problems and that goes against my teachings of accountability for one's actions and decisions and to not judge people you don't know well.

In fact, just two months before, on a long drive back from Philadelphia after dropping off Julie at gymnastics camp, Betty decided to blame black people for most of the country's problems, saying, "They're the ones that commit all of the crimes and most of them are on welfare while we work to pay for it!" This, even though a very good friend of mine, Ken, who is black, is successful and an upstanding person within our community. It was just her and I in the van and, after having had enough of that kind of talk, I uncharacteristically laid into her in a loud, angry voice. I said, "What?! You have the audacity to say that when you refuse to work in the face of our financial ruin and you're as violent as 115 pound women get!" Now I'm flat-out screaming, "Who are you to criticize, you hypocrite! You're my welfare recipient! You're my welfare problem! I work and you don't care where it comes from, you just bitch that it's not enough and refuse to get a job and pull your own weight! You're my welfare parasite!" I had braced for her to hit me or even try to steer the van off the road, but she just sat there staring at me. She must have realized there was a lot of truth to what I said, because uncharacteristic of her, tears started to run down her cheek and she went and sat in the very back of the van in silence for the rest of the trip home.

The trip to the beach this year wasn't much different from the previous years when Betty's brother and sister started yelling obscenities at each other right in front of my kids. It was the same circular argument about who made more money, who out-ranked who by two weeks in the military, and how Peg wasn't really a doctor (she is a pharmacist) and my kids were more or less captive in the nearby hot tub during the worst one.

I was very concerned my kids would think this kind of adolescent behavior from grown adults was normal and they would act the same later in life. I did my best to "unwind" what they frequently witnessed by getting them to talk to me about what they saw and heard and what they thought was right and wrong. Betty's family thinks that how much money you make determines everything in life and the same circular fights reeked of jealousy and hatred. My thoughts are that respect is earned and it isn't always coupled with income. More importantly, happiness and being content in life doesn't necessarily come from a lot of money either. If someone has more money or is more successful than you are in a certain way, you should be happy for them — most likely, they worked hard for it.

The vacation didn't do much to alleviate Betty's stress or anger, because just days after coming home, she became combative with me in the van on a drive to watch a semi-pro baseball game with her family. I knew she was stressed because the FAA wasn't going to be reviewing my application for reinstatement any time soon with the government shutdown looming, and I was sure that that recent news played a significant role in her outburst. Though I don't remember specifically what she became mad about, I do remember her swiping her nails across my face as I drove along the highway. We parked just minutes later and I looked back at the four kids and tried to show them that my bleeding scratches didn't bother me, and therefore didn't hurt, but the girls were crying and the boys looked scared — again. Not only did I have to go into a baseball park with people all around me left to wonder what had happened, but my dad's birthday party was just days later and our friends and neighbors were left to wonder how much longer our family could endure our slowly exposing secret. Now sick of seeing scratches on the kids and I, my mom took a picture of my face when I was playing with the kids at the party.

When the kids went back to school a few days later, I took the time to create a webpage to display all of the pictures I had taken of them (and still do to this day). In an effort to give the kids some sense of normalcy, I showed them the online pictures that were mostly of them playing sports. I tried to make them feel a little like celebrities that had the world in their hands, briefly taking their mind off the dread of our home life.

In the third week of September, Julie and I made brownies after the other three kids went to sleep. She only needed eight hours of sleep compared to ten for the other kids, and occasionally we used that time to try something new and fun, like "9:30 brownies." Betty had just gone to bed, but she was jealous that we were bonding without her, so she came back downstairs when she heard the clanking of mixing bowls and baking pans. She walked in to see that I had set up the camera on the counter, and it was taking our picture as we started mixing the ingredients. Betty said, "Why do you have to take a picture of everything, like you're always trying to prove to everyone how good your relationship is with your kids now?!" I didn't say anything as she sat down at the kitchen table and read the newspaper, waiting for the brownies to be done — a sign that she was there to ruin our time no matter how long it took. When Julie went to cut the brownies, it was obvious they were undercooked. Julie laughed and said, "They're like hot fudge!" I laughed too and, while looking at the back of the box, I said, "Wow! Am I stupid! I read the preheat instructions!" Betty took it from there and said, "You're both stupid, you can't even read the back of a box! You can't even make brownies from a box!" her voice getting louder as she said it again. Julie's reaction was so perfect; she smiled at me as she cocked her head, laughed and said, "Oh well, I kinda like them this way!" as she dipped her fingers in the pan. I reassured her by smiling back and excitedly saying, "Me too!" We both sounded like we had just discovered a new recipe that would revolutionize the entire culinary world and I felt Julie knew she could say what she wanted as long as I was around to defend or protect her — a relief knowing that she wasn't letting her mom's anger control or define her. The pictures I took that night of Julie and I are some of my favorites amongst the 80,000 pictures I have, and I still look at them often. They are a vivid reminder of Julie's independence and strength coming through in the face of adversity — a trait I hope she always has, but never needs.

Now in late September, I was in the best shape of my life, and when I returned from the gym, I made a protein shake — a somewhat messy endeavor with a hand blender and protein powder that invariably set off Betty's obsessive compulsive disorder. This was part of the same counter used by the kids that had to be perfectly clean, and she was still wiping it down dozens of times a day. "I don't know who you're trying to impress!" she said. I looked at her inquisitively as she continued, "You have a beer belly!" She had told me I had a beer belly right after coming home from the beach a few weeks before, so that wasn't new, but knowing that I didn't have a beer belly and it was just jealousy, I just rolled my eyes and shook my head as I smiled. My indifference to her tripe set her off and she went around the house throwing away anything of mine she could find. I just followed her around the house and took it out of the garbage without saying a word; avoiding getting too close to her for fear of being hit or having something thrown at me. She didn't say anything to me either, but when she realized that throwing my things away wasn't making me mad (outwardly at least), she went downstairs and rounded up the kids for her "meeting" with them. These meetings were becoming more frequent, and it was the same vitriol about all of my rehabs, being a drunk, not having a job, losing our house, not having any food to eat, and so on. I just let her go, but my resolve to file, or at least inquire, about a divorce strengthened.

The following morning, I texted and asked her meet me for lunch at the nearby corner restaurant on her way home from the gym. She did, and after we ordered our food, I said to her, "I want to go over some numbers with you; I want a divorce." She looked at me with a stare that told me I had gotten her attention and I continued talking about our assets and debts. Somewhat crudely on the paper tablet I brought, I wrote down our assets and debts and I started doing the math for what I would owe her. When she saw how calm and precise I was, she knew I was serious. By the time our food came, she said she wasn't hungry anymore. I saw tears well up in her eyes, which surprised me because she didn't cry at hardly anything between us anymore; she had grown too callused and vengeful and was too caught up in a one-way struggle for power and control within our marriage. When she cried, that showed me she still held some value for our marriage. When I finished the number crunching (and my lunch), I asked her, "Why were you crying?" She didn't say anything, she just quickly shook her head "no" as if in denial to admitting I could still make her cry. Knowing Betty never gave in, whether it be in an argument or for control within our marriage, I continued on as if she'd said, "Because I still care." I asked her, "Are you willing to get some help?" She sharply said, "Help for what?!" I said, "For your postpartum depression." She grimaced and said, "Christian is five years old; I don't have postpartum depression!" I said, "Well, I don't know who you are anymore; I haven't known you for years." She went to interrupt me but I kept going, "Yes, I know I've handled our problems in a wrong, destructive way, but I got help and now it's your turn to get help." Betty said, "I went on the anti-depressant when you wanted me to and I've been seeing Francine; what more do you want me to do?" I said, "Well, for starters, I'd like you to look into upping your 'low-dose' of the anti-depressant to something more substantial or even try switching to Lexapro, or something else that may work better." She said, "And I'm only on Xanex to help with the stress of dealing with four little kids, I don't have depression and I don't need anything different." When she said this, I sensed her moving in the wrong direction, away from the announcement just ten minutes before that I wanted a divorce, and I said, "Well, I don't know what to tell you, but things had better change if you want me to be around. I'm not living like this anymore and the kids won't live like this anymore either."

Over the next two weeks, she wasn't as angry or depressed, but she wasn't engaged in our family much either — always doing her own thing and taking even more frequent and longer naps than before. Months later, Betty would tell my parents how controlling I was during our marriage, and I said to them, "She avoided me the last five years and I avoided her most of the last seven — how can you control someone you're trying to avoid?"

Because Betty was more of less out of the picture, the kids and I started having more fun inside the house, not just outside where the noise and possible mess didn't annoy her so much. One of my better memories during this period of relative peace happened as I got the girls ready for school. I looked at Julie and devilishly smiled as we heard Noel, a.k.a. "Squeak," come down the stairs, letting Julie know I was going to play a joke on her. When Noel came into the kitchen, I quickly asked her a few questions that were only meant to annoy her. "Noel, do you have your backpack?" "No," she said. "Do you have your sandwich?" I asked. "No," she said. "Do you have snack?" "No," she said. "Do you have your brain?" I asked. "No!" she said. And she looked at me and when she realized what she had said, we laughed until we were on the floor. I then tickled her and asked her, "Where's your brain, Squeak?" to make her laugh even more. She could barely form the words, "It's in my head!" Most families have this type of fun often enough that something like this wouldn't stand out so much. But this was new to us and, more than the minute of laughter it brought, it gave us hope.

The two weeks of relative calm in our house abruptly ended when, in mid-October, Julie and Noel made a Lego trophy for me for being the "Greatest Dad." They also wrote me a very nice note, ending with, "We love you daddy!" We proudly displayed the tall trophy on top of the bookcase in the library and taped the note just below it. The next night, Christian and I got home from the high school soccer game at eleven o'clock and when the girls heard me come through the door, they got out of bed and ran downstairs as fast as they could. Both were crying and Julie said, "Dad, Mom smashed the Lego we made for you!" She took my hand and we went into the library where the Lego was on the floor in pieces. What hurt more than the smashed Lego though, was that the letter the girls wrote me was laying on the floor in shreds too. Julie and Noel were sobbing as they looked up at me for answers. I can still see Noel with her fingers in the side of her mouth, looking up at me for some way to explain or fix it — it being their mom, not so much the Lego and letter. I tried to sound as calming as possible as I said, "It's okay girls, we'll rebuild it just the way it was," and I gave them a long hug. Julie asked, "What about the letter?! It's all torn up!" "Well, we'll just have to tape it back," I said. I was trying to say the right things, but I think Julie knew that even if we taped the sheet of paper that laid on the floor in what had to be thirty piece, it was never going to be the same. We put the pieces of the letter and Lego on my desk and I got the girls back to bed, laying with both of them on Noel's lower bunk until they fell asleep. When I walked into our bedroom, Betty was just sitting on the bed watching TV, again, like nothing had ever happened. She didn't say a word or even acknowledge me, and I was sick with the realization that we were right back to where we were before the talk of divorce two weeks ago. Repulsed by her behavior and afraid I would make the mistake of confronting her, I slept in the spare room. I felt the girls were waiting the next day for an apology or explanation from Betty, but I knew they would never get it — it had been years since we'd last heard Betty apologize for anything.

Two days later, things weren't much different from the last eighteen months. I got the kids off to school while Betty slept in and got up to read the newspaper with a cup of coffee. She then went to the gym and came home and napped for a couple of hours while I got the kids off the bus, got their homework started, and made them grilled cheese sandwiches to hold them off till dinner. I ran the girls to their dance and gymnastics practices and came home to play baseball with the boys in the cul-de-sac and fed them dinner. I picked the girls up, stopped at Subway for their dinner, and came home to get all four showered and in bed. Betty and I had become so distant that I don't even know what she did from the time the kids got home from school until they went to bed; she hadn't even been helping us with their homework the last week or two like she had previously. Whatever she was doing didn't have anything to do with the kids or I and that was fine by all of us. After the kids were in bed, I put their dirty clothes in their hampers, cleaned up the kitchen, and went to get a shower before bed. As I walked into our bedroom, Betty was sitting on the bed in her pajamas with her legs crossed and the TV on, but her head was down. When she heard me walk in, she didn't look up, she just said, "I can't do it anymore." Hearing her sadness, I tried my best to sound empathetic and said, "Do what?" "I can't be their mom anymore," she said. "What do you mean?" I gently asked. "I'm not cut out for four kids. I don't know what I'm going to do, but I can't be their mom anymore. That's it," she said as her head stayed down. Hoping beyond hope that she had hit a rock-bottom, I tried to sound as loving and understanding as possible. "Betty, I'm going back to work very soon, and when I do, we are going to have enough money to hire any kind of help you could possibly want. When that time comes, you just tell me what you need. A cleaning lady, someone to cook meals for us, someone to help you run the kids around. A nanny. You name it." She didn't say a word or even lift her head, she just sat there completely despondent. I tried to convey that I hadn't given up hope on her. "Look Betty, you and I are both so stressed, and I know for you it's mostly about the money. I know we don't have much money left, but please believe me when I say I'm going back to work very soon. And I bet I'm even a captain in a year; we'll have so much money, we won't know what to do with it!" I said in jest. It didn't matter, she just sat there, motionless and unresponsive.

My words apparently had no effect on Betty, because the very next night, she took the kids to my parents' for a sleep-over and told my mom almost exactly the same thing she'd told me when I first walked into the bedroom the night before. Days later, my mom would tell me she thought, "I give you all this help and you can't do it?!" as she cooked dinner for all five of them.

The next week, I asked Betty to meet the kids at the bus stop one day after school while I went to exchange a few cameras and lenses with Ben. When I asked her if she went to the stop, she said, "No, they're old enough to walk home by themselves now." Just like two years ago, I was extremely frustrated that I was about to go back to work and she wasn't doing what I considered of utmost importance, making sure our kids weren't alone at the bus stop. When I confronted her, it set her off and she was screaming at me again. It ended in her gathering the kids for another one of her talks — all of the extremely inappropriate things she just couldn't wait to tell them about their father. This time, I didn't leave, I didn't say anything to her, I just patiently waited — for days. What I waited for was for her to reach the part of her anger profile where she would just act like everything was okay and I should just forget her infraction — because I always did. Not this time — I was resolved to ignore her until she apologized, and if she didn't apologize, I would go as far as filing for divorce.

Four days later, she hadn't apologized and I was out of patience. I fell back on the one thing that seemed to get her to think about where we were headed, because a protracted miserable marriage and emotionally scarred kids weren't enough, and that was divorce. I called a lawyer that morning to have him serve her papers, but he didn't instill much confidence in me. Two other lawyers didn't call me back and I was left frustrated with the whole process. Though by now Betty was in the phase of her profile where she was trying to bring me back, texting me questions like, "Do you want to meet for lunch?" I refused to respond without an apology. I continued to ignore her when I got home, hoping to impart on her that I wanted an apology and permanent change. Betty refused to admit she had a problem and get help and the kids and I refused to live like that anymore. Something drastic had to be done and, in light of the failure to land a lawyer that morning, I made up my mind that night to bluff a divorce.

When Betty went to bed, she laid on the farthest possible part of the bed with her back to me, which indicated to me that there would be no apology forthcoming. I asked her very calmly, "What are you doing Friday morning?" She responded, just as calmly, "I'm not sure, I might go to the gym. Why?" I said, "I talked to a lawyer and I wanted to see if you would be home to sign divorce papers that should be here then." She became extremely angry and said, "I'm not signing any divorce papers!" as she got out of bed and headed to the spare room. As she was about to walk out of the room, she turned to me and yelled, "I don't know where you're going to live, but I'm keeping the house and the kids and all the money! You can live under a f---ing bridge!" I got out of bed and, trying to remain very calm to lend my request for divorce more credence, I said, "That's not how divorce works; you get half of everything and I get half." By this time, we were in the doorway of the spare room and she was repeatedly yelling that I would "live under a bridge." And I, still calmly, repeated to her, "That's not how divorce works." She tried shutting the door, but I wanted her to know I would not accept less than half of anything — especially the kids. The fact that she'd even said she was going to "keep the kids" was bizarre in and of itself, seeing as how she'd had nothing but complete disdain for them up to this point. I stepped into the spare room and repeated, "I will get half and you will get half," my voice getting louder to counteract her yelling. She then slapped me across the face and punched me in the jaw. I grabbed her arms and sternly said, "Stop hitting me." She then tried to kick me in the groin, so I let go of her arms and blocked it by making an X with my fore-arms when I felt her pull her leg back to kick. With my face now leaned into her from blocking the kick, she slapped me again. I was now yelling, "Stop hitting me!" She then grabbed the office chair and shoved it at me. It landed on my foot and a sharp piece from the metal back hit the back of my hand, which only added to the confusion and to my wonder of when, or if, she would stop. She then wound up her arm to hit or slap me again, and I leaned over the chair to grab her arms. I'm not sure if she leaned back, causing me to trip over the office chair, or if she fell backwards, but both of us fell towards her back as I held on to her upper arms. She landed on her butt with her back against the nightstand and I fell diagonally across her, but on all fours. With my head now right in front of her, she scratched me with her fingernails around my neck twice as I tried to stand up. I felt the familiar burning of her scratches around my neck and, for the first time in our conflicted marriage, I lost control of my restraint. I had become so irate, that I reacted to her scratching by sitting up and punching her on top of the head. As soon as I hit her, I regretted it, but it was too late.

In the most heart-stopping of realizations, I heard Julie yell, "Stop!" and I turned around to see her crying in the doorway. I felt incredible guilt that she had heard or saw any of what had just happened and I said to Julie, "Are you okay? I'm so sorry." At this time, Betty also started yelling, "Get over here Julie, he's beating me up!" and Julie slowly went to Betty. Betty then put Julie in front of her as if Julie was a human shield and she repeatedly yelled, "He's beating me up!" Julie was obviously very upset and confused, so I tried to tell Julie that everything was going to be okay. But Betty was extremely irate and yelled, "He attacked me! He beat me up!" over and over. I tried to explain by saying, "Julie, that is not true," but she ran out the door saying, "I'm going to throw up!" Betty and I followed her into the master bathroom and I tried to diffuse the situation by talking to both of them, reassuring Julie, as she threw up in our toilet, that it would be okay, and asking Betty to calm down so we could talk about what had happened "like adults." My calm, controlled voice only incited Betty's anger and undermined her determination to play the victim. Her anger escalated even more and she again started punching and scratching me, but this time right in front of Julie, who had stepped out of the bathroom. Again, I felt powerless to stop her offensive without an offensive of my own. I already regretted hitting her just minutes before, so I gave in to her assault. I put my hands down and I leaned my face towards her, letting her hit me as much and as hard as she wanted. As she hit me, I yelled, "That's it, show me how much you hate me, come on show me! Show me how much you hate your kids! Get it out! Show me all your hate! Get it out! Get it out!" She did exactly that, but an odd thing happened soon after I stopped yelling at her to hit me — she stopped hitting me. She must have wanted me to grab her and yell and try to defend myself because she clearly didn't want to just hit me for the sake of hitting me; she wanted me to fight back.

After she hit me a few more times, I realized Julie was in the bathroom throwing up again, so I tried to make sure she was okay, while also trying to pay attention to where Betty was going; she was certainly at the stage of our fights where she was going to call someone and blame me. I said to Julie, "It will be okay Julie, I love you so, so much and I am so sorry," and I went into the bedroom to find Betty dialing her phone. She looked at me and yelled, "I'm dialing 9-1-1!" I yelled, "Stop!" and I grabbed the phone out of her hand. I was afraid of the police coming to the house and the neighbors thinking it was because of me again, not to mention that my face and neck were bruised and scratched to a point where she would have some pressing questions to answer if the police came. I pleaded with Betty to settle down. "Let's talk about this calmly, like adults," I said. She seemed to get even more irate, yelling, "No, that's it!" like I had been the aggressor. She went and got the house phone, and again, I yelled "No!" and I pulled the phone out of her hand, dislodging the battery and it fell to the floor. She then said, "That's it, I'm going to Helena's!" and she ran downstairs and out the door. I followed her, again to keep our argument away from the neighbors, especially Helena because she had been a friend for so long and she had already seen enough of our maladjusted family. Betty made it to the start of Helena's driveway before I got to her, and I again tried to say in a soft voice, "Come on Betty, don't do this. Let's go inside and talk about it. Come on, everything is going to be okay." Betty kept saying "No," but she looked back at our house, telling me she was close. I said, "I can't let you do this," meaning going to Helena's at midnight. She didn't say anything when she changed her mind, she only turned around and started walking towards our house.

When we got back inside, I again tried to keep her calm by saying, "I will sleep in the spare room, and you can sleep in our bed." She took exception to this, and insisted that she was going to be the one sleeping in the spare room. This most likely stems from the fact that during our arguments, the spare room was where the person who felt they were wronged went. She either felt attacked, or wanted to carry on that illusion to Julie. Doing anything to try to keep her calm, I agreed to her sleeping in the spare room, but instead, she became more flustered and yelled, "I'm going to Helena's!" and ran out the front door. I knew I couldn't stop her forever, and so I decided to stay home and check on the kids. Julie had gone back to her bed and Stephen and Noel were still in their beds (Christian had spent the night at his cousin's). I checked on Stephen first and he pretended he was half-asleep. I knew that wasn't possible with the cacophony of the last ten minutes and I said to him, "I'm so sorry you had to hear that Stephen, but it's okay now. I love you." When I went in check on Noel, she was lying in bed, crying. I tried to reassure her that she would be okay, and that, "Mom will calm down. Just go to sleep, tomorrow is a new day." I repeated "I love you" several times to her and Julie in the upper bunk, trying so desperately to find the words and the tone to calm them and get them to go back to sleep.

At this point, I heard the police pull up. An officer knocked on the door, and I let Officer Fry in. He verified who I was, and asked where Betty was. "I don't know, she said she was going to Helena's, and that's all I know," I said, pointing in that direction. Then another officer came to the front door and introduced himself as Officer Ogdin. Officer Fry asked which house was Helena's and I pointed across the cul-de-sac. Officer Ogdin made his way over to Helena and Tom's house as he scanned the cul-de-sac for Betty. He came back a couple of minutes later, saying there wasn't an answer when he knocked on the door and he asked me for their phone number. Tom answered and Officer Ogdin went over to ask him a few questions. When Officer Ogdin came back, he said he asked

Tom if he knew where Betty was or if he had seen her, to which he said, "No." Officer Ogdin then started looking around the neighbors' houses, checking for Betty. As he was searching for her, Officer Fry used that time to take pictures of my face, neck, hand, and foot (from the office chair landing on it). As Officer Ogdin was about to search the shrubs in our yard, Betty "made herself known," as the report states and came out from behind the shrubs.

Betty was outside with Officer Ogdin, and Officer Fry looked around the house, preparing to ask me some questions. Officer Ogdin came back in and asked me for a jacket and shoes for Betty. I handed him the jacket and shoes and figured it was going be a long night of questioning if she was going to be outside long enough to need those. Officer Fry and I then went into the library and he opened his questioning with, "Tell me what happened." After I told him my recount of the night, he grimaced and asked in a skeptical tone, "Why was the battery ripped out of the phone if she was trying to call 9-1-1?" Just then I realized how that must have looked and my heart sank. I tried to stay calm and I said, "This isn't the first visit by the police to our house, and it would be extremely embarrassing to have to explain to the neighbors why you were here again. The previous two times, I was the one you were called for, and I don't want them thinking I did anything again. So when she said she was calling 9-1-1, I immediately thought of how I was going to explain this to the neighbors and I guess I didn't want the kids witnessing anymore drama either." His eyes stayed locked on mine, trying to gauge if I was lying.

The two officers then reconvened and, after talking for a minute, officer Fry came back into the library and said, "We are going to take Betty in." "What do you mean?" I asked. "We're going to arrest her for domestic violence," he said. My heart sank with the enormity of hearing that Betty was going to jail. I had mixed emotions though. On the one hand, I thought she deserved a big wake-up call and the disgrace of jail. But more than that, I felt bad for her and I felt obligated to protect her from the rest of society as I always had — not to mention that I was afraid of what she would do to me when she got out. I pleaded with Officer Fry, "Please, can she just stay home?" He said, "No." I again asked, and added, "We'll be okay." His answer was firm and definitive, "No, not when your face and neck look like that. Besides, we have to; it's a mandate that goes far above me or even my supervisor — it's Pennsylvania state law." When I heard this, I thought that, as much damage and embarrassment as it was going to cause our family, it would be big enough, sad enough, and humiliating enough to force her to get help with her anger. I now had something to convince her, and any counselor or psychiatrist I may take her to, that she really did have a problem, and my dream that our family could start healing, growing, and be truly happy in the long run now looked attainable — and I felt a huge rush of hope.

I again checked on the kids before going to bed that night, and I said to each one of them as they appeared to sleep, "I love you Stephen. I love you Julie. I love you Noel," hoping that, if they were asleep and having nightmares, maybe they would hear me say those words. I went to bed, knowing I was only going to get six hours of sleep before I had to get Stephen and Julie up for school — even less considering I'd set two separate alarms set for 3:00 a.m. and 5:00 a.m. to check on them — but I hadn't felt this peaceful in years and I fell asleep knowing things were finally going to change.

The Unintended Different Path

Like every other night before I go to bed, I put my phone on silent. It crossed my mind that Betty might call me to go and get her out of jail, but I didn't want to do that until the kids were off to school, so I figured I could leave it on silent and I would turn it back to ring in the morning. When I woke up at 7:00, I looked at my phone and I saw a missed call at 6:22 a.m. I didn't recognize the prefix, so I wasn't sure who had tried to call, but I did recognize the coincidence of an early morning call and Betty being in jail and probably getting one phone call. I called it back, but it just went to a menu for the county jail and I thought, "But she is in the Mercury Township jail, not the county jail."

I woke up the kids, making sure that I sounded calm and reassuring to start the process of healing and forgetting as fast as I could. After I got them ready for school, I took each one into the library and we sat down face to face in the two office chairs. My feeling with kids is that less is more as it pertains to adult relationships, but I had to balance that with how fast they were forced to grow up in the face of my past drinking and Betty's anger — they didn't ask for any of this, nor was it their fault. I started with Julie, and she was clearly shell shocked, so I tried to undo some of the damage by saying, "I'm so sorry that you had to hear and see Mom and I fight last night. I can't imagine how scared you must have been, but it's over now." She asked, "Where is Mom?" I wanted to protect Betty's reputation with our kids, so I lied. "She spent the night at her mom's," I said. Julie smiled and let out a dramatic sigh, as if to say, "Thank goodness!" When I saw that, it was just more confirmation that the kids were afraid of Betty, and I had to fight the tears back to be strong for Julie. My head fell in disbelief and I said, "All I want for you is a happy mom." I looked up at Julie as she absorbed what I had just said. She was shaking her head "no" and her eyes were as big as saucers, as if she knew that was never going to happen. "Dad," she said, still shaking her head. "Mom gets reeeally mad sometimes." "I know Julie, I know," I said. "No, reeeeeeeally mad! One day she punched me in the stomach!" she said. "What?! When?" I said. "Right before the end of school," she said. "You mean this last year, just in May or June?" I asked. Julie said, "Uh huh. And it reeeally hurt!" She had her hands over her sternum, so I asked, "Is that where she hit you, your upper stomach?" Julie's eyes became big again and she nodded yes. I closed my eyes to try and grasp what I was hearing and I said, "That's called your sternum, Julie." Julie just smiled and said, "Oh!" I asked, "And she was mad?" Julie emphatically nodded yes. As resilient and strong as she is, she shrugged it off, saying, "Oh well!" She seemed to move on quickly after our short talk. I gave her a hug and asked her to get Stephen for me.

When Stephen came in, he was distant and still looked sad. He sat where Julie had sat and I said, "Hi Stephen." His head was down and he looked up at me with a half-smile, probably trying to seem happy enough for me not to have one of our father-son talks that he had grown weary of. "I'm sorry for the fight last night Stephen, I can't imagine how scared and helpless you must have felt." Stephen just looked at me, not really sure what to say. "Stephen, I hope you know by now that I'd do anything for you and I know this is no way for any of us to live." He remained silent. With Julie's admission still fresh in my mind, I'd hoped he would open up his thoughts to me. I looked at him and said, "Stephen. All I want for you is a happy mom." He reacted a bit like Julie with his eyes getting bigger while he stared at me. We sat there in silence for a few seconds, and I studied him as he looked straight down. "Dad...Mom gets really mad at me sometimes...and...she hurts me." He looked up at me and I thought I knew what he was talking about. I said, "I know Stephen, I know. I've seen your bruises and scratches and so have my parents and your teachers — probably almost everyone who knows you has. Look, I hope last night puts an end to this fighting and her hitting or scratching any of us. I can't take it anymore and I know you can't take it anymore. So let's just say a prayer for Mom and we'll get you off to school." I sat there with my head down and hands together as if I was praying so that Stephen would do the same, but I was really trying to absorb what I had just heard from my two oldest kids. When I went to bed the night before, I intended to go get Betty out of jail after the kids went to school. But, after hearing from Stephen and Julie, I became scared at the thought of her coming back home with the disgrace of being arrested so fresh. If I was wrong, and jail didn't get Betty to realize she needed help, there would only be one other path she would take, and that is revenge — certainly the odds-on favorite. I quickly realized that no matter what I said to her, there would be Hell to pay and I was becoming very uncomfortable with the thought of Betty around us.

I went and got Noel for the same talk, but she didn't say a word, she just cried with her fingers in her mouth. I don't remember what I said to her, but it wasn't much. I just had her sit on my lap and she buried her head in my chest as I told her, "I love you," over and over. After a few minutes, I asked her if she wanted to stay home from school. She gave me her trademark rapid shake of her head "no" as her fingers were still in the side of her mouth.

Now that the kids were at school, I walked home from the bus stop to organize my thoughts before I went to the police station; I needed to figure out what I was going to do if she was already out of jail and free to come home. When I sat and recounted what had happened just that year, I thought of her acting irrationally and putting all of us in danger as we drove along I-70 in February and how she pushed the kids away when they told her, "We love you Mommy," in July. The kids were scared and knew they were taking a chance in saying that to her when she was so volatile, and she shoved them away. "She's a monster," I said out loud to myself. I didn't even know if she picked up the knife or not or what she would have done with it if she had, but she shoved our kids away saying, "I hate you! I hate all of you!" — that's the part I couldn't get over. After ten minutes of reflection, I knew Betty was out of control and she was a danger to our kids. My resolve to keep her away from us until she sought help for her anger solidified; I just didn't know how I was going to enforce it.

One of the things that had been in the back of my mind since I had woken up was I wanted to explain to Helena what had happened the night before. I walked over to her house with my tail between my legs, expecting her to be disappointed for the reasonable assumption that the police had been called on me again. She opened the door and got her first look at my face and neck. She said, "Oh God, Rob," and she gave me a hug. Such a warm greeting was so unexpected that I couldn't help but cry. "Helena, I am so sorry. I know you probably think the police were there for me again, but they weren't," I said. Helena said, "I know Rob, I know!" "How do you know?" I asked, completely taken aback. "'Rob, we've known about Betty since you moved in four years ago. We saw the bruises and scratches the kids had all the time and I just thought, 'Those poor kids!' I talked to Tom, and we wanted to say something, but we figured you knew.'" I was too ashamed to admit I knew at least some of Betty's abuses and I couldn't help but picture her actually attacking the kids and the kids frightened faces. My thoughts must have been written all over my face, because Helena said, "Rob, it's okay, we know Betty is crazy." She then asked, "Where is she?" When I said, "Jail," Helena said, "Good! That's exactly where she belongs! Rob, I've seen her lock those kids out of the house for hours and hours. In fact, she would lock them out for most of the day and they would have to come over here to get a drink or go to the bathroom." "What?!" I said. Helena continued, "She is a horrible mom and I'm not the only one who thinks that. I had a party here when you first moved in, when Christian was just a baby. He was crawling towards the stairs on our deck and she just sat there while the other moms and I jumped up to get him before he fell down the steps! She just sat there, not a care in the world. Then she put him to bed and came back here; he was all by himself! Ellen Bradley [A woman who lived on our street] thinks she's a wacko too." I didn't know what to say, I just stared at the ground in disbelief that Betty could do that to our kids. As soon as Helena said it, I knew why Betty didn't let them in the house; it was her compulsion to have a perfectly clean and organized house. But I wanted to see if Helena knew that, so I asked, "Do you know why the kids weren't allowed into the house?" "I don't know. I don't think she really wants them around." I said, "Well, you're right about that." Helena kept going, "And Kathy Collins [A lady who works at the girls' gym] thinks she's a horrible mom too. She told me Betty would bring the girls to the gym and leave Stephen in the lobby while she went out shopping." I said, "Jesus. I wonder what else she's done that I don't know about." Helena said, "Oh, I'm sure there's a lot more. Her mom and sister are just as bad. Pat treats Dale like complete shit and I've seen Peg scream at Jon in Walmart. Top of the lungs screaming at him!" I said, "Yea, I've never heard Pat say one nice thing about Dale in the sixteen years I've known them and Peg is that way now to Jon too. And Peg is just mean, flat out mean." Helena said, "Betty's trying to do that to you, but you stand up to her, and good for you." "Thank you, I refuse to turn into her dad; that's not the family dynamic I want. In her family, the women have their kids and then treat their husbands like their personal punching bags to get out all of their hate and I refuse to live like that." Helena finished by saying, "If you ever need anything, Tom and I are here for you. I've known you for over thirty years and I've always considered you a good friend, so don't be shy."

I was so surprised at what Helena had to say that I stopped into Paige's house before going to my parents' next door. She was surprised and saddened to see my scratches, but she didn't know anything about Betty's hidden anger. "Well, I called her to take her to lunch like you asked me to, but she always canceled. Matt and I thought you and Betty were so happy! It's such a shame, because these are supposed to be your best years!" was all she said that provided any insight.

That last stop before going to the police station was my parents'. Only my mom was home and she wasn't all that surprised by my scratches; she had become used to seeing them on the kids and me. When I told her that Betty had been arrested, she put her hand up to her mouth and said, "Is she still there?" I said, "I think so, I'm getting ready to go to the police station now, but I wanted you to take some pictures so we have our own." My mom asked, "Are you going to bail her out?" "I was, but Julie and Stephen told me some things that have me second guessing that. I feel like if I go and get her she will kill me tonight and if I don't get her, she will kill me even sooner," I said.

I went to the Mercury Township police station to see what was going on with Betty and I was greeted by a rather tall officer. "You must be Mr. Black," he said. "Yes, how did you know?" I asked. "Officer Fry briefed me this morning about the domestic last night; your scratches gave it away." I laughed and said, "Of course. Uhhh, is Betty still here?" I asked uncomfortably, not really wanting to know the answer. He said, "No, she spent the night in County." "The COUNTY jail?!" I asked, completely surprised. "Yes, we took her there last night around two o'clock after we booked her here. She complained of a headache and we had her checked out by two different paramedics and they couldn't find anything wrong and so we then took her down. County paramedics checked her out too, but they couldn't find anything either." I just stared at the officer, not knowing what to say. My thoughts went to Betty, a beautiful, petite, upper middle-class white mom of four young kids who had just spent the night in the county jail with some real hardened criminals. As volatile and angry as Betty was, I didn't think she deserved that. She needed psychiatric help, not something like the county jail to perpetuate her anger. Another instance of mixed emotions came over me because I also knew that she would have to look at herself real hard and figure out just what kind of mother she wanted to be to our kids if she wanted to be a part of their life ever again.

The officer must have seen the pain on my face and realized that this was an ongoing issue with Betty, because he said, "Look, someone could post bail for her and she could be out now — heck even on her way home." My eyes got almost as big as Stephen's and he then asked, "Do you know what a PFA is?" I said, "No, what is it?" "It a Protection From Abuse order, it is a way for you to protect yourself by keeping her some minimum distance away from you — I think it's fifty feet." As I looked at him, trying to go through the pros and cons, he said, "You know, she could just get out and walk into your house at anytime, nothing's stopping her." My heart sank and I immediately thought of who she had become over the last two years and the memories of her anger ran through my mind again. I then pictured the kids sleeping later that night, vulnerable to her need for vengeance. I thought, "What if she comes home tonight while we're sleeping. Will she attack the kids? Will she attack me? Will she grab a knife and kill us all?!" Reacting to what was racing through my mind, I put my hand up to my mouth and asked, "Can I get a PFA for the kids too? They're the ones who need protected." "Sure," he said. "Yes. Yes, I definitely want to do that; how do I go about it?" I asked. "You have to go down to the courthouse and fill out some papers and then you appeal it to the judge. When the judge sees your face, you'll get one, you won't have to worry about presenting any evidence," he said. I thanked him and, almost in a daze at what the last eleven hours of my life had brought, I drove downtown to get a PFA against Betty.

Respecting her role as their mother, I filled out the paperwork for the PFA to include the kids and I named three people who could supervise Betty if she wanted to see them. They were my parents and Paige. I knew my mom, who also wanted Betty to grow into the mother my kids deserved, would be willing to accommodate Betty for as much time as she wanted to spend with them. But, just like six months before when I was trying to get Paige's influence into Betty's life, I also wanted some of Betty's time spent with Paige. Paige is happily married, very fit, beautiful yet humble, a successful lawyer, and, most importantly to my wants for Betty in this time of profound uncertainty, a wonderful, caring, soft-spoken mother to Adam and her thirteen-year-old daughter. When I finished the application, I went back and looked at the three names for a long time. I considered removing my parents and Paige, recalling what Betty had done to the kids and especially her words to me just ten days before, "I can't be their mom anymore, that's it." It was hard not to think she didn't deserve to be in their life, at least until she finally looked inward at herself and got some professional help.

After the judge awarded me the PFA, I felt similarly to the night before — there was a lot relief and comfort in knowing she couldn't get to me or the kids. But our family wasn't whole, so I called Francine to see what she had to say about the ordeal. Francine's voice was emphatic and stern. "You need to 302 her!" she repeated several times. "They will run some tests and maybe put her on some meds, but this has got to stop!" "Great, now I have Francine on board with getting Betty some help, and my hope to work towards a family of a happy couple raising four well-adjusted children just became achievable," I thought.

I got home from the courthouse just in time to get the kids off the bus, and after doing their homework, I took them to my parents' while I went over to Betty's brother's house to get Christian. The police had just served Betty the PFA and her brother Daniel was furious. He was yelling, "You set her up! You planned this, just so you could get a divorce and keep everything!" I said to Daniel, "How could I have planned it?! SHE is the one who called 9-1-1, not me! AND I tried to stop her from calling!" He looked baffled for a second, but he still insisted I set her up. A few years before, when one of my kids had scratches, Daniel had said to my mom, "Ohhh! I know all about Betty's scratching!" So I tried to stay calm and appeal to him regarding his sister's emotional state by imploring him to face what I knew he knew, that his sister needed help. "Daniel, that's not it. Betty is so angry and depressed and no one sees it but me and the kids, but I'm not trying to trick anyone. And she's going to end up like Robby; you have to do something." When Robby died, I knew Daniel regretted he hadn't done more to mentor him, and I thought he would be willing to help with another sibling going through hidden, inner turmoil. When I compared Betty to his deceased brother, his wife Kerry said, "Oh! I wouldn't say that!" He was so mad that I mentally prepared to have to physically defend myself. "You had better leave right now, or who knows what I'm going to do!" he yelled. I was very disappointed that Daniel deflected the blame and chose to turn the other cheek; his sister needed someone within the family to step in and encourage her to seek help for her anger and depression and he was the only one that realistically could have stepped in and been a voice of reason.

That night, the Mercury Township police called me asking if Betty could come to get some of her things under their escort. I said, "Yes," and stayed in the doorway of the study, just off the narrow entrance in the house, while I watched her walk past and go upstairs. After a few minutes, I came out into the narrow entrance and uncomfortably stood near the one officer and Pat, who looked at me as if I were the devil himself. After Betty filled her suitcase, I watched her walk into each of the kids' rooms. She didn't say anything, but I assume she went in to see the kids as they slept. I don't know if she did this because last night's arrest had been a wake up call, making her regret that she had been so bad to them for so long, or if it was just a show for her mom and the two police officers so they'd think she missed the kids. When she came out of the girls' room, she grabbed the suitcase by the handle and, oddly for her, let the bottom hit each stair on her way down. The bottom had wheels that she surely she knew had tiny bits of dirt on them and this apparent lack of care that would have been unthinkable just twenty-four hours before immediately caught my attention. As she walked by me, her head was down, but I could see she looked very tired and upset and my heart sank for her. I had always been the one protecting and providing for Betty and it weakened my fortitude for a second. But, as she and her mom walked out the door, I held it open and said, "Betty, I talked to Francine today and she thinks you should undergo some tests. We just want you to get some help." Betty didn't slow down or acknowledge me in any way, she just kept walking. But Pat turned around, and if looks could kill, she yelled, "You're a piece of shit!"

PLAYING THE VICTIM

The next day, I took Christian to preschool and saw one of our friends, Cristy, in the parking lot. Her five-year-old daughter looked up at my face, and even though I was trying to cover the scratches with a turtle neck and a hat, she saw them and asked, "What happened to your face?" I said, "Oh, a camera client's dog jumped up on me, that's all." Taking me by surprise, she said, "I thought maybe Christian's mom did that to you." Cristy laughed and said, "Honey, Betty would NEVER do that!" I just looked at Cristy and nervously laughed as I said bye.

Despite my resolve of the day before to stop protecting Betty and force her to get help, I found myself doing it again, almost subconsciously. I was still hopeful that Betty was going to get some help for her anger and we would eventually be the big, happy family I wanted and I wouldn't want anyone to know what we were like before. Also, I was so used to shielding our family over the years that if I fessed up to Cristy now, or anyone for that matter, I might have to answer some pressing questions about why I didn't do more when I knew the kids were being abused by Betty. I wouldn't have any answers that I wouldn't be ashamed of — I'd made my bed with how people viewed the Blacks within our community and circle of friends, outside of our neighbors, and I was now committed to lying in it.

In the early afternoon, I got a call from the Mercury Township Police Department and they informed me that Betty had filed a PFA against me. I told them, only half believing that Betty could even get a PFA against me, that I would come down so it could be served to me at the station — again to keep the police cars away from our house. When I got there, the same officer that had informed me about the PFA process the day before was there to serve me the PFA from Betty. His smirk told me he didn't think it was fair, but he had to do his job. I asked him, "How can she get a PFA on me when she is the one that went to jail?" He handed me the papers, shook his head and said, "Sorry I have to do this, but anyone can easily get a PFA on someone if they just show up and ask for one. She must have known she wouldn't have gotten one from the Allegheny courthouse, because she went through a lower court, who would have no way of knowing you were the one attacked and that you filed one first." My mind drifted, wondering how someone could slander a person they sought revenge on by playing a victim and abusing the PFA process. I said, "So anyone can get one, it doesn't matter if they're really a threat or not?!" "That's right. And women aren't really challenged for evidence, and sometimes men aren't either. Regardless, there will be a hearing, usually a couple of weeks later, and at that time the issuing court will determine if the PFA is deserved or not. So that is where you get to defend yourself," he said.

Halloween was just two days after our fight and I let Betty have the kids for the first hour of trick-or-treat. To abide by the PFA, my mom stayed with her and Pat, who had also come over. The next day, my mom came down to the house after I got the kids off to school and told me, "Pat and Betty were telling everyone who would listen that you beat up Betty! Just door to door right after the kids got their candy!"

"What?! Could the kids hear her?!" I asked. "Yes, at least most of the time!" she said. "Jesus. What did the people say?" I asked. "They didn't know what to say, they just stood there wondering why she was saying that with all of the neighborhood kids running around," she said. With this, I started to get a sense of where we were headed – divorce. I also got a sense of who I could trust in my neighborhood, as over the next several days, three people told me what Betty and her mom were saying and that they didn't believe them. One was Jeanne, who said to me, "'I told her, 'Betty, I like Rob and I don't want to hear it.'" I thanked her for having the spine to confront Betty, but I couldn't help but think of all the other houses in the neighborhood, who didn't know me well, and who may have believed Betty and Pat.

In the days after Betty wasn't allowed around us, it was hard not think of how nice it was for the kids and I to live like we should have been living all along. They played with their toys, some of which had never been taken off the shelf for fear of being yelled at for making too big of a mess. We ate our food not worried about the clean up until we were actually done eating. And, most memorably for me, we just had a peacefulness about us because we weren't walking on eggshells anymore. I had gotten used to rejection letters from the FAA every ten weeks concerning the process of returning to work. And when I got another one, just four days into our separate lives, I only had to worry about my next step to address what the FAA wanted to see changed or fixed this time, not Betty's acrimony and vengeance for the financial peril I had put our family in (which was, by far, the harder of the two stressors). To keep things as normal and hopeful as possible for the kids, I allowed as many friends to join us as my mom and I could fit into our two SUVs (if I needed her for the extra seats). We went to parks, ice skating, for ice cream, and just about anything they wanted to do. I was an extremely devoted father before, but now I poured my life into my kids, telling Ben I would not be doing anything with our business until I knew things were stable for them again. Ben is a youth minister and his understanding and patience was as welcome as his experienced insights into what was probably going on inside my kids' young minds during our talks.

When I picked up the finished police report from Officer Fry, I read that in the days following Betty's arrest, she showed up at the police station several times. Parts of the narrative read, "She is considering pursuing Criminal Charges against her husband," and "Mrs. Black seemed to have difficulty in controlling herself and left in a highly emotional state." Officer Fry saw the concern on my face and he said to me, as he pointed to a paragraph in the report, "Here, see this part? 'Betty had a clear view of the driveway and street where officers parked their vehicles while responding to the 9-1-1 calls?' We were walking all over the cul-de-sac, knocking on doors and looking for her for twenty minutes — she had to see us. It was obvious to Officer Ogdin and I that she was hiding in the shrubs she came out of as we approached her, but we just can't come right out and say it in the report." He also told me Betty had just submitted some pictures of her own. I asked to see them, and in one these pictures she had some blood in the lower corner of her left eye and four almost perfectly round red marks on her neck. Both struck me as odd, because the blood looked very fresh without a hint of darkening. Yet, according to the report, these pictures were taken several days after her arrest. Also, the marks on her neck were just four small pinkish-red circles, like she had pressed the tips of her fingers hard against her neck right before the picture was taken. She claimed I grabbed her neck, which I didn't, but even if I had, why weren't the marks elongated like fingers? Also, I didn't notice these circles on her neck as she walked past me in the entrance of our house the night after her arrest. I knew that Betty had done these to herself, but there was no way I could prove it. I was very worried about the police's perception of me; I certainly didn't need them thinking they had arrested the wrong person and that I was the real attacker that night. The only sign of Betty admitting that the marks on her neck were bogus wouldn't come for sixteen months, when she didn't submit the pictures as evidence in our custody hearings.

I left the station almost certain divorce was inevitable and I went home and checked on a suspicion that Betty had been on Plenty of Fish in the last few days. When I checked on the site to see if anyone seemed to fit her description, I found "PrettyEyes77" (I used to tell her how pretty her eyes were) on there with an account that had been created just two days before. She was from our town and, besides her physical description (which matched that of Betty's), she only filled in the greeting line and the question asking, "Describe your ideal first date." In an ominous sign of what was to come, she put "Busted" in the greeting and "Seeing you cry" for the ideal first date. I knew it was her, but I didn't fully realize it foreshadowed just how much of an extreme vengeance awaited me.

That evening, I saw a friend of mine from college who had married a woman I considered the picture of class and composure. Mark saw my scratches and I told him about the fight and of my frustration that Betty was so violent at home and yet she would step outside and be "Ms. Happy" to the rest of the world. He laughed and said, "Rob, just so you know, you're not the only one that has a crazy wife who everyone loves." I wondered who he was talking about and I looked at him as if to ask, "What do you mean?" "Oh yeah, Tammy throws lamps, dishes, books, cans of soda — throws just about anything she can get her hands on at me. She screams 'F--- you' all the time. And I'm afraid of her!" Even after all the things that had happened that should have prepared me to hear that a beautiful, radiant woman was not who she appeared to be, it still left my mouth literally wide open as Mark stood there, gauging my response. It's hard to overstate; since I had met her in college I had always regarded Tammy as the consummate lady — beautiful, smart, soft-spoken and always smiling, and if I had not been through what I had, there isn't any way I would have believed him.

Every day that the PFA was in effect, Betty requested to spend time with the kids, which my mom and I were happy to hear. We wanted Betty to want to be in the kids' lives, and we also wanted to keep things as normal as possible for the kids, so we gladly made time to accommodate her requests to see them. And, as long as Betty stayed in compliance with the PFA by leaving when my mom left, I even let the kids spend the night at Pat and Dale's all three weeks the PFA was in effect. I didn't want them to feel like their mom and their mom's family were being ripped from them, especially in these times of uncertainty.

Often, my mom would take the kids twelve miles away to Pat and Dale's house, where Betty was staying. I also asked Paige if she could supervise Betty with the kids, but Paige was busy with her own kids and could only help a few times in the four weeks that the PFA was in effect. My mom would bring the kids back and tell me Pat and Betty were saying all of the things Betty had said to the kids in her "meetings" with them when we were still together. Also, they were turning all of the things Betty had done to the kids when we were together into things I had done to the kids. The not caring about them, the not feeding them, the not cleaning up after them, the not taking them anywhere, the not having one bit of positive interaction all became what I had done to the kids. My mom is the least confrontational person you'll ever meet, and Betty and Pat took full advantage of that. My mom would try to get the kids to leave, but Betty and Pat would say they'd stop talking about me and, "They can stay a little bit longer." The visits with Betty took its toll on my mom, but she did what was right for the kids and made sure they saw Betty every day.

Still in the first few days since Betty's arrest, the kids came back from visiting their mom when Stephen said, "Grammy on the small hill [my parents were "on the big hill"] said, 'All of the Black's have problems, but her family is perfect!' And she meant all of us!" I didn't know just how bad it was at the time, but it became apparent later that Pat was using the time with the kids to bash my whole family and raise hers up. I knew Stephen was being torn in all different directions, and I got him in to see his counselor to help him deal with his emotions as soon as possible. I inquired with Dr. Aaron, Stephen's individual counselor, about family counseling for all of the kids. I spoke with, and chose, Heidi for that very important role.

As the days went by, I could already see my kids changing their attitudes with me. They weren't as happy around me as the first few days and they seemed to be a bit distant and leery about being alone with me. I figured that Betty and Pat were getting through to them somewhat, but I also knew their memories of what Betty had done to them were fresh. I figured they could rely on that memory to really know who had protected them and who had attacked them, so I let the visits continue. Ten days after Betty was arrested, I let the kids spend the night at Pat and Dale's again (Betty had said she wouldn't be there, which kept her in compliance with the PFA), and the next morning, Noel asked me if her mom could come back home. When I said, "Noel, I hope she can at some point, but not yet. Okay?" Noel's emphatic reply was, "But Mom is nice now!" I internally dismissed it because Betty had always been nicer to the kids in front of her parents, but I wondered if Noel really did think that Betty had all of a sudden become a genuinely nice person within such a short time.

Ken is also friends with Betty (sharing the bond of having the same military rank), so when I told him that Betty and her mom appeared to be blaming me for Betty's arrest, he said, "Well, I've been meaning to talk with her, so I'll see if she wants to go to lunch or for coffee just to make sure she's okay too." After they met, Ken tried to be respectful of his friendship with Betty, but he was emphatic when he told me, "Rob, I'm telling you, she is going to play the victim big time! I mean big time! I tried to tell her, 'Don't be the victim, you need to be stronger than that. You need to accept the situation and you need to move forward with your life,' but she wanted no part of it." I thanked Ken and thought to myself, "How can she play the victim if she's the one who was arrested?"

After two weeks of our separation, all of the kids were talking about how they enjoyed their time with Betty and I started to wonder if her change was permanent. I vacillated between letting her come home and filing for divorce, though we still had to have a hearing to release us from the PFAs to be around each other if she was to come home, and it's safe to say that I had no idea which way I was going with our marriage. One night around this time, I was walking out of Noel's indoor soccer game when I saw Betty standing on the other side of a wall. She was supposed to have left in accordance with the agreement she'd made with my mom to leave at halftime, allowing me to watch the second half. So I was surprised to see her standing there, only fifteen feet away, when I rounded the corner and we were in violation of the PFA's distance of fifty feet. When I saw her pretty face for the first time in two weeks, I blurted, "I love you." She sneered at me and said, "There's a reason I have a PFA on you," as if she was the one who needed protection. With a few other people around, I was embarrassed and I said, "Well, we both have PFAs." Her sister-in-law Kerry was then upon us and said, "Come on Rob, you can't be doing this," and I left.

I went home and wrote Betty a letter that I asked my mom to show her that night. I wrote that it hurt me to see her the night after her arrest looking so sad and tired, and that I would explain why I got the PFA later. I also wrote that if she was worried about our money, that I was going back to work soon and should be a captain within a year (almost exactly what I'd said three weeks before as she sat on our bed, despondent). Seeing her at the soccer game brought out some powerful emotions for me and I knew I still cared for her, and that's exactly how I ended the letter. But when my mom told me Betty had just tossed the letter aside after she read it, my suspicion that she wasn't coming back grew much stronger.

Two days later, we had our hearing for Betty's arrest at the local magistrate's office. When we got there, I was surprised to hear that the Mercury Township Police were leaving the decision to prosecute her or not up to me. And without a lawyer to guide me through the pros and cons, I discussed the issues and ramifications with them alone. Betty had her parents and a lawyer there and after the officers came in from talking with them, they informed me that if I went forward with the prosecution, Betty intended to come after me in a civil court for "Beating her up." Surprised, I asked, "What do you mean, 'Beating her up?' She attacked me." The one officer said, "She says you beat her up and that she was only defending herself by scratching and hitting you." "You guys found her hiding in a shrub!" I said in frustration. They just looked at me, patiently waiting for an answer. I asked them, in response to Betty saying that she was going to file charges against me, "Can she do that?!" The same officer said, "I'm not a lawyer, and we're not supposed to give legal advice, but yes, she can." I was dumbfounded and I asked for a few minutes to think about my options. Three things ran through my mind: Betty's case against me would be extremely weak, so I dismissed that as just a scare tactic. If there was any hope of getting back together, going forward with the prosecution would certainly negate it. And the biggest issue to me was that I had just been told by the police that Betty would be a convicted felon if the judge found her guilty — and he most probably would have. If that was true, she wouldn't be able to get a job that made any money, which also meant I would probably be the one who had to make up for her lack of income in the form of more alimony if we did get divorced. Without a lawyer there, I wasn't going to be getting the answers I needed, and trying to extend an olive branch to Betty and Pat, I told the police to drop the charges. All of us then gathered in the small, packed courtroom and Betty was standing a few feet behind her lawyer. When I looked at her, she went and stood right behind her lawyer, acting like she was afraid of me. As the police were talking to Betty's lawyer, I went over to Pat and softly said to her, "I had the police drop the charges, I've had enough." Pat then glared at me and said, "We've all had enough!" I looked at her and quickly realized she was implying that I'd attacked Betty and I just said, "Okay, I'm sorry. Bye."

When I left, I had to drive past where Betty and her parents had parked. Betty and her mom were looking at Betty's phone, smiling and laughing. Curious, I went home and looked at our cell phone bill to see who she may have been texting or talking with and there was a list of outgoing texts so long that it had to amount to everyone in her contacts list. They were all stamped at the same time, so it was a burst text, and people who I regarded as only friends of mine (she had the contact information for some of my old Air Force training friends) were included. I will likely never know what she texted to all of those people, but it would become very clear in the coming days, weeks, and months that exonerating her name from the arrest had become an obsession so strong that there are no words to describe it. It would permeate every aspect of her and she made it, far and away, the single most important endeavor of her life. I suspect that in those texts, she had just declared justice and victory over me — the real abuser having to back down when threatened by her own charges.

When I looked at the cell phone bill that day, I also noticed she had been texting and calling the policeman I suspected she'd had an affair with a lot — and he was texting and calling her too. The calls were usually around midnight or in the morning, but never in the afternoon, which probably aligned with his or his wife's work schedule. Several of the calls lasted nearly an hour, so I ruled out harmless chit-chat and I started to suspect that Betty may have been trying to get Ray to side with her. Though two officers from the Mercury Township Police had arrested Betty, I know policemen can be very unified. And if Ray could convince other officers in the department that I was, in fact, an abusive husband, I wouldn't know who I could trust if the police had to intervene between Betty and I again in the future.

One of the biggest quandaries and heartbreaks I would face would be the parents of our girls' friends taking Betty's side without so much as a chance to tell my side. My first clue that Betty was saying negative things to these parents came when the scratches on my neck and face were still visible. I walked Julie into her gymnastics practice and the lady who runs Noel's Girl Scout troop was sitting in the lobby, talking on the phone. I smiled and said, "Hi Kate," and she glanced at me with a smirk and, without saying a word to me, looked away while continuing to have the phone to her ear (she wasn't speaking into the phone). Those who don't know Betty might say this borders on paranoia, but I know Betty better than anyone, including herself, and the overflowing amount of hate she carries inside has to come out — I suspect she was the person on the phone with Kate; her plan of taunting me by being on the phone with one of her new allies would've been easy to time as I always walked Julie in from the busy parking lot right before practice started. Adding credence to Kate's reaction, over the last three years it has become very apparent that Kate is one of Betty's biggest sympathizers.

What was most disappointing about Kate's presumption was that before Betty and I split, she trusted me enough to have me take pictures and videos of the dozens of Girl Scouts at their functions. Also, just a day or two before Betty was arrested, she came to my house and asked me to put up a sign in our front yard for her husband, who was running for a local office. We had nice, pleasant exchanges — she trusted me until she heard otherwise, and she didn't take the time to ask me if it was true or not, she judged me completely uninformed as to my side of our story. It is extremely disappointing then, to report that the likes of Kate were far more prevalent than those who sought the truth or at least wanted to stay neutral. My stance was, and is, that there are two sides to every story and reasonable people will realize that fact and not judge until they have heard from both sides — to make up one's mind beforehand is pre judging. Kate was a stark realization as to how other parents would view me after helpless and battered Betty told them how long she'd lived with her abusive husband and I would eventually find it almost impossible for my girls to have friends to play with.

Our hearing for the dual PFAs was set for the third week of November. In the days leading up to that, Betty's lawyer called me several times to pressure me to drop the kids from the PFA, but I refused because I still didn't trust Betty around the kids — my memory of the last eighteen months, and to a lesser extent, ten years, still fresh and vivid. I had enlisted Val, a tough ex-DA, to represent me. She and Betty's lawyer went back and forth all morning trying to agree on which one of us would move out of the house and who would have the kids and when. Most of Betty's family was at the county courthouse and I had my parents there for support and to bounce questions off of.

This morning was the first time I had ever heard of Betty wanting any part of the kids' lives, and it became apparent that she now wanted my part too when her lawyer told Val that Betty would "Let me see the kids" if we just gave Betty full custody. Both lawyers conveyed to the judge that we weren't anywhere close to coming to an agreement on our own, but the judge insisted that we try, and said she would only see us as a last resort. Now into the afternoon, Pat became furious and loudly said in the waiting room, "That's it, I'm going to get Julie and she can tell the judge how her dad beat her mom up!" I hoped she was just bluffing, as calling in a nine-year-old, who had already been through and seen far too much, to testify against one of her parents was not in our girl's best interest. But this wasn't about what was in Julie's best interest. This was, at absolutely all cost, about revenge — Pat's revenge on Betty's behalf for the arrest and subsequent PFA.

I can still see Pat walking in and pulling Julie, reluctant and scared, into the waiting room by her arm. My mom exclaimed, "She did it! She took Julie out of school to tell the judge how you beat her mom up! They are damaging Julie! That is just disgusting!" Val just said, "Unbelievable," and shook her head. Pat sat Julie down between herself and Betty and Pat held onto Julie's hand, as if to say, "We're all in this together," like I was some horrible person that the family needed protected from.

I didn't want Julie exposed to any more of this and I asked Pat if she and I could negotiate in a private room with Betty and her lawyer, to which they agreed. Betty sat down across the small table from me, and no longer separated by our fifty foot perimeter, I saw the woman I was married to for twelve years, but I felt like I didn't know who she was or what she stood for anymore. Our lawyers were negotiating when Betty interrupted, "All I want is to be with the kids! I do everything for them and he doesn't do anything! I should have the kids, I'm the one who takes care of them, not him! I'm the caretaker!" as she pointed back and forth between herself and I. When I heard her say this, I really couldn't believe my ears, and I sat there stunned and in a daze for a few seconds. Confused, I blurted "What?" as I looked into her eyes for the first time in nearly a month. I looked at the lawyers, making sure they heard it too. From here on, Betty kept interrupting the lawyers as they tried to come to an agreement, repeating, "I should get the kids, I'm the care-taker!" and anything else she could interject into the negotiations be-tween them. I sat there bewildered, respectful of the lawyers' role, but in complete disbelief of Betty's 180 degree turnaround from just four weeks before when she told me, "I can't be their mom anymore, that's it." I thought, "What about the angry, depressed mom who resented her kids for so many years? I protected them from you and your furious rages, and now you want to take them from me?"

Six hours after we arrived, we finally agreed to split the time with the kids, week on, week off. We also agreed to three hours of visitation during one day for the off-time parent, so we didn't have to go seven days without seeing them. As Val came out of the courtroom, she relayed to my parents and I that the judge was pleased with our agreement, but the judge had decided that, because my parents lived up the street, I had to be the one who moved out — and I had forty-five hours to do so. "Unbelievable," Val said under her breath. "What, that I have to be the one who moves out?" I asked. "No!" Val exclaimed, "I've never met anyone, I mean anyone, more unreasonable or volatile than that little bitch! How in the hell did you stay married to that for 12 flipping years?!" Powerful words from a seventy-two-year-old woman who had spent her whole career in various litigation roles.

With our finances in ruins, I had no choice but to move into my parents' house, as I didn't have the money to afford rent for an apartment. I couldn't decide if I wanted to move as many of my household items as possible in the short time I was given, or leave some things behind to get at some point in the future if we did divorce. Friends helped me with the short-notice move of just some of my things, one of whom was the son of my parents' next-door neighbors. Dan owned a truck and we moved a couple of garage benches and an engine-less motorcycle. Another friend with a truck helped with smaller garage items and I was incredibly grateful for their generosity. With my life so dark, bleak, and uncertain now, I needed their offer and show of friendship more than I needed the actual moving.

Norm and another good friend, Brian, also came over at night to help with some the items from inside the house. On the second night, I was packing up some older pictures of Betty and I and it was incredibly strange to see Betty smiling and looking happy as she leaned into me at a friend's wedding in 2004; it had been roughly six long years since she was pregnant with Noel and I last saw her as anything but angry. Kneeling and losing the struggle to hold back the tears, I looked up at Brian and Norm, who had taken a break. I said to Norm, "I don't know how you did it," referencing his sudden, forced move-out seven years before. I was dejected knowing Betty was the one who went to jail, but I was the one being evicted. "So unfair," was all I could think of as the night wore on.

To add to the things I had to do in forty-five hours, I needed to figure out why I was suddenly getting emails saying the passwords and security questions to many of my accounts had been changed. When I asked the customer service reps from the various companies when the changes were made, I was told they had been changed that day. As several agents commented, "They knew all of the answers to your security questions." I took my accounts back from Betty, one by one, and I wanted to change my standard password to a new one that reflected what I had been going through for the last twenty-four days. "1Crazylife!" fit perfectly. Just months before our split, I had created an excel spreadsheet for Betty and I that tracked the usernames and passwords for all of our accounts and webpages, and fearing the worst, I checked all of my accounts, including the ones where I wasn't notified of any changes. My suspicion couldn't have been more right; almost every account I came across had been changed and I spent hours reclaiming them. From my Yahoo email, to my retirement funds, and everything in between — over twenty accounts in all. The day each of our kids was born, I created an email address for them using their names in the addresses and when I checked on those, I couldn't log in to them either. I immediately contacted Yahoo and I was informed that the accounts had recently been deleted, so I called Betty and asked, "Why did you do change all of my passwords and delete the kids email addresses? Now the kids' first emails are gone forever." She yelled, "They're as much mine as they are yours!" and hung up the phone. Through a lot correspondence with tech support, I managed to reestablish the kids email accounts, but the emails saying "Hello everyone" I sent the day each one was born to Betty's and my parents, and their replies, were gone forever.

In the ultimate test of my sobriety, the next day, I was cleaning out some things in the basement when I came across what I thought was an empty bottle of wine. I took it, and two armfuls of other things, over to a box full of garbage. When I leaned over to dump it in the box, there was wine still in the bottle and it started to chug out onto the floor. I quickly tilted the bottle upright again, but I was faced with the aroma and still half-full bottle of my nemesis. It was one of the worst days of my life and I knew the potential of what remained in the bottle, so I quickly took it over to the toilet and dumped it out before I could give it a second thought — afraid of what could come from that second thought just hours before I had to move out and give the kids to Betty for a week.

I laid in bed that night in my old room at my parents' house, wide awake and wondering if this was really happening. I guess I needed proof, so around 2:00 a.m., I got up and walked towards our house. It had been snowing a lot, so I was mindful of leaving tracks and stayed in the street and away from our house. Or was it her house now? I didn't know, but being court-ordered out of my house and away from my kids left me as empty as I've ever felt as I stared inside the big glass window over the front door. Through my tears, I could see the kids' night lights coming out of their rooms and into the hall as I looked through the big glass window over the door. "Such lucky light, you get to see my four beautiful kids," I thought.

Betty had them all to herself now and I said a short prayer asking that they be okay alone with her. What was stopping her from turning on them again? I didn't know the answer at the time and, afraid of being seen, I didn't have the luxury of time to give it any more thought. I walked back to my parents' house completely dejected and dismayed at the turn of events over the last twenty-five days. Over the next few months, if I woke up in the middle of the night, I always wondered for a split second if it was all just a bad dream. But then my old room came into focus and it was a tangible reminder that Betty had indeed pulled off this impossible switch.

The next day I set to work on getting the two cluttered bedrooms ready for the kids. They would be split into boys and girls, so choosing the paint colors was easy: a slightly deeper blue for the boys and a pastel purple for the girls. I also bought a lot of chalk paint to cover almost one whole wall in both rooms for them to write, draw, and for me to help them with their homework. My mom balked at the chalk paint, but quickly came around when I told her, "We need to do whatever it takes to make the kids comfortable here. They have been through way too much and this will help to make them feel like it's really theirs — not so temporary. Besides, I will just paint over it when the time comes." She and my dad were helping too, by cleaning out the bedrooms and buying beds and mattresses. In the midst of the biggest upheaval in any of our lives, I'm proud to say we put all of the strife behind us and spent three straight days on the task of turning their house into our house.

One of Betty's more shrewd lies, one that afforded her years of payoff and persistent jabs at me, was claiming I took her school yearbook when I moved some of my things from our house. I first asked her for my karate uniform and some scuba gear that I'd left in a pile outside the attic and she eventually returned my email saying she only would give those to me if I gave her the missing yearbook. Even though I was certain I didn't take the yearbook, I did have a little help in my partial move-out, so I went through every possible place it could have been several times. To this day, if I ask for anything from her that I have bought for the kids and it hasn't come back from her house in months or even a year (a GoPro has been captive for seventeen months now), she claims I stole her yearbook and she will not entertain any further discussion until it is returned.

Unequivocal proof that Betty and her mom were on a mission to convince anyone who would listen that I attacked Betty and that I was solely to blame for her arrest came a few days later. Pat and Dale had an appointment with Norm, who is a doctor, and they used much of their time to tell Norm that I "beat Betty all the time," and that I was an angry drunk who'd abused and hit our kids too. What makes Norm a true friend is his reaction and how it reflects his devotion. He said, "Look, I know you didn't hit Betty or abuse the kids; we've been friends since grade school and I know you better than that. I just wish you had confided in me when you were struggling with alcohol. You didn't have to fight it alone; you have to know by now that I'll always be here for you, no matter what and there's nothing we can't do together. Why didn't you tell me?" I just said, "Foolish pride," and I thanked him for his open-mindedness in listening to both sides of the conflict — something that I would quickly learn was far from universal amongst other friends and acquaintances.

This incident was the impetus for what would become my journal as I know it now, no longer scribbled in notepads and post-it notes; I knew her extreme and persistent manipulations would require detailed entries with dates and times and even a key as I needed to organize the myriad of lies and plots against me. It's condensed as much as possible, yet there are over four hundred entries in just the twenty-one months I kept it.

The next day was the day before Thanksgiving, and I took my three-hour visit with the kids that evening so we could keep our tradition of the kids helping my mom make some of the food for the next day. I met the kids outside and Julie came up to me and said, "Daddy, guess what!!" Excited, I said, "What?!" She said, "Mom is nice now!" "Oh really?" I said. We got inside, and in the five days since I had seen them, Stephen and Noel had grown noticeably distant with me, not even saying "Hi" to me or giving me a hug. My mom came to the entrance and saw the less-than-happy faces on Stephen and Noel and she asked what was wrong. Looking at me, Noel said, "Grammy [Pat] said you don't really love us more than anything!" and she started crying. This is the phrase I usually told them when I was done talking to them on the phone. I said, "Noel, of course I do! Where was your mom? Did she tell Grammy to stop saying that?" Stephen interjected, a little unsure why I was asking, "Mom was standing right next to Grammy." I asked, "Well, did your mom say anything to Grammy?" Stephen said, "Mom didn't say anything." Over the next hour, I played and talked with the kids and they warmed up to me before it was time to start making the food. The rest of the night was fairly normal, if a bit strained because of Pat's remarks, still fresh, and their doubt as to the kind of person I was.

When the kids got to my parents' on Thanksgiving, they walked up the sidewalk looking troubled and unhappy. Noel had her arms crossed and walked straight into the dining room, sat down amongst the guests, and immediately said, "I'm bored!" Christian went up to my dad and only said, "I want to go back to the other pap paps to play trains," while Stephen and Julie just looked at me a bit uncomfortably. I let my parents handle it with the younger two, while I tried to get an answer out of Stephen and Julie as to why no one seemed to want to be there. "What's wrong?" I asked. Stephen said, "Grammy told us, 'Be as bad as you can be so your dad and your other grammy don't want you there." Stephen and Julie looked at me with a blank stare, and I said, "Well, you aren't bad kids, and I've raised you to know what is right and what is wrong, and you just do what's right, okay? And I want this to show you that just because someone is an adult, that doesn't always mean they know how to act and conduct themselves, does it?" They shook their heads, no, and I finished our talk by saying, "Let's go in and say hi to everyone and put this behind us, okay?" After eating and chatting with our guests, we went downstairs to play in the basement. One of the games I had been playing with the kids over the last month was "Bad Mood Bull." I would get on all fours and they would lay on my back and I would try to buck them off as they held on and one of the other kids timed them. It's a great way to bond with them, but it also gets them to trust me because I could really hurt them if I was careless. Noel is the perennial champion, and though she seemed to be the hardest to bring around emotionally this night, she did get on and reestablish her supremacy in a raucous evening of screaming and laughter. The kids seemed completely recovered after the four hours, and they left giving big, smiling hugs.

The next day, I was to get the kids at three o'clock for my week and I was still getting their rooms ready when the doorbell rang. It was the mail lady with an envelope that required a signature and my heart immediately sank. I knew what was inside the envelope, but reading Betty's divorce filing left me torn between emotions. I had three hours until I got the kids for my week and I spent most of it walking around the neighborhood collecting my thoughts. They ran from wondering why this wasn't like any of our other fights where we eventually got back together, to wondering who was going to take care of Betty (she is very dependent on others), to the pain of having the stigma of a failed marriage, to exuberance that I would finally be single and free to seek a true friend, companion, and love. But the one open issue I couldn't stop reverting back to was her alone with the kids, unaccountable for her behavior and parenting while I bounced around the country. I wasn't back to flying yet, but I was fairly sure it would be soon with the FAA running out of reasons to keep me from my medical. Trusting her for days at a time with no one to keep an eye on the kids was a daunting risk.

During the walk, I tried to push all other thoughts aside and only think of the kids. I realized that they were far too young to be alone with

Betty and I immediately turned to trying to figure out ways to get her to retract the divorce. I thought of two. One, through friends talking to her, and two, I would simply tell her the things I thought she wanted to hear and ask her to reconsider. The friend I decided to call was Patty, a very nice and understanding common friend of ours that I knew Betty had been talking to. Patty was part of a group of six friends that Betty strongly targeted to abandon their friendship with me after her arrest — and most of them did. During recent uncharacteristic lunches and visits with them, which Betty always made sure my mom or I knew about, she told them how abusive I had been to her and the kids. I asked Patty to talk to Betty and she said that she had been and that she would again. "But I know Betty is pretty sure about the divorce," she tried to gently say. I thanked her and left her with, "Patty, please don't believe what you're probably hearing about me, I hope you know me better than that."

When Betty brought the kids up to my parents' for my first week with them under the new court order, I asked to talk to her for a minute in the small study. We went in and I stood at the back of the room to show as little pressure as possible, trying to remember to say as much as I could about how she had the control — something that she had to have over me like her mom and sister have over their husbands. I looked into her eyes for a couple of seconds, and in a surreal moment, wondered, "Is this really happening?" I carefully asked, "Betty, are you really sure you want to do this, or is this your mom's idea?" "It's not my mom's, it's my idea," she said. I was not expecting her independent and assertive tone. "What if I told you that I want things to be the way they were, before kids. I used to sing to you and tell you how beautiful you are. I miss those times." Giving me some hope, she said, "I miss them too." "Well, we can have them again if you want. That is a hundred percent up to you and it is your decision," I said. Her next comment completely squashed any hope I had when she said, "I actually feel sorry for you." Stunned, I blurted, "What?" "I feel sorry for you. You're older, you don't have a job and you live with your parents now." I believe the diametrically opposed feeling to love is to feel sorry for someone, as that implies there isn't any respect, admiration, or attraction and there isn't anything else she could have said that would have been more powerful to me. I threw in the towel to prevent any more loss of respect, if that was even possible, when I said, "Okay, you've made up your mind." As she looked at me with the same determined and unyielding stare I wore, I thought of a military phrase, "Fight's on." I knew that this divorce was not going to be about a woman who merely tolerated or even downright hated her ex-spouse — this divorce was going to be all about revenge. Revenge because I didn't turn into a virtual punching bag like her dad and brother-in-law for her to vent her overflowing anger on. Revenge for depleting our savings from the time off from work. And above all, revenge for not saving her like she did for me when I seemed hopeless. In her mind, she drove me to rehabs, but when it was my turn to show compassion, rescue her, and show her a way out of her inner hell, I rejected her with a PFA. And Betty had a devoted ally in her mother who was almost as vengeful as she was over the disgrace of the arrest and PFA. Pat would gladly carry out the orders in Betty's multi-fronted mission of hate, often standing right beside Betty while the lies, manipulations, and vitriol against me spewed from her. Betty, the silent conductor, knew if her mom spoke for her, the kids' young minds wouldn't think it was their mom that wanted them to hate Dad — it was just Grammy.

Revenge would come in the form of a vehement, all-encompassing obsession to take everything away from me. It didn't matter if she had a use for whatever it was or not — if I valued it, Betty was going to take it by any means possible. Money, dignity, friends, our family dog Charlie, and far, far, far and away at the very top of my list of things I hold dear, having a significant role and influence in our kids' childhood and upbringing.

Little did I know, the first exchange and my first week with the kids foreshadowed how things were going to be from now on. When Betty left after dropping them off, I realized that she didn't bring anything for the kids. We were missing school backpacks, clothes, winter coats, and gloves. She yelled, "I'll bring that up as they need them!" intending to interrupt my custody time as often as possible and to carry out the illusion that she was the sole provider in the kid's lives. A few hours later, she brought up a few more things, but she blocked my parents' car as they were about to back out of their driveway for a friend's funeral. We repeatedly asked her to move her van, but she became very confrontational and refused. The kids were upset, but Betty dug in and my mom had to get Paige to come over and convince her it was time to leave.

When we got inside, I tried to calm the kids and get them to realize we were going to have fun and an enjoyable evening. They liked their rooms and my parents and I did our best to make them feel comfortable, but it was obvious right away that they felt they had been uprooted from their real home down the street. I knew that the kids and I needed to stay busy, outside my parents' house, and that weekend I took them ice skating and to a unique embroidery store I thought the girls would like. The three older kids seemed distant with me all weekend, and Noel started crying before we walked into the store. When I asked her what was wrong, she asked, "Why can't Mom come with us?" At a loss for words, I just said, "Because we are separate now." Noel, unable to understand the complexity of divorce, said, "But Mom is nice now!" and she started crying uncontrollably. I reacted with frustration, not compassion, and to this day it's still one of the few times I wish I could take back what I have said to them: "She's not being nice to me." All four kids became sad and confused as they looked at me and each other. That only incited me, and after two straight days of frustration, I said, "I don't know what you're upset about, she didn't show that she loved any of us before; this is all a big act." When I saw the girls start to cry and Stephen trying not to show his hurt, I immediately regretted what I had said. I got down on my knees on the sidewalk and said, "I'm so sorry, none of you deserve any of this. I love you, your mom loves you, and everything is going to be okay, alright? I promise." I gave each of them a hug, but the aftereffects of what I had said lasted until the next day.

The next day, the kids were to come home from their shopping day at school with the Christmas presents I gave them money to buy. Unexpectedly, Betty was standing at the bus stop in front of Paige's house when I went out to wait for the girls. Leery of her presence, I slowly walked over. When I got there, she smiled and said, "I hear from a friend of mine, who's a cop, that you got a DUI!" Baffled, I said, "No I didn't." "That's not what I heard and I looked it up on the internet!" she said. As the bus pulled up, I said, "I don't know what to tell you, but rumors aren't going to do you any good." She knew I was right and it incited her anger. The girls came off the bus, looking uncomfortable and confused that their mom was near me. Betty said, as she reached for the bags of presents they were carrying, "Hi girls! I'll take these to our house and we can wrap them whenever you want to come down! Okay?" I said, "I paid for those and I'd like to wrap them with the girls." Betty yelled, "You've NEVER wrapped anything for anyone; it's always been me! You never did anything for me or the kids for Christmas!" I said, "That's not true," and, knowing Betty's penchant to argue incessantly, I got the girls inside my parents' house as fast as possible. As we were walking away, Betty kept repeating, "You were never part of the kids' lives before, why are you pretending now?!" In my notes, I opined, "The whole thing seemed planned as the girls weren't even off the bus yet when Betty asked for the presents."

Julie was eating breakfast the next morning and I asked her what she thought she was going to do when she went back to her mom. She said, "I'm afraid to go back to Mom and go to Grammy's house!" I asked why, and she said, "Because she always says mean things about you." "Who? Your mom or Grammy?" I asked. "Grammy," She said. I said, "Well, tell your mom and maybe she will tell Grammy to stop." Julie looked and sounded confused. "Mom is there," she said. From this I gather Betty wants to portray the perception of complying with one of the biggest rules of co-parenting: don't speak badly about the other parent — she just has her mom do it for her.

The next day, my mom called me as I was dropping off Julie off at gym practice. "Rob, Child Youth and Family is at Betty's and they need the kids at Betty's house as soon as possible," is all I remember hearing on the phone; the rest of the call was a blur of thoughts regarding the custody ramifications of a CYF visit on my record. I went down to our marital house and waited for the CYF agent to come out after she talked with the kids. When she did, I asked her to come up to my mom's house to ask me some questions directly and, though I didn't say it, so she could see for herself how comfortable the kids were in my presence. It was all I could do to keep from breaking down, and Stephen and Noel must have sensed this because as the lady walked into my parents' house, Noel told her, "Grammy is always saying bad things about my dad!" Stephen immediately chimed in with, "And on Thanksgiving, she said for us to be as bad as we can be so my dad and other Grammy didn't want us around!" When I picked up Julie from gymnastics that night, I didn't want to risk any tears in front of her either, so I waited until I got home to tell her that an agent from CYF was doing an investigation on me. My mom preempted my conversation with Julie, and as soon my mom said "CYF," Julie interrupted and loudly said, "Grammy on the small hill did that!" The next morning during breakfast, Noel put her face in her hands and started crying. When my mom asked her why she was crying, she muttered, "I'm very afraid of Grammy." Julie repeated Noel's nearly unintelligible words, "I'm afraid too!" she said in her strong, emphatic voice. My mom said, "Well, you should talk to your mom about Grammy, Noel." Noel was too upset to talk or even eat, so Julie responded, "She always says bad things about Dad!" I went over to hold Noel and I was only partially paying attention to Julie's comment, or I would have asked if she meant her mom or Grammy. But if Betty had done that, it would have been the first time, still to this day, that we would hear that Betty had said anything negative about me — she has a spokesperson in her mother for that side of her.

One evening, I asked Julie to go for a walk. We were putting on our shoes, and she very nonchalantly said, "Dad, Mom didn't punch me in the stomach, she was just turning around and she hit me with her elbow." My mind raced through everything that had happened over the last month. How, instead of getting Betty from jail, I got the PFA against her — in part because Julie had told me that Betty had punched her in the stomach. How that abandonment caused Betty and Pat to become obsessively vengeful. How we were getting divorced. How I was living with my parents. How I was losing a battle to keep the kids' love and respect. I didn't believe that Betty was just turning around and she accidentally hit Julie with her elbow, but the fact that Betty could overwrite Julie's mind with her version of how she wants Julie to remember our family's history brought mixed emotions. I was glad they could have a way to not really remember the bad things in their past, but they were becoming very distant with me, and their distorted memory was costing me the closeness we used to have.

The first week was over, contentious and unlike anything I'd expected. The problem was (and is) that that week wasn't going to be much different than the weeks, months, and years that lie ahead. Indeed, my biggest quandary in writing this book is how to convey to the reader that this relentless targeted onslaught towards my reputation and the constant need to "deprogram" the kids became the norm. There is so much unacceptable behavior pertaining to the kids and I from Pat and Betty that my journal, noting only the more egregious incidents over the next year and a half, still totals that of a typical book — over 80,000 words, all of it in a condensed, bullet format. To keep this book from having the dimensions of an encyclopedia, I have no choice but to leave out most of Betty's instances of playing the victim and Pat's near daily attempts to alienate the kids from me. As was proven time and time again, their behavior was so dreadful that no one would believe me or my mom — at least not 100%. I labeled Betty's extremely adept ability to commit an infraction, and successfully blame me for doing it, "Betty 101." Most people that aren't familiar with Borderline Personality Disorder, gaslighting, and distortion campaigns are probably wondering how it is possible. After all, won't the facts speak for themselves? Sometimes, but I'm convinced that there isn't one situation out there that Betty can't manipulate to her advantage. Additionally, most of the time, Betty and Pat were telling the kids so much, it was overwhelming. And I hardly ever knew what had been said — I had to rely on the kids' behavior towards me and hear them talking to each other to get a sense of it. There would be times that the kids told me or one of my parents directly of course, but it was likely days later when we next saw them and heard about it. During that time, the messages were sinking in and solidifying in their minds to the point that my explanations were too little, too late. Betty, and especially Pat, could distort reality and convince our young kids that I had wronged Betty over and over again.

If you have a hard time believing or understanding how a person could repeatedly manipulate a situation and distort the truth, just imagine the following scenario. Someone who doesn't work but two days a month devotes their life to devising various ways to destroy the reputation of someone they have a vendetta against. They think of the many ways it can fail and painstakingly revise the plan to prevent that. They enlist an eager accomplice. They enlist the unknowing community and even make inroads with the targeted person's own friends. Are you more convinced now? Are you concerned? Concerned that if someone became obsessed with ruining your life, you couldn't keep up with their onslaught of mind games and psychological manipulations? How would you know what their next move was? Despite the absolute best of efforts, you could not stop it. Only the people who know you best, immediate family, neighbors, and close friends would be left trusting you — everyone else becomes visibly uncomfortable in your presence, trying to picture the horrible things they've heard you have done. My mom sums it up best when she simply exclaims, "There is no way we can keep up with all of her lies!"

One only needs to read through all of the texts between Betty and I to understand what I am talking about. To this day, just reading through all of the saved texts I have is enough to make anyone doubt their sanity. There are no better examples of her ability to blatantly lie and contradict herself, just an entry or two above, in all of our texts over those three years. And if you call her out on her contradiction and provide proof, she will deny she ever said the first part, even though her words are sitting there on your phone. If I point out what she texted before, then she will claim that I am harassing or trying to control her. Sometimes her lies span many weeks or months, and trying to dig through the hundreds of texts to figure out what she said and what was going on at the time is even harder to cope with.

There is an odd word for the rare person who tries to convince people of a different reality — gaslighting. It stems from a film in the 1940s where a man convinces a woman that what she thinks is true, isn't. I'll save you the trouble of looking up the definition. "A form of mental abuse in which a victim is manipulated into doubting their own memory, perception, and sanity. Instances may range from the denial by an abuser that previous abusive incidents ever occurred, up to the staging of bizarre events by the abuser with the intention of disorienting the victim. Often done by friends and family members, who claim (and may even believe) that they are trying to be helpful. The gaslighting abuser sees himself or herself as a nurturing parental figure in relation to the victim, and uses gaslighting as a means for keeping the victim in that relationship, perhaps as punishment for the victim's attempt to break out of the dependent role." — Wikipedia. Betty has remarkable success gaslighting not only our children, but with well-to-do and otherwise discerning people. They aren't fools, but she does, in fact, fool them.

From here on, I will leave out most of the lesser and repetitive entries. The reader should know that these instances were still very frustrating, but their repetition prevents their inclusion. If you need an idea of what those would look like, I will cite the very first entry from my notes that would otherwise be excluded as an example: "'Now on Betty's second custodial week, On Friday, I requested to have my three hour visit with the kids Sunday evening from 4:00-7:00. Betty waited until Sunday afternoon to respond and said, 'No, we are going out to dinner.' When I called the kids that night (Sunday), they were at Pat and Dale's watching The Grinch. When I asked Julie, 'Where did you go to dinner?' she said, 'We didn't go out for dinner, we just ate hot dogs here.' I said, 'Oh, I thought you were going to dinner tonight?' She responded, 'No, I never heard that. Do you mean mom? She went out to dinner.'" These entries, where I have difficulty scheduling my visits with the kids and other relatively benign entries during Betty's weeks, will have to be left out, but my journal reminds me that every day brought new manipulations and lies to track and undo. The previous example highlights Betty always had something for the kids to do on the prime visitation days of Sunday, Monday, and, to a lesser, degree Wednesday. They were the best days because the kids didn't have any activities, or had activities that started after the court-established 4:00-7:00 window, but Betty would corner me into Tuesdays and Thursdays by scheduling haircuts, nail appointments, and other frivolous things for the kids. Tuesdays and Thursdays weren't ideal because Julie started gymnastic practice at 4:15. Getting the kids Thursday would also mean I had to go six straight days without seeing them before I got them for my week the next day. Wednesday became the norm for me because I at least got to spend an hour with the girls before they had to be at gym practice. But after a few months, Betty took that away and I settled on what I thought had the fewest compromises of what was left, Tuesday.

I reflect on the rest of 2013 and early 2014 as a very dark time, filled with more of the same things the first month brought — trying to undo Betty and Pat's persistent injections of disdain for me into our kids. Still in early December, when the kids walked into my parents' house for my visit during Betty's week, Noel was very upset. I pleaded with Noel to tell me what was wrong. "Grammy on small hill said you don't love me!" she finally said. Surprised, I said, "Of course I love you Noel, and I will always love you no matter what. No one can ever change that, right?" She nodded her head yes, but she still looked sad. My mom said, "Noel, that is a lie. Your dad loves you more than anything else in the world! That is very wrong of your other grammy to say that and hurt your dad and us so much!" When the other three came into the room, my mom asked them, "Have you ever heard us talk bad about your mom or your other grammy? Or anyone?!" They all said, "No," or shook their head. I said, "Noel, please know that everything I do in my life is for you; I love you so, so much." Still crying, but starting to come around, Noel said, "I know. You painted our rooms, and you bought me a new bed." How could we get her to believe that we did love her? It was our word against Pat's and the best we could hope for is for the kids to split the difference. The damage to my kids was adding up. I felt the more they heard, the more they would believe no matter how much we tried to unwind what they were being told.

Trying to keep the little bit of good momentum going, I took all of the kids into the basement to play soccer. My mom came down to cheer on the kids, but Noel was still crying. Unexpectedly, she went up to my mom and said, "I ruined your Thanksgiving! I feel guilty, I know I hurt your feelings!" as she put her face in her hands again. My mom always seems to know the perfect thing to say, and she told her, "Noel, you made great-grandpa, great-grandma, Aunt Doris, and Uncle Jeff laugh so hard on Thanksgiving! That wasn't your fault; you made everyone's night so happy!" My mom's notes sum up my thoughts even better than I could: "This was twelve days later & she was still feeling the effects of what Pat told her to do!"

One resource Betty and her mom had persistently used against me was the kids' four cousins. Except for the oldest cousin, who was two years older than Stephen, their ages line up within just a few months of each other and all of them are virtually inseparable. Now mid-December, Betty called to talk to the kids much earlier than usual one morning on our landline and Stephen answered it by accidentally pressing the speaker-phone button. My mom and I then heard Stephen's cousin and best friend, Joel, telling Stephen, "Stephen, we're all going to the movies. Can you come with us?" Stephen's "other best friend," Adam, was visiting at my parents' house and he tried to tell Stephen that the movie Joel named wasn't out yet. Obviously confused, Stephen looked at me and I said, "Something's not right Stephen, Adam is saying the movie isn't even out yet." There was a long pause and, as my mom and I both noted, there was an adult's muffled voice in the background when Joel started to sound coached. Joel finished by saying "I'll see you at church and then at Grammy's tomorrow, okay Stephen?" Stephen didn't know what to say, and for much of the time he sat there in silence as Joel kept repeating his question asking Stephen to go to the movies and his statement of seeing Stephen the next day at his other grandparents. The next day was Sunday, and this was meant to taunt Stephen with the tradition of all of the cousins getting to play all over Pat and Dale's large property doing just about whatever they wanted for most of the day and into the night. And Joel couldn't have meant seeing Stephen during Betty's three hour visitation because she had already asked me for (and I granted) Monday for that. Betty then got on the phone and repeated exactly what Joel had asked and said it three more times. Then the oldest and most revered cousin, Mitchel, got on the phone and all of us got to hear the temptations for what had to be the tenth time. I don't fault the two cousins, they were likely only doing what they were "coached to do" as my mom put in her notes. My mom's conclusion after this call was a bit overstated in retrospect, but it fit for how upset we were at the time. "Such child cruelty! Luckily Adam was here and Stephen was here having fun with him. I don't know how you hurt your own child like this. On purpose — planned — knowing full well that Stephen is with his dad."

Far and away, the biggest contradiction I will ever witness is Betty's stance that I was the aggressor on the night she was arrested and that I beat her "All the time." Yet she takes every chance she gets to taunt and berate me. It happens so often that it has its own key in my journal, discernible amongst the other entries with text that is in all capitals and underlined. My stance is, if I really had been physically abusive to Betty, she would be afraid of me and not want to be near me or say anything that could incite me. She is anything but afraid, and she uses the fact that I am the one distressed by her presence to intimidate me every chance she gets.

A great example of Betty's unabashed taunting was the very next day, after the phone call enticing Stephen to go to the movies. I was sledding with the kids in my parents' back yard when I saw her at the top of the hill dressed in sledding gear. As we walked back up the hill, the kids got behind me, clearly afraid of Betty being near me (or were they afraid of me around Betty?). She was smiling and said, "Hi kids! Can I sled with you?!" With their silence, I said, "Why are you here?" "I'm allowed to see the kids on your time! Are you going to deny me that! It's in the court order!" she shot back. I was going to go down the hill again, determined to prevent Betty from ruining our great time, but Betty was starting to walk towards me (maybe to grab my sled out of my hands) when Julie yelled at Betty, "Mom, just go home!" Betty stopped walking towards me, but she just stood there, less than ten feet from me. I thought if I called her out on why she was really there, she might leave. "You came up here under the auspices of just seeing the kids, but it really is just to ruin my time with them. Do you think I'm at all comfortable around you?" I said. "Why? Are you afraid of me?!" she said with a snicker. "Betty! Do you remember what happened just six weeks ago?!" I asked. "Yes, you beat me up! You saw it Julie, you saw him hit me!" I couldn't believe my ears; there were two things blatantly wrong with her statement: she attacked me, but clearly was not afraid of me. And, most importantly, the kids were too young to hear about that kind of violence, regardless of who attacked who. Still not leaving, I tried even more futile reasoning with her: "Betty. Just three days ago [at Noel's indoor soccer game] Christian told me you told him to ask me to buy him a slice of pizza, and then you yelled, 'What is he doing here?' at Christian when I said hi to him when I gave it to him! Then you yelled at me again in front of all of those other parents and kids when all I did was ask Stephen how his day at school was." Though she didn't "yell" at me, her voice was embarrassingly loud and angry. But, more importantly, I wanted her to see the contradiction and know that I'd graduated, with an "A" from Betty 101.

The next day after school, I got to discover, in embarrassing fashion, the first instance of the kids lying in an effort to keep Betty and I separated. When Betty came to the bus stop in front of my parents' and stood uncomfortably close to me, I called her out on an apparent contradiction. I asked her, "What are you doing here? Didn't you tell Stephen I was not to be at your stop last week?" She said, "No, I never said that!" I didn't believe her because she had previously implied I was not to be at her stop, saying "This isn't your bus stop!" and the myriad of lies over the last month prevented me from believing almost anything she said. "That's not what he told me this morning, and if I can't meet the kids at your bus stop after school — even when you won't — then I don't think you should be here either." She stepped even closer, pulled her phone out of her pocket and pointed at me and her phone and yelled, "You can't tell me where I can and can't be and if I can see the kids or not! That's why I'm divorcing you! You're always trying to control me and I won't be controlled by you any more! And if you don't let me see Stephen, I'm calling the cops!" I tried to appease her and let her know she could stay, but also convey that I wasn't going to be fooled either, when I said to her, "Well, be assured I am going to ask him as soon as I get a minute alone with him." She yelled, "Go ahead!" When Stephen and I got inside, I asked him if Betty really said I wasn't allowed at her bus stop (it's easily visible, only 700 feet up the street), he ducked his head and said, "She never said that." I asked him a rhetorical question, "Why did you do that?" He just said, "I don't know." I knew why — because he didn't want his mom and I around each other. I told him that it was okay, but it caused me a lot of embarrassment and it could have become very serious if his mom had called the police on me. I needed to squash any thoughts he had that fabricating things his mom said, or didn't say, was okay, as it would create even more confusion for me and hamper my effort to know when Betty was manipulating in the future. I gave him a hug and he offered a very sincere apology. He let go, but then hugged me again and held onto me for what I called a "Stephen hug," which is a tight, long, loving hug. Also characteristic to the best hugs I will ever know, he would bury the side of his head in my stomach when he started giving them years before, but by this time he was nearly at my shoulder — his hugs a bittersweet reminder of how fast he was growing up.

The worst display of bad behavior my parents and I had ever seen, up to this point anyway, and further insight into Betty and Pat's level of determination, was about to occur in the church where Christian attended preschool. It was his Christmas show and all of the kids would get dressed up and sing on the alter. In past years, I would take a couple of minutes to take pictures of our kids after the show, and I fully intended to do that with Christian this year too. The problem was, it was Betty's custody time and she had been making it very clear at Christian's hockey games, and especially at Noel's indoor soccer games, that I was not to interact with the kids in any way during her time. After the show, Betty and her family got Christian on the altar and took pictures with seemingly every combination of her family possible. My parents and I patiently waited for a full twenty minutes and thought their want for an inordinate number of pictures was just to annoy us. When Pat said, "Okay, Christian, we have to go," I said, "I'd like to get a few pictures of him with my parents." She rolled her eyes and said, "Make it very quick, I have to go to work!" I had Christian and my parents stand off to the side in front of the Christmas tree and, feeling the pressure, I quickly took a few pictures. When I checked the screen, I realized my shutter was too slow, so I said, "Hold on Christian, I need to get one more please." Pat said, "Christian, we have to leave!" My mom politely said, "It'll just take another minute," and Pat rolled her eyes again and repeated, "I have to go to work!" I quickly took another picture and Pat said, "We have to go NOW Christian!" I said, "No, he doesn't," trying to get her to realize the obvious, which was that she had only given us two minutes and I hadn't gotten a picture with Christian yet. As is typical when I stand up to Betty or Pat for what I want with the kids, they become enraged. Pat lunged towards my neck with her arms out and her hands cupped, exposing her fingernails. I instinctively stepped back as her two daughters-in-law, who were nearby and already afraid of a confrontation, immediately grabbed her as her fingers were just a few inches away from my neck. Kerry and Shari were restraining Pat as best as they could, but Pat was obsessed and crazed. She was out for blood — literally. I can still picture the three women, heaped together in one big mass that very loudly, and in fits and starts, slowly made their way to the door a hundred feet away. I was so stunned, that, aside from seeing Betty immediately put her phone to her ear and hearing her yell, "I'm calling my lawyer!" as I knelt down and hugged Christian (while telling him "It will be okay, I love you."), I have to reference my mom's notes for much of what happened inside the church afterwards, and here are those abridged notes:

"As Kerry and Shari dragged Pat out of the church, Pat was screaming 'Bernice, you are a liar' over and over. The two girls got Pat out of the door and poor Christian had to watch his grandma get dragged out of church (though Rob was trying to keep him from seeing it). Betty was already on the phone with her lawyer yelling, 'They won't turn Christian over to me!' Rob Sr. [my dad] went outside to see if they were taking Pat away in the car when she lunged at him with her fingernails too! She was screaming, 'You stole money! You're a piece of shit too! That's how you got all of your money, you stole it!' When we got home, there was already an email from Betty's lawyer about <u>our</u> bad behavior!"

Rewinding back to when I first went over and held Christian, I remember Betty finally hanging up the phone with her lawyer and coming over to me and forcefully grabbing Christian and pulling him away by his arm. One of the toughest and most resilient kids you'll ever see, he didn't appear upset, he just cooperated and walked alongside her with Betty's firm grip still on his forearm.

Perhaps the reason I don't remember much of those ten minutes, from when I picked up Christian to when I was making the first of two trips carrying camera equipment to my car, was because of the magnitude of what happened next. As I was crossing the road to go back into the church to get the last of my camera equipment, I looked up and saw Betty's van turning towards me from my right. I figured she was just going to park next to her sister, who was just off to my left and fastening her four-year-old girl in her car seat, before they went to lunch. I was looking at Peg as I crossed the road when I heard Betty's engine rev up. I looked to my right and I saw Betty's van coming right at me, only fifteen feet away now. Peg screamed, "Betty don't!" and I sprinted across the street and turned to see Betty's van stop a little past where I crossed the road. She glared at me through the passenger window, still leaning far forward and gripping the steering wheel tightly. As I looked at her, I wanted her to know that she hadn't gotten to me — literally and figuratively — so after the first second or two of surprise, I just smiled at her and walked back into the church. Before rounding up the last of my lenses, I stopped into the church office to ask if they had any security cameras in the parking lot, and, not at all surprising for a church, they didn't.

Unequivocal proof that Betty was Playing the Victim (long the original title of this book) came when Jack's daughter, who also worked at the base, told me that the clinic took up a collection for Betty and they bought the kids quite a few presents. I almost didn't believe it, at least until the kids came through the door that evening for my three-hour visit. The first thing they told my parents and I was all of the nice things the people at Mom's work got for them. It had to be around $600 worth of toys, based on what they said, but the bigger question was why did these people, most of whom I used to know, buy my kids presents in the first place? To this day, I don't know what pretenses the fundraiser was conducted under, but I have very strong suspicions that it was Betty playing the victim again. Who knows what she told them, but the fact that these people I'd used to know had bought my kids presents on Betty's behalf, when she was living expense-free thanks to me, was a slap in the face. It was disgusting to know that I was paying for everything Betty needed, including her credit cards (which I didn't have to pay), the mortgage, the kids' activities, the home equity loan, her utilities, and giving her support money on top of it, and yet she had the gall to probably tell someone at the base that she was broke and her out-of-work, alcoholic ex-husband wasn't paying for anything. What a shame for the generous people who contributed money they could have used on themselves or their own children. To top it off, Betty and her mom spent a few thousand dollars that Christmas trying to, in my opinion, buy the kids' love.

What wasn't known to me at the time was that Betty had plans to ask for two $10,000 advances from me and to keep our $12,500 tax return (so high because of the 401k withdrawals in lieu of disability payments) within the next ten weeks. Between these lump sums and the support payments, she would get more money in the first four months of 2014 than probably most of the people who contributed to the "Horrible Dad" fund made all year.

More proof that Betty was playing the victim would come just the next day. As I was in my usual spot in the dining room, journaling what had happened three days before at the show (and a recent comment from Noel, "Mom doesn't yell anymore"), I asked my mom to call Betty to see if she could work out times for the kids to visit Christmas Eve, Christmas, and New Years to prevent involving the expensive lawyers. Betty was far more cooperative with my mom than me, and that translated into a better chance of getting at least some time with them. My mom called Betty, but she quickly asked to speak to me. I told my mom, "No," but Betty asked twice more. I again said, "No, I don't want to talk to her." Betty then raised her voice and forcefully told my mom, "Bernice, this is between Rob and I, not you!" and I reluctantly agreed to talk to her after I heard Betty yell over the phone. I was asking for something I wanted badly, time with the kids, so I was careful to sound very nice. Cringing, I said, "Hi. May I please get the kids tomorrow for our family tradition of —" Betty then interrupted me, twice shouting, "Stop bullying me, I'm not going to be bullied by you anymore!" Stunned, I said, "What? I'm not bullying you," but I may as well have been talking to myself; nothing was going to stop her. She continued, "I've had enough of your abuse and I don't have to take it anymore!" I knew she couldn't have been alone, and powerless to stop her, I hung up the phone as quickly as I could after I realized what was happening. The next day, Christmas Eve, we did get the kids, after my lawyer got involved, and I asked Stephen and Julie if they heard their mom the previous morning. "We were all in Grammy's kitchen," Julie said. My mom and I explained to all four that I'd just kindly asked their mom about seeing them on Christmas Eve, but their mom had reacted by saying those things to get the kids to think that I was being mean to her. I'll never forget Stephen's and Julie's reaction to my explanation. Stephen just gave me a half-smile and quickly looked down — his non-verbal for he doesn't fully believe or agree. Julie stared at me, but with only one side of her mouth trying to form a smile, she was also telling me that she didn't fully believe my side of the story. And to say it again, I couldn't undo all of Betty's lies. If the kids split the difference every time they heard Betty or Pat say something, and believed half of what they said and half of what I said to refute the lies (if I even knew anything had been said), then how long until it added up to the kids not being comfortable around me? Till they were afraid of me? Till they despised me? In the case of my kids, and especially my daughters of nine and seven, the time it took for the three older kids to flip from running from Betty to me, to running from me to Betty, was less than a month.

Christmas Eve went well, besides Betty refusing to let our dog Charlie come, and I was to get the kids back the next evening at 6:30, so I felt good about our holiday so far. But when I woke up Christmas morning, I realized that the kids would normally be opening their presents now and it would be dark before I saw them again. And I hurt. This was the first time I questioned whether it was worth setting this whole thing — the divorce and her war to win the kids from me — off with the PFA. "If I had just gone and picked her up from jail, I would be with my kids right now and all of us would be opening our presents, laughing, giving hugs and kisses and having a wonderful Christmas," I repeatedly thought as I walked around our three grouped neighborhoods for most of the day.

When the kids got to my parents' that night, we had a great time as my parents and I asked what presents they had already gotten and we got to drop little hints at what we thought they had under our tree too. For four hours, we got to put the strife of a shattered family completely behind us and just have fun. It actually felt almost normal too, as when Betty and I were together, we spent a significant amount of our time (and all of Christmas evening and night) at my parents'. When it was time for the kids to go back to Betty, her youngest brother, Stevie, came to the door. He lived in Boston, and it was the first time I had seen him since before Betty and I had separated. I'd always encouraged him in his effort to get into singing and dancing, and in his latest endeavor, to become a model, I'd taken some professional pictures of him when were at the beach just five months prior. I wanted to show him I didn't harbor any hard feelings for him and excitedly greeted him and wished him a Merry Christmas as I invited him in. He was somewhat distant with me and he had some skeptical questions when I told him one of the things we did that year was each kid had to give up a little in what they got for presents so we could contribute to the Child Find of America charity, but he didn't seem to be hateful towards me. So when he asked several times to see the kids, I agreed to let that happen before he went back to for Boston just after the New Year.

We decided that after church on Sunday would work out best, and we met him at the Bob Evans in our community. It was packed with other families that had also just come from church and we were eventually seated right in the middle of the section. Everything was fine until we were halfway done with our food, when Stevie said, "You know I'm a really good swimmer, that's why all of you are good swimmers." I'm a lousy swimmer, so I laughed and said, "Yeah, you don't get any of that from me!" Then Stevie said, "Your Uncle Robby was very strong, and you'll be strong too because everyone in my family is strong." I looked at him a bit taken aback, and said, "Well, I have to say that my family can hold their own and I'm quite strong for forty-four years old." Stevie said, "Oh! Do the kids know you used your strength to beat up their mom?! Do you tell your kids you've been to three rehabs and you don't have a job anymore?! Do they know you're an alcoholic?!" I tried to stop him in his first round, but he kept going over and over like a broken record. He became louder and louder, determined to pound what a horrible person their father was right into their heads. He also pounded it into the dozen other families sitting near us as I saw everyone staring at us aghast. Were they aghast at me or him? Who knows, but it was humiliating and I politely asked him to leave. "No! This is a public place and I don't have to!" he said, with his arms folded, showing me his resolve. When I realized that I couldn't make him leave and the workers, either not caring or pretending not to hear us, weren't going to get a manager, I said, "Okay kids, we're going to go home now. If you're still hungry, Grammy can make us waffles." I stood up and waited for my visibly shaken kids to realize our breakfast was over and I noticed many of the people were still staring at us. Some of them looked at me sympathetically while the rest looked at Stevie in complete disgust.

As we walked to my car, I told the kids, "One, that is not any way for an adult to act. And two, I don't want you believing anything Stevie said. I didn't beat up your mom and I still have a job; I'm just on medical leave right now. In fact, I should be going back to work very soon!" I tried to sound excited about the prospect of going back to work to bring their spirits back up, but my return to flying was still a big, black cloud in the form of a question mark over my head. It didn't matter, as they seemed a bit less down when they started to talk about all of the reasons they didn't like Uncle Stevie, some of which I didn't even know about. I had to be careful that I didn't let them just bash him; I'm doing my best to raise them not to be "haters," but they were disclosing some things that piqued my interest. They talked about not wanting to go to his upcoming wedding. "But he's marrying a guy! That's soooo weird!" Noel said. With that, I knew I had to put an end to it and I said, "Alright, let's not talk about it any more, okay?" Noel had to say one more thing though, "I don't think us little kids should have to hear these bad things that Uncle Stevie was saying." We were halfway home when we passed Betty going in the opposite direction. She had her phone up to her ear and she was laughing. I could only guess that she was talking to Stevie on her way to pick him up and that she must have been very happy to hear of the successful mission he'd carried out for her.

When we got home, the kids were still upset and told my mom what had happened. Stephen said, "Grammy, Uncle Stevie said very bad things about Dad, and he said them to US!" As she looked at all of the kids, my mom asked, "Who is the only one who can judge us?" Stephen said, "God and Jesus!" "That's right," my mom said. Stephen went on, "Grammy wants us to hate Dad and you and Pap Pap, but we know better!" Julie looked at me and said, "I didn't want to see Uncle Stevie, but

I was afraid to tell you." I said, "Well, I think we've all learned our lesson with Uncle Stevie, so you don't have to worry about that in the future." My mom wanted to drive home the point that the kids could trust my family when she said, "What if Aunt Sandi said bad things about your mom to you?" Stephen and Julie answered at the same time, "Aunt Sandi would never do that!" "Why?" my mom asked. "Because she loves us and wouldn't want to make us feel bad!" Stephen said.

Take Everything, Pay for Nothing

From here on, Betty would continue to create a significant distance between our kids and I by putting wedges into our relationship whenever possible. Whether it was Pat saying extremely derogatory things about me to them, likely on Betty's behalf, or Betty's vehement efforts to discourage me to be around or even talk to the kids, their concerted efforts had the results they had intended.

We ended 2013 and started the New Year in style; Betty called the police on me twice in two days, which made a total of three times over the last two weeks. On New Year's Eve, it was because I didn't know Christian left his five-dollar hockey pads in his hockey bag that was in my parents' garage. I tried to explain that the pads were in Christian's hockey bag (that was intentionally left with me), but she didn't want me to have them because she, "Bought them with my own money!" I tried to say Christian wanted to play with them, but she spoke over me, saying, "If you don't give them back right now, I'm calling the police!" I gave her the pads, but when she got them from me, she said, "You should expect a call from the police!" despite my compliance. The call to the police on New Year's Day was because Charlie ran into my parents' house. Charlie got out of Betty's van when the kids opened the door and he ran straight into my parents' house, as I had the door open to greet the kids for our traditional dinner. Charlie is the kids' dog because they bought him with their money — an idea Betty and I had when we started looking for a dog in the spring of 2012. I thought that may make them more responsible for him (it did a little, though I was glad to be the one who cleaned up after him and walk him). Betty got out of the van and ran up to me and yelled for me to give Charlie back to her. I said, "He is the kids' dog and he is staying here." I then shut the door to keep her from coming in. I watched Betty get back into her van and backup and block the driveway. Her oldest brother, Daniel, got out and started walking up to the house. He repeated Betty's stance that they were to get Charlie, or "we will call the police." And I repeated my stance. I watched Betty and Daniel sit in front of my parents' house and make calls for an hour. I took a picture with an SLR every fifteen minutes with my phone off to the corner of the frame to show the time in case the police did show up. Our police department's policy is they do not get involved in custody exchanges or for pets unless there's an unsafe situation, and they didn't get involved here despite Betty and Daniel's assertions that they would.

As I journaled Betty's last two calls to call the police, it occurred to me that she wanted me to go to jail just as she had. What better revenge than seeing my mugshot on a police report, like the one of her? Calling the police so easily also had the benefit of intimidating and discouraging me from walking up and talking to the kids if I had a chance to see them at one of their activities if she was anywhere near — and she always ensured she was. Now knowing the reason for her penchant to call the police, I realized they would be called so frequently that they needed a special key in my journal — bold, and all capitals, purple text.

Another issue that was becoming common enough that I had to create its own key in the journal was Betty's continued refusal to give us things the kids needed. As my mom was the one who negotiated with Betty the most on this issue, I defer to her notes. "Despite repeated requests, Betty refused to give us the kids snow clothes (they only came with t-shirts). No coats, boots, hats or gloves. It has been in the 20's all week, it's all about spiting Rob. Julie called and asked her mom for the clothes, but Betty only said if it snowed tomorrow, would she bring them up. The next day, Julie tried to call Betty from my phone, but it was blocked. Rob and Sophia tried calling Betty from Rob's phone, but they got the blocked call message too. Julie called Betty's house from our house phone, and she got through and told Julie to come down to get the clothes. Julie decided to stay with Sophia, who was home from college and so I went down alone. Betty at first wouldn't answer the door, but did when I rang the doorbell a third time. Betty asked, 'Where are the kids?' and I told her they were at my house. Betty said, 'Well, either the kids come here or you can go and buy them new clothes' and she slammed the door."

I knew I was going to eventually buy the kids new clothes, but if I did so now, it would convey to Betty that I was okay with the fact that she'd broken the court-ordered mandate that, due to my sudden move out, she had to share the kids' clothes. A somewhat concerning precedent when there were so many other rules she could break — and would.

Betty was determined to show the kids that she was the only caretaker, and she went as far as trying to cancel or reschedule the kids' doctor's appointments I had made and rescheduling them for her time in the following days or week. The first time I encountered this, I didn't know that Stephen's allergy appointment had been changed and we went on the original day. When we got there, the receptionist told me he wasn't supposed to be seen until the following week. Sure that I had the right day and time, I asked her if the appointment had been changed. She looked at the notes and said, "His mom changed it." Dr. Orsini and his staff were happy to see Stephen anyway, but I became a bit more distrusting. Just a few days later, Betty called me when she got the confirmation notice from the kids' pediatrician for their yearly physical. She was furious, screaming, "The kids don't need to see the doctor! You're just trying to look like you care now when really you have never cared for them!" I tried to explain that it had been nearly two years since they had an annual checkup, but she just continued her tirade and I eventually hung up. When we got to the pediatrician appointment, the lady behind the counter confirmed that Betty had tried to cancel all four kids' annual appointments, but she didn't cancel them because I had warned her two days before that Betty was likely to call.

It became clearer that Betty didn't want me around the kids and she would do anything to enforce it. One night after Betty picked up a few of the kids' things at my parents', I asked if I could go out to her van and say goodnight to Christian. She didn't say anything, but she hadn't said no, so I went out behind her, being careful to keep a safe distance between us. She got in and I opened the sliding door behind her to see Christian. It was cold, so the van had been running, and no sooner did I say "Hi" than she put the van in reverse and turned the steering wheel so that the front wheel arced out towards me and almost ran over my foot as I jumped back. "What in the hell are you doing?" I asked, but she kept backing up and left with the sliding door still open. She pulled into Paige's driveway next door, got out and stuck up her middle finger.

If she was trying to tell me that I wasn't welcome around our kids when they were with her, I was starting to catch on.

A clearer view into Betty's vision of my role as the father came at the mediation hearing we had in the third week of January. It was with Rob Wilson, the distinguished looking gent who ran the class the kids and I had just attended for families of divorcing parents just ten days before. Betty and I sat down with Mr. Wilson and he went over the format for the mediation and told us that one of us would be alone with him for five minutes to say what they wanted and what they would settle on while the other one sat in the waiting room. After we switched, he would try to get us to bridge the differences, if there were any. During my session alone with him, I quickly admitted to having a prior alcohol problem, as I knew Betty was going to cite that as a primary reason why I shouldn't have the kids as much as her. Mr. Wilson said his previous job had been helping flight crew with substance abuse problems at a different airline and reassured me that this fact wasn't going to be an issue at all. After Betty and I had our time alone with him, we reconvened at the small, round table. Mr. Wilson looked at his notes with a tight-lipped smirk and tilted his head, as if he didn't know how he was going to say what had to be said. "Ms. Black, Mr. Black would like the kids eighteen to twenty days a month, depending on his work schedule, and Mr. Black, Ms. Black would like the kids every day of the month and would allow you to see the kids for a total of three hours twice a month, but no overnight stays." I couldn't believe my ears and I wondered if it was three or six hours total — both being off-the-charts ridiculous. As it sank in, I mindlessly blurted, "What?" Mr. Wilson repeated only Betty's side, and I sat back and said, "Well, I am certainly not going to be with the kids any less than half of the month." Mr. Wilson put his pen down, folded his arms, and with a big fake smile said, "Well folks! This is, what we call in this business, an impasse! Have a nice day." And it was over as fast as it started. As we stood up, I so desperately wanted to discuss a comment he'd made at the class ten days before, but Betty was slow to leave and the opportunity was lost. The comment (only to the adults) was, "One of the reasons a parent is awarded primary, or even sole custody of their children is if the court feels the other parent has an undiagnosed mental illness." His words, his stance, his facial expression, and even how he held his hands when he said it will stay ingrained in my memory forever. I wasn't paying much attention to the three-hour class before that, and I certainly didn't pay attention after; I had heard everything I needed to hear all in one sentence.

Later that same day, after Noel's indoor soccer game, I was walking out of the arena with Betty uncomfortably close behind me. It's a narrow corridor to get in and out, and there were quite a few people as one game had just ended and another was about to start. I picked up Christian as he was getting bumped a lot and I heard Betty yell, "Excuse me, that man is taking my kid!" I looked around and people were looking skeptically at both Betty and me, but they must not have taken her seriously as she was just shuffling along with the mass and wasn't exerting the appropriate amount of effort if someone really had been trying to abduct Christian. I thought back to Disney World, where she had called the police reporting Stephen missing when she knew I had him, and I immediately put Christian down when we got to the door just ten feet in front of us. Her plan was working, because despite the vow I'd made to myself that I would not let her intimidation (or my embarrassment) cause me to do anything different, I just gave Christian a quick hug and said bye. I was so uncomfortable that I left without saying bye to the other kids, who were standing beside or just behind Betty.

Another prime example that Betty wasn't afraid of me (and, in my opinion, invalidating her assertion that I was an abusive husband) came when I had Julie and Christian stay home from school at the end of January. Betty called and questioned me in an angry, condescending voice after getting the notification from their school, saying, "All of the kids get sick when they're at your parents' house!" I said only Julie and Christian were sick and Betty started yelling, "I need to come up there and look around your parents' house and check on the kids NOW!" I wasn't comfortable with her coming over and I started to say, "My parents aren't here, just me and —" and before I could finish, she screamed, "I don't care if you're parents are at their f---ing house or not! What does that have to do with the fact their house isn't clean!" I just hung up the phone, but her texts saying she was going to come up kept going. I almost texted her to make her aware of her absurd contradiction — that she claimed I abused her, and yet she wanted to come in and inspect a house in which I was the only adult. I had it all lined up, planning to say, "If I really beat you up, you would be afraid of me! You don't see battered women taunting the men that abused them because THEY ARE AFRAID OF THEM!" But I realized Betty was so blinded by her hate that she couldn't see the forest through the trees. I knew if I didn't bring the illogical discrepancy to her attention, she would do it again and again, hopefully in front of one of the growing number of acquaintances and parents who initially believed her claims of my abuse and they too would finally see the contradiction I had been forced to tolerate for months.

A few days later, in another brazen display, Betty came up to my mom's front door one night after Christian's hockey game to get a Lego toy he left there. She knew my parents were in Florida and that I was there alone, yet she knocked on the door, only as a formality, as she opened it and stepped in. "I need Christian's Lego car," she said impatiently. I was extremely uncomfortable with her there; what was to stop her from running out of the house and yelling that I tried to attack her again? Absolutely nothing and it fit her front as the victim like a glove. I ran upstairs to look in the boys' room and I also put my phone in the hall with its video camera on to capture any audio that could support me if she did make any wild claims. I stood at the top of the steps and said, "I'll bring it to Christian and say goodnight to all of the kids so I don't have to call later." She snorted, but turned around and walked out. The memory of her trying to run my foot over was still vivid of course, but that time she'd only had five-year-old Christian in the car, and this time she had all four kids, so I assumed she wouldn't try that again with the older ones being able to remember it if she did. In a repeat of just two weeks before, as I opened the sliding door behind her, she put the running van in reverse and stabbed the gas pedal as she turned the steering wheel towards me. I yelled, "Betty!" and she stopped the van as I jumped back. I looked at her as she turned around to look at me with a scowl on her face. Determined to show her that she couldn't keep me from the kids (while being very aware of how close I stood and how far the van's wheels could arc out), and to show the kids that I wasn't afraid (and hoping they wouldn't be afraid either), I went on almost as if nothing happened. I said, "Alright! Goodnight kids, I love you so—" and the Betty jabbed the gas again and turned the steering wheel. I stepped back again, and, as she backed up into the street, I tried to finish as she sped away, "It was great seeing you, I love you and I'll talk to you tomorrow. Good night!" By the end I was probably just talking to myself, the van's revving engine drowning out any chance of them hearing me as they sped away.

Lisa, a very good friend of mine from high school, was also going through some of the same types of lies and manipulations with her soon to be ex-husband. Our dads worked with each other at the same airline and Lisa and I drove to college together for a few semesters, so we knew, trusted, and had a mutual respect for each other. Though we lived 500 miles apart now, we leaned on each other in those incredibly turbulent times by talking on the phone several times a week. On a long drive after one of Julie's gym meets (Julie went back to my parents' in a friend's car), I called Lisa to tell her the latest instance where Betty had contradicted her stance that I physically abused her. Lisa has an education in psychology, and she often has a perspective that helps me cope with the immense stress of Betty's unrelenting "distortion campaigns." During this particular talk, Lisa said, "I've been meaning to ask you, because she has a lot of the behaviors, do you think she's ever been sexually molested?" I said, "I'm not sure; she said something to me when we first started dating in 1998 that could go either way." "What was it?" she asked. "She said, 'I'm not really comfortable around my dad. When I was young, he used to wait for me to come out of the shower and he would do things,' and she started to get teary eyed and she just looked at me and I just looked at her, waiting for her to finish. I didn't know what to say, and I thought it was best to let her do the talking. We had only been dating a month and I just thought she would tell me more when she was ready, but I never heard another word about it." "Rob! That right there tells you she had so much more to tell you. You honestly haven't thought of that until now?" One of the biggest chills I have ever had spread throughout me. "Well, I've thought of it from time-to-time, but I guess I didn't want to believe it. I thought if he really did that, Betty wouldn't want anything to do with him, but she never acted like it happened from what I saw of their relationship, so I chose to believe he never actually touched Betty." Lisa said, "She exhibits all the signs of abuse, and the type of abuse that goes on for a long time." "What do you mean?" I asked. "Well, it's one thing to be violated by someone once or twice, but she acts like someone who had what should be the deepest of trust broken over a prolonged amount of time. This wasn't once or twice. When someone is violated in this way, and it goes on for a long time, the victim usually stops maturing at that age." "Jesus, I used to tell her I felt like I was married to an angry eight-year-old. Now it makes perfect sense." Lisa continued, "Young victims of sexual molestation become children trapped in an adult's body who plays the victim at every chance they get when they get older. This is written about a lot in a book I have. I've thought for a while now she was a Borderline; have you heard of the book *Walking on Eggshells*?" "I'm not sure, maybe. What's a Borderline?" I asked. "Borderline Personality Disorder is a name for people who are not mentally stable as it applies to relationships. I'll send the book to you, I think you could use it to understand why she does the things she does. It has an entire chapter on distortion campaigns, which Borderlines are extremely good at, especially petite, attractive women," she said laughing at the end. "What is a distortion campaign?" I asked. "That's when someone will relentlessly say anything to anyone to try and ruin your reputation. Here's the first definition on a Google search: 'The intent is to destroy the target's reputation and thereby destroy the target's relationships with family and friends, employers, co-workers, doctors, teachers, therapists, and others. The intent may even be to force the target to leave the community, put the target in prison, or even kill the target. As with so many things involving Borderlines and their typical inability to understand or respect boundaries, there really are no limits. They will use basically any means available to them to cause damage to their target, including denigration, endless disparaging remarks, fabrication, false accusations, and even teaching others (including their children!) to lie on their behalf as part of their vilification campaign.' Last thing, because it's not really explained in great detail in the book, have you ever heard of 'psychological projection?'" "No, what does that mean?" I asked. "In essence, it's when someone does something and then accuses you of doing it." "Jesus! That is exactly what I've been calling 'Betty 101!' There's a clinical term for it? Good, that means she can't be the only one crazy enough to try it and therefore I can read about it."

It took sixteen years and the talk with Lisa to admit to myself what I knew in the back of my mind had happened to Betty years ago and what caused her overflowing anger now. That is an immense amount of anger, and it has to come out. Because of the dynamic her family lives under, she isn't free to blame her dad and she found the perfect scapegoat in me and our fight that fateful night. I used to wonder how such an incredibly beautiful young woman could be the way she was, but this was the smoking gun — the telltale smoke long gone after twenty-five years.

When I got the book *Stop Walking on Eggshells* in the mail, I sat down in my parents' dining room and flipped it open to what I thought was a random page. Maybe Lisa had creased the book in a couple of places, but regardless, the first page I looked at was the "Characteristics of higher-functioning, invisible borderlines." As I read through the first two of five criteria, I hadn't even finished the second one when I realized what I was reading was so applicable to Betty that I very briefly wondered if it had been written with her in mind. The book fell out of my hands, onto the table, and I put my face in my hands and started crying.

So many thoughts raced through my head, so fast I am left to guess as to what most of them were. First and foremost, if I had known about this book years ago, perhaps I could have used it to find a way to get Betty some help. Maybe she could have read it and partially helped herself with a little bit of knowledge. Providing some comfort, I also realized I wasn't all alone; there are clearly other victims of the relentless barrage of lies, rages, and distorted truths borderlines are so good at spinning and hiding.

I gathered my composure enough to pick the book back up and finish reading the five criteria, and they were as spot-on as the first two. I got up and took a walk around the block, trying to process the flood of emotions that took me by complete surprise. I tried to prepare myself to open the book again, and I went back and picked another random spot, more towards the end. In a notable coincidence, I saw the title at the top of the page that said, "Male Victims." Below, it describes a "large man, whose wife could knock the wind out of him. 'I was taught not to hit a woman, so what was I supposed to do?'" he says. This was the near perfect description of our physical confrontations, as for four months I had been trying to explain to a few people that no matter how big, strong, or martial-art-trained someone was, they would eventually lose a fight if all they did was defend themselves. Think about it, how do you win a fight, or get the angry aggressor to stop, if all you do is block their slaps, punches, and kicks? What motivates people to stop their attack? It's not grabbing their arms and yelling at them to stop, at least not with Betty — that only incited her more. The next paragraph describes my last few years with Betty to a T. "Many men also believe they should suffer in silence to protect the abuser or avoid being embarrassed." It was this protection I'd provided that Betty turned on me, saying she was the one that had been abused for so long. After all, if I had been abused, wouldn't I have said something to someone along the way? No. I was too embarrassed at my choice for a wife, too embarrassed for my parents, too embarrassed for my children, and especially too embarrassed for myself.

Still just in my first few minutes of reading, other notable lines gripped me. "The Borderline projects that you are such a terrible parent that you shouldn't even be allowed around the kids." "Why do borderlines play the role of the victim? Because it draws sympathetic attention and supplies them an identity or it gives them the illusion that they are not responsible for their own actions." And, "Spouses tolerated regular physical abuse and allowed Borderlines to be abusive to their children." As I continued to read the book, I applied my long-held belief from my studies at work that a highlighter should only be used when the text is profound and jumping out at me, but even by that standard, by the end of the book I had tabs and highlights throughout much of the text. As I read, it was hard not to think of the impossibility that the two authors personally knew Betty and wrote many parts of the book about her. Even if I see the cover now, I get an odd, uneasy feeling, like it is Pandora's Box.

I had a counseling session with Francine a week after getting the book from Lisa, and I was armed with a bit of dangerous knowledge from my readings. Francine had seemed to be a bit distant with me over the last two sessions, both of which occurred after Betty and I had separated, and I had the *Stop Walking on Eggshells* book tabbed to the page that talks about counselors' propensity to be fooled by Borderlines. To paraphrase: *Counselors instead take everything at face value and reinforce the Borderline's feelings of victimhood. This is not uncommon and the therapist may reinforce the Borderline's twisted thinking, making things worse.* I knew Francine was seeing Betty regularly and it didn't take a rocket scientist to deduce that Betty had also been twisting the truth about our relationship to Francine. I was especially frustrated with Francine's chilled demeanor towards me, because twice in the last seven months she had emphatically told me that Betty needed to be detained in a psych ward and be forced to take an evaluation before she should be released. This session with Francine wore on much the same as the last two had as I talked about the stress of Betty's unrelenting manipulations. The more I tried to convey to Francine that, "Betty isn't who you think she is," the more Francine dug in and defended her. I opened the *Walking on Eggshells* book and showed her the page that listed the five characteristics of someone who has Borderline Personality Disorder and keyed in on number five. "Look Francine, it says right here, they use counseling to try to prove they're right and the other person is wrong — to get you on their side to make it two-on-one. That's what she is doing with you, turning you against me!" Francine, possibly feeling threatened by the book, wouldn't look at it and insisted we "move along," which I did. I started to talk about my sobriety and recovery and whatever else I was supposed to be talking about when I met with Francine, before she was turned into a family counselor (she's an addiction counselor), but with my recovery from alcoholism now firmly in my control, my discussions invariably went back to Betty and how she was alienating the kids from me. When I brought it up again, Francine kept interrupting me, defending Betty, and I grew weary of it. I looked at Francine, and, as respectfully and yet as seriously as I could, said, "Please stop interrupting me, I can't finish a—" Francine immediately leaned towards me, sitting as far forward in her chair as possible, interrupted me mid-sentence and yelled, "This is my f---ing office, and I can interrupt you whenever I f---ing want, and if you don't like it, you can f---ing leave!" It was a surreal moment as I sat there motionless and speechless with Francine glaring at me for the better part of ten seconds. I didn't know which way to go with it, my options being to tell her she had to be the worst counselor on the face of the Earth and she was an utter disgrace to the profession, or to demand an apology and move on with the session. "She's an addiction counselor, not a family counselor, and just like the *Eggshells* book says, she is being used," went through my mind and I watched Francine sit back in her chair and look at her notepad like nothing had happened. I then acted like nothing had happened either, finishing our time by talking about my inevitable return to work and how I would cope with the loneliness of the many nights in hotels that used to facilitate my drinking — I didn't dare talk about Betty. Needless to say, that was my last session with her as I would confide in Dr. Lambeau that it had fallen apart with Francine. Trying to be funny and convey the seriousness of the fallout, I told Dr. Lambeau, "Every time I see her now, I feel I need to drink!" to which he pointed his finger at me and said, "Don't you f---ing dare now!"

At the start of my custody week, there were three big issues I needed to talk to Betty about and I apprehensively asked to talk to her after the kids said goodnight to her on the phone. The first was that Stephen's attention deficit disorder had become markedly worse since Christmas, when Betty had bought the boys a TV and a video game console for their bedroom. I said, "Betty, can you please make sure Stephen isn't playing video games too much?" She yelled, "Don't tell me how to parent, that's why I'm divorcing you!" Trying to keep her calm enough to talk about the other two issues, I said, "Okay, but please; you know my concerns with that. Also, all of the kids want Charlie and they've been asking me and you [via text] all night for him, when can I—" She interrupted me by yelling, "I don't have to tell you!" and she hung up the phone. Charlie, the kid's Yorkie, is very comforting to all of the kids, especially Noel. Julie really wanted Charlie to be with us and she had been standing near me to see if I could wrangle him from her mom over the phone. When she heard her mom's yelling, she asked, "Why does Mom always talk to you like that?" I said, "I don't know, but I don't think we're getting Charlie for a few days." The third issue that I'd wanted to address with Betty, that I didn't get a chance to, was that Noel had said at dinner, "Mom said she doesn't have any money." When she said it, I asked, "Noel, why would you say that? I make sure your mom has plenty of money." She said, as she started crying, "Mom said you have all of the money!" I took great exception to that because I knew it wasn't true. I was paying Betty $3,200 per month and I had also been ordered to give her a $10,000 advance the week before. My monthly payments to her were set to go up another $1,400 very soon too. With the money she and her dad were probably getting from her Grandma's recent passing, I knew she probably had far more money than I did, seeing as how I wasn't even working and it was the off-season for the camera business. But it didn't matter if I had millions and Betty didn't have two pennies to rub together or vice-versa, a seven-year-old shouldn't know the first thing of a parent's financial difficulties.

That same day, I was missing $820 in cash off of my dresser, money from selling a camera lens. Knowing the kids were sympathetic to Betty's claimed shortage of money, I became suspicious that one of the kids had taken it. When I told my mom about the missing money, she said, "I wonder if Stephen took it. Paige told me Stephen went over there

Saturday morning and Betty came over right after him when Stephen called her from their phone saying he had a problem with his iPod and he needed Betty to look at it. And Betty came up right away. They were whispering in her entrance and Paige said to me she wasn't comfortable with Betty being there and whispering, so Paige said to Betty it wasn't a good idea for her to be there and Betty left." I said, "Well, that would be logical seeing as how the kids think Betty can't even afford to eat." (She made a comment to the kids that escaped my journal around this time that she couldn't afford food or clothes for herself.) Now ten days later, I told Paige I was missing "a little bit" of money and I asked her if she thought there was any chance Stephen could have given it to Betty Saturday morning. Paige said, "They had an usual meeting in my entrance. They were whispering and I just thought it was weird, so I just told Betty it wasn't a good idea for her to be here on your time. I know you wouldn't care, but I didn't know what else to say." I thanked her and set my thoughts on how to approach Stephen, who surely thought that he was Robin Hood for the day and was only acting out of compassion. I didn't want to squash one of his best qualities, so it would be a very fine line I would have to walk to convey that helping someone could also hurt someone else.

Betty and I would have our first co-parenting counseling session the next morning, and because I wanted to confront her about the stolen money so Heidi would know the level of deceit she (and I) was up against, I decided to meet Stephen at the bus stop and confirm that he had taken the money and given it to his mom. He hung his head low when I asked him on the walk down the street and he remorsefully said, "I did." I said, "Stephen, it's okay buddy! I don't fault you at all, and in an odd way, I'm proud of you! But there's a lot you don't know. Just know

I take care of your mom by giving her a lot of money. And don't worry about taking the money off my dresser, it'll be our little secret, okay?" He looked sad and worried but I gave him a big long hug to remind him that I wasn't disappointed in him and told him, as I grabbed his face, "Stephen! You're the greatest kid in the world and don't you forget it!" He then gave me a big smile and I was free to address the root of the problem.

Knowing that Betty was going to deny the whole thing, the only way I could think of to convey to her that I would not stand for her putting the kids up to stealing from me was to get her to incriminate herself. When I called to talk to the other kids the night I'd met Stephen at the bus stop, I asked Betty, "Did any of the kids give you any significant amounts of money in the last couple of weeks?" She said "No!" as if I was crazy for even asking and I just said "Okay," saving what Stephen had told me for our counseling session the next day. When we started the co-parenting session, I waited for a good segue. When the topic became "working together," I said that I would have difficulty co-parenting with anyone who encouraged their kids to steal. Betty snapped that she'd told me the night before that she didn't have any stolen money and I confronted her about what Stephen had said. Feeling cornered, she shot back, "Well, my lawyer told me to keep the money!" I said, "Your lawyer told you to keep stolen money?!" Betty said, "Paige told me to keep it too, and she's a lawyer too!" I repeated my stance, "I don't think two lawyers are going to tell you to keep stolen money." I knew for a fact that Paige hadn't told Betty that, and she insisted that Paige did, highlighting Betty's trait of lying no matter how obvious it is that she is doing so. "Always leave them with a little bit of doubt," as the saying goes. In the end, she was forced to return the money to me, but she said only $320 was given to her by Stephen, which is extremely hard to believe because, despite the theft, he is 100% honest when confronted and he insisted he didn't keep any of the now missing $500.

Certainly one of the bigger wedges Betty was using create a distance between the kids and I was the fact that she was living in our house and I was living in my parents'. Case in point, Betty had just said to me, in front of all four kids, "Noel only has one house, and it's mine!" when I had taken Noel's dance costumes that I'd paid for two weeks before to "my house." There were seemingly a myriad of other instances that Betty conveyed to the kids they had only one home and they were just visiting me at my parents' house — all to make me feel, as a parent, as temporary and uncertain as my living situation felt.

Betty must have thought that if she could get the kids to steal money, she could get them to steal other things too. As I cleaned the girls' room just a week later, I saw that Julie's medals from a gym meet founded by my aunt were missing. When Julie came home from school, I asked her where they were. Fidgety, she said, "I don't know... well, they're at Mom's house." "Why are they there?" I asked. She said, "I didn't take them, Stephen did!" "Why did he take them?" "'Mom told me to get them out of your house, but I said, 'No' and she said, 'Just get them NOW!' But I said 'No' again. Then mom told Stephen to go in and get them and he said 'No' too! But she yelled at him too and he was scared, so he went in and got them!" she said. "When did this happen?" I asked. "When we got home from Grammy's after church." "Last Sunday?" I asked. "Yes!" Julie said. I got Stephen and when I asked him to tell me about the medals, he must have known Julie had told me because he looked at her and hung his head as low as it could go. I put my hands on top of his shoulders and said, "It's okay Stephen, I just want to hear your side of the story." His head was still down and he stayed silent, so I started him off with a question, "Do you think that was wrong or right?" He looked up at me and snapped, "I was afraid and didn't want to do it, but Mom got reeeaaaaly mad!" I said, "Stephen, stealing is against one of the Ten Commandments." He looked dejected and sad, so I asked him and Julie for a hug and told them I wasn't mad at them, but disappointed in their mom for asking them to steal. I still felt bad for him; what a terrible spot to be put in. But I also had one unanswered question: my mom and I knew we hadn't seen the kids that day and my mom also said she knew she'd locked the door because no one would be home for a while. So knowing he wasn't tall enough to reach the key I kept on top of the porch light, because it is at the very end of even my reach, I grinned with curiosity and asked him, "How did you get in Stephen?!" He smiled and said, with overflowing pride, "I climbed up the wall!" My parents' entrance has a dentil pattern in the brick and he must have used it to climb up to get the key — what a funny sight that must have been!

When Betty brought the medals (and two nice vases of my mom's that Betty had refused to return) back to my parents', I was running errands, but my mom was home. As Betty walked up the sidewalk, my mom said, "Oh my God!" Betty turned around and both of them saw the van coasting down the driveway. The van ran up the hill on the opposite side of the road and started back down. My mom saw Noel jump from the back seat up to the driver's seat as Betty started running towards the van. Noel steered it, whether intentionally or unintentionally, we'll likely never know, into my parents' mailbox. As it came to a stop Betty yelled at Noel, "Why were you trying to drive the van?!" My mom ran over and asked, "Are the kids okay?" Betty turned her anger on my mom and yelled, "The kids are just fine!" My mom, uncharacteristically annoyed, said, "Don't yell at me, I was just coming to make sure you and the kids are okay, and this is the thanks I get." Betty said, "I don't have time for this! I had to go back down to my house to get your medals and vases!" "Well you shouldn't tell your kids to steal from my house!" my mom said. Likely feeling outwitted, Betty, as is very characteristic of her, resorted to intimidation, "Your son is going to be arrested! I'm tired of being bullied!" My mom said, "No Betty, you are the bully." Betty, shot back, "Me?!" "Yes, you are a bully," my mom said. Betty then pointed to Paige's son, Adam, and said "Go get your mother!" When Paige came out, Betty said, "You deal with these people, I can't deal with them!" To add to the confusion, Charlie got out of the van and was now running around the two yards. My mom and Betty came upon him at the same time and Betty picked him up. Betty glared at my mom and yelled, "I'm getting a restraining order on you; I'm going to the police station right now!" Then my mom heard Julie crying very hard, wailing almost, and my mom asked her, "Julie, what's wrong?" Julie said, "You hit Mom!" "Julie! I did not hit her, we were just trying to get Charlie!" my mom said. Betty then got in her van and quickly backed up at an angle that was clearly aimed at hitting my dad, who was standing in the grass by the fallen mailbox. He jumped back and yelled, "Don't hit me, Betty!"

Amongst the funnier texts and calls I've ever had, a long-time client of mine had pulled up as it was unfolding and texted me, "Dude! You'd better get home ASAP!!!" When I called him afterwards to tell him my dad had already been texting me what was happening and to thank him, he said, "'Your ex was very aggressive. You know, your mom is so incredibly nice — she just stood there most of the time while Betty was stomping around and making a huge scene! And I was like whoa! You know, Betty was definitely the aggressor, your mom was just trying to make sure everyone was okay. I never expected to see that side of her, you know? I've known her for what, three years? And she's been so nice all the time, but that was just crazy! I don't know how you were married to that for so long!"

After my parents assessed the mailbox and discussed what had happened, they called the Mercury Township police and got, not coincidentally, Ray. It wasn't a coincidence because Betty had already talked to him about the issue. I was home now, and journaling the incident, when I heard my dad's frustration that he couldn't get the police to come out and document the incident as he talked to an officer over the phone. At first, I didn't know which officer my dad was talking to. My dad eventually handed me the phone and said, "Here, maybe you can get them to come out." When I heard, "This is Officer Rose," I said, "Ray this is Rob." After he told me he wasn't coming out to see the mailbox, I then felt he was protecting Betty too much and it was time to motivate him a little. I told him I had Betty's cell phone bill from November and all of the texts and long, late-night phone calls meant he had a conflict of interest in this matter, and in his marriage, and he should assign it to a different officer — he quickly agreed.

When I read the police report a couple of days later, I couldn't help but laugh at some of things Betty said in the report. That she was "upset" that she had to return the "trivial things" to my parents. She "screamed" at my mom. And Betty, "doesn't want us to interfere with her time by approaching the kids" at Julie's gym meets. My favorite, "She [Betty] stated that she would like to figure out what would make these exchanges less stressful," highlighted her propensity for "psychological projection" — again, the term that describes how someone denies what they did and attributes the blame to someone else. ("Blame shifting" is another term to describe the same thing.) Also in the police report, Betty is advised to stay off of my parents' property and my parents and I are advised, at Betty's request, to only speak to the kids if they come to us — we are not to go up to the kids on Betty's time. And Betty would ensure, through video games and fear, that they would not seek out my parents or me.

An interesting conclusion to this came about the next time I had the kids. Stephen tried to take the blame for the van not being in park when he said he'd bumped the gearshift lever when he went to change the radio station. I said, "Stephen, you can't shift any car out of park unless the brake pedal is being pressed, so you couldn't have done that just reaching from the back." He looked at me and hung his head, knowing he was caught in a lie. What I didn't ask but would have liked to have known, was if Betty had told him to lie for her or if he did it of his own volition, trying to keep his mother out of the spotlight.

As my parents and I sat around the kitchen table that night, discussing the day's drama, my parents opened up about things I hadn't known, that happened before Betty and I split. My mom said, "We were always on pins and needles wondering which Betty would walk through the door. Sometimes she seemed happy, at least as much as she could be, but most of the time she was just nasty! Always complaining and mad at something or someone." My dad chimed in, "Did I ever tell you about when I brought Stephen up to our house when he was being difficult for her and I tried to help her out?" "No." I said. "Well, I walk him back to your house and just five seconds after going in, Stephen runs out crying and says, 'Mom said you're a f---ing idiot!' He was nine years old! So I walked him back into the house and Betty is standing right there in the kitchen with the other three sitting right there at the island! She said that right in front of all the kids and all because I was just trying to help her?!" I said, "She takes gestures that are meant to help her and twists them into she's being wronged, just like Mom trying to get Charlie today." My mom said, "And why did Julie think I hit her mom?! I have never, in my entire life, hit anyone and Julie knows I wouldn't hit her mom or anyone else!" "I don't know, but when I told Lisa the hardest thing I have ever had to do, by far, was watch my three older kids emotionally desert me and align with their abuser, she told me to read up on 'Stockholm Syndrome,' which I did right away." "What is that?" my mom asked. "That's when someone defends and sympathizes with their abuser. They do it to seek the approval of someone who has hurt them."

My mom then said, "You may want to check with the school; something happened a couple of years ago with Stephen that you may want to look into." "What do you mean?" I asked. Mom said, "Betty had said to me, 'Can you believe the school called CYF on me about Stephen's scratches?!' I thought, how indignant! And of course they called, he has scratches and bruises all over his neck and shoulders and they are deep!" "That explains the call I got while I was in Marworth then. All Betty said to me was, 'Stephen and I had a bad day,' but she never alluded to any trouble when I was gone, so I was afraid it ended with her really hurting him. I'll go to the school tomorrow and see if there's any record of it," I said.

When I went to the school the next day, the first person I saw was the school's guidance counselor. I said, "Hi Vanessa, I'm looking to get some information from the school about a time a couple of years ago when someone apparently called CYF because Stephen had some marks on him." Vanessa said, "That was me, what do you want to know?" "Can you tell me what happened? I wasn't ever contacted by CYF, and I'm just learning there was a problem," I said. Vanessa's face looked strained, and she said, "Stephen came in one morning and he was visibly shaken and he had a lot of marks on him, including some bruises on his face. So I asked him, 'What happened?' He said that his mom pushed him down the basement steps, so I called her and she admitted to doing it. So I called CYF." "I'm sorry that happened Vanessa. So sorry. Stephen has had an extremely rough childhood, and I don't like making excuses for him, but I hope that some of his behavioral issues in school are a little more understood knowing that," I said. "We just want what's best for Stephen, Mr. Black," Vanessa said. "Well, if that is true, would you be willing to write a letter saying what happened? Betty and I are getting divorced, and she is trying to have the kids exclusively. She doesn't want me to have anything to do with them," I uncomfortably said. Vanessa said, "I'm going to tell you the same thing I just told her when she asked nearly the same thing, and that is no." I looked at Vanessa, trying to think of a reason why she wouldn't help limit Betty's exposure to Stephen and the other kids. Additionally, I was left to wonder how Betty could possibly find a way to ask the very person who called CYF on her to now testify for her in her effort to be the primary custodial parent. Betty is incredibly convincing as the victim, but she's not a magician. Vanessa's response to me was, and still is, a mystery.

The realization that there might be things Betty had done things to the kids that I may not even have known about made me question if my mom had any pictures that revealed what the kids and I had gone through over the years. Betty had deleted the pictures folder I had created, of just of the kids' marks, a year before we separated, so I was determined to find something in the countless other pictures my mom and I had of the kids since Stephen had been born in 2003. Because my mom had some pictures that I had taken with my SLR and she had a very good point-and-shoot camera, I knew I could take advantage of their clarity and resolution by zooming in on a picture I thought had any chance of revealing otherwise unseen signs of trouble. After I spent nearly the entire month of March going through 23,000 pictures, I ended up finding almost a hundred pictures that the kids had signs of physical abuse (many were of the same marks at different times, and I estimated there were twenty-five to thirty separate instances). Many of the pictures didn't need to be zoomed in as the tell-tale signs of what I was looking for, but afraid of finding, jumped out at me. It was very somber to look back through the years and see the patterns of bruises, fingernail gouges, and scratches that were mostly found only on Stephen and Noel, and I hurt for them, wondering how scared they must have been when it happened. One of the pictures that hit me the hardest was that of Stephen when he was just thirteen months old. It was one of the pictures that wasn't a close up, but seeing the trademark three scratches across his eyes and cheeks when I zoomed in on him made me shudder and I instinctively closed my laptop as fast as I could. I thought of a quote I had just read from a Borderline mother, "I was beating him for just being a kid when I didn't feel like being a mother." This compilation of pictures, and especially the one of Stephen when he was a year old, is the one thing I make myself look at when I invariably question if I really did the right thing for my kids when I sealed our family's fate with the PFA.

The gym meets were a sore spot for Betty and her mom because they didn't want the kids seeing me any more than was court-ordered. Their aggression was made worse by the fact that I looked like an extremely devoted father with my various cases of cameras and lenses and two tripods accompanying me (a typical question was, "Are you with Sports Illustrated?!"). So at one meet, feeling threatened, Betty and her mom got to intimidating Stephen right away. Betty started by telling another parent that I had stolen a camera from her (so she couldn't take pictures) and other lies that indicated I was a lousy father as Stephen sat beside her. For what it's worth, my sister confronted Betty by saying to her, "That is crap!" Sandi texted me, as I stood on an elevated balcony looking down, that Betty was "misbehaving again" and I came down to the bleachers to see for myself. I saw Stephen, now sitting by himself behind the bleachers, and I asked him, "Hey Stephen, why don't you come talk to me for just a few minutes?" and I turned around and walked back upstairs. I glanced back a few seconds later and I was a little surprised to see Stephen following me. Betty and Pat were surprised too, because Betty loudly said, "Stephen, stay here!" I then saw Pat stand up and, carrying Peg's three-year-old son, follow Stephen and I upstairs. Stephen and I sat down, and immediately after we did, Pat sat down and bumped Stephen very hard in retaliation for following me. I looked at her in disbelief, but then I starting to talk to Stephen to show Pat that I was not going to be deterred from talking to my son. When I started talking, Pat talked over me, saying all of the things Betty used to say to the kids in her "meetings." "Stephen, your dad is a drunk and he's been in three rehabs! He never wanted a part of your life before, and he doesn't deserve one now!" In a repeat of just two months before, when Stevie had said what he did at the restaurant, I saw other parents on the balcony looking at us in shock. I told Stephen to follow me, and we went into a nearby office so he wouldn't have to hear any more of Pat's propaganda. As I closed the door, she shoved it open and, bringing to mind when I hit Betty after her assault on me, I shoved the door (and hence Pat) back hard and I locked it. The bleachers were just below us, and Pat used the audience to her advantage by saying, "Rob! Open this door right now! Stephen is afraid of you and I don't trust you in there with him by yourself!" I didn't think Betty or Pat could say anything that could bother me anymore, but the fact that other parents could hear her, and I was on the other side of the door and unable to see who was listening, was very concerning to me. I turned to Stephen to try and undo the damage as fast as possible before turning him over to "The Gestapo," as my family sometimes called her. As Pat continued yelling, I said to Stephen, "As much as I love spending time with you Stephen, I don't want you going through any more of this. I love you more than you'll ever know; you're such a great kid. I hope you know that this is an example of how adults should not act, no matter how angry Grammy is." He nodded his head and gave me a hug. When I opened the door, Pat had just left.

When I got back to my spot on the balcony, I couldn't help but notice a man who was looking towards me a lot. I said bye to Stephen and looked at the gent and said, "I'm sorry." He asked, "Who was that woman with the little boy?!" "That was my ex-mother-in-law; she's a little crazy," I said laughing. He said, "'Well, she told that little boy to jump up and down on your camera equipment, and he did! When I looked at her in shock, she said, 'They're just my son-in-law's, it doesn't matter.'" I wasn't surprised to hear that Pat had her grandson try to destroy something of mine and I took his name and number down, hoping to use his willing recount in court.

A couple of days later, I had my visit with the kids during Betty's custody week. I took them for a walk along a creek before the girls started gymnastics and the serenity and isolation got the kids to open up a little. It started when Stephen said, "I'm sorry for last night Dad." This was referring to his mom trying to sneak him out a side entrance when she saw me looking for him in the crowded lobby after he played the cello during a school concert (when Betty saw me, she said "Come on kids, let's go this way," and they walked away from me). He followed her, but thanks to having to maneuver his cello around everyone, I eventually caught up. I said, "It's okay, I'm used to your mom," even though I wasn't. Julie then said, "I don't want to do the visits anymore!" I asked, "Why," and she responded, "Because Mom is always trying to take away your time!" I told her the visits broke up my seven days without them when they lived with their mom, so I wanted to keep the short visit for now. Christian asked in response, "Are we going to live with Mom?" I said they would live with the both of us and Christian looked at me as if he had more to say. Julie said it for him, "Mom and Grammy were telling the cousins that we are going to live with Mom, not you." I said that wasn't for them to decide, it was for a judge. Noel must have felt left out, because then she said, "And Mom didn't let you say hi to me [and Stephen and Christian] after my soccer game because you were getting me the next day!" In the span of just thirty seconds, each of the kids told me, whether they knew it or not, that Betty didn't want me to have an equal role in their life — if any at all.

The next Friday was another custody exchange, and another police report. This time Pat came to my parents' door and I told her that I was finishing a conversation with a client and that I needed "just a second." As I closed the door, she shoved it open and I, again, had to force it shut against her pushing. Not a minute later, my phone was ringing and it was Paige's number, so I hung up with the client and switched over to hear Paige plead with me to let Pat have the kids' things — like I was withholding them. I explained myself and looked outside to find Pat, somewhat frantically, pacing on the sidewalk near the street and talking on the phone. Apprehensive, I opened the door and saw Noel on her scooter only fifteen feet from the house. I went up to her and nicely asked her to come in and tell me which of Julie's and her clothes stayed at my parents' house and which went to her mom's. When Pat saw Noel walk with me to the door, she ran over and I instinctively picked up Noel and turned my back to her to shield Noel from Pat. Pat yelled, "Leave her alone, this is Betty's time!" and I felt Noel being jerked to my right. I looked down to see Pat pulling hard on Noel's arm. I was about to put Noel down, but Pat let go of Noel and I ran Noel into the house. Once we were inside, I got down on my knees to look her in the eyes and asked, "Noel, are you okay?" She nodded her head and started to cry. "I'm so sorry, if I knew Grammy was going to do that, I wouldn't have asked you to come in. Look, I just need you to show me which of your clothes stay here, okay?" She again nodded and cracked a smile. "Noel, why don't you show me how strong you are; do you think you can carry this bin of things out to the car?" She jumped at the chance to show me, or anyone, her strength and she smiled as she picked up the bin with a grunt. I walked her part way outside, and when I saw Betty standing near her mom, she said, "I called the cops, so you should just stay here." I'd had enough and I said, "When you called the police a few months ago, you went to jail." Pat yelled, "That's because you're an asshole, YOU did it!" I wasn't going to win a two-on-one, and both Noel and her cousin's young ears were standing near Pat and Betty, so I took a few steps back and remained quiet. We waited outside for twenty minutes for the police to arrive. During this time, Betty went over to Paige, who was standing in her driveway, to tell Paige her side of the altercation. When they arrived, the two policemen separated us and we told them our version of the events and then all of us met back up. After I straightened out Betty's lie that the kids weren't allowed to be with me or in my parents' house on her custody time, the policeman looked at Betty and Pat and said, "There wasn't any crime committed here, and you two are just going to have to grow up."

The next time I had the kids for my visit, a few days later, Noel still had some bruises on her forearm and I again apologized to her. Noel was still visibly upset and said, "Grammy hurt my arm, she is very mean!" As much as I initially wanted the kids to have a good relationship with Betty and her family, it was hard not to now think that my kids needed shielded from them. As my mom combined her notes after this with the previous incident at Julie's gym meet, she said, "Again — destructive behavior — putting your own agenda before the well-being of your kids. They will do or say anything to anyone to get what they want. Lie, be deceitful, play the victim, manipulate — these are the behaviors she is teaching the kids are acceptable!" For my three-hour visit with the kids a few days later, the boys didn't want to come out of the house when I went to pick them up and the girls were apprehensive too. It was a struggle that took thirty minutes of my three-hour visit, just so I could see them. I could feel the kids slipping from me and aligning more and more with their mother's cause.

The next day, Betty came up to my parents' to get a toy Noel left there. As she turned to walk away from me, I felt I needed an answer as to why she was on a mission to take our kids (and my dignity) away from me, so

I asked, "Why are you so angry; what did I ever do to you?" She spun around to look at me and with one of the angriest faces I've ever seen, said, "Ummmm, you beat the shit out of me?!" I stood there, completely baffled by her response; no one was around for her to convince that I had been the aggressor (except for Christian, who sat in the van with the windows up); it was just me and her in the yard. My parents, my sister, and I all knew Betty was capable of believing her own lies, but the question that came up after this comment of hers, that we could never figure out despite frequent in-depth talks, was how she could believe I'd repeatedly beat her up, yet she would taunt me every chance she got? She clearly wasn't afraid of me; conversely, she was thriving off the fear she instilled in me. It is common for Borderlines to believe in "Tell a lie often enough and people will believe it" and it may have actually worked on herself. The problem was, she was saying one thing, but acting in accordance with the opposite.

In a comical ending to this brief encounter, because I changed my address with the post office (occasionally still getting utility bills), I handed her a bill through her van's window that had accidentally been delivered to me. As she slowly drove off, she ripped up the bill with both hands outside her van's window. As small pieces of paper that looked like confetti blew around with the wind, she screamed, "I don't have to pay that!" and sped off as she dropped the last of the pieces.

In one incident in late April, I saw Noel take after Betty and exhibit some self-victimization too. She had climbed on top of a tall swingset at a park, and her soccer coach, who was there with his daughter, had told already told her to get down. He was still standing nearby as she stayed on top of the swingset. I had also seen Noel, and though I was a bit apprehensive because it was Betty's custody time, I went under the swing set and nicely asked Noel to let me help her down. She dangled her legs down and I reached up and grabbed them and brought her down. As she slowly slid past my face, I made a silly face and said, "Hi, Noel!" She put her hands up to her face, and I could hear her crying. I asked her what was wrong and she said, "You hit me!" Completely taken aback, I said, "No I didn't, Noel! Why would you say that!" She raised her voice and said emphatically, "Yes, you did!" By now, Pat's husband, Dale, had come up to us and he grabbed Noel's arm and said, "She's coming with me!" I said, "I want just a minute with my daughter." Dale then jerked Noel's arm, hard, as I still had my arms on her shoulders from pleading with her. When he did, I dropped my right arm and grabbed his wrist and looked him in the eye, conveying to him that I would not stand for him jerking Noel's arm. He let go, walked away, and in a big, crowded park, yelled, "He pushed me!" over and over as he pointed towards me. I glanced at the parents and their kids who were subjected to this and I quickly turned my attention back to Noel. "Noel, I would never hit you; why do you think I would do that? I was only trying to help you down so you didn't get hurt." She was still crying and now pushing me away and I knew I wasn't going to get through to her — I had to let her go. I said, "Go to your Pap Pap Noel, I still love you," as she ran away from me.

I stood there in a daze, trying to process what had just happened. In the span of thirty seconds, my daughter claimed I hit her, my father-in-law claimed I pushed him, and my daughter ran to him for protection from me. "Now I'll have to wear a camera or have a witness any time I'm around my own kids," I thought. Speaking of witnesses, I must have looked pretty dejected because Noel's soccer coach came over to me and said, "Rob, are you okay? I told her to get down out of a tree and the swing set several times." I said, "Thank you Jeff, I really appreciate your help. It's Betty's week, and I came to check on the kids over here because I knew that Betty and her dad were watching Stephen's baseball game. I'm an assistant coach, so I really should have stayed at the field, but I was worried about the kids out in the park by themselves." Jeff asked, "Why was Noel crying and...why did her grandpa say you pushed him?!" "I don't know the answer to either one of those Jeff, I really don't. Noel says I hit her and Dale said, well you heard him, I pushed him. I didn't do either one of those, so...," I said as I held my hands out, trying to show my frustration. Jeff said, "Well, I saw most of it, and Mya saw all of it and she is as confused as we are." I asked Jeff's daughter, "Mya, you saw the whole thing?" "Uh huh!" she answered. "And did you see me do anything that would cause Noel to say I hit her or her grandpa to say I pushed him?" I asked. "No! All you did was get Noel down!" she said as she shook her head.

When I got back to the baseball field, Betty had a diabolical smile and I knew she couldn't be more pleased with how it had all played out. I asked, "Do you want to hear what really happened with Noel, or do you want to believe the worst?" I finished with the last part because as I asked her, "Do you want to hear what really happened with Noel," she started laughing and was walking away. Noel's behavior was affirmation to her that she was succeeding in raising our daughter with her values and my values weren't getting through — and Betty took great joy in that, that and the fact that it caused me a visible amount of pain.

Betty wasn't done though. As I walked into the dugout, she came back and approached Stephen as he stood alone in the on-deck circle. I know she couldn't wait to tell Stephen, and that couldn't have been more accurate. Keep in mind that Stephen's team was ahead by only one run in the last inning, and the other team was batting last — Stephen's team needed him to get on base to help get a few insurance runs against one of the best teams in the league. None of that mattered as Betty said, "Stephen, do you know what your dad did to Noel?!" Stephen said "No?" "He hit her so hard, she was crying and then he pushed your pap pap!" Betty said. Stephen looked at her and I could tell it completely knocked his focus off the game. Betty walked away, turning her head to smile at me as I went up to Stephen to reel him back in. "Stephen, that isn't true. I hope you know that," I said, trying to get his mind back on the game. But he was unfocused and struck out. His strike out didn't solely cost his team the game, but they did lose, detracting from Stephen's already fragile confidence.

The next day was Noel's First Holy Communion and she was still very distant with me. When I first saw her through the open door of the waiting room, I softly said, "Noel, you look so beautiful." She scowled and walked back into the room where I couldn't see her. A stark realization came over me: "How do I keep my sanity when all I want is my kids' love and all they want is to find reasons not to give it to me. They WANT to find reasons not to love me, they WANT to believe Betty, they WANT to hate me."

As I packed up my cameras and lenses after Noel's Communion, I saw Pat walking towards my mom. I thought Pat was putting her differences aside and she was going to say "Hi," but then I heard a confrontational tone that one does not associate with being in a church. Pat was pointing her finger at my mom and saying, "This is my church and you shouldn't be here!" I walked across the church as fast as I could as I knew Pat's hostility was only going to get worse unless I intervened. My mom looked upset and frustrated and I'd had enough of this one-way taunting, so I smiled and said, "Off your meds again, Pat?" (For the record, this quote is in my journal in blue text for "Things that I did wrong.") Pat then pointed her finger at me and yelled, "You!" Before she could say anymore, her son, Daniel, ran over to stand between his mom and I. He looked at me with a big grin and said, "How's your career going Rob?" "What?" I said, completely surprised by his question. Once I realized what he was implying, that my career was nearly non-existent because of my past drinking, my look of confusion turned to a big, cheeky smile — I had just received word from Dr. Lambeau that his contact within the FAA had told him I was "Good to go" and, though I would have to wait for the FAA's official letter, I had my physical scheduled for the very next day. But I wasn't going to tell him that, he would find out soon enough. As I stood there all smug, Daniel became frustrated and repeated louder and louder, "How's your career going, huh?" His wife, Kerry, came over and grabbed him. "Not in church, Daniel!" she said as she guided him towards the door.

One of the few good things to come out of that morning was that Kerry's mom and sister approached my mom and I with open arms and big smiles as we were about to leave. Cathy and my mom had always talked a lot the few times a year they saw each other while Betty and I were together. They had a good friendship that endured long periods of not seeing each other till the next family function — and the same applied to Cassie and I. Knowing they were still visible to Pat, my mom was only half-joking when she asked them, "Are you sure you want to be seen with us?" Cathy had the response I yearned to hear from everyone, but least expected from someone within Betty's family, "We know there are two sides to every story." The four of us chatted for a bit longer before a warm goodbye. The brief exchange was so powerful to me that I still have to fight back the tears when I think about it. Knowing that Betty and Pat can't convince everyone (who isn't a close friend of mine or one of the neighbors who knew the real Betty) that I am the worst person to walk the Earth is a great solace when I think of all the relationships I've lost to Betty and Pat's scorched earth campaign.

Over the last six months, as much as Betty had tried to win the kids over from me, she wasn't always 100% capable of hiding her true disdain for them. During one of my visits with the kids, it was raining and my plans of taking the kids to a bike trail would have to wait. Instead, the five of us and Adam played outside my parents' house in the rain. The kids were wearing old clothes and I got out the camera and told them they could do whatever they wanted. Some of my best pictures were captured that evening as the kids ran around and acted as goofy as their ages and imaginations allowed. They dug holes and played in the mud, they jousted with umbrellas, they poured buckets of water on each other — they even laid in the gutter of the newly paved road as the water from the heavy rain got dammed up by their bodies. I got to see my kids happy, carefree, and free — until I took them back to Betty. I'd kept the worst of the clothes and shoes to wash and bring back later that night and I had hosed off the mud and put some dry clothes on them. But when Betty came out of the house, she inspected the kids up and down and I could see in her face that there was big trouble ahead. The kids were wet and not wearing the clothes they had on when I picked them up, so I tried to appease her by saying, "I'm going to wash and dry all of their clothes and I'll bring them back in an hour — promise." "You WILL bring them back RIGHT NOW!" she yelled. I heard the familiar rage in her voice, characterized by fluctuating emphasis and volume, and I flashed back to some of her more violent outbursts that were often preceded by those variations. I went and got the wet clothes and shoes as fast as I could, trying to limit the kids' vulnerability. When I returned, Julie was outside and she was crying as she stood on the porch. As I got out of my car, Stephen walked out of the house and came up to me in the cul-de-sac, crying, and he gave me a big hug. "What's wrong, Stephen?!" I asked. He said, "Mom keeps yelling at us, 'I don't want you anymore, go back with your dad!'" "Stephen, I love you more than anything, and you can always run to Grammy's house or call me if you need to, okay?" I held him and I asked Julie as she stayed on the porch, "Are you okay?" and she just nodded her head. Betty then slammed the front door open and yelled, "Stephen, get back in here RIGHT NOW!" I cupped his face and said, "Stephen, you run out of that house as fast as you can if you think you need to, okay? Drag your siblings and go to Helena's or any of these houses and call 9-1-1 if anyone gets left behind. I'm going to call ten minutes after I leave here to make sure everything's okay. Okay?" He didn't say anything, he only looked at me and just barely cracked a smile, as if to say "Thanks. And wish me luck." I did call, but Betty didn't answer. When I texted her to see if the kids were okay, she only responded, "Of course." Remembering Betty's capability to become violent, I had to resort to checking on the kids by trying to see into her house from the woods in the backyard — a big risk with the court order from when we first separated which kept me from stepping on the property. I could see Betty walking around the kitchen, and the kids' bathroom light switched on and off a couple of times, and that had to suffice that our kids were safe.

Despite this incident, the three older kids', and especially the girls', distance with me only became greater. At Julie's gymnastics meet a few days later, Julie wouldn't say hi to me and she walked away when I wanted to say, "Good luck." But later at that same meet, she saw me at the concessions, which were way off from where the competition was taking place and where her mom and Pat were sitting, and she couldn't wait to tell me how high her scores were on the three events she had already performed. I smiled and gave her a hug, but I was perplexed at how different she was to me when Betty could, and could not, see her. So the next time I had custody of the kids, I talked to Julie about it and her upcoming State meet that was being held on the other side of Pennsylvania. "Why were you so excited to tell me your scores when I saw you getting a drink at your meet, but when you first got there, you wouldn't even look at me?" She grimaced and said, "I'm scared." "Scared of what?!" I asked, half knowing the answer. "I'm scared to talk to you, or Grammy, or Pap Pap on Mom's time, she'll get mad at us. Mom wants us to sit close to her while we're with her...she doesn't really want us to get up." I just smiled and said, "It's okay," but my mind was replaying what she'd said over and over. The two things I kept hearing was "us" and the unsolicited second sentence that, in my opinion, encompassed all of the kids at all of their activities, not just Julie at her gym meets. "Julie, can you come back here for a second?" I asked as she was walking away. She slowly turned around and walked back up to me. "My mom and I will be driving over five hours to watch you at your State meet next weekend; I don't want her and I to be treated like total strangers, okay?" She winced and said, "I'm not comfortable talking to you in front of Mom." I stood there with my arms folded and she knew that wasn't going to suffice. Her eyes got very big and she shook her head and said, "Mom absolutely hates you, and she wants us to hate you too!" As obvious as it was, it took me by complete surprise to hear her say it. She looked at me with sadness and regret, maybe at her own realization of it or maybe because she thought I would use this against her or use it against her mom; probably a little bit of all three. I tried to alleviate her concerns and I surely didn't want to stifle any open discussions in the future with an outwardly negative reaction, so I simply said, "That's okay, Mom is just angry and hopefully she will settle down with enough time." Julie, still in a daze, stared and nodded her head and ran back to her team.

Sometimes I didn't even know who Betty was playing the victim to. Now well into May, the weather was nice and I took any chance I could to play outside with the kids, especially with my return to work imminent. One of the things Betty saw me doing regularly was playing tennis with Noel. Noel would stand in the driveway, and I would be in the street, so Betty would know when we were playing just by looking from the top of her street. One evening, she drove over and partially blocked Noel and I from hitting the ball with her van. She got out, and against the Mercury Township Police's directive from six weeks before, walked up to the front of my parents' house where Stephen and Christian were playing. As I stood across the street waiting for her latest taunt to run its course, she called Noel over and she talked to the three kids, who were clearly uncomfortable. After ten full minutes, I said, "You're not allowed to be in our yard." She spun around and smiled as she wiggled her hips like an adolescent and yelled, "There's nothing in writing!" Remember, this is a 115-pound woman that claims I beat her up for most of our twelve year marriage. I walked back across the street and went inside the house as she and the kids watched me walk by. I grabbed my camera and put a lens on it as fast as I could, but she knew what I was up to and she walked back out to the neighborhood sidewalk, which marked the end of our property. I put the video camera on her and let it run, but she was still smiling and taunting me; her obsession had grown too strong to be able to play it smart anymore. Christian had already gone inside and I told Stephen and Noel to please do the same, but they just stood there on the sidewalk, curious as to how this was going to end. In the video, I ask Betty, "Why were you on my property?" She says, "I'm standing on the sidewalk!" I then ask Stephen, "Was she well into our property?" Betty interjects and changes her story like she is so adept at doing, "No one said I wasn't allowed to come up here!" I say, "The cops did." She laughs and says, "Well, go call them!" It was all a big game of cat and mouse to her and it didn't matter one bit if the kids were scared whenever we were within a hundred yards of each other as long as she got a rise out of me. She got in her van and started it, so I went and stood in the driveway across the street to start playing tennis with Noel again. Betty got on her phone and talked for a minute before she started moving. When she did, she came right at me and I had to quickly move off into the grass. I wasn't expecting her to turn around and go back home, I'd thought she was going to continue straight out of the neighborhood — evidence that she only came up to my parents' house to taunt me and interrupt Noel and I playing tennis. She appeared to still be talking and laughing into the phone when she came at me again as she backed up. When she backed up, she did the same thing she'd done to my dad just six weeks before where she turned the steering wheel and came a couple of feet into the grass where I was standing. She probably would not have hit me, but I took a step back anyway and, to let her know I wasn't amused, I knocked on the back window of her van with the handle of my tennis racket. Still on the phone, she got out and inspected the back of her van. She put the phone near her mouth and said, "Why did you hit my van with your racket? Come on Rob, that's childish," in a calm and collected tone. How she could switch personalities that fast, like a light switch, was disheartening. There was nothing I could do either. I couldn't grab the phone and explain, because Betty would claim abuse, and I couldn't yell what the truth was, because rarely do people associate yelling with being right or reasonable. Another no-win situation with Betty, master of the art. When she finally left, she rolled down her window and said, "Alright kids, try and have a good time until you come home," as if they struggled to have fun with me and to remind them that my parents' house wasn't their home.

In the middle of May, I got the letter in the mail from the FAA that I had waited two years, two months and nineteen days for — the authorization to get my medical and return to work. It was three pages filled with caveats and tenets that had to be met to keep it, but none of that mattered right now; I was going back to work and I was happy and healthy this time. It was Friday and it started my week of custody, so I impatiently waited for Stephen to get off the bus and took him with me to go and pick up my medical certificate from Dr. Lambeau. When I got there, Dr. Lambeau made a point to come into the waiting area and shake my hand. When he did, he looked at Stephen and said, "Isn't he a great guy! I am so proud of him!" He handed it to me and repeated himself, "I'm so proud of you!" and gave me a big hug. For nearly a year, I hadn't thought the FAA would stop dragging their feet and I would ever fly again and getting that little piece of paper was one of the biggest moments of my life. I wanted Stephen to know the enormous weight of what it symbolized, so I showed him the 3" x 4" certificate and said, "See this? This little piece of paper is what is going to buy our next house. And your first car. And pay for your college." I was smiling from ear to ear and he was smiling just as much and when we got outside, we literally sprinted back to the car to go home and show the other kids and my parents.

I was still floating on cloud nine when Christian had his hockey game Sunday. Afterwards, I went into the locker room to start the arduous task of getting him undressed — which, just to be clear, is not as arduous as putting it on. When I walked in, Betty was sitting beside him in the small crowded locker room, talking to him as he started to undress. When she saw me walking towards Christian, she stood in front of him, blocking my view. I said, "Please let me get him undressed." She snapped, "When are you going back to work?!" Surprised, I said "What?" She turned her head around and raised her voice so that everyone in the room could hear her, "Do you have your license back yet?" I said, "Yes," in more of a question than a statement. She then turned her body around from undressing Christian to face me and, with her hands on her hips, asked, "Then why aren't you at work?" I stood there in silence, not willing to engage her. "I said, did you get your license back from being in rehab?!" she said, almost yelling. The room fell almost silent and the parents were looking at her, but she was oblivious to them as she glared at me. I should have left the room, but she stepped aside and I knelt down to finish undressing Christian. As I did, she started again, "I guess you quit drinking then, if you got your license back after three years and three rehabs! Are you finally allowed to go back to work now?!" her voice only slightly less louder than before. By now, the other parents realized that something was wrong and they started talking to their kids to drown her out as they hurried to get their kids undressed. Coach J.R. took over and gave a loud and enthusiastic post-game speech and I picked up Christian to quickly leave the room before he ran out of things to say. I was hoping to step out and see Sophia, who was the daughter of my parents' neighbors and our babysitter from when the kids were infants — someone Betty would not show her Mr. Hyde side to. She had come to see Christian play that morning, but only my dad was standing outside the locker room. I had to get Christian's hockey bag, stick, and my camera bag, so I handed Christian to my dad and implored him, "Leave, get him away from her! She's telling him all those things he should never have to hear!" But when I went to give Christian to my dad, Betty took him right out of our hands. She stood there, just a foot from us, like it was all a game of tag, daring us with a diabolical smile to grab him back from her. My dad threw his hands up and said, "I'm not getting in the middle of this," and took a few steps back. I said to my dad, "I'll go get Sophia." Betty didn't put him down right away, because she would never show me in a quadrillion years that I could get her to do anything I needed or wanted, but once I made my way down the hall, she put Christian down to prevent Sophia seeing her withholding him from us. When I got back, less than a minute later, Betty was gone and I took Christian aside and I just held him and repeated "I love you," over and over, again trying futilely to undo the psychological and emotional damage the only way I knew how.

One of the things that isn't hard to notice about Betty, is that her behavior leaves a path of destruction almost everywhere she goes. In this case, the director of the hockey program had to come up with a new locker room policy. After this, only one parent at a time would be allowed in a locker room for Christian's team. How many times had I seen one parent undress their kid and the other talk to their son, or hand out snacks and drinks. But that was erased on this day.

The incident in the hockey dressing room was an anomaly, because, before that, Betty was always very cognizant of who was around. Her only other compulsion in life, besides the one this whole book is about, is hiding her inner depression and anger. The outgoing, charming front is her thick, multi-layer defense that is almost impermeable and her defenses were right back in place just a few days later at Julie's school picnic. The three of us sat near each other in the grass with Julie's best friend, Dani, and her parents, Rob and Sadie. Though Betty and I didn't say a word to each other, she also wasn't plotting against me, claiming I was being abusive towards her, or yelling at me. As we were leaving, Rob, Sadie, and Dani were only ten feet behind us when Julie said, "Mom, you know how you weren't mean to Dad today?" Betty, I'm sure at a loss for words, said, "Yes." "Can you be like that all the time?" Julie said with a smile. "Well, aren't you little Miss Manners!" Betty said, laughing like Julie must be joking. I don't know if Sadie and her family heard Julie or not, but it is no wonder Betty was so successful in winning over our common friends; hardly anyone besides the kids and I ever saw her evil side. But the kids were too young to catch on to Betty's manipulations and too scared to confront her even if they did. And that is the million dollar question: when will the kids figure out her obsession of taking their love away from me? The handful of people who know me almost always say the same thing: "Give them until they're older or adults and they'll figure her out." But that is of little solace to me as the thing I want most in this life is to be an integral part of their childhood. I am a big kid, after all, and playing sports, building Legos, baking brownies, taking them to parks and museums and all of the little things parents do with their little ones will not be a window of time that spans much longer — their childhood is already two-thirds gone.

One weekend in May, Christian had a hockey game where he scored three goals and played extremely well on defense too. Betty wasn't in the stands during the game, so I wasn't expecting to see her walking into the building as we were leaving. My dad and I had all four kids with us and when Betty saw us walking out, she said, "Kids, come over here, I have to show you what Bob did!" I figured Bob was a new boyfriend, and it quickly became obvious after Betty rounded up all four kids around her phone and said, "Look! Watch him win his wrestling match!" She was overflowing with pride and enthusiasm as she watched the kids watching the match, her eyes scanning to check their level of attention. What bothered me about this was that she never asked Christian anything about his game. She came at the very last minute only to show the kids Bob's wrestling match and she left after telling them how great the other wrestler was that Bob had defeated — her appearance at the rink was all about Bob, not Christian. I felt bad for Christian, and although he didn't seem to be bothered and I had already praised him for his untiring efforts on the ice, I went over and, for a second time, made a big deal about how well he had played.

I wouldn't see or hear much more about Bob for quite a while, but what I did hear from the kids over the next few weeks was cause for some concern. I heard Noel say her last name was going to change to Bob's and, at a different time, Christian asked me if his last name was going to change to Bob's. I don't think Bob had anything to do with that, but he spent the night with Betty and the kids often right from the start of their relationship. Again, that isn't all that far out of the ordinary, but the rest of the story wasn't written yet.

The Future Brightens

At the end of May, I flew to Dallas to start the six weeks of Monday through Saturday training it would take to be requalified to fly again. It felt surreal to be trusted to fly commercially again and trying to say thank you to everyone who'd helped me get back there was indescribable and just didn't seem adequate. It was the pinnacle of a huge success — overcoming an addiction that had left a trail of financial destruction and, at one point, to which I had completely surrendered my life. But there was just one problem: Betty abhorred any success of mine and this was undoubtedly the biggest one of my life. Whether it's getting my black belt and getting into the best shape of my life, or developing a wonderful and loving relationship with the kids, or overcoming alcoholism, she desperately wants me to feel as miserable as she does on the inside, and her pronounced jealously of this triumph would destroy any chance of co-parenting in harmony.

Talking to the kids on the phone had always been extremely difficult, but now that I was a thousand miles away, Betty must have felt she had more latitude to drive the wedge between the kids and I even deeper by making it almost impossible for me to talk to them. She came up with a variety of clever ways to ensure that out of sight meant out of mind. From ignoring my texts and calls all evening until the kids were in bed and then yelling, "Why are you calling here so late, they are sleeping!" to sending them all out to play, to telling me to call the house only to find it was on fax mode, to having them spend the night at their cousins' and my requests to her brother and sister would be ignored, to "The kids don't want to talk to you" when she never told them I called, to claiming she didn't know her phone was on silent, to telling the kids not to answer the phone if it was from me, to any number of things they were doing that she didn't want me to interrupt — I didn't get to talk to the kids much at all while I was in Dallas. At the very best, I could talk to one or two kids once or twice a week near their bedtime. This ensured that the other ones were in the shower, already in bed, or not to be interrupted because they were doing homework. Often, when I did get to talk to whichever one Betty chose, she ensured he or she was distracted by video games or a movie that was so loud they had a hard time hearing me. Though none of this is particularly unique or eye raising to other parents in high-conflict divorces, all of this distraction and frustration was not particularly well-timed as I was trying to study for the oral and simulator tests that, because I felt I was out of chances with Southern, I was under enormous pressure to easily pass.

To be clear, talking to the kids on the phone was frustrating, but for the first four weeks of training, I did have about twenty-four to thirty-six hours at home to spend with the kids. The training was a total of six weeks, but I couldn't come home the last weekend because the simulator phase runs continuously. Betty wasn't cooperative in letting me see the kids and my lawyer had to negotiate with Betty's nearly every time I came home so I could have custody of them. Much to my chagrin then, when I came home that first weekend, Betty had arranged for all of the kids to sleep at friends' houses or at their cousins'. Betty told me I could get them "The next afternoon," but seeing as how I was leaving to go back to Dallas the next evening, that wasn't acceptable to me. I told Betty that she would bring the kids to my parents' house, or I would go through my lawyer. After initially refusing to let me have them, she finally agreed to bring three of them up to my parents' house, but she wouldn't tell me where Noel was. After nearly an hour of negotiating, she finally brought all four to my parents' house. But Betty's adept ability at creating a no-win situation for me unfolded in the driveway right before my eyes. Betty must have told them that all they had to do was say hi to me, because as soon as I asked them if they were coming into my parents', Stephen said, "I thought we were just saying hi." I said, "No, you're staying with me until I go back to Dallas, Stephen." He became very upset and said, "But our cousins are at our house and we're supposed to play and have a sleepover with them!" I had, in his mind, just ripped him from his best friends. I repeatedly told the kids I wanted to spend my time with them and they would have to reschedule the sleepovers Betty had arranged for them. Their reactions ranged from the older three crying and incessantly negotiating to Christian just shrugging his shoulders and giving me a hug. I finally got all four kids, but Betty quickly went back to her house and picked up all four of their cousins, who must have been waiting for the part of Betty's plan where she drove by my parents'. I was still talking to the kids outside, trying to cheer them up and convince them that we were going to have a fun weekend when Betty very slowly drove the cousins by in her van. Their cousins were just following Betty's orders, but they hung out the windows of her van yelling "Bye" and saying all of the fun things they were going to do that weekend. I couldn't believe she could torment our kids like that, and I remember looking over at Stephen and watching his shoulders seemingly slump to the ground as he hung his head straight down. I tried consoling him, but he walked away from me, upset and mad.

There was a silver lining to Stephen trying to get away from me and me catching up to him on the side of the house though, and that was that the next door neighbor, Christine, saw the whole thing from her kitchen window, which overlooks my parents' side yard. She was furious that Betty would "torment" the kids by slowly driving the cousins past as they hung out the window and waved. Besides the cul-de-sac neighbors who'd seen Betty's parenting first-hand, most people that heard my mom or I tell them about Betty's behavior probably wondered if it was really that bad and assumed we had to be greatly exaggerating. And though Christine knew Betty had physically abused the kids and me, she hadn't seen the campaign of parental alienation she had heard about until now. To throw salt on the wound, Betty stopped into my parents' house just after I left for Dallas and told my mom, "Julie is just paying you lip service, she really doesn't like to stay at your house with you."

The second Sunday I was home from training two things happened, though I wouldn't find out about either incident until I came home the following weekend. When I got the kids on that third weekend, Julie told my mom in private that Stephen and Betty were on walkie-talkies as Betty was guiding Stephen through my parents' house, looking for an iPad I had just bought for work. Stephen must not have remembered it was for my job because he looked for it in the evening after I went back to Dallas, and I had it with me. What is most concerning is that Stephen, once again, had to climb the wall to get the key to the front door and he knew he was breaking into my parents' house to steal, once again, at Betty's direction.

The second part of what happened that second weekend was still visible on Noel. She had bruises in the shape of three fingers on her left temple and near her eye, bruises just below and above her left eye brow, and what looked like a fingernail gouge on her ear. I thought that with Betty trying (and succeeding) to win the kids from me, they would be safe from her violent outbursts, but these marks were undeniable proof that Betty was still unable to control herself around the kids if she was provoked. Christian saw me looking at them as Noel talked to my dad, and when I looked at Christian, he whispered, "Dad," and cupped his hands around his mouth to tell me something. I said, "Let's go over here." When we went into the dining room, I asked, "What happened, Christian?" "I ran over a Lincoln Log house Stephen built and we got in trouble. Mom then got mad at Noel and Noel tried to call 9-1-1, but Mom grabbed the phone out of her hand," he said. He didn't say what directed Betty's anger towards Noel, and he didn't know when I asked. I let him go say hi to my parents and, because his recount was hard to follow and it didn't make a lot of sense, I noted what he said right away before I forgot any of the little nuances. After I thought about it for a minute, I couldn't help but think back to what my lawyer had told me about the possibility of the kids testifying. That was, Stephen could be asked and Julie might be asked to testify, but Noel would not be; she was too young. Could it be that Betty went after Noel and not Stephen because Stephen was old enough to be asked to talk to the judge and Noel wasn't? Regardless, Noel was extremely conscientious about the bruises and she told me not to take a picture of her face that evening when I grabbed my camera. Also, she seemed to make an effort to stand with her right side to me for almost the entire thirty-six hours I was home. Though she was especially aware of them when I had the camera out while we played in the yard early the next day, she let her guard down when I took her and her siblings to our community pool the next evening. I managed to get a quick picture that showed, faded though they were, her week-old bruises.

When I called to get Noel in to see her new counselor, Michele, the receptionist told me that Betty was already bringing Noel in to see Michele and I wasn't able to because Betty would not include me on the application. Betty, likely trying to undo Noel's emotional damage so she wouldn't tell me what had happened, openly refused to put me on the application until I told her that I would notify my lawyer. This prompted Betty to raise her voice and say over the phone, "You're just trying to take all of my money!" as Julie was probably right beside her since it was a night where I'd just talked to her (and only her). Betty's comment probably meant I was causing her to spend money on her lawyer to defend her when she shouldn't have to, but my belief was that it didn't have to be this way if she would just co-parent with some level of cooperation.

It's an odd feeling, giving your kids an escape plan from their own mother, but that is exactly what I did after I saw Noel's marks. I didn't want to directly say that it was their mother they needed to escape from and I knew it had to be simple for Christian and Noel's young minds. I told them, "If there is something, or someone, dangerous in ANY way in your mom's house or anywhere you are, get out immediately and go to a neighbor's house and tell them you are in danger and to call 9-1-1. Go to Helena's first. If you're at your mom's house, run up here to Grammy's if you can. Okay?" They looked uncomfortable, but I made them acknowledge what I had told them before they left.

The fourth weekend I was home, I had two extra days before I had to be back in Dallas to start the simulator phase and I used part of that time to take all four kids to our family counselor, Heidi. Heidi said, "Okay kids, Julie last week said she wanted your mom to bring you to group and both parents to bring you to individual counseling, right?" No one answered, and when Heidi looked to Julie for an answer, Julie said, "I only said that because Mom hates Dad; I want Dad to bring us to group too." Heidi's mouth fell open and I think, for once, a counselor realized a small part of what I was up against. The problem was, Heidi was retiring in a couple of months and I would lose that ally in getting the kids to see that just because their mother hated their dad, it didn't mean they should.

If there were any remaining doubts about Betty's intentions of sharing custody with me equally, they were erased when I picked the kids up at Peg's house. I had three days off before my first trip, and Betty came out with the kids and came over and stood beside my car's open window. "I will get them back Sunday at 5:00," she said, glaring at me with her hands on her hips. I said, "I was planning on bringing them back to you Monday." Her anger and voice spiked, "I'm the primary custody parent and I'm only letting you have them until Sunday!" I said, "I'll ask Jenna [my lawyer] and get back to you." Betty moved behind me to where the kids were getting in my SUV and held their door open, repeating, "You have to have them back Sunday," waiting for me to agree while we just sat there in silence. The kids were visibly uncomfortable, and Stephen tried to close the door, but Betty was too strong. Julie started yelling, "Just leave, Mom!" over and over. And Betty started yelling, "You have to have them back Sunday!" I tried to diffuse the situation by saying, "Betty, I will email you what I plan on doing, but please just let us go."

Julie fell silent and Betty said I had to have them back Sunday three more times to show who was in control. After the yelling stopped, I realized we didn't have any of the kids' sports gear for the weekend and I asked Betty where it was. Showing me she would not be deterred, she stuck her head in my SUV and, now sounding like she was sympathetic to the kids, said, "Kids, just try to have a good time with him, okay?" When she started walking away, I asked, "What about their leotards and soccer bags?" She flung her head back and said "Ha!" and kept walking towards Peg's house.

As I look back, there are only a few rare times that the kids verbalize that they know Betty struggles to control herself or her anger. As we ate at Arby's one day in early August, Julie told me that Noel bit her when they were with Betty. Ultimately, Julie wanted me to discipline Noel for biting her, but when I said, "I can't do that; I'm sure your mom did and she shouldn't be punished twice for the same thing." Julie said, "Mom won't discipline her because she knows she can't control her anger." I asked, "What do you mean?" Julie said, "Mom knows if she starts to discipline us, she won't be able to control herself." Again, looking back with hindsight, most of the time when we were married, Betty appeared to know her limits because she would often say, "Rob, come and get so-and-so, I can't deal with them!" Up until the end of our marriage, I reluctantly interjected. I knew what Betty was capable of doing if I didn't step in, but it was hard not to think that if I did almost all of the disciplining, the kids would grow up to resent me.

That discussion in Arby's got Stephen to open up to me and on the drive home, as he sat in the passenger seat, he said he wanted to tell me what one of his cousins was saying about me when we got back. One of the bigger casualties for me in the divorce was that I lost out on seeing all the of the cousins grow up. When Betty and I were married, I often played with them and I enjoyed watching them grow up, but now the cousins weren't allowed around me. It hurt to be completely cut out of their lives by their parents and I couldn't help but to be curious if they believed what the adults wanted them to believe. When we got to his room to talk, he said, "Mitchel doesn't believe what the adults are telling him, he knows you're a good person." I said, "That is very mature of Mitchel. It usually takes until you're much older [Mitchel was 13] to make up your own mind. As you get older, I hope you see things differently and that there comes a point where you listen to other people, but you make up your own mind about something and stop feeling the way people tell you to feel." Stephen said, "Because Mitchel is older, he doesn't have to worry about what Grammy thinks either." Confused at what seemed like a random comment, I said, "What do you mean?" "Grammy smacks Christian and the other kids on the back with a metal spoon — hard! And Aunt Peg is really evil and she smacks us hard too! But they leave Mitchel alone because he is a teenager." Stephen was starting to see that his mother's family didn't live in a way he wanted to and, though I appreciate and respect his friendships with his cousins, I was happy to hear that he was starting to diverge his mind from how the adults conducted themselves.

I tried to get out of my parents' house as much as possible when I had the kids, and in early August of 2014, I took them to Colorado Springs to spend the night and go to the top of Pike's Peak the next day. We first ate lunch at the only restaurant in the country that is inside an old airplane and then we drove to the top of the mountain. The scenery on the way up was so beautiful that it took a couple of hours longer than I thought it would take, due to all of the stops along the way. In hindsight,

I should have budgeted a lot more time for the drive to and from the top because it is as scenic as the peak itself. When we got to the summit, we walked around the somewhat large, flat top and I quickly realized that we all felt a bit weird and winded due to the 14,114 foot elevation. I took dozens of pictures and we looked out for what had to be 200 miles in the clear, cold air. There's a freedom in being on top of a mountain that is hard to describe, but a lot of it is a sense of security, being so far away and above the rest of the world. I remember Christian asking, "Are we on top of the world?!" I smiled and said, "I am!"

We weren't on top of the world for long though. Betty called the kids while we were on the top and she told Julie that they had to be home the next day, not two days later like I'd understood. I talked to Betty after the kids, but she wouldn't trade me a day for one the next weekend, despite the fact that the kids weren't in school and didn't have anything to do. She said that she was going to contact her lawyer the next day and I made sure we were on the first flight home the next morning to ensure we made it home on time. Fair enough, it was my mistake, but I occasionally wished for more cooperation on her part to trade time. On the flight home, I moved around, taking turns to sit with all of the kids. When I sat next to Julie, she held onto my arm and put her head on my shoulder. After a few minutes, she looked up at me and said, "Dad, you're the only one I perfectly trust." It wrapped up a trip that bonded all of us together like few other trips could have, and my hope that the kids would trust, respect, and love me in the face of all the negativity that was being directed towards them was greatly strengthened.

It was such a success that the very next weekend, I flew the five of us to Las Vegas and we then drove to the Grand Canyon. Though a bit rushed over just three days, it was even better than our trip to Pikes Peak with the kids more comfortable being that far from home now. We sang songs on the radio and took in the sights on the long scenic drives, also stopping at the Hoover Dam for the Dam tour on the way. Of all of the pictures and videos I have of the kids throughout the years, my favorite was captured when we got to the Canyon that evening. I told the kids to stay back about fifty yards while I went ahead and stood by the ledge. With the sun getting low and the perfect sky over the Grand Canyon, I turned on my video camera and aimed it at them. As they walked towards me and started to get their first glimpses of one of the most beautiful places on Earth, their mouths fell open and their big eyes and loud gasps spoke of their sheer awe. They stood at the edge of the Grand Canyon mesmerized by the size and beauty of one of nature's greatest creations and, with the camera still recording, Christian was the first to really snap out of it, saying, "Yeah, this is MASSIVE!"

The day we got home, Betty drove up to my parents' house to pick up the kids and she saw Sophia and I talking in the yard. We were discussing the trip, and my back was towards Betty as she pulled up. I heard her footsteps and I saw Sophia's eyes get really big and the next thing I knew, Betty was standing right beside me, almost shoulder to shoulder. Betty had to have heard what I was saying about the trip as she walked up, and because I was extremely uncomfortable with her there, I slowed my speech. Betty took that opportunity to start talking to Sophia about getting her teaching certificate renewed and, realizing she was just taunting me again, I stepped away. But what Betty didn't realize was, for the first time, she had just shown someone — someone whom she wanted believing that I'd battered her all those years — that she wasn't one bit afraid of me.

Stephen was outside when this happened, and when I walked away and towards him, his big eyes met mine. I said, "That was not very comfortable." Stephen said, "I don't like Mom around you, I'm afraid she's going to start a fight with you!" I chuckled and went and got the kids' clothes and toys for Betty to take with her. When I took Charlie to Betty, I said to her, "My parents and I would like to watch Charlie next week while you're on vacation." She looked at me, and now that Sophia had gone back inside her house, she snapped, "No! I've already made plans for Shari [Robby's widow] to watch him!" I said, "You just demanded to have Charlie when I took the kids to Pikes Peak and the Grand Canyon the last two weekends and I let you have him." She yelled, "Go back inside!" which I guess was her way of saying no again. I had sent her multiple texts over the last few days, all unanswered, so I had a feeling that getting Charlie was going to be difficult, but not getting him at all was frustrating and left me a bit down. When Betty and I were together, I took care of Charlie almost exclusively by feeding, walking, bathing, combing, and cleaning up after him. I really like Shari, but she works a lot and I knew Charlie would be cooped up in his cage most of the day, which really bothered me. If he was with my parents' and me, he wouldn't spend one minute in a cage, but Betty's determination to take everything from me, especially Charlie because of how much I enjoyed him, was unwavering.

For the next six weeks, my journal reflects that life was a little like the movie *Groundhog Day*. The dozens of entries repeating my inability to talk to the kids on the phone, the difficulty in getting Charlie while I had the kids, the boys repeatedly missing their soccer and baseball practices and games, or Betty's continued contradiction of trying to intimidate me while claiming I beat her up. But with my return to work still fresh, I felt completely free as we cruised eight miles up and hundreds of miles away. "She can't get to me up here," I often thought.

It didn't happen often, but occasionally, Betty would misjudge people's allegiances. She would air our dirty laundry and tell them all the lies that worked with other people who didn't know me well enough to know any better (or were just gullible). One such person, whose personality is as vibrant and passionate as they get, is Roseanne. Roseanne works at our pediatric dentist's office and she treats our kids with that same vibrance and passion that makes her so unforgettable. She probably treats all the kids and their parents that way, but making everyone feel special is her specialty and she is damn good at it. So when I stopped in to pay a bill for the kids' latest treatments, she stood up from behind the counter and held my face as she said, "Rob! Why is Betty so angry!" I was a bit taken aback, so I smiled and said, "What do you mean, Roseanne?" "Betty! She came in here with your kids and she was full of this SEETHING anger, and she just said the nastiest things about you! These horrible, horrible things about you — right in front of the kids! Stephen was trying to get her to leave by pulling on her sleeve, but she wouldn't stop! I felt so bad for your kids, they just stood there having to listen to her say these horrible things about their own father! I tried to get her to stop, but I couldn't! She wouldn't listen to a word I said! She calls in here all the time and asks why are you bringing them here, like you shouldn't have anything to do with their care! She needs help, a lot of it!" she said, almost in one big breath. I just said, "Yeah, I know she hates me," hoping Roseanne would continue — and she did. "You know, she is sore and bitter! Those kids are suffering; I saw it in their faces and I saw it in their eyes — they're sad! And I tell you, Betty is all about money, that's where her anger went nuts. She said she's giving you all this money and you don't pay for anything! And I know better, I know you're a great guy with a job and you do your part to take care of her and those beautiful babies! And to think when you and her first started coming here, she bragged about you all the time!" Surprised, I asked, "She said she gives ME money?! I just got ordered to pay her another thousand a month. And I gladly pay it because I want my kids to be taken care of. Heck, if Betty and I had a normal divorce, and she came to me and said, '5k a month isn't enough for me and the kids,' I would give her more." Roseanne said, "Look, she is incredibly manipulative and I see right through that pretty exterior. And she is just such a beeeauuuutiful woman!" I said, "I know, she's got that God-given face! But that's what lets her get away with it with everyone else." Roseanne leaned into me and said, "Oh! You know what else she said?! She said, 'I don't want him having anything to do with the kids!' Do you believe that?! You're their father, and you're a great guy and she doesn't want her own children to know their father! And I'll tell you something else, she is ruining it for all of the women who really are victims of domestic abuse!" I thanked Roseanne for not falling for Betty's victim mentality and for trying to get her to stop berating me in front of our kids. She grabbed my face again and left me with, "And if you ever need anything, and I mean anything, you better call me!"

Why is it that no one, besides Roseanne, challenges Betty when she goes off on a tirade about me in front of the kids? I can't help but think how different my relationship with my kids would be if other adults kept my kids' best interests in mind when Betty doesn't and they weren't so receptive to Betty's disparaging remarks. From where I stand, the world could use a lot more Roseannes.

The conversation with Roseanne made me realize that Betty was saying anything she thought could be believed by whomever her audience was. And with the girls unable to play with many of their friends on my time or in my presence anymore, I felt my previous intuition had all but been verified. I tried to talk to the dissenting parents and tell them that I'm not an abusive father or husband, and if they heard anything negative about me from anyone, that I would appreciate the chance to refute or explain what they'd heard. In what became a hard, disappointing lesson in human nature, only one set of parents said what I had hoped all couples would say. When Rob and Sadie answered the door, I said, "Hi, I'm sorry to bother you two, but I think you may be hearing some things about me that aren't true, and I just wanted to offer you a chance to either ask me about it or tell me to just go away." Though smiling, I said the last part because the sudden distance with the other parents really bothered me and I would rather have confirmation that they believed Betty than just be blown off and left wondering if they heard something bothersome. With a big smile, Sadie said, "Rob, don't worry about it, we've known you for a while and we trust you. We know there are two sides to every story!" Rob then said, "Look, if you ever need anything from us, you just let us know. We are always here for you." Here were two people that I barely knew who treated me with more respect and trust than many of my so-called friends, some whom I'd known for twenty-five years.

At the end of September, I found a house to rent just across the street from our old neighborhood (and my parents' neighborhood too). It was important to me to stay in one of the two similar and adjacent developments because the kids had so many friends there and I wanted to be close to my parents so they could help me with the running of the kids to their myriad of activities. I didn't take any furniture from the marital house when I moved out because I couldn't store it anywhere at my parents', so I was starting completely from scratch. A friend of mine with interior decorating skills flew up from South Carolina to help me pick out furniture and a fellow pilot I met in the HIMS program painted the kids' rooms and helped me assemble the numerous Ikea bedroom items. For the fifty-four hours I had from when I moved in until my custody time started, it was a frenzy of painting, buying, transporting, and assembling. I maxed out my credit card and put a big dent in my dad's card too, but by three o'clock that Friday, I had a furnished house that I couldn't wait to show the kids. When I picked them up, I didn't tell them that I had moved out of my parents' house. Instead, I drove them around to look at houses that were for sale or rent, like I was still looking for a place to move to, and they gave me their enthusiastic opinion. I set up my phone to take video of the drive to capture a little trick I was planning. When we finally got to the house I had moved in to, I asked "What about this one?" The kids were yelling, "Yes, yes!" and Julie said, "I love this house!" I said, "Well, if you like it that much, let's go see if there's anyone home that we can talk to." Julie sounded concerned, "Really? Can we do that?" "Sure!" I said. All five of us walked to the front door and I rang the bell. I looked at them and they looked a bit uncomfortable, which was perfect for what I had in mind. "Well, I guess they're not home. Why don't we just go in and take a look ourselves," I said as I reached for the door. Stephen said, "Dad!" as I stepped inside and said, "Is anyone home?" Now the kids were very uncomfortable, and I said, "I don't think anyone lives here, let's look around." Trying not to laugh as all four kids looked at each other, trying to figure out if I had lost my mind or not, I said, "Come on in! This is our new house!" They gawked at me, which turned into huge smiles as they looked at each other in total surprise and started running into the house, literally pushing me aside as they ran past screaming. I showed them their rooms and it was a frenzy of running around and loudly talking about what they would do and where. That evening, we ate pizza on the floor with Adam, as the dining table would take another week to be delivered, and I snapped a picture of five smiling kids wearing varying levels of sauce on their faces. There isn't anything I like more than providing hope for my kids, and this was undoubtedly a happy and hopeful day.

The next afternoon, Betty found out about my move from one of the kids and she drove over with Bob right away. I watched her get out of the Jeep, and she started walking towards me with papers in her hand. In a condescending tone, she said, "You need to sign these papers to sell the house!" I said, "I've told you several times [via email] that I wasn't going to sign those papers because you want to list the house below what it's worth." Now Betty was at my sidewalk and her diabolical smile told me she wasn't there for me to sign listing papers, she was sending me a message that I couldn't escape her. I said, "I don't want you on my property, please get off of it." She came within just a few feet of me, still smiling and tilting her head slightly, as if it were all a game. "Get off of my property!" I said five more times, increasing in volume and serious-ness each time as I walked backwards into my house. I looked out the window and she was still smiling and looked to be in a trance. After a minute, she looked over at Bob's car and walked back to him. They sat in the car in front of my house for ten minutes before leaving and I then went to the Mercury Township Police station and told an officer what had just happened. "I'll call her and give her a warning and also tell her that she will be arrested if she goes onto your property again," he said. I agreed, expecting that to be the last of it, but when he called me back he said, "She claims you're the one who is taunting her, and that you often go to her house and you won't get off of her property when she asks you to get off of it." "What?!" I said. "I am also giving you a warning, that if you go onto her property that you will be trespassing and you could be subject to a citation or arrest for criminal trespass." "But I've never stepped foot onto her property since we separated a year ago and every neighbor in that cul-de-sac could probably verify that! I even park on the other side of the street so she can't claim that very thing!" I said in frustration. "It doesn't matter, she claims you have and it is my duty to advise you not to do it," he said. In a blatant show of defiance, the very next morning I had wide scratches that ran along the entire front fender of my car.

A little insight into what Julie thought of her two parents being near each other occurred when I took her out to dinner for her birthday in mid-October. We found ourselves behind Betty's van and when Julie realized it was her mom, she sat up and, sounding like she was panicking, said, "Quick! Put three or four cars in between us!" "Okay, but why is it so urgent?" I asked. "I don't want Mom near you!" she said, looking at me with great concern. She continued, "There, get that bus in front of us!" and I slowed down and pulled into the other lane behind the school bus. "Julie, what is so wrong?" I asked. "I don't trust her!" she said. "Okay, well let's just go to dinner and not think about it anymore. Okay?" She nodded her head and I started to ask her about her gymnastics routines for the upcoming season to get her mind off of it.

In an odd coincidence, we found ourselves behind Betty on the way home from dinner too. Again, I slowed down and kept a distance, but something must have been wrong with Betty's van because Bob pulled over into the median and we passed them as their hazard lights came on. Perplexed, Julie and I looked at each other as we passed her. I said, "Should you call her to make sure she's okay?" and Julie said, "Yes." Julie called and asked Betty if she was okay, and then said, "Dad wanted to make sure you were okay." I heard Betty laugh, tell Bob what I said and then laugh even harder.

Betty and Pat knew no limits in the people they tried to gaslight, including my own lawyer and mother. The next week was our preliminary custody hearing in front of our new judge. While we were waiting, we sat out in the hall and Pat said to my lawyer, Jenna, "You know he is crazy, don't you?" Jenna couldn't believe what she had just heard, but she didn't dignify Pat's comment by saying anything or looking over at her. Betty laughed, and then said, in complete contradiction to her assertion to the police just two weeks before, "He IS crazy! He won't even come onto my property to get the kids' things! I have to take them out to the curb while he parks and stands across the cul-de-sac and waits for me to go back inside! I don't know what his problem is!" Betty's laughter became even louder as Pat looked at me and shook her head in disgust. A few days later, Pat tried to convince my own mother that I was the problem when she said, "See Bernice! It doesn't have to be this hard you know? See how nice it is when that one person isn't around?!" My mom was tempted to say, "Who, you?" but my mom's composure and class filtered it out. My take is that Pat and Betty were trying to say to my own lawyer and mother, "We all need to bond together against that horrible man!"

Two important things came out of the meeting that the two lawyers had with Judge Wardi, and that was both sides claimed that it was extremely difficult for the other parent to talk to the kids on the phone and that Judge Wardi considered Noel old enough to testify at the hearing scheduled three months from now. When I heard that the judge would be willing to hear from Noel, and not just the two older kids, my mind immediately rewound to four months prior and how Betty had bruised Noel's face. I thought, "Well, Noel's testimony can't be good for Betty's aspirations for custody, but she's still too young to be put in front of a judge." When I got home, I rounded up the kids and I drove home the point when I said to them, "The most important thing in your life, besides oxygen, is talking to your mom every night." Julie said, "But we do talk to her every night on your time." I said, "I know, but we can NOT miss any kids, any nights, for any reason now."

Betty was starting to throw caution to the wind, as her behavior became more erratic and she didn't seem to care much what the kids, and to some degree, what the neighbors thought anymore. In late October 2014, I had Stephen with me and I had to give a memory stick back to Helena that I had put her son's senior year soccer pictures on. I had already texted Betty four times that day, saying the kids had really missed Charlie that weekend and I would like to get him that afternoon, but she didn't respond to any of those. When she saw us pull into Helena's driveway, she carried Charlie out to her mailbox in an apparent effort to tease me with him. Knowing the answer, I asked anyway, "Betty, may we please have Charlie?" She laughed and went back inside behind the glass storm door, laughing and waving to me as she held Charlie. Stephen then got out of the car and stood beside me near Helena's mailbox. Though I told him to get back in the car, he wanted Charlie and thought he could help get the dog from his mom. I asked nicely one more time and Stephen said "Please!" afterwards. Betty then threw

open the glass door and yelled across the street, "I'm calling the police!" and she put her phone to her ear as she held the dog. Stephen
looked at me with panic all over his face and said, "Come on, Dad, let's
go! She's calling the cops!" I was now quite used to the police being
called and I tried to pass some of that calm onto Stephen by saying,
"Okay, she's not going to give Charlie to us. I'll text her tomorrow and
ask again." We got into my car and Stephen said, "She's ruining everything! I should've told you this was going to happen. Mom said to us
yesterday we weren't going to get him and I told her all of us wanted
him, but she didn't care!"

In an odd ending to this incident, Francine called me about half an hour
later, demanding to talk to Julie. I politely asked "Why?" and Francine
said, "I don't have to have a reason why!" and hung up the phone. I sent
two texts to Francine offering for her to call me, but she didn't respond
to either. Betty was so good at making puppets out of our kids that she
had moved on and set her sights on our counselors and she easily made
one out of Francine. Betty then tried to do the same with the kids' counselor, Heidi, just a couple of days later. I found out when Heidi called to
remind me of an upcoming appointment for the kids. When I said, "That
is my custody time, Heidi, but I don't think we are coming in until next
week. Are you sure?" She said, "Oh. Never mind; I see my notes say
Betty is coming in alone." Heidi was retiring and, even though I doubt
Betty had much success winning her over, she would cease to be our
kids' counselor in two weeks and it simply didn't matter anymore.

Further proof that the time my kids spent around Betty and her mom
was driving them from the values I wanted ingrained in them happened
a couple of days later. We were driving home from ice skating when I

heard Stephen tell all of his siblings, "Barack Obama is only the president because all of the blacks went out and voted for him and the blacks cause all of our country's problems!" I yelled "Stephen! Stop that, you will NOT say that again! Do you hear me! That is very wrong and it isn't true! You never, and I mean NEVER judge a whole group of millions of people with one general statement, do you hear me!" I was yelling by the end, but I wanted my point made — and it was. I didn't have to ask where he heard it because it sounded just like Pat, and to a slightly lesser extent, Betty. There were times when Betty and I were married that I had to leave the room and make sure our kids couldn't hear them as Pat would go on similar tirades about blacks, Mexicans, or Democrats. Betty wouldn't contribute so much as she would emphatically agree with her mom, trying to back her up with examples like, "Well, almost all of the people in jail are black!" Pat always had someone else to blame for her lot in life, and I knew it was only a matter of time before I was faced with having to undo her rants and teach my kids that they alone are responsible for where life takes them and if they are happy later in life — or not.

One of the issues I had grown increasingly suspicious of was the kids telling Betty negative things about me just to please her. One night, I had to discipline Stephen by taking money off the "Reward Board," a way I tried to reward and punish the kids where they earned money that they could spend on anything they wanted. All of them seemed to really value this system and he was trying to save up for a certain Lego at the time and he became very upset when I deducted a few dollars for an earlier infraction of his. When Betty called soon after we'd gone over the Reward Board and I'd deducted the money, he went into Christian's room and shut the door. When he came out, I said, "Your conversations with your mom are none of my business, unless you are trying to get sympathy from her by exaggerating or lying." Stephen said, "I told her you were a little mad, I'm sorry." I said, "It's okay." He then said, "I try to tell her the good things too, but she won't listen!" "What do you mean?" I said. "Like when Christian told Mom that he got to shoot the BB gun all by himself, I tried to tell her that no, Dad was there. But she told me to be quiet when I said you were there; she only wants to hear the bad things!" I said, "Doesn't she want to hear what really happened — the truth?" Stephen said, "No, only the bad things."

Something that had become a big concern for me was the kids' apparent lack of sleep. They were coming into my custody time with dark circles under their eyes and the two who are most irritable when tired, Stephen and Noel, went at each other even more than when they were rested. Before a counseling session with the five of us, I expressed this to Heidi and asked her if she could uncover what time they were going to bed when they were with Betty. As we got started, Heidi asked, "Does your mom have different rules than your dad?" Only Julie didn't immediately exclaim "Yes!" Heidi then asked, "Like what?" Stephen went first, saying, "Mom lets us do whatever we want, just so we don't bother her." Heidi asked for an example and Stephen said, "I get to go to bed when I want." Julie said "Nuh uh!" Stephen looked at Heidi and said, "Well, I go to bed at 10:00, but I get to stay up and watch TV or play video games in my room until I fall asleep." Heidi looked at Julie and said, "What about you?" Julie said, "My bedtime is 11:00 on school nights, but sometimes I stay up until 1:30." Now Noel's turn, she said "I get to stay up until 10:30 on school nights, but I get to watch TV as long as I want." Heidi asked, "You mean you have to turn the TV off at 10:30?" "No, I have to be in bed at 10:30, but I get to watch TV as long as I want." Heidi looked at me as if to say, "It's worse than I thought!"

Heidi said, "Wow. You do have different rules at your mom's house." Stephen, rather annoyed, then said, "Yeah. And I have to actually sit here and talk the whole time." Julie looked at me and, trying to get Stephen in a little bit of trouble, said, "Yeah! When we're with Mom, he gets to sit in the corner the whole time during our counseling sessions and play video games!" I looked at Stephen and he clearly was not happy with Julie, so I knew it was true. Seeing as how Stephen could use the counseling the most out of all four of the kids, I couldn't help but wonder why Betty would even bother taking him — unless the counseling was all just for show.

A WRONG PREDICTION

My parents, and especially my mother, had grown weary of the near constant drama and the feeling that the next scheme Betty was working on was right around the corner. The next day, I told her what Stephen had told me, "She only wants to hear the bad things," and of Betty's appointment with Heidi. My mom became angry and said, "She has nothing more to do than sit at home and think of all these things to do to you! And you pay her to do it, she gets so much money, she doesn't have to work! THIS is her job, trying to destroy you!" I said, "And she is very good at it, perhaps I should give her a raise," trying to make her laugh. This everyday strife was taking its toll on her though and it wasn't funny. She went on, "We can't keep up with her! When we finally figure out what she just did and we work on undoing the damage, she already has the next two or three out the door!" I was trying to give her some hope and I told her what I had been thinking for the last month. "Mom, our custody hearings are only two months away. Some time very soon, she is going to settle down because she won't want to risk getting caught acting like that," I said. My mom said, "I don't know, she is obsessed! And she is just as good at hiding it and fooling everyone!" I said, "Yes, she is obsessed, but she is very smart in the ways of hate and she won't risk it. Don't worry, she'll settle down soon," I predicted.

Only twelve hours after I predicted that Betty would settle down soon, I got a call from my mechanic down the street while I was on a trip and in the van going to the hotel in Ft. Lauderdale. I had taken my SUV to Dave because the brake pedal had started slowly going to the floor four days before, the day I'd gotten custody of my kids. I live on a big hill, so I drove my mom's car when I had the kids, and I just pumped the pedal if I had to drive the SUV when I was by myself. I wasn't about to work on my brakes with temperatures in the single digits, so I'd left it for him to work on as I started my weekly trip. "Rob, this is Dave. You thought this was a bad master cylinder, and I did too from what you told me on the phone, but I got news for you, I think someone tampered with your brake line," he said. "What?" I said, as I looked up at the other pilot sitting across from me in the van. Rick and I had worked quite a bit together and he knew from my elevated tone that something was wrong. Dave then said, "Someone had to loosen your brake line; I've never seen anything like it." I said, "Which brake line had been loosened?" and Rick looked at me like I had two heads. Dave said, "The right front. The banjo bolt was loose and it has some fresh marks around it." I thanked Dave and looked back over at Rick, whose eyes were as big as saucers. "A disconnected brake line?! Holy shit! You have to call the police — right now!" he said. Dave didn't even know I was getting divorced, so he wouldn't have had a reason to jump to false conclusions. Even so, I thought there had to be some other explanation as Betty probably didn't know how to loosen a brake line, so I was hesitant to call the police. Rick then said, "If you don't call them, I will!" and I laughed and made the call. The Mercury Township dispatcher said they would send officer Phillis to look at the bolt the next day, as he had many years of restoring and working on cars and he would be qualified to make a determination of whether the bolt had been intentionally loosened or if it somehow came loose on its own.

Coincidentally, Rick and I were on the way to the hotel again the next day when my phone rang with the police's number on the screen. I fully expected to hear that Dave was wrong and the bolt had just worked its way loose. He said, "Mr. Black, this is Officer Phillis with the Mercury Township Police. I looked at your vehicle and I agree with Dave, someone tampered and loosened the bolt." I asked, "Are you sure?" He said, "I have been working on cars for 30 years, and I can say I am CERTAIN someone loosened your brake line. What would you like us to do?" I said, "I'm guessing we can't prove it was my ex, or anyone in her family. She used to help me work on the brakes of cars I fixed for friends, but not much besides pumping the pedal. I don't think she would know how to loosen that anyway." Officer Phillis asked, "Is there anyone she knows who would know how to do this and would carry it out for her?" "Well, her uncle hates me and he is crazy enough. He doesn't live too far from us, and I would put most of my focus on him. Her dad — not quite as crazy, but he's a close second. I certainly can't rule him out. My ex did something weird this past weekend [Betty staged that I lost the kids' phone on purpose, so that she couldn't talk to them as easily] that her boyfriend sent me an angry text for, but I doubt he would do it — I hardly know him," I said. He responded, "If you don't know for certain who it is and don't have video surveillance, then I'm afraid all we have is a loose bolt." What disappointed me most, including not being able to catch whoever did it, was the fact that the bolt was loosened the night before I got the kids for four days. All's fair in love and war, and our divorce was all out war to many of the people in Betty's family.

That night I started to look at outdoor surveillance cameras, but I was deterred by the myriad of choices online and the fact that there were only a few "wireless" sets (having only a power cable), none of which got favorable reviews. I postponed any decision until after the holidays, still thinking Betty would slow down as the hearings got closer. As busy as my life was, and hence the lack of time I had to devote to finding a set, it turned out to be a big mistake.

On Thanksgiving of 2014, both Betty and Pat, in two separate incidents, acted in direct contrast to someone who they claimed was a violent, abusive person. That afternoon, I got an email from Betty telling me where she and Pat and were staying in Cincinnati for Julie's gymnastics meet in December — presumably to taunt me while we were there. It said, "We all booked rooms at the Hilton for Saturday night." Now, I don't know about you, but I personally can't think of a time where I've heard of a victim of domestic violence telling her alleged attacker what hotel she was going to be staying in. Later that night, it was Pat's turn to contradict their stance that I had been physically abusive. When I went to Pat's house to get the kids for Thanksgiving dinner at my parents', I parked at the end of her driveway to avoid any confrontation with Pat or Betty. I heard Pat yelling at me from the top of the driveway, "What are you doing?! Get up here, and get the kids! They can't walk down there, it's raining!" It was really just misting, but I got out of my car and told Pat that I would come up and get the kids and carry Noel (she was wearing an ankle brace) anyway. As I walked up their thirty-yard driveway, Pat appeared to be alone (Dale was actually just inside the glass door rounding up the kids), and she started yelling again. "There's something wrong with him, he's crazy! Look at him, he won't even drive up here!" she said. She shook her head in disbelief as I picked up Noel and rounded up the other kids as they came out of the house. Pat walked towards me and she was less than ten feet from me as she kept pointing and yelling, "There's something wrong with you! You don't care about your kids; you were going to make them walk down there in the rain! What kind of father are you?!" Again, I assert that if Pat really believed I had a propensity to be violent, she wouldn't talk to me with such blatant disrespect. Would I yell like that to someone who had a supposed history of beating people up? Not unless I had a death wish.

Throughout the last six months, I'd occasionally talked to Jenna about having Betty undergo a psychological evaluation before the scheduled custody hearings. I told her what the teacher of the class for divorcing families had said regarding an undiagnosed mental illness and I knew Betty couldn't go from undiagnosed to diagnosed without testing. Of course, I would have to go through an evaluation too, and they would cost an estimated $8,000. But the price was actually welcoming to me as I figured if there was going to be that much time and psychiatric knowledge devoted to making sure both of us were fit to be parents, Betty had less of a chance to fool them. Whenever I talked to Jenna about the evaluations, I didn't get the enthusiasm I was hoping for, and I requested a meeting in her office one afternoon so I could go through the pros and cons with her and my mom face-to-face. I started our meeting with, "Jenna, you know I want these evaluations, why aren't you chomping at the bit to request them?" "Rob, it's not that easy. First, both of you will be watched as you interact with all four kids in a room, and from what you tell me, the kids have emotionally gravitated towards her and away from you. They could see how the kids interact with her and think everything is okay and she would be found to be perfectly sane and it all would backfire on us. We have a better chance at trying to prove she is unfit just by the court proceedings and her arrest, but even that is going to be an extremely tall order. Unless she is actively beating the kids daily or on drugs, the Allegheny court generally will not give the mother less than fifty percent of the time with the kids. That's just the way it is," she said. I looked at my mom and she was now clearly on Jenna's side and I was alone in my belief to continue on with the evaluations. Jenna then said, "You've said it yourself, she has fooled every counselor she's come in contact with. What makes you think she won't fool them? I've seen her myself, she is petite, pretty, and she is extremely convincing." "Well, one is just an addiction counselor and the others were just licensed practicing counselors. None of them had any college education in psychiatry — I don't think. I have to believe that she won't be able to fool actual doctors, who have probably seen her type before." My mom chimed in with, "Rob, it would be a dream come true for Betty to be found perfectly normal and she would not only use it in court, but against you for the rest of your life. How many people besides Dad and I, and your neighbors, believe her side of the story? Isn't it just about everybody else? I think Jenna is right and this could really backfire on you." I felt the best thing to do was to force the evaluations, but I didn't want to create a distance with Jenna right before I needed her and I to be a cohesive team in the courtroom, so I very reluctantly decided against the psychiatric evaluations.

In mid-December, I went to get Stephen from Betty to start my custody time (he got home from school twenty-five minutes before the others). I had been advised by the police to get video of the exchanges because Betty had been so contentious and she was becoming more and more brazen about walking up to me. During the last exchange, I'd walked around my car while Betty kept switching directions, trying to get to me right in the cul-de-sac, and we'd looked like a couple of little kids playing a slow game of tag. With that still fresh in my mind, I pulled up and parked across the street and I set the camera in plain sight on top of my hood. Pat was already in Betty's driveway, and I could see Stephen looking at me out the rear window of her car. I waited for fifteen minutes until Betty pulled in and Stephen and Pat stayed in their car until she did. Betty got out and immediately went into a rage, pointing her finger at my camera and yelling, "You can't do that! That is illegal, and you are going to jail!" I said, "Betty, just stop. Stephen can hear you, the whole street can hear you." "You are going to jail!" she incessantly repeated. I'd had enough and said, "Betty, I am NOT going to jail. As much as you want me to, your revenge is not going to happen." Betty shot back, "Revenge for what?! I didn't go to jail, there isn't any record of it! Show me a report, show me a police record!" She was screaming by the end and I just stood there, waiting for the madness to stop. Pat finally let Stephen out of her car, but he looked dejected and sad. Still fifty feet away from him, I said, "Stephen, what's wrong?" "I don't want to go with you," he said. I asked, "Why, big boy?" "I just want to stay here, I don't want to go," he said. I nicely pleaded with Stephen at least eight times and the answer was the same each time. After ten minutes, he finally moped over towards me and I put my arm around him and said, "It's okay buddy; let's just go home and get a snack and find something fun to do. Okay?" When I did, Betty laughed and loudly said, "I should get a picture of this!" probably implying that I had to pull Stephen along to get him to go with me. She wasn't done though. "It'll be okay Stephen. I'll be with you tomorrow, okay?" she said.

When we got home, I asked Stephen why he embarrassed me like that. He said, "I miss my cousins!" I asked him, "Did someone tell you could play with them today?" He said, "Mom and Aunt Kerry did. They said I could be playing with Joel if I didn't have to come here." He started crying and I held him on the couch and said, "I'm sorry Stephen, I would love for your cousins to be able to play with you here on my time, but they just can't. I don't know what to say to you. Look, I lost all of my time with those four boys too, I lost out on being Uncle Rob for their entire childhood. I miss them so much too!" I couldn't help it, but tears started to well up in my eyes too. The four boys are great kids, if a good bit mischievous, and I missed playing with and talking to them. I had lost something I deeply valued in watching them grow up into young men and that was very hard for me to accept. Stephen looked up at me and saw me hurting and put his head on my shoulder, now trying to comfort me.

Occasionally parents, who believe Betty's side of our story more than mine, get funny little glimpses as to who is the real aggressor. At the gymnastics meet in Cincinnati, the same meet where Betty had told me what hotel she was staying in two weeks before, Betty followed a couple on the drive and ate dinner with them, their daughter Abby, and Julie. I met up with them in time to go to the pool, and Betty walked side-by-side with us and chatted on the pool deck as the girls swam, as if us being around each other was no big deal — it wasn't, to her. When it was time to go to our rooms, all six of us got on the elevator and Julie asked, "What is our room number?" I didn't want Betty to know what room we were in, for obvious reasons, so I said, "1728," when really it was 1623. Earlier, Julie had left something in Abby's room and her dad called me after Julie and I got into our room. Tyson said, "Rob, Julie left her hair band here, and when I went up to your room at 1728, some guy, who certainly was not you, answered the door in his underwear!" We both laughed, and I said, "My room is really 1623 Tyson, but I can come down and get it." When I got to his room, he looked at me funny and said, "I called downstairs and they didn't have your name listed, so I couldn't figure out where the hell you were!" I chuckled and said, "I didn't want someone on the elevator with us to know what room we were in, so I intentionally said the wrong number. I also told the front desk that they were not to tell anyone I was staying here." He smiled, looked at me inquisitively and handed me the hair band. I'm not sure who Tyson and his wife believe, but their daughter is one that appears to not be allowed to play with Julie when I would be the only adult around the two girls. "A tiny, little victory," I thought.

Just a couple of weeks later, Tyson and I would have another laugh when Betty notified me that my personal email address had sent an unsolicited and dangerous email to her military address, and she implied in several texts that I had been on pornographic websites. She knew I greatly enjoyed using my cameras, and especially the professional lenses, to capture Julie's and her teammates' routines. At the beginning of the season, I made sure to get permission from everyone involved, but after the first meet or two, most of the parents were asking me to make sure I got as many of their daughter as possible. Because the coaches, the parents, and the gymnasts looked forward to seeing their latest performances posted on my website, Betty was probably determined to take this part of my hobby away from me by telling the other parents of the alleged suspicious email. But I was on to her ruse to disgrace me and I promptly contacted her boss and the department that monitored the base's email to get the facts. Her supervisor said, "I was here all weekend, so I don't know what she is talking about." One of the communication techs summed it up best when he said, "With China and North Korea trying to hack into our communications almost daily, I'm sure we'd already know about this if it had the slightest bit of truth to it; we wouldn't be hearing it from you." From their reports, and the fact that Betty refused to send me any proof of the hack, I knew her claim was bogus. That evening I saw Tyson at a gym practice and, expecting Betty to still go ahead with tainting the nature of my picture taking to the other parents, which I could now immediately denounce, I said, "Get ready Tyson, it's going to get weird." He smirked and said, "What? You and Betty?! Honestly Rob, can it possibly get any weirder?!" We laughed, but his eyes stayed focused on me and he had an air of seriousness about him. In the end, being proactive by contacting the base and asking Betty for a picture of the email, or for her to forward the email to me, deterred Betty from trying to paint me as the sexual deviant she wanted the parents to believe I was. Though I'm almost certain she tried anyway with one or two of the moms she was close with, I had secured proof that it was all a ploy if they ever approached me.

In the fall, I had theorized that Betty wasn't taking Stephen to baseball practice, Christian to his baseball and soccer practices, and Noel to her soccer practices because those are sports I knew how to play and the kids could practice with me. The girls' gymnastics and Christian's hockey were safe, Betty thought, because I couldn't practice those sports with them. The gymnastics is obvious, but the only reason I couldn't practice hockey with Christian was that it was difficult to get time on the ice. I know how to skate, so when Christian and I heard there was going to be a father-son hockey game to be played the morning after their holiday party and free skate, both of us got very excited. We boasted about who was going to "crush" who and Christian would fling his arms down like he was "dropping the gloves." I'd then put him in a headlock and pretend to beat him up while he hit my back. On the evening of the party and free skate, I went to the rink and waited for Christian. After fifteen minutes of looking for him, I sat at the end of a hallway and I then saw Betty. She was alone and appeared to be looking for someone. Figuring Christian was there somewhere and probably putting on his skates, I stood up and walked out onto the ice, which Betty saw. When she saw me, it was as if she'd found what she was looking for, because her head stopped swiveling and she promptly turned around and walked back to the parking lot. I went onto the ice and skated around for a few minutes while I waited for Christian. I saw another parent, who said, "Hi Rob, I think Betty was just looking for you," which struck me as odd, of course. A minute later, the head coach of the team then skated up to me, smiled and said, "What are you doing here?" "I'm here to see Christian for the party and play during the parent-son game tomorrow morning," I said. He cocked his head, smirked, and said, "Your ex said it was your time with him tonight and tomorrow, and that you wouldn't be bringing him to either one." I said, "That's not true, JR. I actually took the weekend off from work to be here tonight and tomorrow, but it is Betty's time with him." I grew concerned that Betty had been scouting to see if I was home or on a trip, and if she could determine I was home, she wouldn't bring Christian to either event. To find out, I only had to text her, "Where is Christian?" Betty replied, "He is with Bob." "Is he coming to the party tonight?" I asked. Betty responded, "No." I then asked, "What about tomorrow's father-son game?" and she texted, "No. He will not be there." I said, "I can come and get him for the game and bring him back to you if it is a matter of transportation or logistics." She replied, "No. It's not." When I got the kids a few days later for Christmas Eve, Christian really was "crushed." It takes a lot for Christian to cry, but I saw tears well up in his eyes when my dad said, "All of us waited for you at the game, Christian. Why didn't your mom bring you?" It was an unfair question that my dad regretted right away. We knew it wasn't

Christian's fault and there was nothing he could have done to be there — Betty was the only one who would do the "crushing" that weekend.

Another incident involving Christian and hockey happened just a week later, and it was a good example of how Betty could project blame in a way that I couldn't contain the damage from. When I talked to the kids on the phone, I asked Christian if he was going to his hockey practice on Saturday. He asked Betty and I heard her say "No" in the background. I then asked, "What about your game on Sunday, Sweet Pea?" and he again asked Betty and got the same response. I then heard him start to cry and he tried to repeat Betty's "No." Betty then got on the phone and, extremely angry, she said, "Why are you making Christian cry?! What did you say to him?!" I explained that I'd only asked if he was going to the hockey practice and game that coming weekend. She then repeated over and over, "What kind of father are you?! Why are you are making him cry?!" I just sat there listening to it, knowing she was only saying it to beat into the kids' heads that I was the one who'd made Christian cry, not her. After she finally grew tired of repeating herself, I calmly asked, "Betty. May I please talk to Christian?" Betty said, "Here, Christian, just don't let your father make you cry again." He didn't say anything, so I said, "Christian, please don't be upset. I'll take you skating and I'll make sure you go to the practices and games when I have you. Please don't be upset, it will be okay." He is such a great, resilient kid, and he managed to say "Okay."

Since the time Christian was only a year old, I'd known he was going to be a great kid. I used to say "I could have a hundred of him," and that still holds true to this day. He is just the most pleasant, easy going, and yet competitive boy. Such rare qualities combined into one child who has had a lot of bad examples set for him, yet he goes about life unfazed and happy. Somehow, his intuition of what is right and wrong always surfaces and older kids and adults alike would do well to take a few pages from his book.

An ongoing issue for months now was that Betty was still turning the kids over to me completely exhausted. Again, Noel and Stephen act the worst when they are tired, and they were so unhealthy-looking at the start of my custody time that I hesitated to take them out in public until I caught them up on their sleep. This often meant that the entire first day of my custody (which started at 3:00 p.m.) was spent getting them long naps, eating dinner, getting washed, and getting them back to bed. Their faces wore their state of exhaustion and the dark circles under their eyes were so pronounced and sunken that I took pictures and sent them to my lawyer in an email asking, "Is this grounds for a CYF investigation?" Ultimately, it was up to me to file the complaint she said, so I called CYF and asked one of the intake agents if any level of sleep deprivation would be grounds for an inquiry. According to the woman I spoke to, this is a gray area within the organization and it almost certainly would be "unfounded" even if it was considered extreme. I knew Betty wasn't doing it all week, just a day or two before my custody time started and with our hearings only a few weeks away, I didn't want to look like I was creating problems or being uncoopera- tive with Betty, so I chose to drop it with CYF unless it continued after our hearings. The benefit for Betty in doing this was that the kids got to stay up late, watching movies or playing video games, and it con- tributed to their view of freedom and a general lack of rules in Betty's house. This, of course, added to the appeal of living with her and it noticeably contrasted with my early and rigid bed times. Betty also knew it would put a big dent in my already-not-enough custody time by forcing me to get the kids naps when we could have been doing something fun. And even if they did get a nap, they were usually still tired afterwards; their irritability caused arguments and their lack of energy caused them to balk at any activity that required walking or skating.

I had been dating Lauren for two months and I had developed a lot of trust and respect for her over that time. After I finally introduced my kids to her and her kids, she saw how tired my kids looked and acted. As the weeks went on, she got used to only meeting for a short time on my first day with them as they needed long naps after school and early bedtimes that night. The next week, Lauren and I discussed at length what could be done to get my kids more sleep on Betty's time. As she is a teacher, she suggested I request a conference with the teachers and counselors to convey my concerns for the kids' lack of sleep right before my custody time. Due to work constraints, I hadn't planned to talk to their teachers until a few days into Betty's next custody window. But when I went into the school the next day to sign out Christian and Noel, the school counselor, Vanessa, brought Noel to me to discuss her concerns. Noel was crying and she looked alarmingly tired. Vanessa said, "She's been having a rough week." Trying my hardest to sound understanding, I said, "Noel, what's wrong?" She didn't answer, she just kept crying into her hands and rubbing her eyes. Vanessa said, "She seems so tired. She's been acting this way for a while now. Was she with you last night, or with her mom?" I said, "Her mom. The kids' apparent lack of sleep is becoming a very big concern of mine. To think they had a two-hour delay this morning [due to single-digit temperatures] too." Vanessa said, "Well, if there's anything you need, please just ask." Christian then came out and my heart sank as I saw how tired he also looked. I felt I couldn't make any plans that evening with Lauren, or she and I would have others looking at us like we were the horrible parents neglecting our kids. I felt powerless and though I thought my kids were nearly in a state of suffering, there wasn't anything I knew I could do to help them. If I confronted Betty, she was likely to say something familiar like, "Don't tell me how to parent! That's why I'm divorcing you!" or, "You're always trying to control me!" and she would get the kids even less sleep to spite me and to show me that I didn't have any influence over her.

On the drive home, Noel fell asleep within seconds and Christian laid his head against the window and he dozed off too — on the three-minute drive home. As I got Stephen and Julie after school, it was obvious all of the kids (with the possible exception of Julie, who was only a little tired) were very sleep deprived. Stephen, who despises naps and early bedtimes, walked into my house and said, "I'm soooo tired, I'm going to lay down," and fell asleep on the couch. Later, I vacillated between contacting Betty and just letting it go. But in the end, I decided to send Betty a text that questioned the recurring problem of why the kids were so incredibly tired, especially after a two-hour school delay. Betty's only response was, "So can the kids give me a call?" We went back and forth three more times and she never answered me, she only asked to talk to the kids. Another no-win situation: if I kept demanding an answer, she would likely claim I was denying her the right to talk to the kids or I was harassing her. Or both.

One sure way to divide kids and get them to feel you don't love them is to favor one over the other(s). Over the last couple of months, my once-tight bond with Noel now had a distance to it. I asked her, "Noel, are you okay? Are you comfortable in our new home yet?" She said, "Yeeeaaah, but Julie is your favorite and you do everything and buy everything just for her." I said, "Where did you get that idea?! I love all of you the same. I just don't have any favorites. Why do you think that?" Noel said, "Grammy on the small hill told us, she said you don't care about the rest of us." I said, "Ms. Noel, again, I love all of you the same. Please don't think that, that is just not true! You know, you and I have such a special relationship, and it was even better before your mom and I split — I really hope I have that with you again someday. Sometime very soon." She looked at me and gave me a half-smile, but it was another issue on which I couldn't undo all of their doubt. If Pat or Betty say something about me to the kids, I might be able to give their young minds a little reassurance (if I even find out about it) and I might be able to reel them back in a little, but I couldn't ever erase all of what they heard, every time, and Pat and Betty's obsession to alienate me from the kids was slowly chipping away at our once close relationships.

That night, I heard Noel crying an hour after she went to bed. When I asked her what was wrong, she said, "Mom is struggling with money." I'd had enough of Betty playing the victim to our kids and I got the other three, who had just gone to bed but weren't sleeping yet, and brought them into Noel's room. I sat on the floor while they sat on the bed and I said, "Noel just told me your mom said she 'is struggling with money.' I need for all of you to know that I give your mom a lot of money every month, and she can spend it on herself AND you. She also works a little bit for some extra money, and she probably has more money than I do. So please do not worry about your mom and money. Do you think I would not take care of you no matter who you spent your time with? Everything I do and every dollar I make is so that you are able to have the things you need and want no matter who you're with. My parents had very little money when I was your age, and they never once made me feel bad for it. Even so, it affected me well into being an adult and I do not want that for you, so I will tell her to stop saying that to you." They looked at me and I took that as they understood a little of what I was saying. "I make enough money to support all six of us in two houses, so there's nothing to worry about. You let the adults handle adult things and you handle the kid things. Okay?" They stared at me with half-smiles and half-blank faces until I told them to go back to bed. Again, I was losing the war I had chosen not to fight and it showed at times like these. I was undoing only a small fraction of what they were hearing from Betty and Pat and I was left to wonder what other lies they had been told that would widen that emotional distance.

Over the next two weeks, an odd story unfolded. It's so odd that I am uncomfortable expecting whomever I may be telling it to to actually believe it — as it says in *Stop Walking On Eggshells*, "People who don't know a Borderline as well as you may not believe your account of their behavior." It started the night after the money talk when I got a text from Betty that said, "Noel called me, she wants to come home." I replied "At 8:30?" Betty said, "She's crying and she is afraid to be there." I went into Noel's room to see what was going on, and she was under her covers and pillow, crying, and the "kids' phone" was sitting on her night stand. I said, "Noel, please tell me why you are crying and why your mom said you want to go to her house." "I can't tell you!" she said as she sobbed. "Yes you can, Noel," I said. Almost yelling, she said, "No, I can't!" "Noel, please tell me what is going on. I can't help you if you don't tell me," I said. "I'm scared," she said as she started wailing. I asked, "Scared of what, Ms. Noel?" "I can't tell you!" she insisted. "Well, can you tell me why you want to go back to your mom's?" Noel had come out from under the comforter to look at me and managed to say though her crying, "I miss Mom." I said, "Noel! That is great! Why wouldn't you want to tell me that?" She said, "After Mom got nice, I got used to it." Trying to sound as cheery as possible, I said, "Good, that was my wish for you the morning after her and I got in the big argument!" She continued, "I used to like to be with the both of you, but...and Mom got all nice." I said, "That's fine Noel, it really is! Isn't that what I wanted for you?" "Yes," she said. "Good, then let's just go to sleep and you can be happy that both of us are nice, okay?" I said. She nodded her head and I scratched her back until she fell asleep. When I got up to leave, I saw a string of texts from Betty asking when Noel was going to be there and why I was ignoring her. As I walked down the hall to my room, I saw the last text that questioned if I had Noel's best interests in mind by making her stay at my house and I shut my bedroom door hard in complete frustration. In a feeling much like the night fourteen months before, I immediately regretted it, but it was too late — Noel started crying again when she heard it and I went back into her room and comforted her until she fell asleep.

It would be nine days later before another clue came into focus, when Stephen opened the front door for us to go to the bus stop one dark morning. He stood there for a minute while I put my shoes on and looked outside at the fresh snow. As I did, a thin layer of condensation was collecting on the clear glass storm door. Stephen then said, "Why does that say 'Warning?'" I glanced up at the door and said, "That's a UPS tag, Stephen, they'll see my signature and drop the box off today because I wasn't here to get it yesterday," referring to the piece of paper stuck to the small glass window to the side of the door frame. He said, "No, here. It says, 'Warning.'" I looked up and Stephen had a puzzled look on his face and he was clearly looking at the big glass door, not at the door tag stuck to the side widow. "I don't see it Stephen," I said. "Here, right here!" he said as he pointed up just above his head. I hunched over to his level, and turned and twisted my head. "I see it. But it's backwards," I said, trying to figure out why someone would use their finger to write on the glass and why it read "gninraw." We were already a bit rushed, so we headed out and I drove him to his preferred bus stop in front of Adam's and my parents' house. When I came back, the sun was starting to come up and I couldn't see it anymore, and I decided to postpone the detective work until the sun went down that night.

That afternoon, I went over to my parents and told them about the glass. My mom asked, "Have you cleaned that glass since you moved in?" I said, "Yes, right before Christmas, I cleaned both sides before I hung up the wreath between the front door and the storm door. Guess that means she did it within the month." My mom looked at me a bit skeptically, like she didn't want to believe Betty had done that and there must be some other explanation. My dad said, "Last week, I think it was the Thursday before you got them, Betty came up to me in our driveway with Noel and said, 'Did you hear that the police were called for a break-in in Broad Hill Courts?'" "Did you ask her what house it was?" I asked. My dad said, "No. I didn't really know what she was talking about because I thought we would have heard it from Jack and Sandie [Their good friends that live just 150 feet from my front yard] if it was true."

Periodically throughout the day, I would check the door, but it was very difficult to see any of the letters. During nightfall, I looked out the glass door, and it was still difficult to make out much of what had been smudged on the glass. I then turned on the porch light, crouched down to where Stephen's eyes were, and looked again. I saw it perfectly now. The "Warning" was on top, "I" was just below it, and "was here" was below that. The letters were big, about four inches tall, and I started to look to see if there was anything else that I could discern on the glass. I then saw four sets of swipes around, but not across the writing. They had three fingers in each and they resembled claw marks. The fingerprints where she stopped the swipe were clearly visible too. Still to this day, and in writing it now, I get a huge chill when I realize what those swipes represent — they are Betty's claw marks that she would leave across Stephen's, Noel's, and my faces — and my neck the night she was arrested. I couldn't believe what I was seeing, and I stared at the swipes in a complete trance as goosebumps came up all over me. I then called Christine's husband, Niles. He knows far more about photography than I do, and I asked him if he could come over that night to get some pictures of the glass door. He seemed to look forward to doing a little sleuthing when he said, "Sure!"

I went back to the words, trying to see it all at once. I opened and closed the door slowly to the get the porch light to shine on the glass just right. As I was barely moving the door, I noticed the letter "a" in "was" was backwards, so I took a closer look at the smudges. I then realized that the message was written from inside the house, but backwards, so that it could be read from the outside of the house as I walked up. I thought of the movie *The Shining*, where the little girls put "redrum" on the mirror and another enormous chill came over me as I became Jack Nicholson when he read the mirror.

When Niles came over, he looked at the glass door with the porch light shining on it, his face scrunching up, trying to see everything I saw. As I said before, there are only a few times that people have had the privilege of seeing the other side of Betty and when they do, they quickly realize the level of psychosis I have been dealing with. When Niles saw the warning, he studied it and thought of how exactly we would get pictures of the message. "Niles, did you see the claw marks too?" I asked. He said, "No, where?" "Here, look off to the side, near the frame." His mouth fell open as his eyes found the series of three finger swipes on the glass. He said, "That is oooone f---ed up bitch." After he looked at the swipes more closely, he said, "Look. They're all in threes. Isn't that how she always scratched and bruised the kids and you? Always with three fingers?" I said, "Yes, except for the night she got arrested, I had five scratches on my neck that night." I looked at Niles, and he looked at me, both of us realizing the flaw in that at the same time. Niles said, "How could it be five? Do you have the pictures your mom took the next morning?" I got out the pictures of my neck from the morning after Betty had been arrested and I looked at them for the first time since they had been taken. It jumped out at me right away, now that I knew to look for it; there were two scratches that almost completely overlapped. There were six scratches on my neck, not five — three from each swiping of her nails.

Niles and I spent the next two-and-a-half hours getting pictures of the door, taking our time to get dozens of pictures at different angles to the porch light, using a tripod and various lenses. We also got extremely close-up pictures with a special lens and the fingerprints are probably as clear as anyone in the FBI could hope to produce. I knew that I was going to ask the Mercury Township Police to take fingerprints off the glass to see if they could get a match. And I wanted them to know, in case anyone within the police department had thoughts to protect Betty, that my camera and lenses had the resolution and clarity to get the prints all by themselves. I was not going to let Betty get away with it if I had anything to say about it.

That night I laid in bed and thought about why Betty would risk getting seen or even caught when she had a restraining order that stated she would be arrested if she were to come onto my property. She also had fingerprints on file from her arrest and also with the military, so her smudges, which she had to know were going to leave fingerprints, struck me as exceptionally foolish. I knew she lived to intimidate me, but this seemed like an extremely uncalculated risk.

The next morning, I called the Mercury Township police and told them of my suspicions. After an hour, the officer had what he needed from the glass door and he told me the results would take a month. I gave the officer a set of the pictures Niles and I had taken to ensure they realized that I knew there were fingerprints easily visible and identifiable with a camera. I also had to do "elimination prints" at the police station. A different officer called me that evening, and in so many words, expressed some concern for my safety and offered my property to be put on the "extra patrol list," to which I wholeheartedly agreed.

I left for my weekly trip that day and I came back home the night before I got the kids again. I was shoveling my older neighbors' driveway when the gent next door to them asked me, "Did you get called by the police about your door?" I said, "Yes, they were here a couple of days ago taking prints." He said, "No, this was a couple of weeks ago. Your door had been open for a few days, so I called the police and they came out. They looked around and made sure no one was inside and took some pictures of quite a few footprints in the snow in your backyard that they thought were suspicious." I said, "This is news to me; I wasn't ever called. Though I just rent and maybe the police called the owners. What day was this?" He said, "Let me think. It was two weeks ago, so the seventh or eighth." "Well, I was on a trip then, so thank you very much for keeping an eye out for my house," I said. I went back to shoveling the snow and I used that time to try and put the story together. I know Betty, and most likely she had done something or left something behind that would definitively tell me she had been inside the house. I didn't see anything right away, but more evidence would come when the kids and I invited Lauren, her kids, and Abby over to make candy apples that evening. Stephen was acting like the tour guide to Lauren's kids, and he showed them the covered rear porch. He looked at me and said, "Dad, why is the fan on the porch on?" I went over to look, and when I saw the fan on the back porch spinning, I said, "I don't know. I don't think anyone has used this switch panel for the porch since we moved in a few months ago." I eliminated the eight kids at our house that night by asking them and each one said they hadn't touched that panel. That night, I also discovered three camera lenses were missing. With that, and the footprints in the snow and the porch fan being left on, I had the signs I'd known Betty just had to leave.

To round out the night, and story, I put Noel to bed very early because she was so emotional and had been crying at random times. We were having a lot of fun that night at our make-shift party, but nothing I did or said seemed to matter. I scratched her back in bed and asked her, "Noel, aren't you comfortable in my new house yet?" She didn't say anything, she just cried harder. Something was very wrong, and I then suspected she was afraid of being in my house. "Noel, did you know the police were here?" I asked. She paused and said, "Yeah." "Did you know when they were here, or why?" "A couple of weeks ago, someone broke into your house." I said, "Who told you that?" "Mom," she said. "Okay, when did she tell you?" I asked. "A couple of weeks ago, right after it happened," she said.

Because the incident was as hard to figure out as it probably was to read unfolding in bits and pieces and out of order, I stayed up that night for four hours literally putting the pieces of the puzzle together. I typed and printed what I knew, and when I'd come to know it, and when it actually happened and I cut those pieces of paper out and taped them to a piece of paper that had the two weeks dated across the top of the page.

─────Parents are in Florida─────

Noel is extremely upset when I get her, school counselor says she is "Concerned". Noel has had a rough week and seems extremely tired". Noel is very tired and "uncomfortable" and "scared" when we get home. Wakes up in the middle of the night and sleeps with me. First time she has done that in the 14 months of separation.

1/23

Neighbor calls the police because he has seen the main door open "for a couple of days."

I tell the kids my parent's are in Florida.

I go on a trip that morning. Kids get their stuff after school.

Most likely the night of the "Warning I was here" marks.

1/20

Noel is still "uncomfortable" and emotional.

Noel calls Betty that morning and says she wants to go to her house. First time that has happened in the 14 months of separation.

Noel again comes into my room around 12:30 and sleeps in my bed.

I go to the police to do the "elimination prints" and give Officer K. my pictures. Neighbor tells me of his call on 1/7. Stephen sees the back porch fan on. I realize someone has been in the house, and I look for missing camera equipment. I notice three lenses are missing. Noel is despondent in our home.

Stephen sees "Warning" on the door. I call the police, they dust for prints. Niles and I take pictures of the door at night.

Noel is upset and "scared" to be in our home, says she misses mom. Says she "wants Charlie... for comfort." Betty battles me in giving Charlie to me - happens at 5:15 pm, two hours later.

Mercury Police Officer K. and M. respond and M▬▬ respond to my call about the stolen lenses. I put my house on the "extra patrol" list. Tell Noel and she seems to like the idea.

Noel is still "uncomfortable", but is noticeably better than Friday.

2-Jan 3-Jan 4-Jan 5-Jan 6-Jan 7-Jan 8-Jan 9-Jan 10-Jan 11-Jan 12-Jan 13-Jan 14-Jan 15-Jan 16-Jan 17-Jan 18-Jan 19-Jan 20-Jan 21-Jan 22-Jan 23-Jan 24-Jan 25-Jan 26-Jan 27-Jan

What became clear was that Betty used the fact that the kids went into my house to get their things on January 6th in the custody transition. She either got the keypad number from them, or, more likely, relied on them not locking the door. They didn't know how to lock it after unlocking it, and for the first three months I lived there, my mom would go over in the evening and lock it for them after they left. But she and my dad had gone to Florida early the morning I'd left for work, which Betty knew about from talking to my mom. The opportunity had been made even more tempting because Stevie was home for a couple of weeks and he could drive her close to the house and be her lookout. And there it was all laid out on my dining room table. Betty had broken into my house, wanting to leave it looking broken into so that the police would be called, to scare Noel into thinking my house was not safe, so that Noel would be more likely to testify that she wanted to live with her mom at the upcoming custody hearings starting at the end of January. The only thing that didn't make sense — why she knowingly left her fingerprints on the glass — was explained the next morning when the Mercury Township Police advised me that Betty's arrest record had been expunged and her fingerprints were not accessible anymore. The expungement probably empowered Betty with a sense of being nearly uncatchable and that was probably just the impetus she needed.

I wouldn't hear back about the fingerprints from the glass door for two more weeks, but I didn't need any more proof that Betty had done it than when I went to get the kids' things from her the morning after she found out about the investigation through our custody court filing, due a week before the hearings were to start. She went out of her way to make sure I had everything — still to this day, the only time that has happened — and she spoke in a nice soft tone to me, very different from the annoyed, barbed tone I was so used to. She looked tired and said, "Okay, bye now," when I left.

An incident that showed just how determined Betty was to tell everyone that she was the primary parent — and probably trying to put the stigma of her arrest behind her and earn trust with that knowledge — came just a few days later. We had a meeting with two guidance counselors, two teachers, and the principal to have our yearly discussion regarding how Stephen was doing in the program he was in to guide him through school with his pronounced ADD. The principal opened the discussion with, "We have a lot to go over in a short amount of time, so let's get started." After a few minutes, Betty looked at her phone, lying on the table, and said, "Excuse me, I'm getting a call from the school and I'm the primary parent. I need to get this." I thought it was odd because when she went to pick up her phone, I looked at it and it was completely silent and the screen appeared to be black. One teacher preempted Betty and said, "Let me check to see if it's our school," and she got up and went to the main office. She came back and said, "Nope, not this school." After a few more minutes of discussion, Betty said, "They're calling me back, I need to answer this." This time, I got a very good look at her phone and it was completely inactive. She was gone for a few minutes and when she came back she exhaled and said, "Okay," like she was relieved. After the meeting, I called the elementary school that the other three kids attended and the lady who runs the front office answered. With all of the issues surrounding Betty and I, she was very in tune with our kids. I said, "Hi Holly, it's Rob Black. We got two phone calls just fifteen minutes ago from the school, so I just want to make sure everything is okay with my three kids." She said, "Hi Rob. Hold on please," and she checked with the kids' teachers. "Nope, no problems today, Rob. I don't know who may have called you, but it wasn't anyone from this school," she said. The fabricated calls were all a ruse to have a reason to tell the personnel from the middle school that she was the primary parent. It didn't matter how much of Stephen's educational plan we had to cover or how important the material was or even how valuable the teachers' time was, she was on a mission.

A COLLISION OF OPPOSING OBSESSIONS

After I got home from the trip in early January, I took the next three weeks off from work and I spent every minute possible at my dining room table preparing the presentation to show the judge the side of Betty only the kids and I had ever seen. Having the entries in my 80,000-word journal dated wasn't good enough, and with half of the entries repetitive and centered around not being able to talk to the kids or not being able to get their needed clothes, sports equipment, or Charlie, Jenna and I would need a way for the more significant incidents to stand out. I got my journals ready by color-coding, using boldface and all capital letters, and underlining it in accordance to a ten-character key I made — all of it so that Jenna and I could easily reference the most egregious incidents amongst the 450 in the heat of the moment. I finished my thirty-page "Good Stuff" journal and printed hundreds of pictures that showed the loving relationships the kids and I had before and after the separation. I also had pictures of the house I was renting and what I had done to it, such as paint and print a lot of pictures of the five of us to make it feel warm and inviting for them — I wanted to have something positive to show in court to contrast the inevitable plethora of negativity. My mom and Lauren came over on a few evenings and we discussed the possible issues and what was likely to be relevant during the hearings. On the back of all the pictures, they labeled and dated both the good and the bad, again for Jenna's easy reference. Nine stacks of pictures were on my dining room table the day before Jenna wanted my material to review it before turning in as potential exhibits. One each of the three different groups, the good, the bad, and the glass door — for Judge Wardi, Betty's lawyer, Alexis, and Jenna. As I got the journals printed, and readied all of the other items needed to take to Jenna, I stacked them on the table to reflect on all the work and wondered, "Will this be enough?" before I put it all in two big boxes. I asked Jenna to set aside most of a day to go through it. But when we did, I was a bit frustrated with how little she thought we were going to actually have time to admit as exhibits. I wouldn't realize how long it took until the hearings started, but getting just one picture submitted for evidence is quite the arduous task with the opposing lawyer likely to find anything and everything wrong or inaccurate about it to keep it from being admitted. But I accepted the small stack of pictures we whittled down to and hoped for the best.

Near the end of January, we started our custody hearings that were supposed to take three days, including one day for the three older kids to testify at Betty's request. Betty and her witnesses went first and I felt Jenna did a great job discrediting each of them. Sometimes I'm reminded that I don't know Betty as well as I like to think and I had assumed that with her being in the military, she wouldn't lie under oath. Much to my dismay, she took the oath and promptly started lying. From saying I never wanted anything to do with the kids and that she was the only caretaker in their lives to the lie that I'd bought a whip to lash our dog. As an example she used to bolster her stance that I didn't want any part of raising our kids, she testified that I couldn't have cared less that Christian had another ear tube surgery in March of 2013 and I didn't go because

I didn't want to. The real story was that his surgery was on a Thursday and I had seven clients getting cameras and lenses that day. I asked the clients if I could move them to Friday, but many said no. Betty and I agreed that I would just call her to talk to Christian several times before and after his surgery. My phone records prove that, and I have a video of Christian coming home where I ask him all about it and apologize for not being there, but I hadn't known Betty was going to fabricate this story. And though I had printed the phone records for that time, they weren't submitted as exhibits. I later refuted this story in my testimony, but it became just another "he said-she said" story without the video and phone records being allowed. I still have the printed phone records to one day show Christian that I didn't stop thinking about him the whole time he was away from me that day. This story was just one facet of what I called Betty's "Lie and catch me if you can" strategy in court. Like the last fifteen months, the facts and the truth were not to get in her way.

Betty's testimony about the night she got arrested was predictable in that she accused me of following and attacking her. But she made a mistake by saying that I'd wrestled her onto the bed and pinned her on top of the mattress and said that that is what caused her back to be bruised. Right after she said that, she looked at me, and I was laser focused on her eyes when I whispered to Jenna, "That's a lie," without taking my eyes off of hers. Betty could read my lips and she didn't say anything for an uncomfortably long time as she watched Jenna write in her notes. Betty's face then turned a very unusual color, gray. I was surprised to see her like that, with a distinct lack of confidence and obviously stressed, and I half expected her to pass out on the stand. I thought, "Good, you're lying, your whole case is based on lies and you now know you're going to get caught." As would become apparent later in the hearings, Betty must not have realized her blunder of saying she'd bruised her back on top of a mattress, because she told the story the same way months later at our financial hearings. Betty finished her rendition of that fateful night and got off the stand five minutes later, her face still gray.

One of the more surprising things to learn was that Jess, the lady who ran our kids' private preschool, was going to testify for Betty. Helena, who was one of my witnesses, had told me several days before that she wasn't surprised that Jess was testifying for Betty because, until recently, one of Helena's good friends worked for her at the school. The friend said that while we were married, Betty would drop off the kids and go into Jess's office with her and complain and cry about the kids and how "horrible" of a husband I was. Jess's blind allegiance to Betty was very disappointing because I'd been nothing but nice to her from the very first day — always offering to take pictures for her at special functions, as well as helping to set up before, and clean up after. Now Betty's boss when Betty worked two days a week at the preschool, Jess on the stand said that she was so afraid of me she'd had her husband wait in the parking lot in his car on the days she knew I was bringing or dropping off Christian. Throughout much of this book, my disappointment in human nature should stand out — 90% of the people I knew chose to believe Betty's description of me instead of what their own eyes and ears had told them over the years — never asking me for my side of the story. Jess is my standard for people who want to believe the worst in others as, for eight years, she chose to completely ignore my actions and her own eyes and only believe Betty's deceitful words.

One of the dynamics I noticed in the courtroom from the start of our hearings was that the judge's natural demeanor appeared to be unhappy and annoyed. In the days before our hearing, I read that he had been recently appointed to the position of Family Law Judge amid some controversy. Maybe he had greater aspirations than a family law judge, or the daily grind of going through contentious divorces wore him down, but whatever it was, his resentment showed. Interesting to me, he would repeatedly enter the courtroom looking like there were a dozen other things he would rather be doing, but then have a big smile for his tip staff and court recorder as they greeted him. They were younger, attractive women and I knew on the first of five days when he looked delighted to round them up and include them on a questionable issue, that he sought their opinions and approval. I realize seeking their opinion on certain matters is normal, but his complete change in demeanor when he addressed them was pronounced. I didn't think much of it at first as he was a slightly older judge (upper fifties) and he may have been just mentoring the two women in their mid-twenties.

Betty's mom was discredited in embarrassing fashion when she admitted to having to be physically restrained to keep her from attacking me and my dad during the Christmas show. But to her credit, she did admit fault when she said, "I don't know what came over me, I'm not like that!" At least the first part may have been true. She and Dale both testified that "Betty frequently had bruises on her arms!" When Pat said it, I thought, "Yes! God damn right she had a lot of bruises on her upper arms! That was from all the times I had to restrain her from hitting me!" Pat and Dale had just unknowingly supported what I'd known for fourteen years — that I was the one attacked during the time we dated and throughout our marriage. I saw Jenna sit up a bit, telling me she'd heard it too. The tipstaff woman looked at me after both Pat and Dale said that — probably trying to either figure out if I was capable of hurting

Betty, or trying to figure out why I'd bruised only Betty's arms. Despite the fact that she was all of approximately twenty-five, the tipstaff woman had probably heard about a lot of fights between couples during her time in the courtroom, and she probably wondered why I wasn't being accused of bruising Betty's face or body. After our eyes met for a second, I looked off to her side, but I could see her from my periphery. Her eyes stayed on me for about ten seconds with Pat's testimony and about five with Dale's before looking away as she probably assessed if I was capable of hurting Betty. I had a feeling that, as Judge Wardi mostly looked down to concentrate on listening, this young woman became his eyes of the courtroom. After all, she had nothing else to do after swearing witnesses in but watch everyone, gauging reactions, body language, and facial expressions.

Jess and another one of Betty's witnesses, who worked for the township, were discredited because they had to admit they had never seen me behave in any way other than calm and respectful. During the break, Jenna said to me, "I think everyone in that room was left to wonder why in the hell they were even there! What a waste of time just to hear, 'Uhhh, he never said or did anything that would cause me to be concerned and he always spoke to me in a kind and respectful manner,' after I asked them about their personal interactions with you."

After Betty's side of the testimonies finished on the second day, we broke for lunch. We had, in my opinion at least, just trounced Betty and her stance of being a victim. I also got a call from work as we walked out and I was told that they were offering me a training spot to upgrade to captain. To go from thinking to I may never fly commercially again to being entrusted with such a great responsibility in a relatively short time was an indescribable honor. I was on cloud nine and I thought I had life by the horns, but my testimony was coming up after the break and I knew any celebrations would be far too premature.

After I was sworn in, the first thing Jenna asked about was what happened the night Betty was arrested. I knew it was coming at some point in the day, but I'd thought it would be after a few warm up questions. Caught off guard, I took a few seconds and regrouped my thoughts and my mind to talk about something I wanted everyone in that room to believe beyond anything else (even more than the fact that I was a devoted father), and that was that I never once attacked Betty. To concentrate on remembering faded details and to keep it in chronological order, I told the story with my head down most of the time, though I would occasionally look up at Jenna. With the judge directly on my right, I couldn't see him without turning my head, but with the young tipstaff woman now behind and just off to Jenna's right side, relative to me, I couldn't help but notice some of her reactions as I tried to focus on that life-changing night. When I said, "And I sat up and hit Betty once — she says three times, I remember once, but it doesn't matter! She wouldn't stop hitting me!" she leaned forward a bit and she looked a little sad. Just seconds later, when I said that Julie had walked over to the spare room and the first thing Julie saw was me hitting Betty, she appeared to start putting her hand to her mouth, but stopped. What happened next that night and how Betty and I ended up in our master bathroom has always been the fuzziest part to me and I kept my head down and even closed my eyes for some of the time I talked about that. As I got to the part where Betty had again started to hit and slap me, I said, "I gave up trying to stop her and I dropped my hands and leaned into her and said, 'Go ahead, get it out! Show me how much you hate me! Go ahead, get it all out!' and I let her hit me for as long and hard as she wanted." I looked up at Jenna for the first time in nearly a minute and when I did, I saw the young woman's mouth quiver as she struggled to control her visceral reaction. I briefly stopped my testimony because tears had welled up in her eyes and I couldn't help but be mesmerized by her reaction for a second. I then looked over at the deputy, who was seated nearby, and he was leaned far forward with his mouth wide open and he just stared at me as if in a trance. During the next break, I started to process what their pronounced reactions could have meant, and it was hard not to think that they wouldn't have acted in that way if they felt I was lying.

During my testimony, we submitted pictures of some of the kids' bruises and scratches over the years and I couldn't hold myself together as they were passed around and copies landed on the small desk that was the stand. They'd hurt to see when I had cropped, printed, and organized them (even the lady at Costco had had tears in her eyes when she asked me about the nature of the pictures), but hashing out what my kids had been through in court and having their bruises and scratches analyzed by lawyers and judges was too much for me and Judge Wardi asked if I needed a minute. True to form when Betty is faced with the truth, she reacted to the pictures by smiling and looking out a window for a few seconds. When it came to the picture my mom had taken one summer day as the kids played on a water slide in her back yard, the one that showed the worst bruises and scratches on Stephen's face, I had printed two versions. One was the original picture which was zoomed out a ways and the other 5x7 had been cropped in. But there was something obviously different with the cropped picture; it had an unusual amount of what is called saturation, which is really just color contrast. When Alexis asked me about it, I immediately admitted that it looked "over processed." She asked me if I'd "altered or doctored the photo in any way," and I said, "No, but I don't know my complex editing program well; I only use it to brighten, darken, and sharpen my pictures, which it does without losing detail or adding artifacts. The cropped picture looks to have too much saturation; maybe the program has a default setting that it processes the pictures with, and the crop would be adding the saturation a second time from the original because the crop is the original edited a second time." Because RAW photos keep more detail when edited and professionals use it extensively, professional editing programs are made with editing "RAW" pictures in mind, not Jpeg. RAW is exactly that, it is not an acronym. RAW is the picture as seen by the camera's sensor, and without any of the eye-pleasing color, contrast, and saturation automatically added into Jpegs, they look flat. Having only one dose of color added, the original picture looked normal and accurate, and it was accepted into evidence. But the cropped picture, showing far more clearly the level of abuse Stephen suffered at Betty's hand because it had been zoomed in, was dismissed without any contention from me or Jenna. I had printed the pictures at the last second and I noticed the significantly more vibrant green color of the grass in the background, but skin tones, specifically Stephen's face and scratches, were only slightly more vibrant and I didn't think it would be an issue. After all, he had signs of abuse, Betty did it and that's all there was too it — so I thought. I was rushed, and I'd sent the huge stack of pictures to Jenna for her to prioritize the day before she needed them, leaving me without enough time to figure out why the cropped picture was more vibrant and print new ones.

I was disappointed that Judge Wardi wouldn't be able to see the abuse close up, but we had the original admitted and I didn't give the rejected picture any more thought as the afternoon wore on. During the next break, Jenna stopped me right outside the door and she looked at me like something was very wrong. With Betty and her whole family just twenty feet down the hall, she somehow loudly whispered, "Rob! What the hell was going on with that cropped picture?" "What do you mean?" I asked. "That picture is going to cost us big time! Alexis thinks you doctored it, the judge thinks you doctored it. Hell, I'm not even sure you didn't doctor it!" she said. I said, "But it's not doctored, you can't even do that kind of stuff with Lightroom, that's Photoshop, which I don't have or even know the first thing about! I can get a friend of mine, who used to do media authentication for the military, to verify its authenticity." Jenna said, "Rob, we don't have the time left for that! Besides, the judge isn't going to take the time to hear this case like it's a murder trial! That was very, very damaging to us!" Her anger turned to disappointment and her shoulders slumped and her hands, full of papers and notes, dropped. Using the pictures that showed the marks Betty had left on the kids was something I'd pressed Jenna hard on from our very first discussion because she didn't want to use them, saying they weren't a good idea and they could even backfire. "Was this Jenna's excuse if the ruling didn't go our way, or was her fear legitimate? What was the big deal? The judge admitted the original into evidence and he saw that Betty physically abused the kids, how could I be more wrong than her?!" I wondered. I stopped wondering, and like only I can do, tried to turn a negative into a positive when I said to Jenna, "I'm kind of glad it happened because, I have to admit, I wasn't sure if you really cared about this case or not, but clearly you do." Jenna didn't say a word, she just looked at me, still wondering how we, or she, would recover from what she thought looked like a blatant attempt to deceive the judge.

When we went back in for the rest of my testimony, Jenna asked me some questions that contradicted Betty's claims that I didn't care for the kids and that I abused her and the afternoon went on somewhat predictably, refuting Betty's testimony. One noteworthy point out of the afternoon was when Alexis questioned me on taking the kids to Denver and Pikes Peak without telling Betty until we got there. Remembering the time in Disney World when she'd called the police on me, I'd feared that if I told Betty I was taking them, she would say no out of spite, or even call Southern or the TSA at the Pittsburgh airport and tell them that the kids weren't allowed to go. She could tell them it was a court mandate or whatever else she wanted to make up and, not having the time to refute her claim, the only peak we would reach would be that of my frustration. Regardless of my reasons, Judge Wardi seemed less than pleased and, admittedly it is something I should have found a better way to handle.

On the third day, my character witnesses were heard from. The first was Helena, and I thought she would be somewhat reserved in what she said about Betty, who was sitting just twelve feet from her, but she was very blunt when she told of the times she'd seen Betty acting abusively towards the kids. Though she did get to talk about the time Betty left Christian at home and in bed alone when he was just fourteen months old, and how the kids would frequently be locked out of the house all day and evening and be forced to go to her house for something to drink and use the bathroom, she didn't get to say everything she wanted. I didn't know why at the time, but when Helena walked down off the stand, she walked right past me with a sad and concerned face. I just assumed it was because she felt bad that I was fighting for time with my kids when the issue of primary custody should have been a no-brainer.

But, when I talked to her that evening, she said that there must have been a disconnect between Jenna and her assistant, whose job it was to get everything Helena had to say out of her and give it to Jenna to word in the form of a question. "I didn't know what happened. The next thing I knew, I was being dismissed when I had so much more to say! Annie even thinks she saw the kids made to sleep out in the van overnight, but I don't think I can speak for her. Is it too late to bring her in to testify?" Helena said. I said, "I'm so sorry Helena, I feel we really blew it somehow and I should have been more on top of it, making sure Jenna had all the questions lined up that I needed to be asked. And it's too late for Annie; our list of witnesses were due in last week. Plus, she's only fourteen and I just don't want her having to do that at such a young age. Betty can be extremely aggressive as you know, and the thought of Annie possibly having to face her in the cul-de-sac is just too much for me to be comfortable with." Helena insisted that neither she nor Annie minded, but I did and the fact that Annie sounded like she wasn't certain the kids were made to sleep out in the van sealed it for me. Also, I thought with all the evidence piled up against Betty in the form of her arrest and especially the pictures of the kids' marks, we just didn't need to aggravate the judge by pleading for a late witness to say a lot of the same things Helena already had.

One of my witnesses, who had been the one that witnessed Pat have her grandson jump up and down on my cameras, testified via phone conference and it was over as fast as it took him to describe the incident. It almost didn't matter — Pat had already lost all credibility and this seemed unusable in our effort to prove Betty wasn't a fit mother. It felt like we were just gloating and I didn't want Jenna and I to seem vindictive to the judge and Jenna agreed and kept his testimony to just a minute.

My mom's testimony closely resembled the tight-rope she felt she had been walking on for ten years. She thought Betty was suffering from depression, but she was compelled by the need to be as much a part of her grandkids' lives as possible. Jenna had been telling us from the beginning that, despite Betty's history with the kids, the Allegheny County Family Court was extremely unlikely to give any mother less than fifty percent custody. That, and the complications my erratic work schedule brought, might mean I could get even less than half the time with the kids. My mom hedged her bets on the stand and only said that she felt Betty was easily overwhelmed with the kids and she was concerned about all of the marks she used to see on them. But for the rest of her testimony, she only spoke about what a great father I was, not why Betty shouldn't be allowed around the kids unsupervised. When Alexis was finishing her questions for my mom, she asked, "Do you own a rifle?" Confused, my mom looked at her and said "What?" Alexis repeated the question and my mom looked around the room like she couldn't believe the question. "No. No, we have never owned a gun." I was almost as surprised as she was, and knowing Betty's devious mind, I became concerned. But my parents had never owned a gun and I had to rely on that fact. Alexis asked, "Never?" Mom said, "Never."

My dad's motivations, and therefore testimony, weren't much different than my mom's. He didn't want to rehash all the things Betty had done to the kids and he chose to stay on more benign issues. Jenna did ask him, "Is Betty timely with getting the boys to their activities?" My dad said, "No. Christian just had hockey tryouts last week and he missed over half of it. I called and texted her a couple of times that morning to see if I could help or take him and she didn't respond until he was supposed to be on the ice at noon, saying, 'I'm on my way.' He had to get all suited up and it was half over by the time he got out there. That is pretty normal for her." The truth is my parents can't think of one time she has had either boy to any activity on time, but we agreed there would be no burning of bridges between my parents and Betty. The accounts of Betty telling our four kids, "Your grandfather is a f---ing idiot!" and the like would be set aside to keep a mostly open channel of communication with Betty in exchange for more of a role in their grandkids' lives — or so we all thought.

My sister didn't testify because Jenna and I thought her testimony would be redundant after my parents', to which she agreed. But Sandi ended up regretting it when she heard about Jess being so afraid of me that her husband waited in the parking lot, saying, "I never once saw one mark on her — ever! Even when she wore bathing suits and tank tops! While you had scratches all over you! She mauled you over and over!" Like my parents, Sandi also very much wants to be in my kids' lives, but she differs from them in that she isn't afraid of Betty's inevitable backlash and she would have unabashedly described what it was like having her in the family for the last ten years. I also quickly regretted not having her speak her mind on the stand.

My last witness was my parents' next door neighbor, Christine. Christine is petite but mighty, being the quintessential lady most of the time, and a determined force to be reckoned with when she wants to be — making her, in conjunction with her observations, an obvious choice as a witness. When she got on the stand, she'd talked about how concerned she'd been for the kids when she would see their frequent marks throughout the years. When she did, Betty smiled and turned her chair to the side and looked away. Again, smiling and quickly gauging other people's responses before looking away is Betty's normal reaction if she is caught, and it wasn't lost on me here. Christine also said that she witnessed, through her dining room window, Betty's drive-by with the four cousins hanging out the van and enticing my kids to stay with her when I had come home from training in Dallas. She said, "Just to ruin Rob's custody time by upsetting the kids. I watched him take Stephen to the side of the house after the cousin drive-by, and very patiently and calmly try to calm him down and reel him back in. I don't know of any other parent who would have been that patient with Stephen that day, he was extremely upset!" She also testified that I was a "very hands-on dad" and I could often be seen playing with my kids outside. But the one story she told that I had never heard from her left me wondering how many other untold stories of Betty's carelessness were out there, never to be heard. Christine said, "Three years ago, Betty came to me and said, 'Do you believe someone had the nerve to call the police on me?!' When I asked her why, she said, 'Because I left Christian and Noel out in the van when I went into the store and when I walked back out, some lady told me the kids weren't safe in the hot van! I told her, "I can see them from the front of the store and I cracked a window," but she didn't care!' So I asked Betty when this was and she said, 'Earlier today,' which would have been in June three years ago." Jenna asked, "So it would have been hot?" "Yes," Christine said. Jenna then asked Christine, "Did anything else strike you as odd about this?" Christine said, "Well, she was outraged that that lady thought she had the right to call the police. Betty had parked in the street at the front of the mall, where the van could easily have been hit by another car on top of the fact it was very hot outside. Also, the checkout counter in the store she said she was shopping in is in the back, not the front. So Betty couldn't have seen the kids from there. This isn't the first or last time Betty kept the kids in the hot van when they slept, she would do it when she brought the kids to Bernice's too." Trying to take in that Betty had left the kids in the hot van during the summer, and recalling the times I'd heard about other kids that had been left in the car and their fate, I became grateful that they had survived the age when they couldn't have let themselves out. I didn't care if Christine's testimony had bolstered our case or not, it pained me to think of how vulnerable Noel and Christian were, just five and three years old at the time. I said a little silent prayer, thanking God for putting that unknown woman there that day, and for any other time I didn't know about when he was watching my kids when no one else was. As Christine told this story, I noticed the tipstaff woman look at Betty with disbelief and disgust. Again, her stare told me she was trying to picture what she was hearing, and over the course of this day, I caught her unapproving gaze directed at Betty quite a few times.

All of the testimony dragged on so long that we only had time for the adults testimony, not that of the three older kids. Betty had asked that they be allowed to testify, and though Judge Wardi discouraged her, he allowed them as long as there was no negative talk and questions from the lawyers. Judge Wardi and the lawyers discussed when they could get the kids in, and it would be two months before they could find a date and a courtroom that was open. When we left, Jenna and I stood just outside the courtroom as Betty went up to her family. Pat had been crying and she sat there looking dejected. I thought, "I don't know if you're crying over how you were disgraced, or if you realize your daughter is the monster I told you she was years ago — but good, you finally realize what she has done to me and the kids and it's about time that the courts know what you and your family stand for. They will now be raised completely opposite of that horrible dysfunction."

The next day at Noel's gym meet, Pat couldn't hide her sadness and she cried for most of the time I saw her. Betty sat there next to her, looking straight ahead with a blank expression for most of the meet as she occasionally talked to Bree, the mom of Noel's best friend, sitting to her other side. Most likely Betty was dismayed that I'd turned the hearing around to reflect the real story, undoing her fifteen-month obsession to manipulate and distort the truth to win custody and take the kids from me. I didn't know it at the time — I just thought Betty was pensive from how prepared I was with the pictures and how blunt and revealing our neighbor's testimony was — but in hindsight, the two months between the adults' testimony and that of the three older kids told me she was plotting that day at Noel's meet. Plotting how to turn it all back around in one fell swoop with the kids' testimony.

The next Monday, just three days after our hearing, Lauren called me and said another teacher, whom she had known for years, had approached her to warn her about me. Her peer had met Betty and Pat at a support group for people who had lost a loved one to suicide and they'd apparently exchanged phone numbers at a meeting. Pat and Betty then made multiple attempts to "desperately and relentlessly" contact Lauren's co-worker, who was now gravely concerned for Lauren's safety around me, saying, "He is extremely dangerous to be around," and I was "a player" who would shamelessly cheat on her over and over. The co-worker pleaded with Lauren for half an hour while she tried to defend me and her choice of a boyfriend. Lauren tried to get her to understand she knew me well and that Betty and her mom were flat-out obsessed with destroying my name to anyone who would listen, especially to someone who knew of or had a great relationship with my four kids. After all, our kids liked and had a lot of fun with Lauren and her daughters, and they wanted to spend time with me in part because of Lauren. Lauren refused to talk to Betty throughout our relationship, and this was Betty's way to try and get to her anyway — to get Lauren to leave me out of fear of the unknown. After the half hour of often tense exchanges, Lauren's peer reluctantly agreed that she was "a good judge of character" and she would try to give Lauren the benefit of the doubt despite the violence and deception she had heard I would soon carry out. Two weeks later, when Betty realized that Lauren had not been deterred, Lauren had three scratches on the hood of her ten-day old car. They were spaced like someone had put nails or something sharp between their fingers and ran them along the paint.

The next weekend was a big gym meet for the girls, but they were so late that Julie missed warm ups and Noel, whose meet was on Sunday, walked in as the National Anthem was playing. The coaches approached me, wondering where they were both days and voiced concern that this was becoming too common, but I had no answers I could comfortably tell the coaches. The girls looked so tired, Julie especially, that I didn't post some of their pictures that I took of them standing with their team-mates on my website. The kids loathed my early and rigid bedtimes and, knowing this, long nights spent watching movies and doing whatever else they wanted appeared to be one of Betty's key ingredients to winning over the kids and I was utterly powerless to stop it.

When I went to get the kids a week after the hearings, I waited inside my car across the street for ten minutes. After I called the house phone and Betty's cell and then texted Betty asking her when the kids were going to come out, all unanswered, Betty and Noel came out and stood on the porch. I got out and stood by my door and I could see

Noel was crying. Betty smirked and said, "The kids don't want to go with you. Stephen and Noel said you are mean and they are scared of you." Surprised, I said "What?" Betty became irritated and raised her voice, "The kids! They. Are. Afraid. Of you! They. Do. Not. Want. To. Go!" I pleaded, "Betty, please don't do this." She stood there with an ear-to-ear grin as Noel cried into Betty's stomach, like going with me was an indescribable tortuous Hell. "Miss Noel, what's wrong?" I asked as gently as I could. She didn't say anything or even move. Betty then reached behind Noel and opened the glass storm door and yelled inside, "Stephen, your dad isn't leaving." Stephen appeared and stood behind the door with a scowl and his arms firmly crossed. He wouldn't open the door more than a couple of inches, to provide him that extra protection that I guess 100 feet didn't afford him. Obviously upset and annoyed, he yelled, "I don't have to go with you, and you can't make me go!" "Stephen, please. I'm begging you, please don't do this, big boy." He then repeated himself over and over like a broken record to convince me he wasn't budging. I stood there with my head straight down, wondering what I had done to deserve this treatment from Betty and the kids. I also wondered if Helena happened to be listening, as she had told me she could sometimes hear Betty yell during previous exchanges. I just stood there waiting for Stephen to wear himself out. When he finally stopped, I said, "Stephen, it is court-ordered that I get this time with you. And I miss you so much, I don't even care about a court-order right now, I just want to see you and spend some time with you." He didn't say anything, he just closed the door and stood behind the glass with his arms still folded and he now looked downright angry. I could see a hint of sadness too though — probably torn that he couldn't negotiate better and instead had to resort to saying hurtful things to try to get what he wanted.

After all was said and done, I spent forty-five minutes across the cul-de-sac pleading with Stephen and Noel. Julie and Christian came out when they realized Stephen and Noel had finally caved and we left in a heap of hurt feelings and broken hearts. It's only two minutes to my house and, except for Noel's continued sobbing, we spent the first in total silence. I looked back at them, hoping, because Betty was now out of sight and they didn't have to carry out her plan of despising or acting afraid of me, that they would start to warm up to the thought of spending time together. The older three looked at me like they just couldn't believe I had ripped them from their mom and I lost my composure and yelled, "Don't you EVER do that to me again, do you hear me?! That was flat-out humiliating!" Stephen's face turned to regret, Julie started crying, and Noel cried even harder. Christian, as usual, just sat there a bit embarrassed by his siblings' behavior, knowing he hadn't done anything wrong.

When we got home, I told Stephen and Noel to go to bed, as they looked extremely tired. I also wanted to use the time to calm down and figure out why they didn't want anything to do with me. Lauren came over and got Noel settled down in bed, and I took Julie to gymnastics practice. I said to her on the drive, "What happened to the times we used to have? We used to bake brownies and play together. Heck, I even tried to learn back handsprings just so we could have fun together. Look, I'm happy your mom is good to you now, but why does that also mean I have to give up being your father? Is it one or the other — you're not allowed to love both of us?" Julie just looked at me with a grimace, hoping I would stop asking questions she didn't want to answer. When we got to the gym, I realized she was a few years too young for those pressing questions and I said, "I'm sorry, I just want you to know how much I love you and the way you, Stephen, and Noel treated me today really hurts."

When I got home, I went to check if Stephen was sleeping but he was still awake. I said, "Stephen, if you can't sleep, you're welcome to go get up." He sat up on the side of the bed and looked at me with the saddest face. He started crying and tried to say, "I'm sorry." I said, "I'm sorry too, but I don't know what I'm doing wrong." Stephen said, "I don't know who to believe!" When I asked him what he meant, he said, "When Mom and you got in the big fight!" I asked Stephen, "Who is telling you anything about that night?! Why do you have to try to figure out who is right and wrong when you shouldn't know much about that horrible night in the first place?" He said, "Grammy and all the cousins are saying you beat-up Mom!" I said, "No Stephen, that is not true and I will tell you and Noel exactly what happened if you want me to." He said, "Yes, I do." I heard Noel talking to Lauren and I asked her to postpone baking the brownies they had started to come into Stephen's room.

I asked Noel, "Do you want to hear what really happened the night of the big fight? I can leave the really bad stuff out, but I want you to hear what really happened, not what your mom and grammy want you to believe." She said, "I don't want to hear about you and Mom hitting each other." I was a bit relieved to hear she only wanted to hear the beginning of that night — because Stephen was three years older, and because he wanted to believe his father wasn't an abusive person, I could be a bit more descriptive to just him. I told them what happened up to the point where Betty started hitting me and told Noel to go back to Lauren to keep baking. She ran as fast as she could back upstairs.

When I was done explaining that night to Stephen, I asked him, "Do you think I should have done anything differently?" He said, "You shouldn't have hit Mom back." I said, "I respect that Stephen, and I couldn't be happier that you believe you should never hit a girl. And there are times that I agree with you; I should not have hit her back that night." He looked up at me like he was open to more of what I could say. "Look Stephen, I always thought until the end of time one of my most important teachings to you and Christian would be you never, ever, EVER hit a girl or a woman, but…I don't know how to say this. How about this, if someone comes up to you on the playground and hits you, what do you do?" "I walk away," Stephen said. "Great, I thought you would say that. What if they do it again for the rest of the week?" Stephen hesitated, but said, "I walk away." "Okay. How about if they hit you for twenty days or a hundred days?" Stephen repeated his answer, but now a little unsure of himself. "Well Stephen, I'm not sure if it is right or wrong to keep walking away. The message you're telling this person is, 'It's okay to hit me,' and at some point, I think you need to stand up for yourself and hit back. We are constantly teaching those around us what we will and will not accept and my message to your mom that night was I will not take it anymore. I'm not raising you to be somebody's punching bag, as long as you recognize what is likely a one-time altercation and what will likely continue until you show them you won't take it anymore." He asked, "What do you mean?" I said, "Everyone has their number Stephen. How many times do you just walk away when someone hits you? Mine was about thirty. That's probably the number of times your mom hit me before that night before I hit her back. And the night of the big fight, I pleaded with her to stop. I yelled at her to stop and I grabbed her arms to make her stop. I respect your stance that you would just keep walking away time after time, but you and I are different in that regard.

I eventually hit back." Stephen cracked a smile at me and he gave me a hug. I thought, "New ground, I should have told him what really happened that night a long time ago."

One afternoon, I got a call from the Mercury Township Police and I was informed that they got the fingerprints off of the glass door, but they couldn't match them with Betty's. Thinking the police were protecting Betty and they didn't even try to match the prints, I said, "I can see them as plain as day with the pictures I took, how can she get away with this?" The officer said, "Well, we can't match them up with Betty's prints because she recently had her arrest record expunged." "So that means it never happened?" I asked in complete frustration. "It happened, but her name and prints have been removed from the file." "What if she killed someone or committed some other really horrible crime?! I can't imagine that you wouldn't then try to match her prints, which I know have to be on file somewhere!" "This crime isn't to that level Mr. Black, and I'm sorry, but there isn't anything more I can do." Exasperated, I said, "Okay, may I please talk to the Chief of Police?" "Sure, let me put you through," and I left a message with the Chief. When he called me back, I conveyed my concern that Betty might be getting protection through an officer that had had an apparent affair with her. "I will look into that with Officer Rose, but that surprises me. I'm not saying I don't believe you, I just didn't think he was like that." "I'm not trying to get him in trouble with you or his wife sir, I just don't want him protecting someone, whom he has an allegiance with, that is also trying to ruin my life," I said. "I understand, but when it comes down to it, all she was doing was trespassing. The officer was correct in telling you there is nothing we can do about the prints — at this level," he said. I couldn't believe my ears; how Betty got away with staging the break-in and didn't get caught with her fingerprints all over the glass still, to this day, absolutely boggles my mind.

One of things I did for Stephen over the last four years was I took him to get allergy injections. But taking Stephen into a doctor's office every week or two didn't fit Betty's agenda of her being the only caretaker — and part of Betty's strategy to alienate the kids from me was to appear "to be the only caretaker." (This quote is from when we first separated, and she also had this exact phrase in several emails from that time.) The *Eggshells* book confirms this is a trait amongst Borderlines: "Another role common among people with BPD is that of helper or caretaker. This more positive role may help provide them with an identity, heighten feelings of control, and lessen feelings of emptiness." Right before I got the kids at the next custody exchange, I texted Betty, "Did Stephen get an injection this week?" She replied, "I told you a few weeks ago I talked to Anna at the office and she said now would be a good time to stop and see how he does going onto (sic) the spring. So no I was not taking him." This is not what Anna, who is the only one Stephen trusts to give him the shots, said to Betty. Anna said to me, "Betty is twisting my words! I didn't tell her she should stop bringing him. She was really pressuring me. I said if she wanted to stop at any point in the year, this would be the time, but I told her that would be a very bad idea and that his allergies would probably come back with a vengeance this spring. I did NOT encourage her to quit bringing Stephen!" Over the next month, while I was in Dallas, Betty refused to take Stephen to get an injection. By the time I came home in late March, and he was far behind in the dosing schedule and he was having significant reactions to the spring allergies.

To further the point of how far Betty would go to appear to be the only caretaker, ever since we separated Betty had been "updating" Childrens Hospital's contact records by removing me from their reminder list of upcoming appointments. Frustrated that I was missing Christian's appointments, I would have to call periodically to get put back on. When I did, I asked the person taking the call to make my contact permanent or not let Betty remove me, but I got the same response each time: "We can't stop a parent from updating a child's records."

At the next custody exchange, Lauren came with me to pick up the kids from Betty's house. Again, we parked across the cul-de-sac and waited for the kids to come out. Julie came out of the house first and said hi to us and went back inside to get the others. Betty then came out and stood on the sidewalk and stared at us, indicating there was going to be trouble. When Julie came back out, Betty yelled, "Everything you said in court was a lie!" It was loud enough that I thought she meant for Helena, who was inside her house, to hear it. I said, "No, I didn't say one thing that wasn't true." Then there was a minute of relative calm as we waited for the other kids. When Noel came outside, Betty, having her audience of our kids and Lauren, again yelled, "And you had two affairs!" I said to Lauren through the open car window, "I am so sorry you have to be part of this." I turned to Betty and said, "So?" I'd hoped she would come to the realization that our marriage, and hence her control over me, was over — in essence, she couldn't control me now if she couldn't control me then. Julie and Noel were trying to give Betty a hug goodbye, but she denied them until she'd yelled I had affairs two more times.

Just an hour after I left with the kids, Betty texted me and accused me of using Julie as a messenger that morning, even though Betty was the one who'd made Julie call me about where I would be picking the kids up. When I replied, "You're the one that had Julie call me — from your phone!" Betty texted, "Can I talk to the kids or not?" I replied, "You just had them, is it an emergency?" Betty replied, "Are they allowed to call or not?" I texted, "Can you please answer my question?" She responded, "Just to be clear, you're disallowing contact with my kids. Noted." I didn't know it at the time, but Betty most likely used this exchange to convince the kids that I wasn't allowing them to talk to her and that I was using Julie as a messenger — two big no-no's in custody battles.

I suspected that the kids were afraid to show any affection towards me and Noel made it very clear after her gym meet that weekend. When I said, "Great job, Miss Noel!" and reached out for a hug, she turned and looked around. When she finally saw Betty in a crowded corner of the gym with her back to us as she talked to Bree, Noel gave me a very quick hug and appeared to try to keep her eyes on her mom. Afterwards, she immediately turned back around to see if her mom had seen her give me a hug. I didn't want Betty to change the way I acted with my kids, but I had to temper that once unwavering stance with how uncomfortable my kids had become interacting with me in her presence. Noel's emotional state has always been more fragile than the others, even more so after the staged break-in at my house, and I knew that it was best to start limiting my affections towards her anytime her mom was around. In a classic case of being put in a no-win situation by Betty, she was likely to use any perceived distance I had with our kids to show others that I didn't care about them.

I left for captain training in Dallas towards the end of February. The training prevented me from coming home and I had to rely on the phone to talk to the kids. But I did not get to talk to all four kids during one call in the twenty-five days. Reminiscent of ten months prior, I had to repeatedly ask to talk to the kids and call Betty's cell and house just to talk to one or two kids once or twice during the week. At one point in my training, I thought I was coming home for a weekend. Betty was about to go on a trip that weekend with Bob, and Peg was going to be watching the kids. On the phone, I told Peg that I might come home that night and I wanted to know where she would be with the kids. I could hear her trying to muffle the phone, and I heard her and Betty have a quick exchange, but I couldn't make out what was said. When Peg came back, she said, "I'm not telling you." "They are my kids, you can't tell me where you're taking them?" I asked. Peg said, "No." Always the victim, Betty emailed her lawyer right away and said, "He was very angry and Peg is afraid he will make a scene." I had never made a scene before, and Peg and I, up to this point anyway, had maintained some mutual respect. After I showed how much I wanted to be a part of the kids' lives in court, that was now gone in the womens' all-out war to get the kids to believe that they didn't need me, and, by greatly limiting our conversations, to forget about me. I felt I was becoming just a memory to my kids, fading in the distance, and Betty and Pat's stance, even more than before, had become, "You just send us your money and go away, we'll raise the kids."

I was to come home from training in mid-March and my mom and I were going to drive Julie to her gymnastics State meet five hours away that next weekend. Lauren wanted to go with us, but when I told Julie, her eyes got big and she grimaced as she shook her head no. "Why not?" I asked. Julie just looked at me in silence, still wearing the pained face. "Do you not want Ms. Lauren around your mom?" I asked. Julie nodded her head as her eyes got big again. I couldn't help but wonder, if Julie is afraid of or embarrassed by her mom's volatility, why does she empathize with her 100%?

Betty called my mom and asked her, "What hotel are you staying in for Julie's State meet?" My mom, still desperately trying to keep an amicable relationship with Betty so she could see the kids as much as possible, told her, "The Hilton Reading." I said to my mom, "That was not a good idea, I don't want to be anywhere near her." I called the hotel right away and, when asked, the lady who answered said, "Someone called here this afternoon and asked if someone with the last name of Black had reserved a room in the last couple of days. I told her, 'I am not allowed to give out that information.' She then asked if her husband, Mr. Black, had made a reservation, and I told her again, 'I'm not allowed to give out that information.' She got flustered and hung up." I said, "Can you please ensure that it is annotated on our reservation that no one, under any circumstances whatsoever, is to know my mom's room number? There is a good chance that if the person that called you finds out what room we're in there will have to be police intervention. I'm Bernice's son; she may go as far as to have a male call and impersonate me to get it, so I need this to be absolutely water-tight." She said, "Yes sir. We will ensure that no one, except Ms. Black [my mom], knows the room number."

At the State meet the next morning, we were the first ones into the gym as it opened. I settled on the far right side of the school's bleachers for the best vantage point for my cameras as I looked at the apparatuses already set up on the double-basketball-court-sized floor. The bleachers were almost as wide as the floor and they were also high. Ample seating certainly had to be one of the reasons the meet was being held there, so when Betty, Pat, Dale, and Bob walked in and sat right behind me, my mom and I looked at each other, wide-eyed, for a second. Betty was just off to the side of me, with her right foot just a few inches from my back side. Pat was right beside her and Dale and Bob were right behind them. I looked back at them as Pat and Betty chit-chatted like everything was perfectly normal. I then looked around the rest of gym and there were large areas of open seating that were still available, and I knew their close proximity was only meant to intimidate me. So I grabbed the cameras I wanted for Julie's first event, the uneven bars, and I moved to the complete opposite side of the gymnasium, over a hundred feet away. As I set my tripod back up, Betty came over with Pat and she stood just a foot away, directly in front of my camera's lens. Betty's taunting wasn't new to me, but this was the first time she had been so blatant when Bob was around. My first thought was, "There Bob, who do you believe attacked who now?!" and I stood up and looked down the bleachers to see if he was looking over. He was talking to Dale and looking out into the gym, so I just had to assume he'd watched her walk over there and stand in front of my camera — after all, if he believed Betty's assertion that I beat her up and that I was still a threat to do it again, he would feel obligated to watch out for her if she'd ventured away from him with me in the vicinity. I picked up my tripod from the first row of seats and moved three rows back to get the lens above Betty's back and I set it up again. When I sat down, Betty looked back at me and she moved up two rows to stand right in front of me again. When she sat down, she would have sat right on my feet, which were on the row in front of me, had I not moved them. Pat sat right in front of Betty, and I again looked over at Bob, who now appeared to be texting or playing a game on his phone. I finally thought of the obvious, put a wide lens on my camera, and took a few pictures of Betty and Pat, and also of all the empty seating, to possibly use against Betty in court. I had to go to the bathroom after Julie was done on the uneven bars and when I got back, I noticed my handbag was now right next to Betty and the compartments were unzipped, which I took another picture of. Betty and Pat then left and the gent sitting behind me, who earlier had asked about my cameras, asked me, "I assume you know that woman that was sitting in front of you?" I said "Uhhh, yes, that's my ex-wife. Why?" He said, "She took an awfully big interest in what was in your bag." "Did she take anything?" I asked. He said, "No, but she may have had she not looked back at me and seen me looking at her with her hand literally inside your bag." I had my computer and three lenses in there, and I made sure everything was accounted for. My notes from that day say it best, "Betty's message to me: You cannot escape me, I WILL get to you. And I will take everything I want, to include your freedom and dignity."

As I write with the perspective of passed time, I have to relive the stories in my journal and Betty's psychosis is much clearer than when all of these first took place. When something happens, I'm mired in the thick of trying to figure out who has heard the worst lies you can hear (and how likely they are to believe them), or if I'll ever see Charlie again, or how I'll get the nice things my parents and I have bought for the kids that Betty won't let the kids take out of her house, or how many times I'm going to ask her if I can talk to the kids, or how she is going to claim I beat her up for years and then turn around and taunt me, or what lies the kids are hearing about me — when these things happen, I get mad or frustrated, but I settle down over the next couple of hours. One of the occasional frustrations was that Betty would put me on speakerphone when it was loud where the kids were and she either created even more noise in the background or she could listen to my conversation with them. Betty knew that the last thing the kids wanted to do was interrupt their time playing or eating to talk on the phone and that their distracted or annoyed one-word answers frustrated me, but I could at least talk (or just say "Hi, I love you. Bye.") to all four kids during their get-togethers and parties. One such time came near the end of March, when Betty and some of her family took the kids out to eat for Christian's birthday. With how clear the background noise was, I figured I was on speakerphone as I tried to talk to him. I said, "Happy birthday, Christian!" He said, "Thank you." I said, "You were born at 5:15 and thirty seconds seven years ago, Sweet Pea!" That's when Betty grabbed the phone out of Christian's hand and loudly said into it, "That's when I! I pushed him out!" Caught off guard, I said "What?" Betty then said, "I'm the only parent, I'm the only one that has given birth to them!" and she handed the phone back to Christian. When I relayed this to my mom, she said, "At one of the gym meets, Betty told me, with a couple of the other moms there too, that she was the parent because she is the only one that has given birth to them, but I didn't really think she meant she was the only parent." These are the things that are so bizarre that they actually help me deal with the frustration of her suspected Borderline Personality Disorder and psychological projection. After all, would a person who is perfectly sane say these things? Dr. Darnall backs this up when he writes the obsessed alienator says to themselves, "That's my baby! He has no right to have him or her."

I still felt some sense to protect Betty's reputation, despite the constant hell she put me through. When she wouldn't give me the girls' leotards at the custody exchanges, I would balk at asking the other moms if one of my girls could wear one their daughter had grown out of. Julie was the smallest on the team, so it was only a matter of making the calls and then washing and returning the borrowed leos the older gymnasts had grown out of, but I was embarrassed that I couldn't get Betty to give them to me (I also didn't like having to borrow something). One of the moms said, "Why don't you just buy a couple of extra leos and leave them down there?" I said, "I thought of that, but I'm pretty sure Betty would eventually find out about them from the girls and they would be gone too." In addition to causing me a lot of frustration, one of my theories was that by denying me the kids' equipment on Friday at the exchanges, Betty could run whatever it was they were missing to them right before they needed it on the weekend, looking like she was coming to their rescue. Missing sports equipment is an exchange staple of Betty's and this is just another one of a myriad of similar journal entries that has repeated over and over since the first weekend we separated.

By now, it should be painfully clear that in the time before the kids' testimonies, Betty turned up the parental alienation to a level I could never have foreseen. I couldn't keep up with her persistence, and I couldn't undo the damage to my relationship with the kids nearly fast enough. The phone had been Betty's most used weapon since the beginning, and as we drew closer to them testifying in the middle of April, she had seemingly endless ways of ensuring I couldn't talk to any of them on her time, regardless of how early in the day or evening I started pleading with her via text or called her cell phone and house. If I called, or texted asking for the kids to call me, she would call me back and only let it ring for a split second — too short to be able to get to my phone. Then, after I called back and said I didn't get to talk to the kids, she would say she didn't have time for my games of hanging up on her. On my custody time, she created (and still regularly does) the illusion that I didn't let the kids call her by frequently texting me, "Are any of the kids allowed to call?" She called my phone when I had the kids and hung up after a ring or two, then took a screen shot of her outgoing call to tell the kids the next time she had them that she'd tried to call but I hadn't answered or I'd rejected it.

In the middle of April, we had three hours in court one day to give Betty a chance to explain or defend herself from my testimony two months before. Almost line-for-line, Alexis asked Betty about my testimony, and my witnesses', and Betty denied it or accused me of doing what she'd actually done. I wanted to jump up and yell, "Everything she's saying is a lie!" — instead, I had to sit there and painfully listen to it.

I also found out that Betty had gone as far as to send an email asking to be able to talk to the kids on her birthday a couple of days beforehand, but she had sent it to an address she knew I never checked. I'd created the address for her and I, right before we were married, for websites we felt we couldn't trust or we wouldn't use more than once. The address is far more closely associated with me because it was simply my email address plus the number 1, and now she used it to claim that I wouldn't let her talk to the kids on her birthday. When I checked the address that afternoon, there were several other emails from her going back to the month we'd separated. The emails discussed subjects as important as where I needed to pick up the kids and what I needed to know about their medical conditions or homework and school projects — proof of what I had long suspected, that Betty places a higher priority on spiting me or making me look bad than the welfare of our children. I thought of a comment I'd said to Ken just a month into our split, "Her hate for me exceeds the love of our children," that had probably sounded a bit overstated at the time. How could I foresee that she would use any and every means to play the victim and make me look like an inattentive and careless father who dissuaded our kids from having a relationship with their mother? I couldn't, and the kids' false perception that I wasn't allowing them to talk to her, including on her birthday just a week before their testimony, ended up being very damaging to my case.

Another issue that shot holes in my case was the rifle my mom had been asked about during the adult hearings. Betty brought in pictures that she'd had Stephen take just a few days before, of a rifle under my bed at my parents' house. The pictures were a complete surprise as I had never seen the gun, and yet there it was lying under my bed. Any of the kids could have found it during a sleepover or when just playing around and of course that is what Alexis said. It wasn't locked up and everyone in the courtroom was left to wonder how easily one of the kids could have found it and shot it and... draw your own conclusions.

That evening, I went over to my parents' to discuss the gun and we found it still under my bed. I had bought the smallest, least powerful gun possible, a .22, when I lived with my parents, but with my mom's firm stance on no guns allowed in the house, it stayed in my storage shed five miles away. A .22 is puny by gun standards, so there was no mistaking the gun I'd purchased for this ratty, yet very big rifle that I'd never seen before. As much as I tried to convince my parents, I'm not sure they believed me. It wasn't until we told Christine next door about the gun that she shed some light on a possible clue. My parents had been in Florida for a week in late March, two weeks before the hearings in April. During the time my parents were away, Christine said she saw a black car parked in the driveway. It wasn't there long, and the next thing she knew, it was gone. We knew the only thing keeping Betty out of my parents' house was the verbal warning from the police, something she would demonstrate over and over meant nothing to her. And she knew all of our hiding spots for the key. We're still not certain, to this day, how that rifle that no one in my family had ever seen got there, but it's hard not to think Betty planted it. What we did know was that Betty had told Stephen to take pictures of it and she brought the pictures into court, giving Jenna and I no time to refute the origin of the rifle with serial numbers or other checks.

Another reason we were scheduled to be in court for the entire morning was to present evidence of my testimony that Betty had blocked my phone from being able to call or text her cell and home. We had video of the recordings and the automated messages that had Verizon's code for blocked calls, but Verizon would not send a representative into court to verify the code. And despite the video I had taken with a separate camera, and Sophia as a witness to the video and blocked calls, Alexis asserted that because I "doctored" the pictures of the kids' scratches and bruises, I could also doctor the video. It was a very frustrating day for Jenna and I, and it ended with Judge Wardi looking skeptically at Jenna and saying he would "Just give it the weight it deserves" — which I took to mean he didn't know who to believe. His level of annoyance to my claim that Betty blocked my calls to the kids that morning stayed consistent with his feelings on the issue from the January hearings — he didn't care. I still felt good about our case overall though and over the course of the morning, the tipstaff woman — who was my barometer for how things were really going — appeared to still be on my side. I didn't want to overthink it, but I saw her looking at Betty a couple of times like she was still trying to figure out who Betty really was.

As the judge walked out of the room, I looked at my phone and saw that Holly from the elementary school called me and left a voicemail, saying that Christian had fallen during recess and he had a couple of scrapes on his face. When I told Betty of the call, she became agitated and said, "Well they had to call me too! I'm the primary parent!" She picked up her phone and said, "They didn't call me, and I'm the primary parent! Why wouldn't they call the primary parent? They know I'm the primary parent and they didn't call me!" Jenna and I finished gathering our papers and walked out and, after I rewound Betty's remarks and counted the four times Betty had said "Primary parent," it dawned on me. I thought, "Betty thinks that if she is the primary parent, it will completely exonerate her from the arrest. We never took our fight over who was right or wrong to court, so this was her way of being able to tell everyone that the courts found her innocent that night eighteen months ago — and consequently, I would be guilty. It would also have the effect of getting the kids to believe that she was a good mother to them all along — the past abuses either weren't really that bad or they were just very vivid bad dreams, never really happening."

The last thing Judge Wardi said to us that day was he questioned why the three older kids were going to testify and he asked that "we" should reconsider. So that afternoon, I sent Betty an email saying that I did not think the kids should be made to testify, and that, "It wasn't in their best interest to miss school and go through the stress and uncertainty of testifying before a judge." Betty responded, "I think that going back to a 50/50 arrangement is not in the best interest of anyone, and they will be testifying."

On the morning the kids testified, the two lawyers went into Judge Wardi's chambers and my parents and I, and Betty and her mom, waited in the chairs in the hall. Pat held Christian almost the entire time so he couldn't talk to us very easily, and Betty made it a point to put a book she was reading, *How To Disarm The Narcissist*, just inches from my face. She said, "Ha!" as she did, as if she had found the secret to happiness. When the lawyers came out, Jenna told me that Judge Wardi had repeated that he didn't want anything negative brought up. I was comfortable with this as I didn't want the kids being forced to relive bad memories, but if the kids had been made to answer questions about what their mom had done to them, it would have helped convey to Judge Wardi that Betty should not be allowed around the kids unsupervised.

The kids went in and talked to the judge one-by-one and they came out looking relieved that it was over. After Stephen was done, I chatted with him, but the girls were noticeably distant with me, staying at Betty's side and impatiently waiting to go home with her (her custody time had started while we were there). When Jenna and Alexis came out of Judge Wardi's chambers, I knew the second I saw them fifty feet away that it wasn't good. Alexis was laughing and smiling as she said hi to Betty and her parents and Jenna looked worried as she quietly walked up to my parents and me. By this time, Betty's dad and sister were also there and it was a cacophony of laughter and loud, interrupted talking amongst them as I tried to say bye to the kids. The boys came up to me and gave me smiles and hugs, but the girls couldn't leave fast enough. I looked at Jenna, hoping against all odds that she had a favorable explanation. She said, "Here, sit down." I said, "This can't be good, how bad is it?" "Rob, your kids don't want to be with you and it was very damaging to our case," Jenna said. My heart sank, and though I was focused on what she was saying, I couldn't hold back what became a steady stream of tears. "Julie said that you don't let any of them talk to Betty and you use her as a messenger," she said. "What? It is just the opposite Jenna, and I have an entire journal nearly an inch thick that proves it!" I said. Jenna looked at me, knowing there was nothing we could do to undo the damage, and said, "Noel said you threw her against a wall and dragged her down the stairs and you slam doors." "What?! There was one time I had her against the wall, but I certainly didn't 'throw' her! She was smashing an umbrella in her room and I heard Betty trying to get her to stop when Betty said, 'Rob, you had better get Noel, I can't deal with her anymore,' and I knew that meant Betty was close to saying or doing something really bad, so I went upstairs and saw Betty standing in the master bedroom door waiting for me to see how I would handle it. I went into the girls' room and said, 'Noel! Stop smashing the umbrella!' and she laughed at me. Just a few days before that, she had taken a big stick and purposely tried to hit Christian in the eye and she hit him just below it and it left a bruise, so I had had it with her and her destruction and so had Betty. I felt Betty was going to kill her if I didn't do something more drastic, so when Noel laughed at me, I picked her up and put her against the wall to make her look at me eye-to-eye, but I didn't 'throw' her and I wasn't abusive! I made her continue to look at me for a few seconds to realize how serious I was, and she started crying. Then, knowing she was starting to get the message, I said, 'Noel! When mom or I tell you to stop doing something, you stop! Do you hear me?!' and I put her down and made her throw away the umbrella so she knew she had ruined it," I said. "Well, Noel is afraid of you and that was clear when she spoke to the judge," Jenna said. "What happened to no negative talk?! And how could there be any negative talk without saying the hundreds of things she had done to them over the years?!" I said as I felt it all caving in. Jenna said, "The girls just said that, he didn't ask.

It was very clear Julie and Noel want to be with their mom and Judge Wardi isn't going to go against them." "What about Stephen?" I asked. "He was fine, he really loves you — loves both of you — but he wants to be with his cousins more than anything else and he isn't allowed to be with them on your time and that was also clear. He didn't damage our case as much as just reinforce that the kids want to be with Betty and they don't see their mother as abusive." I couldn't believe it, and I sat in the chair staring at the ground in a complete daze. "Jenna, how in the hell could we lose this?! This was a classic case of good versus evil — and evil won! Evil fricking won! Betty proved that all you have to do is lie, and I didn't tell one lie the entire six days! How can that be?! How can I respect the oath I took and Betty won because she lied?!" In the first time I had ever heard Jenna raise her voice, she laughed and said, "Rob! They EXPECT you to lie!" like I was a naive fool for not knowing. "Well, what if you don't?!" I said. Jenna didn't have an answer. "This whole f---ing court system sucks! There are posters all over the walls of this huge f---ing building that say 'We're here for the kids' and 'We want what's best for the kids' and 'Kids this and kids that' but this God damned court couldn't care less about what's right for the kids! It's like a fast food restaurant! Get in, and get the f--- out — we don't have time for you and we don't care! There are hundreds more after you and your time is over!" I looked at Jenna and she appeared to still be process- ing the inevitable ruling that would certainly turn out be a humiliating defeat for her. If my worst fears were true, I'd lost to someone with an undiagnosed mental illness, and Jenna, the consummate, soft-spoken lady at all times in the courtroom, had also lost to an immoral, far less educated, blurting, and otherwise inferior adversary in what should have been an easy case. As luck would have it, the tipstaff girl walked by as Jenna and I sat there in those moments of silence. She looked at me quickly before looking ahead again, but she saw me differently now, like she was disappointed in me.

On the drive home, I thought about how Betty had pulled off a once unthinkable switch: "If I were the judge, and he had to listen to Jenna and I talk about how Betty had repeatedly abused the kids, and I, somewhat successfully, was accused of 'doctoring the pictures' that we submitted as proof, and the kids came in and told him that they wanted to be with their mom and that I was actually the abuser, why would he believe me over the kids? Because I had f---ing pictures and I didn't 'doctor' them and I can prove it by having them analyzed! Damn, there isn't time devoted to custody hearings like it's a murder trial, turning over every stone." I pictured the fifteen minutes from when the lawyers came out of the judge's chambers to when I saw the tipstaff woman leaving — she and Judge Wardi discussing what an unbelievable con-artist they thought I was.

I tried to think of all the good things I had and the bigger problems one could be facing, but it didn't erase the fact that this was one of the worst days of my life. I pulled into a gas station to just think and I looked at my phone, hoping there was a message that had some kind of positive news, or at least something to distract me for a few seconds. I saw two emails for both Christian and Stephen, reminding parents of baseball games that both of them had that evening. Hoping to watch, I texted Betty and asked if she was going to take them to their games. Seconds later, I got a text that said, "Message to 7245555555 failed: Denied." I couldn't believe she would block my phone again, just days after being accused of that very thing in court and thirty minutes after the kids' testimony, so I tried to send the same text again and I got the same reply. I then called Betty's cell and got the exact same automated recording I'd heard in early 2014 when Betty had blocked my phone for that week. I called her house and my number was blocked from that line too. I knew Betty was very unlikely to take either of the boys to their games, so though it may seem contradictory and a bit concerning, I called scheduling and asked if they had any trips that needed covered. There was one — it flew from Chicago to Boston that evening and I took it. I knew that operating a commercial plane validated my want to feel trustworthy when friends, the courts, and even my own kids didn't think that of me anymore and it was the perfect escape.

When I got to the Pittsburgh airport to catch the next flight to Chicago, I had a police officer listen to the Verizon recording when I tried calling Betty's cell and home numbers again, in case I ever needed verification. I thanked her and took her name and I contacted Jenna with the information. When I got to Chicago, I had over an hour before I had to be at the plane, so I journaled and occasionally tried calling and texting Betty's phones again, but they were still blocked.

I got busy dealing with weather and the need to add fuel to go around a line of thunderstorms near Lake Erie on our way to Boston and those same thunderstorms were going to force us to fly a little further south than normal on this route to avoid them. When we flew around the weather, we were just north of Pittsburgh and I looked down from 41,000 feet and gazed at how peaceful the town we lived in appeared to be. The shimmering orange of the street lights was the only perceivable movement and I felt gratefully insulated and disconnected from my ground-based problems. I was free, going 600 miles per hour, amongst people that trusted, respected, and worked with me — none of that available where I looked eight miles below me.

Lauren had been an invaluable resource in keeping my sanity over the last five months, and I'd leaned on her countless times while we were together. Though we were just friends now, she was always there for me and I called her several times to help me process what appeared to be the final nail in the coffin in my effort to keep Betty's influence on how our kids were raised to a minimum — at least until she showed she could parent with their best interests in mind and not hers. She kept telling me, "Rob, it's going to be okay. Your kids are going to come around." But I knew that if they did, it would be years later. The one thing I wanted most, their childhood, would be gone.

The next several weeks would be filled with countless rejected phone calls to the kids on her custody time, missed games and practices for the boys, and extreme difficulty getting Charlie, the kids' things, homework, and unfinished school projects that were due on my time. I could not, no matter how hard I tried, get special shirts for field trips or themed school days on my time — anything the kids needed for school, she would take to them herself, even if it meant they would get it late. If she felt any obligation to at least pretend to cooperate before the hearings, that was all gone now.

So many police reports have been filed between Betty and I, that, just like many other aspects of our contentious divorce, it's not possible to include them all and keep this book to a reasonable length. But there was one in early May of this year, 2015, that stands out because an officer from the Mercury Township Police strongly questioned why I didn't get another PFA against Betty. I had driven the kids to a soccer field just down the road from my house, and Betty and Bob stopped when they were driving by. Bob parked next to my two-week-old van and Betty got out and stood near it as she started talking to the kids. I asked her why she didn't give me the soccer and hockey equipment for Christian's and Noel's games they had the next day when I had gone to her house to get their things earlier that afternoon. Betty said to the kids, "If he won't do the right thing and come and get your stuff, I will bring it to you." Our conversation degraded further when I said, "You need to do the right thing and just give me the equipment when I come to get it." Betty yelled, "I don't have to give you everything the second you want it!" Bob gave me the finger but said to Betty, "Let's just go get it." They left and brought the equipment to me minutes later and Bob set the equipment near the front of my van. When the kids and I went to leave, I noticed three scratches along the passenger side, very similar to the ones on Lauren's car. I called the police to document it and Officer Henche, who had been a responding officer to a couple of the other calls, showed up to take this report. After I told her what had happened, she looked at me with an air of skepticism and asked, "Why haven't you gotten a PFA on her?" "My lawyer thinks that it will damage my case to get custody of the kids. I'll look uncooperative and it'll look like I'm doing it just to make her look bad," I said. Officer Henche, who is quiet and subdued, just looked at me as if she was wondering if that could possibly be true. It was hard not to think that her skepticism was because she thought I could be staging all of these problems to compile police reports to use against Betty later, or to play the victim myself. For a year and a half, Betty had been trying to get me arrested and to convince the police department that it was really she who was the victim, and I was very sensitive to any indication that the Mercury Police were starting to side with Betty.

THE EVERY-OTHER-WEEKEND DAD

Five weeks after the day the kids testified, I was just watching the clouds go by underneath us at cruise altitude when I thought to check my phone. I saw that an email from Jenna, titled "Custody Result," had come through earlier in the day. My heart instantly started pounding and I stared at it, wondering what was awaiting me if I opened the email. When I finally rounded up enough courage to open it, I read, "The result is not favorable to us." I dropped my phone and said, "Oh my God." The other pilot, wondering if I had just discovered something terribly wrong with our plane, looked at me and said, "What?!" "I just got confirmation of what I already knew, that my ex won our custody dispute," I said matter-of factly, trying to alleviate his fears that something was wrong with the plane. I could only stand to skim Jenna's summary in bits and pieces but it was painfully clear that I was to have the kids Friday afternoon till Tuesday mornings every other week — I was now an every-other-weekend dad. My thoughts raced: "How could I possibly be reading what was in front of me? The kids used to run from her to me, and now they run from me to her — all because she has erased the past from their minds and replaced it with what she wants them to believe! She has molded her own version of history! Of reality! She doesn't really want the kids, she just doesn't want me to have them! She thinks, 'How dare I be their father. You don't deserve to be their father, you just have to pay for everything and go the hell away!' She's also going to wave this flipping ruling in front of everyone's face and tell them, 'See, even the courts believe he beat me and the kids, and they will only let him have the kids every other weekend because of it!' All I want in life is to be an integral part of my kids' childhood, and she has taken that from me out of spite and hatred. She knows that's all I've ever wanted and she is hitting me where it hurts — and it does hurt."

As I started to come to grips with the ruling, my thoughts changed to, "Her ability to lie and manipulate was just better than my mom's and my ability to explain them," and "It looked to be an impossible dream at the time, but this is what you told the kids you wanted for them the morning after she was arrested, and you got what you asked for. Ha, be careful what you wish for, you just may get it." As we descended, I tried to see some positives in the outcome and thought that I could use the time away from the kids to work overtime. I owed a staggering amount of money to three credit cards that were maxed out or even over the limit, including the one my dad had lent me to furnish my rental house. Between my parents and the credit cards, I owed over one year's worth of income and I was nowhere near being able to buy a house like I had wanted to by that summer. Plus, the kids and I would make the best of our three-and-a-half days at a time together, and now that Betty had fooled the court and gotten what she wanted, she would probably just leave me alone and I could live in peace. But then the reality smacked me in the face again, and the realization that I had lost the battle to win custody of the kids stung me right in the heart like a thousand needles. I briefly thought about sending a message to our schedulers when we were descending, to tell them I would need to be replaced when I landed, but my emotions came down as our altitude did. Even more than the time just five weeks before, I needed to know I was worth something to someone and my job provided that.

It only took till the next day to get the first clue that Betty had no intention of moving on and stopping the spite after the ruling. When I texted her to have the kids call me, she did, twenty minutes later, but there was so much background noise I could hardly hear anything and Noel couldn't hear me. I spoke loudly into the phone, "Ms. Noel, what are you doing?" "We're getting ready to sing happy birthday to Anthony [one of their cousins] now," she said, sounding a bit sad. "Right now?" I asked. And then, what sounded like Betty's entire family started singing. "Noel, go ahead and sing to Anthony, I don't want you to miss it," I said. But Noel didn't seem to hear me and she didn't sing happy birthday to her cousin. At the end, I heard Betty laughing loudly as if she was near the phone. "Noel, why didn't you sing?" I asked. "I don't know," she said as she became more sad and frustrated. Noel felt left out from the singing, which she probably resented me for, and Betty got to reinforce to her that I was just a nuisance. It was an ideal scenario for Betty, as she also got to rub in my face that the kids and their cousins were inseparable. The biggest disappointment to me was that Betty could have easily had the kids call me before or after the singing, but she'd rather use the kids to spite me. From this, I knew she wasn't anywhere near putting down the guns and she was now going to rub in the custody ruling every chance she could get — even if it meant she had to create chances.

Attached to the email I got from Jenna, where she gave me a very brief summary of our new custody order, was the full-blown report from Judge Wardi. It was too painful to open the report, but my mom had read it during the two days since I had forwarded it to her. She called me and said, "You're not going to believe this, but Judge Wardi didn't even mention Dad or I, Christine, or Helena in his report! He didn't say anything about our testimony — nothing. It's as if he knew all along how he was going to rule and nothing was going to change his mind." I have never known my mother to lie about anything, but I just couldn't believe what she was saying about Judge Wardi's report. After all, wouldn't he be obligated to put all of the relevant testimony in his comprehensive report, not just what Betty and her family had said? Apparently not, because in what has to be the most bizarre part of our whole divorce — disconnected brake lines, staged break-ins, and attempted hit-and-runs included — he did not.

While I am one to naturally assume positive intent with everyone, it's hard not to think Judge Wardi didn't have an agenda. Just as egregious of an omission as leaving out all of my neighbors' testimony, he also left out any mention of the pictures showing the kids' bruises and scratches on their faces. Judge Wardi also blamed me for not being able to take the kids to a class on divorce twenty-five miles away from where I lived when many of the roads in Pittsburgh were closed due to snow and ice that morning, despite the fact that I took them to the next available class. I provided proof of the weather with multiple copies of weather reports and news video, but that didn't seem to have mattered. Even more disappointingly, he twisted my words, and the context in which I said them, to fit his apparent agenda in the report. In one instance, he completely fabricated what I'd said to bolster his point. How I would love to sit down with him and match up his "findings" with the audio recordings from the testimony. The disparity between what he wrote and what was really said and what really happened in the courtroom was so great at times that it was as if his report was from a different case. It's hard not to think Judge Wardi had some external motivation — I can think of nothing else that makes sense of it all.

This book is partially about people who do not put forth the courage, effort, and time to learn both sides to a story, but Judge Wardi was paid well and entrusted to do just that. His failure highlights the biggest flaw in divorce litigation that our state, and maybe our country, faces — one person, and only one person, has the ultimate power to decide what is likely the biggest decision that will ever be made for our children — who will raise them. This decides everything they become for the rest of their lives. Their values, their traits, their customs and courtesies, their drive, their level of responsibility, their care (or lack thereof) for others, who they respect and why, who they look up to and why, who they want to be and why. When we think of what we have become and who we are, most people retrace their steps back to their upbringing and how their parents guided them.

Though few, there are judges who are biased and careless — they pre-judge this immensely important decision and they have the ability to justify it if they want. If the judge is corrupt or incompetent, there is very little recourse. In Pennsylvania at least, the Family Law judges run almost autonomously. When I asked Jenna about an appeal, she said, "The Pennsylvania Supreme Court is likely to give the case back to him and tell him just to review it. They could make suggestions, but regardless, it will stay his case." Translation, I would just annoy and aggravate Judge Wardi by, in essence, saying to him, "I didn't like your first answer; give me a different one." I hope I sound disgruntled, disappointed, and let down, because I am.

The ruling left my parents, my sister, and me stunned for weeks — it's still hard to believe eighteen months later — but just a week after it was handed down, my mom ran into one of the neighbors from our first house. She called me on the drive home and said, "Rob, I just saw Michele and I told her that Judge Wardi ruled in Betty's favor. She couldn't believe that she has primary custody of the kids! She said Bonnie [another neighbor] thought Betty was a terrible mom because she had seen Betty force the kids to sleep in the hot van in your driveway! Michele also said, 'Betty has always seemed disconnected from the world' and she waved her hand in front of her face as if there was nothing there." Frustrated, but not a bit surprised at hearing another neighbor's observations, I said, "Between our two houses, how many neighbors have said the kids were forced to stay or even sleep in the van? Four? Christ, how many times could she have killed them? Then there's Gretta [another neighbor] who said to me, 'We always knew when Betty was home, we just had to listen for the screaming.' The few who know the real Betty describe her as a 'terrible' or 'horrible' mother — the courts have been an impossible failure and let-down." "Yet she's the one with the kids! She wouldn't dare do that now and risk getting caught and you getting the kids half the time!" my mom said. I said, "Well, at least we know they're safe now, not with a mom that's scratching them across the eyes, leaving welts on their faces, punching them in the stomach, throwing them down a flight of fifteen stairs, screaming at them and calling them little effing bitches, and leaving them to sleep in a hot car all the time. She's now so obsessed with taking the kids away from me with all of this competitive parenting and niceness, she'll never hurt them again. Ironically, it's like I have to give up their youth to ensure their safety; she wouldn't dare hurt or be anything but a good mom now – my price of getting the kids a normal mom, if you can call her that, is my fatherhood."

That night, I laid in bed thinking about everything my parents and sister and I had to endure over the last twenty months. It was hard not to think almost everything we valued had been taken from us and I thought of the movie *The Grinch,* and the Whos down in Whoville he stole from at will. Like the Whos, we would go on making the best of the situation and trying to see all the positives in our lives in the face of someone who had proven to be unstoppable — we could not let Betty's spite, anger, and manipulations ruin our lives and dictate who we became. But unlike the Whos, we would not find a solution — this was an everyday and life-long vengeance.

The next day, I drove to see Dr. Douglas Darnall, the author of the definitive book on parental alienation, *Divorce Casualties.* A couple of months before, I'd started reading his book about kids who are alienated from one or both parents by the other parent and I primarily wanted to see if he could offer any more insight into my situation that may not have been covered in his book. During the last several months, I had been compiling and organizing my notes that were in my phone and computer in preparation to start writing this book, and I knew I wanted a book to help other people who may be divorcing someone with suspected Borderline Personality Disorder who would also psychologically project and gaslight — I can't be the only person in the country who is divorcing someone with all or part of that toxic mixture. In addition to his expert opinion on my situation, his book is so accurate in so many parts with regards to what my kids and I were going through that I knew I was going to need his permission to quote him here.

Dr. Darnall and I talked for more than two hours about the various considerations to writing a book of this nature, and he shed even more light on my situation. He agreed with me that Betty was "certainly" an obsessed alienator, based on what little I had time to describe, and that the only way obsessed alienators let up just a little is "to make their behavior public, because they want everyone to side with them and against the evil parent — you. But obsessed parental alienators never fully quit — they are not capable." On the long drive home, I couldn't get my mind past two other topics we'd discussed. The first was Dr. Darnall early on in our session said, "So many times people, like you, who are divorcing an obsessed alienator, are so flustered and emotional at the custody hearings, that the judges think they're unstable. The judge doesn't know that you've been put through hell and it costs you credibility and often custody time." I couldn't help but wonder if that applied to our case, as I had been quite emotional when I spoke of the kids' marks.

The second topic, which we spent considerable time on, was Dr. Darnall's belief that the book had to have an uplifting ending. When he said, "Your story has a lot of unresolved conflict and heartache; how is it going to have a positive ending?" I said, "As of now, barring a miracle, it isn't." Dr. Darnall and I went round and round about the possibilities for a pleasant ending to the book, but I had just lost the battle to convince the courts that Betty was not fit to be unsupervised around our children. Writing a book about how to document, journal, and defend yourself against your Borderline ex in court had become an unfixable paradox that brought questions that had no answers. How could I write a book with an ending that gave any hope while sticking to absolute truths? If I couldn't finish the book, how could I start it? I couldn't.

I'm not sure why Betty's next attempt to paint me as a terrible father bothered me so much, as it wasn't that high up on the scale compared to others. Regardless, the day after I met Dr. Darnall, Betty came to pick up the kids and Julie came back inside my house to tell me her mom wanted to switch upcoming weekends with me. I told Julie that the next Sunday was Father's Day and I would have them anyway, so a switch really wouldn't be a switch, it would be taking a day from me. And if I did switch, I wouldn't see them for nearly a month after Father's Day as her mom would also be taking them on her vacation over my one up-coming weekend. Julie started to cry and said, "But Mom said there's a party at Grammy's that weekend and all of our cousins will be there!" I said, "I'm sorry," but Julie ran out of the house and straight into Betty's arms, who had been standing on the neighborhood sidewalk. Julie was crying and wailing and they hugged each other for so long I doubt any-one would believe it — over five minutes. Was the inordinate amount of time to show my neighbors, one of whom did immediately question me after Betty left, that I must be so horrible, Betty has to comfort the kids when they leave? Was it to reinforce to Julie that I wasn't a coop-erative parent? It's as if Betty was saying to Julie, "I'm so sorry he's your father." The next time I had the kids, I took an unprecedented amount of Reward Board money off of Julie to let her know I was not going to stand for her playing the victim too, and for also not taking the time to at least think about my very valid reasons for not trading weekends. I had been put in another no-win situation and I wanted her to understand my reasoning. Perhaps that's what irked me so much about this incident; I saw Julie's woe-is-me, victim mentality growing and she was turning into her malevolent mother.

Winning the custody verdict seemed to have empowered Betty with a sense of invincibility because she clearly upped the taunting a level or two afterwards. In fact, her mom and dad must have felt the same because they joined in with Betty. They appeared to view the custody exchanges as ripe opportunities to be as difficult as possible by yelling, questioning, and taunting me. After enduring their tirades, my parents and I then had to go to different places to pick up different things for the kids on their tight schedules. Again, I can't include them all, so here are my notes from just the next two exchanges.

I went to the Betty's parents' house to get the kids, and while waiting for the last one (Julie) to come outside of the house, Betty and her parents started questioning me about why I was going to take Julie to Dr. Crocenni for wheezing when she exerted herself at gymnastics practice, which her coach said I should have checked (Betty had declined to take Julie when advised the week before). Pat said in a loud, angry tone, "She doesn't have asthma, she's only nervous when she's around CERTAIN people!" implying that I made Julie nervous to the point it caused her to wheeze. To my surprise, Dale uncharacteristically joined in, saying, "If she wasn't so afraid of you, she wouldn't have a problem. What makes you think you're the expert? You're not the expert." I said, "I'm taking her to the doctors, they're the experts on these matters, not me." Pat then said, "Why are you going to see her (Dr. Crocenni), she just wants to take your money!" I said, "I've known Terry since seventh grade, I don't think she's out to take my money." Betty shot back, "Ha! You sat next to her for six years of school and she doesn't even remember you! You were a nobody then, and you're a nobody now!" and she started laughing. I said, "I don't think that's true, and she is very nice and I trust her with our kids." The taunting continued from Pat and Betty about taking Julie to Terry, but I was too concerned with rounding up the kids and getting out of there ASAP to listen anymore. Meanwhile, Bob just stood there watching it all happen. I occasionally looked at him wondering if he was ever going to step in and try to tell Betty that it was time to knock it off. He was a West Point grad and I held him to a higher standard than to just passively watch his girlfriend belittle me over and over in front of our four kids, but sure enough, he just stood there content to look at his phone as if this was all normal. Betty then said, "Stephen doesn't have his baseball shoes here." I said, "Why not? He has a game tomorrow and yesterday I asked you not to make me run all over to get their things like the last four exchanges. And his cleats were the only thing I specifically asked for you to bring." Betty smiled and said, "I didn't bring them." I said, "Well, we're leaving; you can put then in my mailbox tonight." Betty said, "I'm not going in your mailbox, you'll call the police on me again! And, it's your weekend with the kids, YOU have to get their things, it's not my responsibility!" At this point, I'd rather go buy Stephen his third pair of cleats than beg Betty to tell me when and where I would be able to get them, so we got in the car and left. When we got home, my mom called me and said, "Betty just texted me and said that you didn't take Stephen's medicine for his strep throat and that she would not be bringing it over — if you wanted it, you or I had to go and get it." I said, "I didn't even know he was on any medicine, and I asked her, I don't know how many times, if I had everything because I didn't want to run back and forth like the last two months. It's going to be this way every time now. In fact, it's likely to get worse because it'll get reinforced every time she does it that there's nothing we can do."

The next weekend, I asked Stephen if I could to talk to his mom after he and I talked, to see what time I could get the kids for Father's Day. Betty was very snippy and hostile towards me, causing me to ask, "Why are you so angry towards me all the time?" She switched her tone, started laughing and said, "You think I'm angry?! I'm not angry, you are! Are you listening to me?! You're the angry one!" By the end, sounding...angry. "Okay Betty, okay. I'd like to get Charlie tomorrow when I get the kids please," I said. She responded, "I'm not bringing Charlie, you only have the kids for a few hours! Besides, he's going to stay at Peg's." (I really had the kids for ten hours for Father's Day.) When I offered to get Charlie at her sister's, she said, "No! You are NOT getting him!" I asked, "Why not? He shouldn't have to spend the day alone at your sister's." Betty said, "Because I'm not giving him to you! He's not your dog and there is nothing in the court's decision, NOTHING, that says I have to give him to you!" As much as I missed our family dog, I would have to settle for getting just the four kids for Father's Day — and the kids' cooperation was by no means certain with the party at Pat and Dale's.

Not all stress and strife, occasionally our exchanges were good for a laugh too. When I went to the church to pick up the kids after Mass on Father's Day, Betty came out of the side entrance and poked just her head around the end of the tall brick wall that lined the sidewalk as she looked for my car. Only seeing her head without even her shoulders visible made her look like she was floating and it reminded me of a cartoon character when they manage to stretch their neck and look around corners. She was startled when she saw me standing only thirty feet away, but she tried to act normal as she rounded up the kids. She and her parents took a very long time to say bye, reminding them of all the fun that awaited them at their party once they were, as Pat said, "Done with your dad."

When Betty and Bob picked up the kids at my parents', Betty told the kids, "And we still have a lot of games for you to play, and all of the cousins are waiting for you too!" If this was a mother that had good intentions, and wanted her kids to be well-adjusted and co-parented with her ex-spouse in the best interest of the kids, that quote would sound quite normal. But it was nothing but unabashed taunting by Betty. She also, as I predicted to my parents, brought Charlie with her — a show of control seeing how she wouldn't let me have him for the day. When she left my parents' house, she turned her van around one house down, rolled down the windows, and slowly drove past my parents and me. They were waving and playing a song that Betty, Bob, and all of the kids were singing loudly as Betty held Charlie and waved his paw "bye" at me. "There goes the big, happy family," was all I could say to my parents.

One of the more memorable verbal jabs Betty threw at me came the next time I picked up the kids. The marital house had just sold and I was getting the kids from her new house one neighborhood over. While the kids were still rounding up their things, Betty came outside, put her hands on her hips and smiled at me. Ready for the worst, I said, "Yes?" Betty turned to her side and put her arm towards her house and said, "Ha! You should write a book!" I was taken aback because I really was planning to write a book, but I had only told my sister and parents. I was already pretty sure why she'd said it and I didn't want to ask any questions and fuel her need to berate me. She had started her life over, and somehow managed to erase her past, and it had all come at my expense. The favorable custody ruling was still fresh and she had just bought this nice house, mostly with the money I was paying her every month. Her comment to me meant she knew, just as I did, that she had pulled off what I called, and once considered as the title for this book, "The impossible switch."

Also, for what it's worth, Betty must have realized that leaving Charlie at her sister's house over twenty minutes away worked so well for her during Father's Day that she did it for this exchange too. But, because Charlie wasn't part of the custody ruling, my parents and I were still so glad to get him at all that we accepted driving around on Betty and Peg's narrow schedules to pick him up.

Days later, Betty and I were sitting in the orthodontist's office, waiting to hear what the doctor had to say regarding Stephen's need for braces. A bit amusing to me, and along the lines that Betty was gloating over winning the custody dispute and was now looking towards the upcoming financial hearings a few months away, she had set her phone's incoming text chime to that distinctive sound an old cash register makes. She and I were in the small waiting room when she held her phone up towards me. Seconds later I heard the unmistakable, "Cha Ching." She smiled and her eyes stayed fixed on me — she'd taken the kids from me, and now it was time to take the money.

And, without the fear that her actions and words could be used against her in court, that was our norm for the exchanges going forward. I'll save the specifics of some of the other noteworthy times for the website as a reference for others divorcing a Borderline, but suffice to say, this would continue. Always withholding something, always belittling, always uncooperative, always taunting.

A Thing of Beauty

Over the last year, the three older kids were always distant with me for the first few hours of my custody time after spending nine days with Betty, but they would eventually warm up and become more comfortable with me. Rewinding to the end of May, the custody ruling had just come out and the three older kids acted like I was the worst thing that ever happened to them after I picked them up from Betty. I felt hopelessly lost. Dejected, and in private, I told my mom, "I wouldn't care if I got hit by a bus," later that afternoon. I didn't mean what I said to her as I still had hope my kids would eventually, over many years, come around to appreciate me. But that was very uncertain and all I was certain of at the time was that I was losing everything that mattered to me and I was as emotionally lost as one could get. Again, I relied on my job to provide my sense of self-worth.

I picked up an overtime trip in the middle of June that had a layover in San Francisco on the second night. When the new copilot and I got to the plane at 4:30 a.m., I offered to save her some time and preflight the outside of the plane and get the long, often-greasy, metal pins out of the landing gear. When I came back up into the jetway, the passengers were lined up and slowly boarding. I found myself trying to get around a rather large gent who, despite my repeated requests, didn't much seem to care that I was in a bit of a hurry and I wanted to get by him. I heard a snicker just behind me that sounded like a woman who was amused. Without looking at who had taken an interest in my dilemma, I put the gear pins just an inch away from the passenger's behind, motioned to her, and said, "I ought to give him a little motivation." When she laughed, I did too and I turned around to see, standing right behind me, the most beautiful woman smiling and looking into my eyes. She was so attractive that I felt a little intimidated, but she had a warm, genuine smile and we chatted for a couple of minutes until I went left into the cockpit and she went right into the passenger cabin. She sat near the front, so I knew she would probably already be gone by the time we got the cockpit door open after our post-flight checks. Willing to try just about anything, I told the flight attendant something I've never offered in my sixteen years as an airline pilot: "If that lady in 5D would like a drink, I'll buy it and pay you once we land in Chicago." The flight attendant laughed and looked at me, wondering if I was serious, and I had to say, "I'm serious!" It's so unusual for a pilot to say that — especially at 4:30 am, that I couldn't help but laugh too. I didn't know how else to convey to the woman I'd met in the jetway that I was attracted to her. I thought I'd never see her again, but I figured she would at least stick around to thank me for the drink on the remote chance she took the flight attendant up on my offer. After we landed and opened the cockpit door, the woman was gone and the flight attendant told me she'd said to tell me thank you, but she didn't want a drink. That was my only flight that day, so I waited four hours to fly home to Pittsburgh to get my kids the next day.

As the newspaper article from 2007 says, on my commutes to and from Chicago, I serve the snacks and also go through the cabin picking up trash for the flight attendants. When I served the snacks to the passengers on the flight home this day, I saw the woman I had met in the jetway in San Francisco. I hadn't seen her on this flight yet, because as a passenger, I'm usually the first one on a plane and I sit in the last row. Our eyes met and we both laughed. I asked her, "What are you doing here?" She said, "I'm going home." I couldn't help but ask, "You live in Pittsburgh?!" and we again both laughed at my stupid question. "Okay, I meant to ask, 'Where in Pittsburgh do you live?'" She said, "I live in Badger. Where do you live?" I said, "Mercury." And we both took a few seconds to look at each other and, in a partial trance, tried to comprehend that we met 2,500 miles away from home that morning but lived only fifteen miles apart. I broke the silence with "No way. Well, I'm Rob." She said "Hi, I'm Bobbie," and she stuck her hand out to shake mine. "What were you doing in San Francisco?" I asked. "I work for a tech company out there, so I travel back and forth a lot." "Ha. I can't help but wonder if I've flown you before today then," I said. "It's quite possible," she said as she looked at me with those beautiful blue eyes. There was some silence and I felt a bit awkward just standing in the aisle and holding the basket of snacks, so I said "Ahhh, would you like some peanuts or pretzels?" She said, "No thank you," but when she did, she lightly touched my forearm. I'm no expert in the ways of female thought processes, but I do know that a woman won't touch you if she doesn't feel some respect, admiration, or attraction. I just said, "Okay," and smiled at her as I resumed serving the snacks. When I finished, I sat back in my seat and, with the time I had to wait for the attendants to finish serving drinks before I went through the cabin to collect garbage, I thought about Bobbie touching my arm. Except, I didn't remember her name — when she'd said it, I was too caught up in her striking looks and it was all just a blur. I also forgot to look for a wedding ring, but I thought, "What the heck," and put my name and phone number on a napkin with the intention of asking her if she was married before I gave it to her. I went through the cabin picking up...garbage, and I came upon her. She looked up at me and smiled and I found the courage to say, "Hi. Are you single?" She gave me a tight-lipped smile, looked down, and said, "No." "Damn!" I thought, "You didn't ask if she was married, you only asked if she was single!" I'm not usually quick-witted on my feet, but, with her less than enthusiastic answer, I said, "Well, if you have any friends that look just like you, here is my number." We both smiled and I got back to picking up trash.

Ten days later, I hadn't heard from her and I was commuting back to Chicago to start another trip. When I was about to go into the jetway, I heard "Hi Rob." I turned around to see her, but again, I couldn't remember her name. I just smiled and said "Hi," and started down the jetway. When I got to the airplane, Ashley, the boarding agent, was standing there. "Hi Rob, how are you?" she said. "Good, Ashley, but I have a dilemma. Can you please go up to the boarding area and check if you can see the name of the blonde woman standing just a few people back? Maybe on her boarding pass?" I asked. Ashley said, "Sure." She came back down and said, "Bobbie." "Thank you so much, Ashley!" I said. When Bobbie came on the plane, she saw me sitting towards the back. She looked at me, smiled, and said, "You forgot my name, didn't you?" "Ahhh, just a little," I said. I ended up having to sit in the cockpit on the way to Chicago, but I left my suitcase in the back. When we landed, I waited for the passengers to get off to go back and get it. I saw Bobbie coming towards me, but I was very cognizant that she hadn't contacted me since I gave her my number the day we met and I didn't want her to feel like I was pressuring her in any way, so I just said, "It was nice seeing you again" as she passed me. She smiled and asked, "Do you happen to have time between flights?" I stumbled when I said, "Ahh, yes. Yes, I do." "Can I wait for you up top?" she asked and my heart sank. I only barely remember saying, "Sure."

When I saw her waiting for me in the gate area, she said, "Do you want to go somewhere and talk?" I, of course, said, "Yes" and we walked to a restaurant that had a booth tucked away in a corner. On the way, she said, "I don't know what I'm doing here." To which I said, "It's just a conversation; just two people talking. Friends do that all the time; you don't owe me anything."

During our two-hour talk, she confided in me that she was married, but she was in an abusive relationship. Some of what she had to endure was so bad that the physical abuse I went through pales in comparison. But she had "resigned this life" to raising her girls and sticking out her marriage with their father regardless of how unhappy she was. "That sounds familiar," I thought. She also said that her girls were growing up seeing her submissive behavior with her husband to try and keep the peace and she also knew that she needed to raise her girls in a more healthy, equal, caring, and respectful environment.

As we talked about our marriages, it quickly became apparent how scarred both of us were from our spouses. She told me of a time that her husband had wanted their girls to think she was a neglectful and uncaring mother, putting work ahead of them. She looked at me as she described that day in their car and she started to get tears in her eyes as she said, "I hit him. I hit him back, Rob." She couldn't believe her marriage had become so distant and when there was any interaction, it degraded into belittling, berating, and battling very quickly. Then she said, "I don't mind traveling as much as I do because it brings some predictability to all of our lives — especially my girls." Though I was getting divorced now, that sounded just like me two years before. Here we were, two people with incredibly similar situations, who lived near each other, and we met clear across the country.

Not all of our afternoon was spent on gloom though. We also discovered that we had similar tastes and a passion for music since we were kids. We both recognized music's powerful ability to take us back in time and relive our youth with just a song from that time. We quickly realized that her name is the last two initials of my four initials — which I had been using for my website and email address for years. We were the same age and her girls were very close in age to mine. We both had an interest in photography and flight. I'm not the most spiritual of people, but we felt right there and then that fate, or even God, had guided us to each other and our meeting was as close to a miracle as I'll be a part of. There was just one problem — a friendship was all we could have; Bobbie was married. At the end of our conversation, I told her, "You are incredibly special and I am here for you in any capacity you want — or don't want. I can be your friend if that's what you need, and there isn't any pressure to ever want more." She said, "I don't know where this is going, but I feel very drawn to you," and we parted with the tightest and longest embrace I've ever had. Though we hardly knew each other, it was hard not to think I had found the person I was meant to be with for the rest of my life.

In the ensuing weeks, Bobbie wrestled with the thought of not carrying out her vows with her husband and she felt guilty that she would be violating one of the tenets of marriage, but a few weeks later we met again. On a clear summer day at a local park, we laid on a blanket and talked about many things, but they all involved what a future might look like together — and we knew we were at the dawn of something incredibly special.

MOVING ON

I f it feels like neither Betty nor I had moved on after we separated, I would have to say that's pretty accurate. I could have moved on, but when she used the kids to get to me, it drew me in and the dread of always wondering what she was going to do next often kept her in the forefront of my mind. Right before I met Bobbie, I'd had enough of Betty's taunting and I sent her an email asking, "When are you going to move on?" I highlighted the contradiction that she taunts me and then says I attacked her during our marriage. She then claimed the email was threatening and she promptly sent it to her lawyer.

A few weeks later, after I had met Bobbie, what anyone else thought of me, besides my children, didn't seem to matter nearly as much. Though Bobbie was still living with her husband, she had decided that her marriage was irreparably broken and she was going to separate with the intention of getting divorced. We were now spending every available minute with each other and we were already so close that, instead of Betty and the kids' distance with me being front and center in my mind, it was now off to the side. My internal focus became to remember that, despite their beliefs, I couldn't be any better to my children, I couldn't control Betty, and to appreciate what a wonderful person I had in Bobbie — and I moved on.

Right before Betty would learn about Bobbie, she took another verbal swing at me on the phone. From this, I knew once she found out about my new girlfriend, she would not be happy. Betty called to tell me that I needed to sign the title off to the dealership for the van that she had just traded in for a new one. We had already had some contentious discussions regarding the van, because it was worth around $5,000, but she had a friend at the dealership say it was only worth $1,000. This was so that I wouldn't get as much credit for the residual value at our upcoming financial hearings (her friend took the difference off of her already discounted price and I thought that was fraudulent). I said I would sign the title when I got home from work and she raised her voice, "I know you can't work all the time and I am too busy to deal with you! I have the kids — I'm the full-time parent! I work two jobs AND I take care of the kids! You're all alone! You hear that? You are all alone!" She laughed when she said the part that I was alone and right there I knew how miserable and lonely she wanted me to be. And once she heard I was dating Bobbie and realized how happy and content I was with her, it would only be a matter of time before there would be big trouble. To give her a clue that I wasn't alone, I said, "That's not true Betty, and I still have a role in the kids' lives — I am their father." She responded "Ha! That's what you think!" I gave up and tried to move the conversation back to the title, but she started crying and saying that I was being "abusive" and to stop yelling at her. Knowing someone else must have been with her, I quickly hung up the phone before more damage could be done.

Betty met Bobbie in Pat and Dale's driveway when we went to pick up the kids just a couple of weeks later, and they had a quick and pleasant exchange. But just an hour later, at my house, Stephen told me Betty was outside and she wanted to talk to me. I walked out and Betty was standing in my driveway, near the house, which is against the police order. I told her repeatedly to get off of the property, to which she said, "I'm not on your property and you come onto my property all the time! And I have a police order saying you can't come onto my property!" I said, "No such order exists, but I don't go on your property anyway." She said, "Yes, there is!" With Stephen still outside, Betty then said, "And what about Lauren, are you still seeing her?" I said, "No, why?" Betty said, "Because Julie wants to play with her daughter and I want her number so that those two can play." I said, "Thea is fourteen years old, and I am not giving you Lauren's number. She doesn't want you to call her or to have any contact with you." Betty then said, "How many girls are you dating at one time now?" Confused, I said "What?" Betty said, pointing to my house where Bobbie was, "Are you seeing her and Lauren at the same time, like you did with me? Seeing a whole bunch of girls at the same time like when you were married to me?!" I said, "I am still friends with Lauren and I am dating Bobbie, which really isn't any of your business." Betty went on yelling about how I see more than one woman. I told Stephen to go inside, but he went into my car and shut the door instead. I went inside the house and told Bobbie and the other kids that Betty was out of control and I wanted to make sure everyone stayed inside. Bobbie had already known something was wrong because she'd heard Betty yelling. Trying to diffuse Betty a little, Bobbie opened the front door, waved and said, "Hi," to her. Betty said, "Hi" back, but in a very annoyed tone and then she drove off. Within minutes, Betty sent me two messages to my iPad, which I believe the second was meant for Bobbie to see (she'd been holding the iPad when she said "Hi" to Betty, playing music on it for Julie and Noel). The first was asking for my plan to take the kids to their school orientation so she could be there with me. The second message read, "To respond to your comment you said in the driveway of your house. No one deserves to be cheated on or abused no matter what the circumstances. It took me a long time to realize that but I am glad I finally did."

For what it's worth, Betty also sent an email that evening, saying, "I have not heard back from you about Noel's and Christian's orientation. I would like to go but need to know when you are going over so I can meet up with you and the kids." As I asked before, can you imagine a petite female victim of domestic violence going on to the alleged attacker's yard and taunting him, then refusing to get off his property when he repeatedly tells her to, and then immediately sends him two messages asking where he was going to be that night so she could meet up with him?

Knowing how determined Betty had been in trying to convince Lauren that I was a physically abusive cheater, I wanted Bobbie to be prepared to be confronted by her with the same attempts to win her over and/or scare her off. I knew after the incident in my driveway that the clock was ticking on Jekyll turning into Hyde and I felt the pressure building to preempt Betty. I had a dilemma though — no matter what I said to Bobbie, it would be too much now, but not nearly enough for when she would inevitably be confronted by Betty later. I had already prepared Bobbie a little in small bits and pieces by saying things like, "My ex isn't cooperative," "She is a very angry person," and "There is a lot more you'll eventually want to know."

Just a few days after Bobbie and Betty had met, Bobbie had driven up to meet me for lunch after Stephen's orthodontist appointment and she waited for me out in her car. I had a few minutes before he was going to be seen, so I went out to warn her that Betty might confront her when she got there. "There is nothing I can say to fully prepare you for what you will be subjected to by Betty. But let me be very clear that in the beginning, the first month or two, she will be exceedingly nice to you, just like everyone else. She's going to try and win you over by getting you to like her and then she'll tell you everything she's told everyone else," I said. Bobbie said, "Rob, I am a big girl. You don't have to protect me. Besides, I think she will be fine around me. I'm going to treat her with respect and let her know that the bad blood between you two doesn't mean she is a bad person; sometimes two people grow apart and that's all there is to it. And I'll show her that I respect her as your kids' mother and we may even be amicable towards each other." I now knew that there would be a great clash of mindsets and agendas between the three of us and Bobbie's futile hope and optimism was going to be trampled like a herd of elephants. I would rather be the one who did the trampling, so I looked intently into her eyes and said, "Bobbie, listen to me. Please! You need to be prepared for what she is going to say to you. She is going to see how attractive you are, see that you're a great provider for your girls, and see how close we are and she is going to do everything, I mean everything, to take that away from us!" "Rob!" Bobbie said, trying to interrupt. "No, you have to hear me out, she is evil. Pure evil! If you don't believe that, you can ask my parents, that's the phrase they use to describe her too!" I said. Bobbie just stood there with her arms crossed, looking disappointed in me that I wasn't going to let her start from scratch with Betty. I had to be careful not to harm our relationship by trying to prevent harm, so I said, "Okay. Let me just say this. After she realizes she can't sway you, she is going to resent and hate you too. I just need you to be prepared for it and okay with that because that is as certain as the sun coming up tomorrow." Bobbie just stood there and looked at me as if to say, "Are you done yet?" One of Bobbie's endearing traits is she is full of love and she sees the good in everyone, but I feared she would be disappointed or even hurt if she got to see first-hand that, on the inside, Betty is a broken, hopelessly lost soul.

Occasionally, I am not able to predict Betty's actions and how and when her disdain for me will manifest itself, and this was one of those times. I told Bobbie that it would take a month or two for Betty to give up trying to win her over with niceness and pleasantries, but it was all of five minutes from when we had that talk till Betty was standing outside Bobbie's parked car. Bobbie was on a call for work, but Betty stood uncomfortably close to her window and Bobbie had to tell her sales team that she would call them back. Bobbie got out of her car and said, "Hi Betty, how are you?" Betty said, "You need to know who you're with!" Bobbie said, "Certainly you have known him a lot longer than I have, but I'll figure out my feelings for myself." Betty said, "He was not good to me and the kids. In fact, it was so bad that I'm going to be going on a speaking tour to share my story with other victims of domestic violence." Bobbie said, "Betty, what I understand is sometimes two people don't see eye-to-eye and they aren't meant to be. And I'm glad you've had the opportunity to move on." Betty twitched and she was left speechless by Bobbie's simplicity and unwillingness to judge. At this point, I had come out of Stephen's appointment to check on Bobbie and, when I saw them, I asked Bobbie, "Is everything okay?" She responded, "Yes," and Betty walked back to her car.

After this happened, Bobbie took a little more interest in the things Betty said and did so she could make up her own mind. Just days later, one of the more persistent and frustrating things Betty had been doing, that I felt was just out of spite towards me, came up. It was time to sign Christian and Noel up for fall soccer and I texted Betty, "Christian and Noel want to play soccer this Fall. You don't have to take them if you don't want." I knew Betty was going to say no to signing them up because she didn't want any of the kids to play sports that I could practice with them and having no obligation to take them would leave her without a valid reason for her refusal. She responded to my text as I predicted — she didn't want them to play soccer. Keep in mind that Christian is a great soccer player with potential to compete on travel teams and, with enough effort, possibly even get a college scholarship years down the road. Of all the sports he is good at, soccer, in my opinion, is easily his best. And Noel is in a league all by herself when she plays soccer. Noel is so good that I never saw her play a game where she wasn't the best player on the field and I often felt bad for the opposing teams that had to try to stop her. She is gifted with great speed and her gymnastics make her legs very powerful for kicking. Add in her unspeakable determination to score goals and win, and my aspirations for Noel went far beyond even college scholarships. I responded to Betty again, saying how much Christian and Noel told me they wanted to play and Betty responded, "I already gave you my response." I registered them anyway, and less than an hour after I did, I got a text from Betty saying, "Why did you register them both for soccer? We never discussed or agreed to it. It conflicts with Noel's gymnastics and she cannot miss for soccer and Christian will have hockey." I responded, "There is very little overlap in their sports and when I took them to soccer games and practices in the spring there was hardly any conflict." Betty responded, "I will not be taking them and I will be contacting Alexis. Are you drinking? Because you are not making much sense." Through this and other events, Bobbie began to see Betty for who she really was — someone who put her spite for me ahead of what was best for our kids. Noel and

Christian playing soccer sometimes meant they had to be taken from one practice to the next, but neither the kids nor I minded. I (and Betty) also had the help of my parents, who lived up the street. They couldn't wait to help shuffle the kids around if I had to be at one of the other kids' activities. Christian and Noel would let Betty convince them that they didn't want to play, but they would tell me they did want to play. They had been excited to play before, and it pained me to know they were being put in the middle. I kept them signed up, hoping that Betty would eventually acquiesce after realizing how much potential they had and how much they enjoyed it.

The next weekend, Betty became more brazen in her effort to break Bobbie and I up when we went to Betty's house to get Christian's hockey bag. Betty wouldn't give it to me when I first picked up the kids, so I thought a separate trip with only Bobbie there would make Betty more cooperative. When we pulled up, Betty was on her porch and she looked sad and stressed when she saw us. Betty came up to the open passenger window and talked to Bobbie about how bad it was for the kids that I brought so many different women around (they'd met two girlfriends over twenty-two months) and that I am on Match every day. I asked, "Who have I brought around the kids? And I haven't been on Match for months." Betty said, "Here, I have proof!" as she showed her phone to Bobbie. Betty didn't actually show anything to Bobbie except a blank phone screen though. Betty's anger was escalating and so was mine — a combination that usually didn't end well. Afraid she might reach in and hit or scratch Bobbie, I drove away without the hockey bag before anything could happen.

That night, Stephen asked me, "Was I thrown down the steps at the old house?" I asked, "Why would you ask me that, Stephen?" He said, "I kind of remember it, but mom said it was just a dream." I looked at him for a few seconds, searching for a way to tell him that it wasn't a dream without sounding too harsh towards his mother. "It was real, Stephen, Ms. Vadessi told me about it when it happened a few years ago. But it's okay, your mom is much better with you now." This provided a lot of insight into how Betty had probably masked the times she'd punched, scratched, bruised, and screamed obscenities at the kids — it was all a dream. She had other methods too, like denying it ever happened, saying it was really me, or saying it was an accident. Our kids' young age and their unwavering trust in this new, nicer mother made the kids easy to dupe — or gaslight — and Betty knew attributing their memories to just dreams would clear their minds of what she used to do to them.

On Tuesday, the kids went back to Betty and I went to work. When the kids came to pick up their things from my house after school, Bobbie was still there, finishing up some things for work. They said, "Hi," and gave quick hugs to each other before the kids left. Bobbie went to the door to wave bye as the kids were still getting into the van and she saw Betty standing on the grass. Bobbie said, "Hi Betty." Betty said, "You know that all of this happiness will wear off, don't you?" Bobbie said, "Well, I guess time will tell." Betty then pointed at Julie sitting in the back of the van and said, "Julie knows how he is!" Bobbie said, "Betty!" with her arms out as if to question, "Why would you say that in front of your kids?!" Betty then said, "Oh! They all know what he's like! Julie, tell her what Daddy did to us!" conveying to Bobbie that she thought the kids had been hardened by me over the years. Meanwhile, the kids were sliding around in their seats and looking down and away, visibly uncomfortable. Bobbie said, "It's not appropriate for them to be hearing this and for you to think it's okay for you to talk like this in front of them! I'm removing myself from this situation and I'm going back inside." Betty then said, "It will be no more than eighteen months, that's all it took for him to start giving me the hand! You just wait, I'm giving you just one more year and it will be you who is getting the hand!"

Just minutes after Betty left, my dad, who had been out for a walk, stopped in to say hi. When he did, he found Bobbie crying. Bobbie now realized that everything I'd told her about Betty was true. Betty had just said, in front of our four kids, that she had been beaten by me and that Bobbie would be beaten in time too. Bobbie saw first-hand that Betty's obsession took far more precedence than our kids' welfare and she hurt for them.

Occasionally there are things that happened after Betty and I separated that were so poignant to me that I didn't journal them — their memory is powerful enough to remember in detail. One such time was in mid-September when I was talking to Stephen on the phone. He had been sounding down, distant, and annoyed over the last few months when I talked to him, but it was only on the phone that he sounded that way — he was happy when he was with me. The next time I had custody of him, I asked, "Stephen, why do you sound so down when I talk to you on the phone?" He said, "What do you mean?" I said, "Stephen. Do I really have to explain? You sound miserable and every one of my questions is answered with one word or a grunt." He looked at me, sad and like I should know better than to ask, and said, "I'm not allowed to sound happy on the phone with you. Mom and Grammy yell at me if I sound happy when I talk to you on the phone." As I type this, I'm saddened to think about the pressure they were under to live this way. I immediately regretted pressing him on some of the previous phone calls when I'd repeatedly asked him to tell me what was wrong. After Stephen told me this, I didn't want to put the kids in a bad position and I didn't ask to talk to the kids but once or twice a week. This didn't help our growing distance and it hurt to talk to them after three or four days and hear, through their frustrated, one-word answers, that I was still just an annoyance or inconvenience.

I said before that being with Bobbie gave me a sense of calm throughout all the strife, but there were times when Betty did get past that insulation. I went to Betty's house to try to get the order form for the kids' school pictures, and when I got there, I asked her if the kids could come outside so I could say hi. Betty opened the door and, sounding completely annoyed, said, "Kids, do you want to come out and say 'Hi' to your dad?" I heard a couple of them say "No," and Betty shut the door, turned back towards me, and smiled. She raised her voice and said, "See? They hate you just like I told you they would! They know what a horrible, abusive father you are! They don't want you here and they don't want you in their life, so just leave!" This got through and it hurt. Though I would never show Betty, I was completely dejected. I went home and went against my stance of waiting one or two days to journal (the amount of time it took for me to be able to leave emotion out of my entries). I wrote, "Can my kids of ten years from now please come and hug me? And tell me they will come to understand the truth?"

To make matters worse, during this week, Betty had been playing the role of the victim like a fiddle. Just an hour after my kids didn't want to say hi to me, my sister told me that Betty had put that October was Domestic Violence Awareness Month on Facebook. Sandi said to me, "And her mother responded 'I'm very proud of you!' You are the one that got mauled, not her! You are the one that should be saying that!" To top the week off, Betty put a Domestic Violence Survivor sticker on the back window of her van. It had been given to her by Cristy — the same woman who had said, "Betty would never do that!" when her daughter asked if Betty scratched me.

I thought of what Roseanne had said a year before about Betty ruining it for the real victims of domestic violence, and I had to wonder how many other people hid behind such a front. I'm sure the percentage is extremely small, but I doubt Betty is the only one who waters down and disgraces such a benevolent cause.

Now two years after we had separated, Betty sometimes did things that still surprised or even baffled me with how brazen she was. In October, I called the photographer who took our district's school pictures to order packages for each of our kids. He said, "I have been told I cannot let you buy any of your kids' pictures." Perplexed, I asked, "What do you mean?" He said, "I don't want to say much more, but if a parent, who is the primary parent in a divorce, says I am not to sell the pictures to anyone else, I have to abide by that." I asked, "Did she single me out?" He said, "I can't answer that." I said, "Bill, this is Rob Black. I started the lens rental business around Pittsburgh and I'm a photographer of sorts. As a professional courtesy, can you please just tell me?" In a funny, indirect way, he confirmed it when he yelled back to his business partner, "Hey Dave, I know the guy whose ex-wife won't let him buy their kids' pictures!" He then said, "I'm sorry, Mr. Black, you were saying?" I laughed and said, "I love a person who can improvise."

For one of the custody exchanges in October, I thought if my mom went and got Charlie and a few of the kids' things, Betty would be more cooperative than if I went. When Betty answered the door, Charlie was jumping up at my mom's feet so she picked him up. My mom said, "Hi Betty, I just came to get some of the kids' things. Stephen would like his Fitbit too." Betty shot back, "Stephen doesn't want that, YOU want it and you're not getting it!" My mom said, "Betty, Sandi bought that for him and we would like it for this week-end." "You're not getting it! Rob has taken things he hasn't given back to me!" Bob then came and stood behind Betty, and she contin-ued, "You read all thirty-three pages of the fact-finding report from the judge! Even Judge Wardi could see what kind of person your son is! He knew he was a liar! You know all the terrible things he did to me while we were married!" My mom said, "No Betty, I only know what you told me — I wasn't there. I'm only trying to have an amicable re-lationship with you." Betty yelled, "You have your head up your ass!" as she stepped towards my mother. My mom stepped back as Bob turned and walked away, not wanting to get involved. "And that's my dog!" Betty yelled as she yanked Charlie out of my mom's arms. My mom said, "Betty, I'm just trying to have an amicable relationship with you, but it's obvious that's not possible." As she walked out the door, my mom turned around and said, "But you know what Betty, that's your fault."

This exchange was one of the worst and I could not, despite repeated texts and calls, get Christian and Noel's soccer gear that day for their games the next morning. The next morning, Betty finally agreed to bring their soccer bags right as I was leaving for Noel's game. We were in a rush and I didn't check to see that Betty hadn't put Noel's jersey in the bag. I texted Betty from the field, "We are missing Noel's jersey. You said I had everything." She texted me back with this:

How many female victims of domestic violence do you know that would be so brazen as to send a text like that to their alleged attacker? Betty then brought the jersey to the game after it started, looking like she had come to Noel's rescue. She walked by me smiling and gloating at how easy and fun it was for her to visibly frustrate me.

Halloween was coming up and according to the court order, I had the kids for our community's trick-or-treat night this year. When I got to Betty's house to get the kids, Betty came outside and, without any provocation, yelled, "I don't need your money!" This was presumably because our financial hearings were set to start in a month, but otherwise, I have no explanation as to why she would randomly say that. She then leaned into her house and said, "Kids, do you want to go with your dad for Trick-or-treat or not?" Stephen and Christian came outside and gave me a hug and got in my car. But Julie and Noel were standing in the doorway, hip-to-hip with their mother, and yelling that they didn't want to be with me and they were going to go trick-or-treating on Saturday with their mom and cousins (Saturday was my custody weekend). I said, "Girls, please. Let's just go and we'll have a good time. We'll be back in just a couple of hours." Julie yelled, "We don't care! We're not going!" Noel repeated Julie for emphasis. We went round and round a couple more times before I tried to break the stalemate: "I was going to take you to a haunted house Saturday night, but I will let you go with your cousins if you just come with me." Obviously, Betty had planted the idea to go with their cousins in the girls' heads and she was quite happy with the result judging by her expression.

I had to come up with a plan to make Betty cooperate and to also get the girls to come with me. I also needed to fix several things that Betty had been doing to frustrate me during the exchanges. One was that Betty had been locking the kids out of the house on the days I took custody of them (forcing me to bring the kids by her house only when she was there. Once she got home, she made me wait twenty minutes as the kids got their things and she talked to them to drag out the process). To top it off, she had not been giving me Charlie the last several exchanges either. So I drafted an agreement for her to read and, if she wanted the kids for a second trick-or-treat on my time, she would agree and sign it. It wasn't complicated or demanding, I was just asking for her to be reasonable.

The things I requested were:

1. I get Charlie on all of the days I have the kids [She couldn't tell me the kids didn't want him to go like she had so many times before].

2. The kids always have a way into your house on my custody time — you cannot chain the door.

3. We are responsible for getting the kids' things at the end of our custody time — not the kids [which she used to make excuses for missing things].

4. We should text if we will be more than 10 minutes late for a drop off or pick up [she was consistently late and at a recent drop off, she was thirty minutes late].

5. Please consider when I am at work, I only have 30 minutes on the ground [she knew this and if the kids called me, it was usually around an hour after I asked, according to my phone records].

Betty claimed I was being unreasonable with my demands and she and Bob went to Paige's house to show her the agreement. Stephen asked to go to my parents', so that we would be next door to Betty as she talked to Paige. Stephen, God love him, was running back and forth between the houses being the mediator between Betty and I, negotiating the smallest of details so that he could trick-or-treat with his cousins. After nearly an hour of negotiations, we were left with just the first two points; the last three had been struck by Stephen, one-by-one, as he negotiated with his mother so she would sign it. I really wanted Stephen to be able to go, and he knew that, but Betty recanted at the last second and again didn't want to sign. She sent an email saying, "Don't waste your time. I was only trying to do something the kids wanted to do. If you don't want to let them go, it's on you." I called her bluff and told her the whole thing was off when she recanted and said she would sign it. She signed the agreement in Bob's truck as he sat next to her and watched. She handed it back to me and I looked at her signature, almost expecting her to have signed it with ink that would start to disappear. The kids went with Betty and their cousins trick-or-treating for a second time, and I was ecstatic thinking I had a new way of getting Betty to be reasonable — put it in writing.

The next Monday, Betty's lawyer contacted my lawyer and said that I had "put Betty under duress" and "forced" her to sign the paper. The email accused me of acting "inappropriately" and the signed paper was now "void." How Betty could claim that I'd put her under duress and forced her to sign the agreement with her six-foot-two, 250 pound, heavyweight wrestler boyfriend sitting two feet from her in his truck as I waited on the sidewalk fifteen feet away was a bit of a mystery to me, but she'd found yet another way to manipulate which of the kids' items I got, and when. And I still couldn't get Charlie.

Though it was something that I once would have thought was blasphemy, I was contemplating not paying for the girls' expensive private gymnastics program anymore — especially when the school district had a very good school program that cost exactly 1% of what the private lessons did. It was previously unthinkable because Julie is good at gymnastics and she enjoys her team immensely; it is a big part of her identity.

Noel is in the middle of the pack as far as competition scores go, but she also likes her teammates and the camaraderie of the sport. I believe she does it, for the most part, because she sees Julie getting on the podium and getting medals and she wants that too. But as their disrespectful attitudes grew worse, I felt that switching them to the school team was a proper measure — at least until their attitudes improved. My significant financial debt had nothing to do with it, just to be clear — I would pay any price, make any effort and do anything for my kids if they appreciated it.

One of the things Bobbie and I were careful of, was when and how to introduce our kids to each other. My girls are loud and, at times, a little crass. Her girls are polite and quieter. Bobbie certainly didn't like how my girls behaved when they were around Betty, but she also knew that once they were in my custody, they acted like I had raised them. We were both a bit concerned, but after five months, we thought it was about time they met. Our six kids would probably be step-siblings at some point, and we weren't going to leave the success of their meeting to chance. They met just before Thanksgiving in 2015, and they had a great time together at a place that had a bowling alley, a huge arcade, and a good restaurant. It was a raucous time of laughter, yelling, and squeals for nearly two hours — all made possible by spending lots of money. When the night was over, the girls hugged each other, my boys said a nice and proper "Bye" and Bobbie and I wore smiles from ear-to-ear. "Wow, could that have gone any better?!" I asked Bobbie. "Only if we were all going home together!" she said.

The next day, my girls asked when they could see Bobbie's girls again and, though we felt it may have been a bit premature, we let the girls have a sleepover at Bobbie's that night. They bonded so fast and so closely that, for the next few weekends, we had to plan our days around getting them together as much as possible.

Occasionally, I would hear from the two boys' teachers about missed homework assignments and projects. I talked to the boys and tried to convey to them how important their schoolwork was, but internally, I knew part of it was just boys being boys and it wasn't on the forefront of their playful minds. But one weekend at the end of November, Betty refused to give me Christian's school backpack and timeline picture project, which was due on my custody time. (Interestingly, when Betty wasn't home and I got the project from Bob a day before it was due, he said, "Betty is going to kill me for doing this," as he handed me the unfinished timeline.) I could not get the backpack from Betty before Christian went to school on Monday, so I had no choice but to contact his teacher and tell her that any homework he may have had would not be done. The teacher said, "He has missed a few things over the last couple of months." When I relayed this to Betty, she said, "I send you the emails, you're just irresponsible with the kids' homework!" It dawned on me she probably wasn't sending the emails to my main account, which she regularly sent emails to, and I checked the same account she had used to falsely convince the kids and Judge Wardi that I wasn't letting the kids talk to her on the phone. I saw multiple emails with projects and homework assignments for both boys, including a big project Stephen had missed earlier in the year because of her deception. The emails still sit in that account today, a reminder that I need to be ever-vigilant with regards to getting the boys' homework done. The girls, for the most part, enjoy their school work and they won't forget what is due so Betty has not tried that with them.

Now early December, our financial hearings got underway. I quickly liked the slightly older judge, because after she introduced herself, she said, "And I have been doing this a very, very, very long time, so don't think you can pull one over on me." I was overflowing with hope that I might have met the first counselor or judge who could see through Betty's victim mentality. Betty told the story of the night of the "Big Fight," as the kids called it, and she again said I'd bruised her back when I threw her on top of the bed. The judge looked at her a little funny, but she let Betty continue. This was relevant to our financials for at least one reason — Betty had racked up a solid four figures in counseling and chiropractor visits because of how hard she claimed I'd hit her that night. After Betty finished that story, Alexis asked Betty if I beat her when she was pregnant, and Betty responded, "All the time." The judge looked over at me, trying to quickly gauge my reaction and I looked at her, trying to gauge her reaction and how gullible — or not — she was. The judge then asked Betty if she had gotten her own health insurance through the military yet. When Betty said "No," the judge firmly said, "Well, don't you think it's about time?!" And I heard the first person ever to question Betty in a way that casted doubt on her actions. Betty's testimony wasn't that memorable otherwise, except for the last thing the judge asked her. The judge asked, "How many jobs have you applied for?" Betty said, "Four." The judge said, "Four?! In over two years, you've applied for four jobs?!" They then discussed Betty's lapsed teaching certificate and the judge strongly encouraged Betty to do what it took to get it reinstated. Betty agreed. Then the judge asked, "What four jobs did you apply for?" Betty said, "They were all in the Allegheny County Courthouse Family Division for clerical work." The judge couldn't believe it and she shook her head as she took some notes. Surprised Betty would admit to that, I looked at her and thought, "Four jobs, all in this courthouse?

Sitting in traffic and spending an hour driving each way to and from work? Making very little money? Seems very transparent that you just want to influence the court rulings."

With all of the contention about my sporadic employment at Southern, my camera business, our huge debt, and our military retirements, we ran over the time allotted and we would have to reconvene in mid-January. Betty dug her hole a little deeper when our two lawyers and the judge were trying to figure out what day we could meet. Everyone was going through the possible days, willing to push commitments aside like my trip, depositions, and hearings to get our last day in. When we found a day, six weeks later, Betty was the one who said, "I'm not sure I can do that, I have to work!" The judge knew Betty made very little money working part-time at the private preschool and we ended the day with all of us, her own lawyer included, looking at her in disbelief.

Now just before Christmas, I saw Julie texting some things to her mom about how much she didn't like being with me and how she couldn't wait to go back "home." I rounded up all four kids and talked to them as they sat on the steps and I sat below them in the entrance. I said, "Look, I'm glad you have a great relationship with your mom now, that's what I've wanted for you all along. But your new relationship with her shouldn't come at my expense. I know I'm strict. I know you can't stand your early bed times. I know you don't like when I tell you you can't have soda after three o'clock. But that's the kind of parent I am, and I'm not going to get involved in some popularity contest and change my beliefs on how to parent just because you get to do almost anything you want at your mom's house. We have a lot of fun, but I also have a lot of rules, and I am very rigid with all of the ones you don't like — like bedtimes."

They just stared at me, not wanting to face the fact that no matter how much they said or tried to convey that they now liked to be with their mom more, I wasn't giving in. I continued, "Your mom and I are two very different people, that's why we're not together anymore." Julie said, "No, you're not together because you beat-up Mom!" I said, "No I didn't, Julie." "Yes you did!" she exclaimed as she started to cry. "Julie, do you remember what your mom was like before that night? She wasn't like she is now, she just wasn't." Julie looked at me with a face I'll never forget, like I was everything Betty wanted Julie to think I was. "Look Julie, I did everything I could to get her help when we were married. I tried to get her to counselors and doctors, to have friends take her to lunches, we went on trips, I'd do things for her, I'd clean the house, I'd buy her things, asked her to go on medication. Julie, that's all I knew to do." All of us sat there in a partial trance when I put my head down to hide the fact I had started to cry. I softly said, "I couldn't help her anymore, Julie." Julie then started crying uncontrollably. I never asked why, but judging by her face when I said I couldn't help her mom anymore, I took her back a couple of years. She may have briefly remembered what her mom used to be like and knew that I really couldn't have done any more for her.

It didn't seem to matter what I said anymore though, because the next night, Julie texted Betty to call the police on me (Betty didn't ask why). The doorbell rang at 9:15 that night, and when I opened the door, a police officer was standing there. My face must have been somewhat contorted, because he smiled and said to me, "You have absolutely no idea why I'm here, do you?" I said, "No, none at all." He said, "Well, someone called us." As he said that, we heard Julie running down the stairs saying, "That was me! I told my mom to call you!" All three of us stood on the small porch and the officer asked "What's the problem, young lady?" "My dad made me go to bed and I have a math test tomorrow! And he yelled at me!" Julie said. The officer looked at me, trying to stay serious. "He did that?!" he asked. Julie threw out her arms and said, "Yes!" as if to say, "Just take him away now!" Then, to my surprise, Betty slowly drove by with her windows down and music playing loud enough for us to easily hear so I would know she was watching. Trying to ignore Betty, and sensing it was my turn to talk, I said, "Julie has been very mouthy the last several months, and she has also been procrastinating going to bed when I tell her to. She'll tell me she's getting a shower, or getting something to eat, or she has homework to do and I've been telling her bedtime is the time she is in bed — not the time to do things she should have done before." "But I have a test tomorrow!" Julie said. I said, "Julie, I have repeatedly asked you to not wait until bedtime to get your things done. And I just can't take your disrespectful tone with me anymore and I wanted you to know you will be punished for it. You know I'd never stop you from studying, and because you only need eight or nine hours of sleep, I was going to get you up forty-five minutes early and help you study." The officer said, "See Julie, we parents don't always show our hand." Julie said, "But at Mom's we get to do anything we want! With my dad we have to go to bed so early and he even tells us when we can't have any more caffeine!" It was all the officer and I could do not to burst out laughing. He asked, "You hardly have any rules at your mom's house, and your dad makes you go to bed and tells you to stop drinking soda every day?!" Julie again said, "Yes!" He asked, "Julie, does your dad ever hit you in any way or has he ever abused you in any way?" Julie shook her head no. The officer deflated Julie's hopes for me to be arrested when he said, "You know, I have a daughter and I do the exact same things your dad does. She has to do her homework after school, she's not allowed to eat and drink whatever she wants, and she has a bedtime that is earlier than most of her friends." With that, I said, "Julie, now please go upstairs and go to bed; I'll be getting you up at six o'clock to help you study for your test." The officer and I tried not to laugh too loud as we ended the conversation by chatting about the pitfalls and occasional frustrations of being a good parent. For what it's worth, the police report ends with, "Julie herself admitted that she was upset because her father is more structured and is more of a disciplinarian than her mother. I found no evidence and have no reason to believe that Julie was in any danger. It appears she was upset about having rules to follow."

We got up at six o'clock the next morning and studied as if nothing ever happened. An interesting conclusion to this incident came when I told Stephen what had happened the next morning. When I said to him, "Nothing happened with Julie to cause her to tell your mom to call the police," he said, "Mom will probably just make something up!" It appeared to me over the last couple of months, that Stephen, in many different aspects of life, was starting to develop an independent mind. He was not just believing everything he was told to believe without questioning it — I wish I could say that about others in our community.

It was now coming up on New Year's Eve and the custody order states that in odd years, I am to get the kids on holidays that aren't conducive to splitting. I was starting to dread getting the kids for New Year's though, because it was Betty's normal custody time — and Betty takes great exception to me getting the kids on her time, even when it's court ordered. Julie had sent me a text message from Betty's phone the day before saying, "I am not going with you I don't care what the court order says I AM

NOT GOING WITH YOU!" When I called the girls to try to reason with them, I heard Betty in the background tell Noel that she was going to spend New Year's Eve at Peg's with her cousins. Noel then hung up on me, and I sent Betty a text asking why she would tell Noel that and if she was going to encourage the kids to go with me. She replied, "It's none of your business what I say to her. I don't answer to you. And no. They do not want to go. They have made it very clear to me and I know Julie has to you."

Bobbie decided to drive to my house to help me get the kids from Betty for New Year's Eve, and we were both a bit antsy and nervous about how we would be received. When we got there, Stephen opened the front door and, sounding a bit regretful, said, "Dad, I don't want to go." I said, "Why, Big Boy?" He said, "Our cousins are having a party tonight and I want to be with them." I said, "Okay. May I ask you to come with me this time and you can be with them tomorrow after I bring you back around noon?" He thought about it and came outside, gave me a hug, and sat in my car. Christian then came running out of the house and said, "Hi Dad!" as he gave me a hug too. "Where are your sisters?" I asked of the boys. Betty, standing in her doorway, said, "They are right here and they do not want to go." The girls then appeared and stood to each side of Betty. "Why don't you want to go?" I asked. "We hate you! Just leave us alone; we want to be with our real family!" Julie said. Noel chimed in, "Yeah, and we don't want to go to some stupid hotel and swim, we want to be with our real family — our cousins!" Noel then looked up at Betty and smiled — she had nailed her lines. Betty looked at me with a face that told me that this was just one infinitesimal spec of the payback that lie ahead of me for getting a PFA on her two years before. "What do you mean? I'm your real family?" I said. Julie yelled, "Just go away! Just leave us alone and stay out of our lives!" Noel then said, "We hate you;

you're not even our dad anymore!" This went on for another minute or two while Betty stood between them, alternating between a vengeful stare and smiling. They went back inside and Stephen said, "I'm sorry, Dad, but I want to be with my cousins too." He then got out of my car, gave me a hug, and walked back inside. He was twelve and not quite old enough to make up his own mind about which parent he wanted to be with, but how was I to force him to be with me when he was polite and his sisters weren't going and they were incredibly rude? When he opened the front door to the house, Charlie got out, and when he saw me, he ran over and jumped until I picked him up. Betty then quickly walked towards me. Before Betty could take him out of my hands, I put him inside my car and Charlie sat on Bobbie's lap. Betty then walked around to the passenger side and threw open the car door hard enough that I thought it was going to break the door. She grabbed Charlie from Bobbie's hands and yelled, "That's my f---ing dog!" She quickly stepped back onto her property, where she knew I would not set foot on.

Christian, Bobbie, and I left and I decided two things right there. One, that, within reason, whatever Christian wanted this day, he would get. Going all the way back to when I'd moved in with my parents, he was the only one who consistently came with me when I went to pick him up and he was always happy to see me. Two, I would not be paying for the girls' private gymnastics anymore. If not for Christian, I'm not sure even Bobbie could have kept me sane — the sadness and stress of picking up my kids had taken a huge toll on me.

Just a few minutes after we left, my phone rang with Betty's number showing on the screen. I didn't answer it at first; there wasn't any good that could have come from her calling me now. It rang two more times just seconds later and I finally answered it. It was Julie, who said, "I want to talk to Christian!" I gave Christian the phone and I could hear Julie telling him he needed to get back to his mom's and that they "Would be having a lot of fun with their cousins tonight." Christian said, "No, I want to be with Dad," and he handed me the phone. I said, "Julie, what are you doing?" She said, "He isn't safe with you!" I laughed and said, "Have a Happy New Year, Julie," and I hung up. I saw a message had been left on one of the previous calls, so I rounded up the courage to listen to it. I held Bobbie's hand as I heard Julie leave me a message in which she sounded almost possessed. Saving this voicemail for any future court hearings, should they come up with regards to custody, is one of the harder things I have had to do since I was forced to move out. It is a harrowing reminder of who she is becoming and I would much rather delete it and pretend like it never happened. My notes from the day end with, "Hating me has become a sport."

It was also about this time that my daughters became distant with Bobbies' daughters. My girls would complain about the smallest of things that Bobbie's daughters did or said (or they would make things up), and my girls started avoiding and excluding Bobbies' girls. All of my kids know that excluding another kid that wants to play with them is one of the fastest ways to get in trouble with me and yet, I could not force Julie and Noel to play with or even acknowledge their presence. As I was about to get my kids again in early January of 2016, I asked Bobbie, "What do you want to do this weekend?" She said, "I don't even know if they'll be together anymore." I said, "I was afraid of that. Your girls are such incredible sweethearts; they don't deserve that kind of treatment from my girls." Bobbie said, "You don't even know the half of it. Ella found this under her pillow." She handed me a piece of paper and I read it out loud, "I HATE YOU." We did our due diligence to make 100% sure it was one of my girls, probably at the sleepover they'd had just before New Year's. It was easy though, as Bobbie's other daughter Addie reacted in a way that unequivocally told us she hadn't done it and no other kids had been in the house for a couple of weeks. It hurt me as much as Bobbie, because it had taken her five months to feel comfortable enough to have our kids meet and I couldn't stop my girls from who they were becoming. Bobbie is very protective of her girls, and especially of Ella, who is quite timid and unsure of herself. This note scared Ella and I had had enough of my girls growing up to be haters.

My mom and sister had had enough too, and when I got custody of the kids the next day, we took the two girls into my old bedroom at my parents' house and we had an intervention. My mom started, "We are going to have a family meeting." Noel said, "This should be fun!" But the expressions on my mom's, my sister's, and my face said that this was not about fun. I cut to the chase and told the girls this was about their behavior on New Year's Eve and their blatant hatred for me as they'd stood in the doorway with their mother. Julie tried to placate me by dismissing what she'd said and how she'd said it that day, but my sister interrupted her, "Julie! You stood hip-to-hip with your mother at her house, yelling at your dad how much you hate him! You can't now just say, 'Oh, it wasn't that bad!'" I interjected, "No way Julie! No way! You behaved horribly. You got caught. You now have to be accountable. Bobbie and I stood there and listened to you say some of the worst things you could say to someone over and over." My mom said, "Girls, your dad does so much for you. Nearly everything your mom has is because he works and takes care of your mom and you." My sister said, "He gives your mom more money than most families make in a year, and he does it because he wants you to have nice things at both places." I was torn between not getting the kids involved in anything to do with money and saying whatever it took to get my girls to realize that I would do anything for them, including giving their mom money to spend on them. I said, "You know, at work I sometimes take kids to see one of their parents who lives hundreds or even thousands of miles away. They may only see their one parent once a year. Often, it's because the other parent doesn't want their kids." I quickly realized that my girls probably wished I'd do that: give up on them and just let them be with their mom, but I never give up on something I believe in and they knew it then, and they know it now.

When I brought up the note found under Ella's pillow, Julie started crying and emphatically said, "I didn't do it! I didn't do it!" Noel wasn't so reassuring in her denial, and she was, by far, the ruder of the two to Bobbie's daughters. Despite the fact that the writing looked quite a bit like Noel's, albeit, like it was trying not to look like her writing, I didn't say anything more about the note because I had to allow for that 1% of uncertainty that it wasn't hers.

We wrapped up the twenty-minute talk with hugs, tears, smiles, and, I hoped, a new understanding. My girls have an adept ability to say what one wants to hear and how they want to hear it to get out of trouble, so I was not leaving this to chance. How could they sit hip-to-hip with Betty and Pat every other Sunday morning in the very front row of church and still say such terrible things to me? How could they go to class for one hour after church just to learn about God and then act this way? How could they believe there is a God and he is watching over them and yet behave this way? I didn't know, and I figured I would leave it to someone who might have more success than I in trying to understand that contradiction. I had to think of one more way to pound it into their heads that I would not just let them turn into haters, and getting Julie to talk to the pastor was all I could think of. I took only Julie to see the pastor that day because Noel looks up to her and I knew that if I could just show Julie the error of her ways, Noel would come around right behind her. Singling out Julie also made the focus on her more intense. I talked to the pastor in private before Julie went in and I told him my concerns while Julie waited in the hall. I then let Julie go in, but I gave her a hug first to let her know I cared about her. This wasn't punishment, this was for her to sort through her emotions and to try to get her to live the other 167 hours of the week like the one spent in church. She came out fifteen minutes later and we left without saying anything. That was fine by me — I wanted all this serious dialogue to sink into her mind and get her to think about who she was growing up to be. The only thing I said to her on the twenty-five minute drive home was, "When you were little, we used to watch all those shows that the mean kids were always caught and either made to look bad, or they came around and joined the good kids. Right now, you are the kid we used to boo and cheer against and I'm trying to get you to come around to the good side."

When I called to get my girls in to see the family counselor after their New Year's Eve rant, I was told by the one receptionist, "We will not see you and your kids." "When, this week?" I asked. She said, "No, we will not see you at all." She didn't sound rude, she sounded like she was simply repeating someone else's guidance. "Why?" I asked, not really believing they couldn't see me at all. "Is that even legal?" I thought. "We just will not be seeing you anymore, Mr. Black, there isn't any more that I can tell you." "Hasn't their mother brought them in recently?" I asked. "Yes, she has," she said. "And Michele can't see me with the kids?" I asked. "Correct. That's all I can tell you, but that is what has been given to me," she said. "My kids need this counseling to try and undo the things their mother is doing to them. And Betty will not sign off on a new counselor at a different practice because she is accomplishing her objective with NHA. She's afraid a new counselor may actually uncover her. And you're telling me NHA won't see my kids with me, so I'm left with zero options for getting my kids counseling?!" I said in complete frustration. "I don't know what to tell you," was all she could say. In a different call, to see if I could get a different answer, I was told by a manager, "We deem your case to be too high conflict to be able to help you." Of course, I asked, "But NHA will see my kids with their mother. And I'm not asking to be seen, just my kids. So it's really me that is the impediment, right?" She repeated, "I have nothing more to say to you, Mr. Black," several times before we hung up.

On the inside of the front cover, I say that I was failed by our counselors. After Heidi retired from NHA in late 2014, Michele became our new counselor. Judging by Michele's reluctance to listen to me and schedule me, it would appear that Betty had talked with her during the first couple of sessions, before I met her. Perhaps Michele so completely bought into what Betty wanted her to believe about me that she may have actually started to reinforce Betty's version with the kids — maybe by the questions she asked, maybe by reinforcing that they would heal with enough time, maybe by telling them they needed to forgive me, maybe by just simply making the same confirming "I'm sorry you have had to go through that" comment that so many common friends and members of our community likely say too. After all, what are people supposed to say when faced with such stories? If this was the case, then how could Michele then facilitate my family counseling session? She couldn't. Over the past year, when I'd asked for a recommendation for a different counselor among the dozens within NHA, I was never called back. Though Michele had likely harmed my cause, she would at least question my girls' behavior on New Year's Eve — had I been able to take them. Not letting me bring my kids in at all anymore was NHA's most egregious failure though and left me wondering who I could rely on to tell my girls their behavior was deplorable. It wasn't working coming from me or my family. This book, in large part, is about the failures of people to make the effort to learn both sides to a story — the real shame here is that is the very basis for being a counselor. To think it was I who'd paid hundreds of dollars to NHA for Betty's visits with the kids to help accomplish her mission of hate.

It was now the end of January and the last day of our financial hearings was upon us. It was my turn on the stand and just like at the custody hearing, Jenna started with the night of our fight. I told the story the exact same way — the way it really happened — but, unlike at the custody hearing, I prefaced it with why I'd asked for a divorce in the first place. I spoke of the events leading up to the argument — that Betty didn't meet the kids at the bus stop when I had to meet Ben — and Alexis objected and claimed that I was telling a different version of the story. The judge looked at me and I responded, "I'm saying what I said in the custody hearing. It's the same, I'm just telling it all at once instead of in bits and pieces." The judge seemed satisfied that I was telling the truth and we quickly moved on.

The judge agreed with me that the girls' private gymnastic lessons were too expensive for the amount of debt I had. She said, "Unless you think your girls are going to the Olympics, this is just crazy!" I believe Betty wanted the girls to stay in the private lessons because I had to pay for 89% of our kids' expenses (I really paid for all of the expenses because she refused to reimburse me for anything), so it was a pretty big loss for her that frustrated Alexis. Alexis then lost some credibility when she tried to go through every purchase I'd made while we were married. She first brought up a shaver I bought off Amazon in 2012 when the judge told her, "We are not going through everything they bought before they separated!" Also, Alexis's propensity to stand up and forcefully blurt out of turn frustrated the judge, and within the first hour the tone was set for the rest of the day. I thought, "After 27 months, finally, something is going my way."

The judge then questioned why I had so much credit card debt. I said part of it was because I'd moved out of the marital house and into my parents' house, so I only took some of my personal items. When I moved into my own house ten months after I moved in to my parents', I had to furnish it with credit. The judge asked, "Didn't you ask Betty for some things out of the marital house?" I said, "I did, but she wouldn't give me anything." "Anything?!" the judge skeptically asked. I said, "Anything. In fact, it got to the point where I was asking for just four spoons and forks from her the day before I moved and she said no in a text." The judge looked at Betty and said, "Is that true?!" Betty said, "No! That is not true at all!" The judge looked back at me and I said, "Actually, I have the texts right here." Alexis was then asked to read the texts that confirmed Betty had denied me anything from the house to include, "Just four forks and spoons." Despite all the hell Betty had put me through, I still felt bad for her and I wanted to crawl under the table as the judge's realized she had just been lied to again.

When we moved on to our financial accounts, Betty, through Alexis, accused me of depleting the online investment account without ever telling her when I grew the rental business. I told the story of calling Betty into the room in 2012 and asking her if it was okay to liquidate the account, and Betty's words of "I trust you." The judge made it clear that she didn't believe that Betty wouldn't know $50,000 was missing with her access to all of our financial accounts — not to mention there was a bunch of new cameras and lenses being delivered to our front door for days. I knew after this recount that I had finally met the first person to call Betty out on her lies. Not that it would ever be enough to make her to stop though.

Jenna pointed out that it appeared that Betty had changed my address for the online account to her new address in late May. I didn't have any money in the account, so I'd never changed the password from the one Betty knew. Also, to rub in the week-old custody ruling (at that time), Betty had changed the number of dependents from four to zero and deleted our kids' names. The judge was visibly concerned and she looked around the room before settling on Betty and asked, "Is that true?! Did you do that?!" Betty was fidgety and said, "No, I never did that!" The judge asked, "Well then, did you ever get any mail or notification of the address change, which would have been sent to your house?" Betty was smiling like she does when she knows she's been caught and said, "No." The judge's mouth fell wide open to let Betty know she wasn't fooled and she shook her head as she made a note. This judge ran her hearings in a way that put Betty at ease though. The judge's ability to smile and look over at Betty just seconds after catching her in a lie put Betty at ease and facilitated her doing it again and again.

Flustered, Alexis again stood up and blurted, "Aren't you being difficult, and making every part of your divorce between you and Betty contentious?!" I was prepared for this "blame shifting" tactic and I pointed to the big stack of videos, pictures, printed emails and texts of Betty taunting me over the last two years and said, "It is Betty that has made it so unspeakably contentious and I have a stack of proof in pictures and videos right here." The judge had previously said, "Oh, I like pictures!" expressing her interest in what I had brought in that morning, and knowing that, Alexis sat down. But, for some reason, the whole divorce seemed personal to Alexis and her mounting frustration was clearly visible. She became very fidgety when, unlike at the custody hearing, I calmly answered the questions.

The day wasn't perfect for me though, and I had some hard questions to answer as to why I would have so much debt and yet buy a brand new van just months before. I explained that my car's transmission had failed by the dealership, and they were willing to give me the full value for it anyway if I bought new. But the judge must have felt I should have found another solution because she shook her head at me too.

As the day came to a close, the judge asked me if there was anything I wanted that I hadn't taken with me during the hurried move in late 2013. I wasn't ready to be asked that, and all I could think of was the big metal storage rack Stephen and I had built right before Betty and I separated. Betty had repeatedly refused to let me have it because its sentimental value is very high to me. I taught Stephen the basics of how to measure, cut steel, and weld during a time of unspeakable uncertainty and dysfunction in our family — our escapes to the shed are memories as bright as the light the welding arc produced in the darkness of the very last days of our marriage. When I said the metal rack was all I wanted, the judge said,

"Ms. Black, you have ten days to make it available for him to pick up." Betty raised her voice, and said, "But I am using that!" Now, Betty was furious. The judge said, "Ms. Black! You have ten days to make that available to him; that is all he wants!" "Well, he's not allowed on my property and I don't want him near my house! And I have stuff all on it, and I can't even get to it!" Betty said. The judge said, "So this is what it has come to? This is all he is asking for, out of all the property you got to keep, and you WILL make it available to him!" Betty was now loudly interrupting and talking over the judge as they went back and forth, and I again wanted to crawl under the table. The four days of financial hearings ended in a big melee between Alexis, Betty, and the judge, with the judge and Alexis both forcefully saying, "Just stop, Betty! Just stop!" True to form, if you go against Betty, even if you are a judge, she will lash out and try to intimidate you.

An interesting story came to the surface the next day. In the hearing, Betty had been asked by Jenna if she was pregnant and Betty said, "No." But a friend of mine told me he'd heard Betty was pregnant and due in early August. I immediately did the math, and that would have made the date of conception in early December. More of this story developed over the next month, and much of it needs to be left out for what I hope are obvious reasons. But in the end, I couldn't help but wonder if Betty set out to get pregnant after she saw my girls developing a relationship with Bobbie's daughters just weeks before. "You want a sister? I'll give you a real one," I envisioned Betty thinking. Of course we didn't know the sex of the baby, but this was what crossed my mind several times.

THE END GAME

t was apparent that the intervention we had with the girls, and the talk Julie had with the pastor, did a little bit of good, but its effect faded fast over the ensuing weeks. Now in the middle of February of 2016, Bobbie came with me as I drove Julie and Noel to a gymnastics meet (the same gym meet where Pat had her grandson jump on my cameras two years before). My mom also came, but she drove separately and met us there. The drive went by very fast with the girls singing, laughing, and talking with Bobbie and me. When we got there, Bobbie and I sat down in the bleachers during the warm ups and we talked before I planned to go up to the balcony. As the meet got closer, I started taking my cameras up, and Julie sat down with Bobbie to talk and go through the snacks we had brought. When Betty arrived, Julie walked towards the entrance to greet her. Julie then approached Bobbie with Betty following her and said, "Ms. Bobbie, can I go and sit with my mom?" Bobbie smiled and, trying to be respectful of Betty, said, "Absol—" Betty scowled and loudly interrupted Bobbie and said, "You don't have to ask her!" as she nudged Julie along. Incited, Betty then made a point to wait for me to come down from the balcony. When I did, Betty said, "I WILL be taking Julie home tonight." Because she sounded so sure of herself, I was a bit taken aback and I didn't say anything as she walked away.

Bobbie had to get her girls right as the meet ended, so my mom drove her back to get her car at my house. After the awards ceremony, I went and asked to get a couple of pictures of the girls with their medals. Julie said, "Okay, but after that we are going home with Mom." I said, "Not tonight, Julie, it's already 8:30 and I'd like you in bed in an hour." Julie started crying and Betty came up behind her and said, "Why are you making her cry?!" I said, "I just told her that she was coming home with me." Betty said, "No! They want to come home with me and they are old enough to decide for themselves!" I said, "No, they are not old enough. I want to get a few pictures of them, then you can talk to them for a while, and then we are going home." I took a picture of the two girls and then I asked Julie to take a picture of Noel and I. Noel would only stare for the first picture and she was visibly upset for the other two. Afterwards, both girls were clinging to Betty and couldn't wait to get away from me and go home with her. Betty repeated, "The girls ARE going home with me!" I said, "Betty, I'm not doing this here in front of all these people. I'm taking my equipment out to my car, where I will wait for them. Please just say goodnight and tell them to come out to me when you are done." Betty wouldn't look at me and I went out to my car, hoping for the best.

The last of the coaches were walking out, but Betty and the girls were still inside. Bob and Pat then came outside and waited by Betty's van, which was right by the front door just twenty-five feet in front of me. A minute later, I saw my girls walk out, crouched down and leaned over. They were easily visible to me through the clear glass doors that led into the gym, so I'm not sure why they thought I wouldn't be able to see them. When they came out, they were still leaned over, and went around the front of Betty's van and into it from the other side. I got out of my car, and not wanting to touch Betty's van or force the girls to come with me, I appealed to Bob. "Can you please tell my girls they need to get into my car and come with me?" I had, for the most part, appreciated his very passive demeanor up to this point because it kept him from engaging in the alienation campaign like Betty probably wanted, but now I needed his interaction. He looked up from his phone, but just stood there in silence, unwilling to help. I asked Pat to please tell them they had to go with me, and she said, "You're welcome to try and get them." She said it like, "I don't know what's wrong with them," but I knew better. She, in conjunction with Betty, was behind my girls' behavior that night — and ultimately the last two-and-a-half years. Betty stood on the other side of the van, where I could see her through the glass. As I walked up to the van, her smile gave away her excitement for what was awaiting me when I opened the van's door. When I did, I was immediately met with four shoes in my face as my girls had slid down in the seat and were trying to kick me in the face as they screamed, "Go away! Just get out of our lives! We hate you and we never want to see you ever again! Go away!" Noel went as far as spitting at me and I knew I had to give up. I had never been so humiliated in all my life, and when I saw Betty fake laughing on the other side of the van, I felt the same rage as the night of our fight when I'd hit her back. I closed the van door and yelled, "Are you happy now?! Happy that your obsession of getting them to hate me is a success?! You have so much to be proud of, brainwashing our kids into thinking I'm the abusive parent! They'll remember what you did to them one day! They'll remember what a piece of f---ing shit you were to them and they'll remember when you punched them in the stomach and pushed them down a flight of fifteen stairs! They'll remember all the welts, bruises, and scratches across their faces and eyes! They'll remember you calling them 'Little f---ing witches and Little f---ing bitches!' They WILL remember and God help you when they do!"

I called Bobbie and my mom and told them what Julie and Noel had said. Bobbie said, "What happened?! We were having so much fun and we had such a great time, and then they go and do that?! I thought this after the New Year's Eve debacle, but they have turned into monsters! Complete monsters!" "I know," was all I could say. My mom's reaction was very similar; she couldn't believe that we'd gone from having so much fun before the meet started to the girls kicking and spitting at me in a matter of two hours. I was in such a daze that I don't remember much of the drive; all I knew was I wanted to get my boys from Paige to get the most needed hugs of my life. They would remind me that I was still a parent to two great kids.

After I brought the boys home, Betty pulled up in front of my house and both girls walked in. Julie said, "I'm getting all of my things! And you stole my iPod! I want that back too!" I explained that I didn't have her iPod, but she didn't believe me. "You stole it! You put it somewhere where I can't find it and you stole it!" she yelled. "Julie, I didn't steal it. I haven't even seen it since you got here Friday," I said. "Well, you stole it and I want it back!" she said. "Take the things you brought Friday, and if I find it, I will text your mom," I said. She said, "I'm getting all of my things out of your house when you're gone this week!" She had recently taken a laptop of mine to her mom's and left it there without telling me and, on the phone, claimed she'd lost the diamond earrings I'd bought her for Christmas when I asked where they were. In the background, I heard Noel say, "Julie, your earrings are right in front of you!" and I figured she was trying to "lose" them. With that in mind, I said, "Julie, you are not to come into this house anymore without me, my parents, or Bobbie here. Is that clear?" She didn't say anything, she just folded her arms in a sign of defiance. Trying to sound calm, I said, "Julie, if you come into this house without one of us here, I will call the police. Is that clear?" She yelled, "I hate you!" and then walked out the door. Noel, who had been silent the whole time, was right behind her and said, "You're a piece of crap!" Amongst all of the thoughts of pain and despair, I couldn't help but also think, "Here are two little girls who say I used to hurt them and beat up their mom, and yet they talk to me in the most incredibly disrespectful tone without anyone around to protect them. Who does that sound like?"

They got into Betty's van and left, but they made a right turn towards my parents' neighborhood instead of a left towards theirs, so I called my mom and told her they may be coming. My mom answered the door while I was still on the phone and I heard Julie say, "I need to look for my iPod." "Go ahead and look around Julie," my mom said. After a minute of looking, Julie was almost hysterical and said, "I can't find it! Dad took it! He steals all of our things!" My mom said, "Julie, that is not true! Why would he do that? Did you look in his car?" "Yes!" she said. I then heard Betty yell, "He steals all of the kids' things!" And as she continued yelling at my mom, I hung up and called the police. According to my mom, while I did that, Julie was still in a frenzy, yelling, "And he beat up Mom! I saw him hit Mom! He beat her up!" During the commotion, Bob, who had stayed by the van, was now at the front door too. After Betty called my mom a bitch, my mom said, "Bob, get her out of here!" The three of them started to walk back to the van when Betty turned around and yelled, "You're a nobody! That's why you don't have any grandchildren anymore!" My mom then said, "I hope you have a lot of good memories of me and all of the things I did for you, Julie." Never one to let someone else have the last word, Betty yelled, "You never did anything for her!"

The next day, Stephen found Julie's iPod between the seats in the back of my car. My mom texted Julie, "So I hear Stephen found your iPod in the back of Dad's car? I guess he didn't steal it?" In a clear indication that Betty has formed Julie into a younger version of herself, Julie replied, "Well, I didn't accuse anyone." Julie has learned that if she says what she wants her version of the story to be, no matter how blatant of a lie it is, she'll feel exonerated and will not feel any remorse. I can only hope she doesn't actually start to believe her own lies.

The police got to my parents' house right after they left and it was Officer Henche who had responded. After hearing what happened, Officer Henche, who knew that Betty was not allowed on my parents' property, said, "You have two options. I can give her another warning, or I can arrest her." My mom, still not wanting to sever all ties with Betty because of the kids, chose the warning. Officer Henche spent two hours at Betty's house trying to get her to realize that my mom had chosen not to have her arrested and that she needed to respect the order to stay off of the property. Officer Henche later relayed to me that Betty was incredibly difficult and never admitted any fault or remorse for the two hours she was there. Only Bob eventually said that she shouldn't have gone on the property and offered any voice of reason during the time Officer Henche spent there. I thought, "Finally, Bob has said something to try and reel her in."

As much as being kicked and spit at and hearing about the confrontation with my mom bothered me, the thing that hit me the hardest was reading Stephen's iPod the next morning. Betty has all of the kids and Bob included in a group text and I saw Julie's texts back and forth to Betty. They were conversing as if they knew Julie had left the iPod at either the gym meet or in my car, yet both of them had just accused me of stealing it. Neither Julie nor Betty ever mentioned me in the eight texts back and forth as they tried to retrace their tracks. Betty gaslighted Bob the next morning when she texted him, "Julie texted Bernice and she didn't get a response. I don't know what to think anymore. I just want the kids to be happy. I am worried about all of the stress on the baby with all of this." Bob replied, "Just do your best to stay calm, the worst is over. If this happens again, don't engage and just leave. It's all we can do at this point."

After I read this, my first thought was, "Bob's a West Point grad? This has to be the most gullible military officer of all time. If the enemy told him they were going to attack from his left, would he believe it and send all of his troops there?" As much as I'd wanted to confront him about doing something about Betty's behavior before, that looked futile now. I still needed to keep this big kid/passive man from joining forces with Betty and Pat and I thought, "Do not wake the sleeping giant!"

If you're divorcing, or divorced, from a Borderline, you may be familiar with their insatiable need to kick you while you are down. Betty's overflowing hate means that once she starts letting it go, she can never get enough of it out, especially since she has to act normal 97% of the time. The next morning, she drove Julie to the bus stop in front of Adam's house that I drive Stephen to. I would normally have taken Julie too, had she spent the night at my house. This was pure unadulterated taunting at its finest — Betty teaching Julie it's not enough to win, you need to humiliate your victim to make it complete. Betty parked her car at the bus stop and the both of them sat there smiling at me like it was all a big game they had just decisively won.

Betty wasn't done rubbing it in though. I wouldn't find out until I tried to pick up Stephen and Christian at the start of my next custody window, but Betty went to each of the kids' schools that day and took my parents off the list of trusted people who could pick them up. They were lined out and her initials were beside it. I knew each of the two administrators well, Holly being one of them, and my parents were reinstated.

In the police report, Betty is on record saying, "I went to the door because I heard Bernice yelling at Julie," which can't be true because Betty is the one that went to the front door with Julie when they first got there. Betty is unspeakably good at deflecting blame, and my girls were learning from the master of the art.

Though this horrible episode had been over for days, Bobbie had bad headaches for half the week. She also said one of the most searing things of this whole divorce: "If I think of Satan now, I think of a woman." My parents were visibly stressed and emotionally down. Sandi could barely stand to hear anymore. I wasn't eating and I got about half as much sleep as I needed all week. The physical toll on my family was steep and several times I heard my mom say, "Dad and I can't live like this anymore, we're too old and these are supposed to be our good years!" Though only sixty-seven, they were right. And I couldn't help but think that my girls, if they ever came around, would probably be in their twenties, at the youngest, before they realized that they had been accomplices to Betty's mission of hate and taken my parents' time to be grandparents away from them. My mom couldn't play tennis with Noel or teach the girls how to cook and bake. For both of my parents and my sister, there would be no walks around the neighborhood talking and laughing. No Easter, no birthdays, no Thanksgiving, Christmas, or New Year's Eve — no holidays spent with them at all, it was all gone. I would add that even more disheartening was the loss of the day-to-day inter-action. The holidays and birthdays make up but ten or so days a year, but the other 355 were also empty, and that's the part that really hurts.

When my parents and I talked about this the next day, my mom said, "I want to think at some point Betty will get caught, but even if she is, she's not capable of learning. She is only capable of lying and manipulating." I said, "Her ability to successfully lie and manipulate perceptions is simply far better than our ability to keep up and explain them. If you realize that, and just add in I'm not allowed to have anything that makes me happy, that has to be all of what Betty is about." My mom said, "Well, just add in that we're not allowed to be happy either because we love you. No one is allowed to both love you and be happy."

Betty drove Julie to my house the next night to get some more of her things — she was moving out. As carefully as I could say the words, I said, "Julie, before you go, I'd like to talk to you for just a minute." I sat on the steps and she stood by the door, looking impatient. "I want you to know I don't agree with you growing up to be a hater," I said. "Everyone hates someone," she calmly said. "That's not true," I said and added, "What about my mom? What about me?" Julie responded, "Grammy has to hate someone, she can't be that nice. And you do too, you hate Mom." "Julie, I don't hate your mom. I just don't like what she has done to my relationship with you. Big difference." I knew I wasn't getting through to her, so I said, "What about CCD and church? You sit in the very first row of church with your mom and her family every Sunday and then go to CCD. Aren't those teachings about caring for everyone and forgiveness? Not hating someone?" She just looked at me. Sensing I was making some progress, I asked, "What about Jesus or God? They wouldn't want you hating your own father." Julie, sounding calm and assured, said, "Jesus created us to hate." Stunned, I just watched her walk out the door.

Dr. Darnall says it takes about two years for the obsessed alienator to completely win over their targeted children and turn them into "parrots of hate" — and that's almost exactly how long it took for Betty and my girls. I'm not sure how a person, even a child, is able to be entirely reprogrammed, but my girls are proof that it is possible given enough time.

Just days later, Betty tried to schedule an appointment for Stephen with Dr. Orsini without me knowing. I only found out because I called to order new allergy serum for myself and the lady behind the desk confused my son and I. To be at the appointment, I'd stayed home from a trip I was supposed to start, knowing Betty was going to twist anything Dr. Orsini said to make it sound like Stephen could stop his injections. Again, the injections were my thing with Stephen and Betty wouldn't allow me to be a caretaker in any way, even if it meant our son stopping his needed allergy injections. When Betty walked in and saw me already sitting in the waiting room, she glared at me as Stephen gave me a hug in front of her. It's odd not being comfortable getting hugs from your own child, but it infuriated Betty and my presence alone already had her red in the face and looking for payback. Anything I said to Stephen, she forcefully countered, even if it was as simple as, "I miss you, Big Boy." When I said to Stephen, "I would like to see you continue the injections; they are really working for you, even if you don't know it." Betty interjected, "He can decide what is in his best interest!" Maybe she hoped the fear of getting the shots would be enough to override any perceived benefit and he would elect to stop them. I said, "No, he is not. But even if he was, let's see what Dr. Orsini says first." Betty knew I was mostly trying to ignore her and she said, "Stephen, come over and sit with me." Again, Stephen knew there would be consequences if he continued talking to me and going against his mother but, starting to become more independent and assertive, he said, "Just one more minute." Betty was not going to be outdone though. She had to have the last word, so she immediately got out her phone and said, "Hello? Hi Julie, I'm waiting at Stephen's appointment and I wanted to see what you wanted to do this weekend? Do you want to bake cookies or brownies? Okay, I'll be home to see you soon." This was a jab at me because the upcoming weekend was my custody time and she wanted to drive home the fact I wasn't getting the girls.

When we were seen by Dr. Orsini, Betty tried to get him to say anything that had any amount of doubt as to whether Stephen should continue the injections or not. Dr. Orsini is the nicest and most soft spoken gentleman you will ever meet, and his concern for our son's health and well-being has always been his first priority. Yet when Betty could not get him to say anything other than, "Stephen has done well with the injections and he should continue to get them," she raised her voice to the point of almost yelling and said, "I don't like the way you're talking to me!" Betty had become used to people conforming to what she wanted them to believe and say over the last thirty months, whether it was counselors, judges, friends, members of our community, or our daughters, and when she came across the rare person that didn't, she invariably lashed out at them. Dr. Orsini said, "Okay. I'm done here. He is your child and it is your decision." He walked out of the room, looking concerned with his head down. I looked at Stephen, who no doubt didn't like getting a needle stuck in his arm every other week, and I asked him, "Stephen, what do you want?" He knew he was nearly symptom free because of the shots, and he said, "I want to stay on the shots." He looked at Betty and, trying to appease her a little, said, "Just one more year, okay?" She was furious and she looked at him with that half-smile that I knew meant Betty was burning up inside that someone dared to go against her. The only thing that alleviated my fears that she would again turn on our son and hurt him once they were away from me was the fact that it would interfere with her obsession of winning over the kids. Stephen surely remembers what his mother had done to him years before and, right in front of her, made a decision to keep getting the painful shots. He officially went from the timid and irresponsible child, whose maturity often seemed to be that of half his real age, to a young man right before my eyes in a matter of ten minutes. Another instance where I have to type these blurry words as I look through tears.

She left with Stephen closely behind and when they walked outside the waiting room, I watched them from the doorway to further gauge her potential to become physical with Stephen. When she saw me standing back in the doorway to the waiting room, she said, "You're just using him [Stephen] like you use the girls, and that's why they hate being around you! And I'm getting a second opinion from Dr. Simon! He's been our doctor for longer than he has!" as she pointed towards Dr. Orsini's office. Dr. Simon was the surgeon who'd performed Christian's ear tube surgeries, but he had no expertise in allergies. She just had to have the last word.

To drive home the point of just how far Betty would go to discourage me from being a caretaker, she called the police when I took Stephen to his next injection just a week later. So he didn't fall even further behind in his shots, I'd wanted Stephen to get an injection the afternoon our custody switched back to her. I called and texted Betty multiple times, asking her if she could take him to the office after school that day. Or, if she couldn't, I asked her to reschedule for when she could take him. After I hadn't heard back from her all day, I texted to tell her that I was picking up Stephen after school and taking him to get the shot. I also said I would bring him straight to her house "at 3:25." She responded to that text, saying, "I contacted the school and they are aware that you will not be able to sign them out again without my permission and I will be contacting the police that you removed him form (sic) school without permission." Sure enough, when Stephen and I pulled up to her house, the police were there waiting for me.

It wasn't as if the girls walked out of my life and I was left with just my boys. The girls, and especially Julie, pressured the boys to stay with them during my weekends too. While I was on the phone with the boys, asking them what they wanted to do with me during my upcoming custody weekend, Betty would say subtle things in the background like, "All of you kids should be together." Knowing full well the girls had disowned me as their father and they weren't leaving her, that of course meant, "You should stay with me this weekend." The girls weren't so subtle, saying, "I would stay here this weekend if I were you!" to Christian the mornings of our custody changeover.

As I said before, buried in all the stress and strife is an occasional good dose of humor. My portion of any costs associated with the kids was

89% — Betty's 11%. And proof of paying those in 2015 was due to the other parent for reimbursement by the end of March. (For the record, I still haven't been paid for 2014 or 2015.) Buried in Betty's declaration of what I owed her for her child care and activity expenses was $8.90 for... toothpaste. I did the math and figured Betty could buy 25,000 tubes of toothpaste with what I was already paying her. My parents, Bobbie, and I saw a passing chance to laugh and we got as much mileage out of it as possible. Even Jenna, normally very stoic, got a good laugh when we talked on the phone.

Our school's spring break was at the end of March and Betty was not going to let me take the boys to my parents' house in Florida. Jenna brought the issue up as a motion in court and I was granted the week with the boys by a new judge. But before we could get the motion heard, Betty quickly began scheduling doctor's appointments, birthday parties, and her ultrasound during the four weekdays I had requested. To this judge's credit, he saw through the recently scheduled events and allowed our vacation. But there would be a cost to this small win.

We were going to leave the Saturday after I got custody of the boys, but Stephen missed school every day that week with the flu. On Wednesday I texted Betty four times, asking her to call me to talk about Stephen's symptoms. A call had gone out that day to all parents in the district that pertussis was spreading throughout the community and to be vigilant. From my texts, Betty knew I wanted to know why Stephen had missed three days of school and what his symptoms were, so she called me twice, but hung up both times without saying a word. I texted her multiple times afterwards to try to get her to answer, but again, she was elusive and would not tell me anything. On Thursday, after he had missed four days, I called and asked Betty to take him to see a doctor the next day so he could get on some medicine and feel better by the time we left. She yelled, "I'm the primary parent AND their caretaker! I'll decide what they need, not you!" and she hung up. When I called to arrange to pick up Stephen from her Friday, she told me, "And Chris is here and sick now too. And with his ear tube surgeries, I don't want him on an airplane." I said, "Well, I'll assess that and let you know before we leave tomorrow." She became irritated. "He. Is. Sick," she said. I tried to appease her somewhat when I said, "I'm not going to take him if I think he won't be able to clear his ears." She then hung up the phone.

During the time between the call and when I went to pick them up, I started thinking. I looked at Bobbie and said, "Do you think it's odd that Stephen has been home from school sick all week and now Christian is sick the day before we leave for vacation?" Bobbie, said "No." I said, "I didn't either, until I realized the girls are in school, so they must NOT be sick." Bobbie threw both of her hands over her mouth and said, "No! No, tell me she didn't!" I said, "Well, I doubt she somehow got Stephen sick on purpose but once he was, it would be very easy for her to get Christian sick just a day before we leave. Maybe that's why she didn't take Stephen to see the doctor, she needed to wait until Wednesday or yesterday to get Christian sick so there wouldn't be time to get him better before we left." Bobbie stood there with her mouth wide open in complete disbelief and said, "Who does that?!" I said, "Well, enough people that it has a name [Munchausen Syndrome By Proxy]. For the record, there isn't any way we can prove that and she may not have even done it; it may be a coincidence." Bobbie's face conveyed to me exactly what I was thinking and she said it before I could, "Knowing her the way I do now, I think there is a much better chance she did it than not." Six months after meeting Betty, Bobbie had gone from believing everyone had good in them and everyone deserved the benefit of the doubt to believing the worst when it came to Betty.

During the two hours we had till I got the boys, Bobbie had an idea. "Let's go buy Stephen a phone, and that way you can talk to him when Betty doesn't let you," she said. I said, "That works both ways you know?" "What do you mean?" Bobbie asked. I said, "If I get him a phone, she's going to pelt him with call after call and text after text." "He's almost thirteen, he's not going to want to text his mom all day," Bobbie said. "No, but she will use it to continually remind him of what he could be doing if he was with her. Like playing with his cousins," I said. Bobbie looked at me, wondering what we should do. I then said, "What the heck. With a few exceptions, he has been a great kid the last eight or nine months and he should be rewarded."

I have always wanted any phone I bought for the kids to have a memorable number, so the assistant at the store kept going through the numbers that would randomly flash on his screen until Bobbie and I found one we liked. It was perfect, as it had the model number of my favorite commercial airplane in it and the excitement of giving it to him replaced the concern. Stephen was excited to get the phone of course, and he wanted to let everyone know he had it ASAP. He stepped into the other room and called my mom. My mom said, "I wonder who this is?" as she looked at her phone. She answered it and Stephen said, "Hi Grammy!" Everyone laughed and I looked over at Bobbie as if to say, "Good idea to get the phone." A few minutes later, he called his mom. They talked for about ten minutes, but he looked less and less happy as he listened to Betty talk. When he got off the phone, he said, "I don't want to go to Florida." I asked, "Why?" He said, "My cousins have the whole week off for spring break too and Sunday they're having a party." I said, "Stephen, Grammy bought tickets because the flights were full and I took the whole week off from work. We are going and we'll have a great time." He didn't say anything to me and he didn't have to — his face told me there would be trouble getting him to cooperate and get on the plane Sunday.

Throughout the evening, I tried to have fun with the boys and get Stephen excited for our trip. Most of the time, he wouldn't even look at me. I decided to give it a rest, and get him some rest, as maybe a full night's sleep would make him more cheery and cooperative. That night, Betty called him again and they talked for another ten minutes. He was even worse after this call than the first and he forcefully said to me, "I'm not going!" as he hung up. I said, "Stephen, you are going and you are not going to ruin our time." "I'm not going and you can't make me!" he said. I said, "Stephen, why are you doing this?" He said, "Mitchel and Joel [his two older cousins] want me to come over Sunday and play with them!" "Stephen, this vacation has cost me a ton of money in tickets and missed work and you are going." "No! I am not!" he yelled. I stuck with the original plan of putting him to bed early and hoping for a rosier outlook in the morning.

Sunday morning, while I packed the kids' things, my mom took Stephen back to the store to have a problem with his phone fixed. On the drive back, Betty again called Stephen and my mom could hear Betty as Stephen sat right next to her. Betty said, "Stephen, don't you want to play with your cousins? They're home from school all week." Stephen said, "Yeah, I do." Betty then said, "Well, just stay home." When they got back from the store, I looked at Stephen's phone and Betty had also sent texts saying "Just stay home" and "Mitchel wants to talk to you." Mitchel trying to talk to Stephen was most likely at Betty's direction, to tell Stephen about all of the fun they would be having that week and to convince him he should stay home. For the rest of the three hours until our plane left, Stephen said he would only go to Florida if we came home just a day or two later. I said, "Stephen, we have six days there and we're going to have fun every one of them." As we walked through the airport, you would have thought we were taking him to boot camp if you had seen his dejected demeanor. Meanwhile, Christian, the perennially great kid as always, had been jumping-up-and-down excited since I'd picked him up the day before.

As we went to the airport and got on the plane, Stephen vacillated between being distant and angry, to being somewhat happy — or at least not mad. When we walked into my parents' new house late that night, he was tired, but he was excited to be there and looking forward to waking up and playing in the enclosed pool off the back porch. "I knew it," I thought. "I knew if we could just get him down here, he would be fine." But getting Stephen to go to Florida incited Betty and she called him twice the next morning. After those calls, Stephen was combative and angry that he couldn't be with his cousins and he set out to ruin every minute of our vacation until we agreed to take him home. This wasn't Stephen's fault as much as it was Betty's, but at nearly thirteen years old, I believed his want for more independence, and hence responsibility, worked both ways. Besides Adam, his two oldest cousins were his only real friends and spending time and playing with them was his version of paradise — not a house in Florida 1,000 miles from them. Betty knew this and, through Stephen's new phone, used this well-known fact against us.

The first five days seemed like *Groundhog Day* with Stephen angry and argumentative. It created problems with my parents and I because there was nothing we could do to abate his attitude — we were simply along for the ride until we took him home. On Thursday, I remember thinking, "I don't think I have ever been this stressed. Ever." I then made Stephen an offer to try to keep my sanity. The upcoming Sunday was Easter and, according to the custody agreement, I got the kids for most of the afternoon that day this year. So I told Stephen that I wouldn't exercise my rights to Easter with him and Christian and he could stay and play with his cousins — if he was good. He cracked a smile and said, "Okay." I learned something right there — this was more about control than actual time with his cousins. After all, Stephen was getting only a small fraction of the time with his cousins that he'd initially wanted, but he now knew that he could get part of what he wanted. My problem with it was, I didn't want him to think he'd gotten what he'd wanted, gotten that control, because he'd made our lives hell — he needed to know (or at least think) that he'd gotten what he wanted because he had negotiated for it. I had a long conversation with him about his behavior, and if he thought he deserved more control over his life because he was getting older, then he needed to act like he was nearly thirteen. Very telling of the lesson he learned, Stephen's behavior has been significantly more mature since this happened nearly a year ago.

If anyone reading this was wondering why I didn't buy my kids a phone when, in the previous chapters, I'd said I had extreme difficulty talking to them on Betty's time, this incident should clear that up.

An interesting thing happened during the days when Stephen was combative. I had him talk to his mom on speaker phone the third night because I wanted to hear exactly what she was saying to him to make him so upset. By this point, she had somewhat given up on trying to get Stephen to come home early and, after a run-down of what Mitchel and Joel were doing for the rest of their spring break, she spent the last few minutes talking to him normally — normally for any parent, that is, just not Betty. Because I hadn't listened to any conversations of theirs since we'd separated, I heard, for the first time ever, Betty talk to our son like she cared for him — not the burden she made him out to be before that night thirty months before. It was so foreign and powerful to me that I had to leave the room so Stephen wouldn't see the tears well up in my eyes as I again realized that the whole divorce was worth it if it meant she treated him with care and respect.

Highlighting how oblivious to the obvious I can sometimes be (outside of work), on the flight to Florida days before, it dawned on me that Betty had probably never told her mom what really happened the night she was arrested. They are so closely bonded that I thought, for two-and-a-half years, that Betty had told Pat what really happened that night and then they came up with a plan to exonerate Betty's name from the arrest. I previously thought Pat said something like, "We'll say he attacked you, put some bruises on your neck and eye, and you play the victim like your life depends on it, and we'll take him to the cleaners." But my realization on that flight was that Betty had probably told Pat her spun version of that night on the drive back from jail the very next morning, and what Pat really said was probably more like, "You are divorcing that abusive S.O.B. and we'll take him to the cleaners!"

FOOL CIRCLE

Losing the ability to monitor my kids around Betty's dad was certainly at the top of the list of things that concerned me about our separate lives. At the end of April, Stephen had a school concert that Betty's parents, and my parents and I attended. We sat a few rows back and off to the side of Betty and her parents, and I didn't like the manner in which Dale was making his one grandson sit on his lap. When I had custody of the kids the very next day, I talked to Christian, who was the same age, about being cautious around his grandfather. Christian, of course, asked why, and I felt like I had to say enough to concern him but not too much to make him afraid of Dale. "I don't really trust him Christian. I will tell you more when you're older, but that's all I can say about it right now," I said.

I didn't get Stephen that weekend, but I talked to him two weeks later when I saw him next. I told him the same thing I'd told Christian two weeks before, but I added, "I have reason to believe he may have done something a long time ago and I believe he is still capable of being inappropriate with kids." I also told Stephen I would tell him more when he was older as he had many questions about what little I could tell him. I then said to Stephen, "Please watch your grandfather very closely when he is around your sisters. They may despise me, but I'm still their father and I still need to do everything possible to protect them — to include getting you to watch out for them when I can't." Stephen was growing up quickly and, wanting more responsibility, and he gave me a big-eyed nod.

The reason I didn't get Stephen that weekend after the concert was that Pat picked up Stephen after school without telling me. I went to Stephen's bus stop to get him that day, but he wasn't on the bus. I asked Adam if he knew where Stephen was and he said, "I think I saw him getting picked up by his other grandma." I went home thinking Pat was taking him back to Betty's house, but I didn't know and I had to wait for Christian to get off of his bus near my house, so I couldn't run around looking for him. Right before Christian's bus pulled up, my phone rang with Pat's number on the screen. I answered and Stephen said, "Hi Dad." "Where are you, Stephen?" I asked. "I'm with Grammy. We're almost at Aunt Peg's and then we're going to Grammy and Grandpa's house," he said. I asked, "I thought you were coming here, Big Boy? What happened?" "Well, Pap Pap is opening the pool this weekend and Grammy said there's a big kids' party all weekend with the cousins and us," he said. "He's opening the pool in April?" I asked with a bit of skepticism. "That's what Grammy told me," Stephen said. "So you're not coming to me this whole weekend, Stephen?" He didn't say anything, so I said, "Let me talk to your grandma please, Stephen. Before you go, can I get you at some point this weekend?" "I don't know, Grammy said we're going to be doing fun things all weekend," he said. Stephen put Pat on the phone and I said, "Why did you take Stephen from school and not tell me?" She said, "He got in the car, I didn't make him get in!" I said, "You lied about opening the pool and that it's a 'kids weekend.' What is a kids' weekend? And I have never, in seventeen years, known Dale to open the pool before Memorial Day. It's chilly outside and you're going swimming?" I said. "I don't have to tell you what my family is doing!" she yelled as she hung up the phone.

I then called the police and explained the situation. "What options do I have?" I asked. The dispatcher said, "I can send an officer to your house to talk with you and you two can decide what you want to do." When the officer arrived, he called Pat to ask her directly why she'd taken Stephen. During the conversation with the policeman, Pat said that she'd left the school where she'd picked up Stephen and Julie and picked up her other granddaughter at the private preschool Betty worked at just a quarter-mile from my house. The policeman then asked her, "If you were so close to Mr. Black's house and you had his son on his time, why didn't you stop in and tell him so he didn't have to worry about where his son was?" I heard Pat yelling over the phone that I beat up Betty and I was a horrible father to our kids. The officer replied, "Don't yell at me; I don't talk to kids about adult matters and I don't talk to adults acting like kids." The officer tried many times to get Pat to answer why she hadn't contacted me before taking Stephen, and as the police report says, "She could provide no reasonable answer." He gave up trying to get Pat to answer the question a few minutes later. The officer looked at me and said, "I have grounds to go and arrest her, but I'm leaving that up to you." I said, "No, that would only make this whole thing even worse and the kids would blame me for putting her in jail, not her." What frustrated me about my decision was that I could have had Pat arrested and yet she wouldn't care that I didn't — it's not like she's going to realize that I'm not such a bad guy after all, thank me, and then help mend my relationships with my kids. I didn't get Stephen at all that weekend and Dale, of course, didn't open the pool for another month.

Going back to the night of the concert, when Bobbie and I left the school parking lot, we passed right in front of Betty as she waited at a stop sign. I had my window down, and I casually waved thinking Stephen was in there with her. She pulled out of the intersection extremely fast, for a minivan anyway, and seemed intent on hitting the back of my car. The light just a hundred feet ahead of me was red, so I was slowing down and now trying to keep an eye on her when she swerved into the right lane. As I came to a stop, she pulled up beside me. She was partially out her window as she pointed and yelled at me. Bobbie and I don't remember what she said to me, because it was overshadowed by what she said to Bobbie, "And you're a bitch too!" Bobbie said, "Me? I'm a bitch? What did I ever do?" Betty then put up her middle finger and left just as fast as she'd pulled up to me. On the drive home, I felt bad that Bobbie had tried her hardest with Betty and yet still had to endure being yelled at. It's not as if Bobbie avoided Betty or just said a causal hi when they saw each other, Bobbie went out of her way to say to Betty, "Wow, you look great," and "How do you feel?" This was an effort to extend an olive branch to Betty as her pregnancy visibly moved along. I said, "I'm sorry. No one is allowed to love me and that's why she hates you, it's not you personally." Bobbie said, "There are two things someone can't take away from you unless you let them, and that is hope and love. And that's why I'm a bitch, because she can't take away our hope and love for each other. It doesn't matter how nice and loving I am towards her kids or her, I'll always be a bitch for not hating you. And she expects your kids to despise you too, and there are consequences if they don't. And that's why we cling to our tiny little successes with them because that is all we get. Remember, love always wins." I said, "I'm not so sure love always wins. She has taken almost everything I value — everything but the boys and you. And she is working feverishly on the boys now too. And even if my girls come around, they'll be adults before they realize what happened and Betty would have taken the very thing I want the most, to be a part of their childhood." Bobbie looked at me and grabbed my hand, knowing I was right.

That same week, I went into Julie's classroom for a program at Southern where we can volunteer to talk to the kids about careers and why learning and doing well in school is important. Over the three or four visits we talk about science and keep the discussions loosely related to aviation. I wasn't sure how Julie would receive me in front of fifty of her classmates, but I made sure my uniform was spotless and that I was very well prepared. When I first walked in, Julie wouldn't look at me, but halfway through the first class, she was looking up and smiling as her classmates were very interactive with my discussion and questions. They were having fun and Julie must have felt it was okay after a while and she started raising her hand when I asked questions. I had taught the science material to my kids from time-to-time over the years, so I smiled and said, "You have a bit of an unfair advantage here, Julie, but you can answer anyway." One boy then said, "Wait! Do you know her? Are you Julie's dad?" When Julie realized that the other kids liked what I was saying and were fully engaged in the class, I think she took some pride in the fact that I was her father.

After the class was over, I asked her to meet me off to the side of the classroom while the other kids packed their books to change rooms. She walked up to me as I crouched down a little to meet her eye-to-eye and so I could talk softer with her friends just twenty feet away. She said, "I really liked it!" I said, "I'm glad, Julie, but that's not why I wanted to talk to you. I want you to know I do not like your behavior towards me and I do not agree with how you are being raised, but I am always here for you if you need anything. Always, no matter what." Julie looked at me more seriously and said, "If I come with you next weekend, do I have to come the next time after that? Grammy's having a big party that second time that I want to be there for." I said, "No, I will never force you to come with me; I will let you make that decision. I am so happy to hear that you may come with me Friday though, and I can't wait to tell my mom and dad and Aunt Sandi." With her mouth now full of braces, she smiled and I thought I might have found a way back into her life.

The next day, I called Betty's house to ask the boys what they wanted to do when I got them Friday. I didn't want to ask Julie anything just yet, as I knew her coming with me was not a certainty and I didn't want her to feel any pressure. After I talked with Stephen, he said, "Julie wants to talk to you." Julie got on the phone and said, "Dad, I'm not coming with you Friday. I'm sleeping over at a friend's that night." I said, "Well, I hope you know I can take you to your friend's too, Julie." There was just silence, so I repeated what I had said. Julie then said, "Well, her and I are going to a dance competition the next day." I didn't want to force the issue, hoping that Julie would feel more free to come and go without any significant pressure.

This is pure speculation, but I believe that Julie went home the day I was in her class and told her mom that she would be going with me Friday. Then Betty probably arranged a sleepover with a friend whose mom believed Betty's stories about me (there seem to be plenty of those moms in the community), and they wouldn't want me around. Far fetched to most people, but not for those dealing with suspected Borderlines.

Though Julie was showing signs of coming around, I wasn't sure if Noel had started to miss me or not. I got my answer from Noel towards the end of May when I needed to get Christian's soccer shoes and jersey to him. I drove to where he and Noel got off the school bus up the street from their mom's house. I was standing about twenty feet away from the bus, and to the opposite side of where the kids got out. Noel stopped Christian from getting off the bus and she looked scared as she took quick glances at me and then looked up at the driver, who was wondering what she was doing. After a minute of this, Noel then ran off the bus and down the street in a sprint as she occasionally looked back at me, presumably to see if I was following her. Good ole Christian walked off the bus, smiled at me and said, "She sure was in a hurry!" I laughed and said, "Yes, she certainly was!"

One of the things Betty does to take away my custody time is to use her vacation days over my weekends. The very next weekend I was to get the kids, it was my mom's birthday that Friday and Betty used two of her fourteen vacation days to keep the kids till Sunday. When it was time to get them on Sunday, I headed over to Pat and Dale's with my dad, who wanted to come and video the exchange in case Betty or Pat tried to do or say anything. On the drive over, I thought about parking off of their property to avoid fueling any confrontations. But when I got there, we could hear a couple of the kids around the back of the house playing where the pool was, so I drove most of the way up their driveway. When I got out of my car, Julie and Noel had just come out of the pool and they were walking towards me. When they saw me, they both screamed and ran back into the gated pool area and hid in the storage shed. I walked up to the gate, and as Stephen saw me, he walked over and stood behind Betty and said, "I'm not going." I asked, "Why not, Stephen?" He said, "I want to play with the cousins." I said, "Okay. Christian, are you ready to go?" and he said, "I don't want to go." Betty smiled at me like it was all a game of cat and mouse — and she was the cat. I asked, "Why not, Christian?" He said, "We're having a party." By now Charlie had run over to me and was jumping up and down at the gate, so I opened it and let him out. When I picked him up, Betty yelled at me to put him down and ran up to me and started grabbing and jerking my arm as I turned away from her. Julie and Noel were yelling, "I hate you!" I said, "This is my weekend with him under our new agreement." (I got Charlie only once a month now that I wasn't getting the girls.) I've heard that Betty's family didn't treat Charlie well, and he was clinging to me and shaking from the first second I had him. My dad and Charlie are good buddies too, and, hoping I could talk Christian into going, I took him to my car and Charlie licked his face while my dad kept trying to take video. Betty saw my dad taking the video and she yelled at him and reached into the passenger side of my car and hit him in the face and then knocked the video camera out of his hands. Again, even with grabbing and jerking my arm, yelling at me and my dad, and punching my dad and his video camera — all on video — this is a woman who drives around with a Domestic Violence Survivor sticker on the back of her van and whom 95% of the people who know her believe I beat her up for all twelve years of our marriage.

I then went back to the pool to see if I could talk to Christian. He came out of the fenced in area and I said, "Look, Christian, I know you want to stay here, but I really missed you and I really want to spend time with you." He just looked at me, not knowing what to say. I didn't want to force him, and he didn't want to hurt me by saying he'd rather stay there, so I said, "Okay Christian, you can stay. Just promise me I'll get you next time without any trouble. Okay?" He said, "I want to be with you, Dad," and I gave him a hug, trying to hide my face so he wouldn't see the tears his comment suddenly pulled from me. While I was hugging him, Noel and Julie were still declaring how much they hated me. Noel then stuck her butt out at me and said, "You're not even our dad anymore! You lost all of your kids!" With Julie and Noel just a few feet away from me, with Noel's butt sticking out and the two girls now laughing, I said, "You two look like you're really afraid of me after all of those horrible things you say I did to you." I was hoping they would see the obvious contradiction. Pat and Dale then started questioning me. "Why are you on our property?" Dale said. "What do you mean?" I asked. Pat yelled, "You are not to come onto our property and we called the police!" I said, "Eighteen months ago, you yelled at me for NOT coming onto your property to pick up the kids, so which one is it Pat?" She stood there, dumbfounded, as she realized I was right. Dale interjected, "Well the police are coming, so now you need to stay here." Out of patience, I said, "I'm going to wait for them off of your property, and you can claim I'm now trying to leave." I got Charlie off of my dad, but something was wrong with him. Just as he had done with me minutes before, he was clinging to my dad and shaking. We'd never known him to do that, and I've heard Stephen say Pat and Peg didn't like him, so I couldn't help but think he was being mistreated somehow. Regardless, I was going to be mistreated too if he didn't go back to Betty.

As I got in the car, Betty yelled something to my dad, something I don't even remember from all of the other things that were said. But after she did, she threw herself into Bob's arms as if she needed his protection. In one of the more vivid memories from the last thirty-three months, I can still see the both of them holding onto each other. Bob's face was that of someone who was protecting the helpless mother of his unborn baby and Betty acted like she was the victim of yet another battering by me — this after she was the aggressor for ten straight minutes. My dad had had enough, and said to Bob, "Does Michele know you're having a baby with Betty, Bob?" This was in reference to an email I had just gotten from Betty's lawyer that read, "Bob is married to someone else and he has no intention of getting divorced." I'd received the email after I'd had Jenna ask Alexis if Betty and Bob were going to get married (so I would know how long I was going to be paying alimony to her and whether or not to accept the judge's financial ruling that had just come out). I gritted my teeth and loudly whispered to my dad, "No! You can't say that!" He looked at me like, "What does it matter now?" I said, "I'll explain on the way home."

My dad and I talked to the police officer while standing just off Pat and Dale's property, and my four kids and their cousins were starting to come to that part of the front yard — possibly told to leave the pool and go there by Betty or Pat. There was a trampoline there, and they bounced on it and laughed while looking at my dad and I. When we were done telling our side of the story, the two policeman went to go talk to Betty and her parents. Julie and Noel then started laughing at me and Noel alternated between sticking her butt and tongue out at me. As we drove off, they were laughing and sarcastically yelling "Bye!" I was humiliated by my daughters' behavior and I thought, "They are at a point of no return. They are going to despise me the rest of my life."

On the drive home, I explained to my dad why I hadn't wanted him saying what he said about Bob still being married. I said, "Right now, he has not joined Betty and Pat in their effort to alienate the kids from me and that's the way I want to keep it. That's the way it has to be at ALL cost. He has passively stood off to the side when I know Betty would love nothing more than for him to start joining forces with her and to also start acting like their father. Because ultimately, that what she wants — to butt me out of their life and for him to take my place." My dad said, "But she says that she finally found someone to really love her and how he is such a great role model for your kids. How can he be either when he is married to someone else and he has no intention of divorcing this other woman?! And she's due to have his baby in two months; they are both terrible role models!" he said. "Things are different in society now though Dad. Look, I don't want the kids knowing about Bob being married. There will be a time for it, but I'd rather it not be from us; we'll just look vindictive for telling them," I said.

In the police report from that incident, one officer suggests we do the exchanges at a neutral site, such as at a police station. I had been trying to get Betty to do this since early 2014, but she refused. Now with it in writing, she didn't have much choice unless she was willing to risk exposing the real reason she didn't want to have the exchanges at the police station — she used that time to taunt me. When I met Betty at the police station in early June, I walked over to where Betty had parked, but I was careful not to stand too close to her van. Stephen rolled down his window just behind Betty and he put his head down without saying a word, so I knew he didn't want to come with me. Christian was nestled in the back seat between the cousin that is his age, Anthony, and Noel. He wasn't moving or making any effort to get out, so I asked Christian if he wanted to come with me and he said, "Anthony is sleeping over at Mom's house tonight." I said, "But Christian, you didn't come the last time either. And you'll be on vacation next Sunday, which is Father's Day. And the weekend after that, you'll still be on vacation. I'm not going to see any of you for a month and it will have been almost two months from the last time I had you." He just looked at me with a blank face and I decided not to pressure him anymore. "What about you, Stephen?" I said through the open window. "No, I don't want to go," he said with quite a bit of remorse. Frustrated, I asked Betty, "Are you going to tell them they should go with me?" She didn't answer, she only smiled. "What about Stephen's GoPro? I haven't seen that in a year," I asked. She said, "I told you I don't have it! Stop asking me about it!" I said, "Stephen said it is at your house." Betty then got out of her van and went inside the police station and I was left there with the kids. As I stood there, Noel looked at me and smiled sarcastically, as if she knew hurting me was all a big game. I'd had enough and calmly said, "It's real funny, huh, Noel? You think it's funny to hurt me?" She then snorted, trying to stop herself from bursting out laughing. I then said, "You're really afraid of me, aren't you, Noel?" She chuckled and looked up to Julie in the front seat. Julie yelled, "Just go away, Dad!" Noel continued, "Yeah! Just go away! You're not even our dad anymore!" I said, "I'm not? Who is, Noel?" Julie looked back at Noel as if to say, "Don't say it." Noel then said, "You're not even a dad anymore, you LOST all of your kids! How sad is that?!" I am far from perfect, and it briefly crossed my mind to say, "I lost you until it comes time to pay for college, and then we'll see how lost I am," but I found some restraint. I said, "Okay. Have a great time on vacation," and I left.

The girls had their biennial recital the next day, and my mom came up to me before the show started and said, "Look in the program; you're not going to believe it." When I did, there was a full-page color ad from Betty and her family that said, "Love your biggest fans, Mom, Bob…and

<u>All</u> your cousins!" I looked at my mom and said, "Jesus. I thought she was obsessed before. Now she takes out a full page color ad? And Betty capitalized and underlined 'All'?!" If there was a bright spot, at the end of the show, despite Betty's efforts to keep the girls from my parents and me, Julie actually came out into the lobby and said hi to us. I couldn't keep the tears back in front of hundreds of people, so I gave her a quick hug and said, "I'm proud of you Julie," and I went back into the auditorium to pretend to gather my camera equipment. Noel then popped her head into the dark auditorium and said, "Thanks," for the flowers my parents and I got her (and Julie) and she ran off as fast as she could.

Towards the end of June, Jenna filed contempt of court charges against Betty for enticing the kids to stay with her and not encouraging them to go with me during my custody time. Betty, Bob, and the kids were in the middle of their vacation, but within minutes of sending the email to Betty's lawyer, my phone was ringing with Betty's cell number on the screen. It was Stephen, and he was mad. "Why are you taking Mom back to court and getting us a guardian [Guardian Ad Litem]?" he asked. I said, "That really shouldn't concern you, Stephen, that is for the adults." He said, "But then we'll HAVE to go with you!" I said, "Exactly, Stephen. I'm not talking to you anymore about this." He said, "Well, I'm still not going to go with you!" "Let me talk with your mom," I said. I heard Stephen say to Betty, "Here, Dad wants to talk to you," but the phone hung up. I called back and I heard Bob say, "Hello," in an irritated and annoyed tone. I said, "Hi Bob, is Betty there?" With the same annoyed tone he said, "She doesn't want to talk to you." I'd had enough of the disrespectful attitude from two people whom I was financially support- ing and I said, "And you do?" He yelled, "No, and don't give me shit!" I said, "You started it with your tone, not me." He sighed and then snickered, so I said, "It's real funny. Real funny how Betty has gotten the kids to hate me, isn't it?" He shot back, "That's right! They do hate you! They like me more than they like their own father! How does that feel?!" I asked, "Do those same kids know that you're married to another woman and have no intention of divorcing your real wife, Bob?" It degraded to the point that we were both yelling over top of each other. I was yelling, "You're a parasite!" and Bob was yelling, "How does it feel?!" over and over.

Betty had declared her vacation through the last day of my custody, but she actually came home thirty-six hours before that time. Betty's stance with regards to the contempt charges was that she always tried to foster a good relationship between the kids and I and she tried to get the kids to spend time with me. Yet she'd declared her vacation days with the kids to run right to the end of my custody time, despite the fact that she was going to be home the last day-and-a-half I should have had them. She knew that I had not had custody of any of the kids for six weeks, and through her vacation time, tried to make it eight weeks. In the end, through tireless negotiation and the realization that she was now going to have to answer to a judge for her actions, she let me have the boys Monday afternoon until the next morning. Even though this was my custody time and they were back in town, she was still indignant, saying, "I let you have the kids on my vacation!" in a subsequent conversation.

As luck would have it, I was outside cutting the grass in the hours before I got the kids Monday morning when Betty drove by. She looked over at me and, as she saw me, a big smile came over her face. She knew, as did I, that in the heated argument with Bob just days before, I'd accomplished something she hadn't over the two years — I awakened the sleeping giant. Now flanked by Pat and Bob, Betty's vision to nullify my role as our children's father was more attainable than ever.

My next custody weekend started the second week of July. I met Betty at the police station and though the girls wouldn't even look at me, the boys jumped out of the car and gave me big hugs. "Hi Dad!" they said. "Hi boys! How are you?" "Great!" they said, and we made our way to my parents' house for a quick visit. When we got to my parents', Stephen and I were finishing up a conversation in the car, so Christian got out and went inside. Stephen had said something odd and I wanted him to clarify before we went into my parents'. "We're not allowed to sleep over at Grammy's anymore," he had said, speaking about Pat and Dale's house. I was concerned and asked him, "Why?" He said, "Well, really we're not allowed around Pap Pap alone anymore. But we're also not allowed to sleep over either." I asked, "What brought this about?" He said, "One night during a sleepover, one of the girl's friends ran out of the room all of the girls were sleeping in and yelled, 'He is trying it again!'" "Trying what?" I asked. Stephen looked at me with a raised brow and big eyes and said, "I don't know, but it can't be good! Grammy was walking around the next day with a piece of paper saying, 'Look kids, this is what your grandfather has done!' and saying that we wouldn't be allowed to sleep over or be around him alone anymore. But I didn't know what was on the paper, I really couldn't see it." "I really can't stand when she uses her grandchildren as her therapist," I said, trying not to convey to Stephen that part of my mind was rewinding to the times Betty and Bob had gone on trips and left the kids with Pat and Dale and another part of my mind was trying to figure out if I needed to call CYF or not.

After our conversation, I sat out in the car and thought about what he had just told me, and I went back to the piece of paper that Pat was showing the other grandkids. Could it be something Betty had drawn, at Pat's request, thirty years ago, trying to express how she felt about what her father had done?

I spent over an hour trying to figure out how I could call CYF and report what Stephen told me without involving him; even going as far as calling CYF and giving them a hypothetical situation. I was met with, "We don't deal with hypothetical situations," from the somewhat annoyed lady on the other end of the phone. With that, I knew that I would have to include Stephen and, now thirteen years old, he would be somewhat equipped to handle the inevitable fallout from his mother and Pat. "How big will the fallout be, and will he be safe?" were the questions I asked myself over and over before and after I made the call that evening.

The next day, the CYF agents visited Betty and the girl from the sleepover. Though I don't know what they said, it was enough to where Dale was quarantined from children pending a more comprehensive interview. I was visited by a CYF agent, and I told him what I knew and of my observations of Dale over the years, which I will not include here. Suffice to say, Dale was in big trouble. And so was Betty, because based on the timing of it, she and Pat had known Dale still had a problem going back well over a year before this. They continued to let the kids and their friends around him unsupervised after this incident, despite the no sleepover rule and family quarantine Stephen had told me about. If Dale was found guilty, and Betty was found to have put our kids in danger, she would likely lose her primary custody status — or even worse. The young girl's mother, her only parent, didn't seem to be too engaged in her life, but

Betty no doubt had some work to do with the both of them. Betty had been told from the outset that CYF wanted the second interviews to be as close as possible to the first, so she had a limited time to find the words to keep her father out of jail and her failure to protect our kids from being uncovered. For three weeks, Betty dragged out getting the kids to the forensic interviews, during which time I conveyed to the CYF agent my concerns that Betty was coaching our girls and their friend on what to say. In the agent's words, "We can't force her to come in."

When the agent called to tell me about the interviews, he said, "All of the girls denied anything inappropriate ever happened with Dale." I said, "Didn't the friend make a disclosure a month ago?" "Yes, but this time she said that he was just trying to wake her up in the middle of the night and he touched her down there, but it was an accident." "Do you really believe that, Rodger?" I asked. "No, of course I don't. But we can't make her say what really happened either. If that's the story she wants to stick to, then that's all we have." "What about my girls, did they say anything had ever happened to them?" I asked. "Both of your daughters, especially Julie, could not, no matter what, stay on the question asked of them. They immediately diverted their answers to the kind of father you are every time. They said you scare them and are very mean. And they did not call you their father either, they referred to you as 'Rob.' And they did not mention you when we asked who was in their family. It was very frustrating. And you should know that they also said your girlfriend had been inappropriate with them and your boys too." "Really? How so?" I asked. "They said she would lay down with them at night and they were very uncomfortable." "Ha. Funny how that's what it has become now that they have an agenda. Rodger, I can assure you that Bobbie is a very caring and loving person, but she would never do that. If there is any shred of truth to that, it is because my kids would ASK for Bobbie to come into their rooms and scratch their backs when they went to bed. In fact, they would argue with each other for who got to be first. I know the one night Bobbie's arm got tired and she layed down as she scratched Stephen's back, but she was on the edge of the bed, not up against him. I saw her and I didn't think anything of it, but Betty made a big deal of it when the kids went back to her, so Bobbie stopped doing that. Bobbie also layed down with Noel one night that Noel was very upset, and Bobbie was just trying to comfort her, but again, it wasn't anything that alarmed me. I actually welcomed how Bobbie was able to calm Noel," I said. Rodger said, "Well, unfortunately, that's not all. You should know that your girls said that you had been inappropriate with them, not their grandfather." "What?!" I nearly yelled. "They said you gave them showers when they 'were five and six years old,'" he said. "Rodger. I'm sorry, but I really don't think there's anything wrong with that," I said as I calmed down. "Don't worry, we didn't either," he said as he laughed a little. I just couldn't stand the thought that my girls had tried to swing the whole investigation around to focus on me, so I said, "In fact, Rodger, Julie would ASK me to come into the shower and comb conditioner through her hair as recently as 2012. So she would be what, seven or eight years old? She ASKED me." He said, "Don't worry, Mr. Black, you are not under investigation — not even close. Oh, and you should know that, like you warned us, Noel did accuse you of slamming her against a wall. But when I said, 'Your father told us you would probably say that and he says he only put you against the wall,' she got upset and admitted she had lied about it. She said you were right." Noel's admission and honesty about that day gave me hope that she might eventually tell the truth about other things I had been accused of and I was overcome with emotions. I thanked Rob for his time and effort and hung up the phone, stunned from what I had just heard.

A different agent, who was also in the room when the girls were being interviewed, called me a few days later to ask if I wanted a copy of the report, to which I said, "Yes." She informed me that, in her interview, Betty was adamant that the accusation against her father was all a ploy to take custody time away from her and that I had fabricated the whole thing. I said, "Ultimately Leah, I'm just trying to make sure Dale doesn't go after my girls. It sounds like he has a long history of being sexually inappropriate with young girls and people like that don't just stop. They can't." She said, "Mr. Black, it is clear something happened to the girl, but we can't make her say it. If, at some point in her life, she wants to talk about it, she can — there is no statute of limitations for this."

Through a friend, I was told that the girl had told their daughter that Dale did touch her "In a weird place and in a weird way." And she said it just days after the interviews. I said to my mom and Bobbie, "Betty is so good at manipulating other people's minds, that she can not only keep her dad out of jail and keep her record clean, but she can actually take the enormity of a molestation charge directed at her and her father and somehow make ME look like the child molester."

When the report came in the mail, I learned that Dale had "likely" (it appeared he had his arrest expunged) been arrested for "Indecent Exposure years ago," adding credence to both what happened that night to the girls' friend and to what likely happened to Betty when she was a little girl. The rest of the report was even harder to read as I saw, in text, my girls complete disdain for me. They had clearly been coached during those three weeks between interviews and Betty and Pat's mission to get my girls to become parrots in their campaign against me seemed complete. The most painful thing is knowing that my daughters are living with a family that is very much like a cult. They are choosing this way of life though; they embrace it and discard me and my family, who only want the chance to love them. They are willing to repeatedly lie about me and the kind of person I am, and support Betty and Pat's propaganda throughout our community and court system. They want to be with the person and family who they need protected from, not the person who is trying to protect them and raise them with love, accountability, and morals. Hate is now ingrained throughout their minds and thoughts, and I am powerless to change who they have become and who they will be.

In a bittersweet coincidence, the day I got the CYF report in the mail, Bobbie found three pages of Julie's diary while looking for some make-up in her room. They were dated a year-and-a-half before and had been torn from the book and hidden under some old clothes. Bobbie and I read how happy Julie was to be with me and how much fun she had on my time. To think of how loving she had been towards me just half-way through the two years Dr. Darnall talked about and how different she was now. When we found the rest of the diary, it noted inside the front cover that she had ripped these older pages out. Probably fearing any evidence of our good times being found, she ripped out the pages to carry out her mother's objective of painting me as a person whom the kids had always been scared of.

There was an impossible-to-measure amount of good to come out of the whole CYF ordeal though, besides Noel finally admitting I only placed her against the wall that day she smashed the umbrella years ago. Like Christian always has, Stephen sees me for who I really am. I don't know why, and I don't care to know why, but he is excited to see me now. He smiles from ear-to-ear and gives me one of his trademark "Stephen hugs" when he sees me for the first time in nine days or even after just being away from me for part of the day. He is incredibly well-behaved with me and he has become the caring leader I saw in him for a short while during the end of the baseball season in 2013. He is responsible and grateful. He knows I'm going to put him to bed early and he accepts it. He accepts me. Christian accepts me. And they love me. That's all I ask of my kids and I get it from both of my boys.....

An Unforeseen Chapter

left the five periods at the end of the last chapter because they represent the words, "and both of my girls." Those periods also represent the undying hope that I have not lost them forever. They represent unconditional love. And they represent that I am a father to four children, not two.

This book was being sent off to print just when my girls had decided to see me again — this chapter is a last second add-on. The change was mostly due to a new counselor, one that I decided on when I sought "reunification counseling" with Julie and Noel. Through Jenna, I got the legal authority to change counselors and after numerous phone calls, I selected Tamryn. Reunification counseling specifically focuses on high-conflict divorces where children are alienated from one of their parents. The biggest impediment, which we have run into, is that it can't address the root of the problem, but through many small steps, and considerable time, the goal is to gradually get the children to want to have a relationship with both parents — not just one. After quite a few sessions, and many conversations with my girls that broke down into heated disagreements, I asked them, "Do you want to want to have a relationship with me?" I'd felt my girls were lying to defend themselves over the incidents from the winter and I posed that question at the end of this particularly frustrating session as I was getting up to leave. Tamryn explained the confusing question to them once I'd left and she told me, only minutes later, that my girls wanted to try spending some time with me.

Their visit was only supposed to be for an hour that weekend, and the girls wanted it to be at my parents' house, not mine. And though they changed their mind at the last minute, and didn't come to my parents', I sensed some hope. Through Tamryn's patience, calm demeanor, and devotion, she has started to slowly turn the girls' minds around from the person I am being made out to be. Because it was actually Julie's idea to see me after one of the sessions, I delayed the publishing to see if this small bit of hope became something more. I am happy to say that my girls did join me after the next counseling session for an hour. In fact, both girls said they wanted to stay longer and they called their mother and asked if they could spend two more hours with me before going back to her. Near the end of those two hours, they called and asked to spend the night at my parents' with me and the boys. What was most telling of that precious time was how happy the girls were — and I made it a point not to do extravagant things to try and win them over. We simply met at my parents' and talked and laughed, walked through the neighborhood and talked and laughed, and ate a dinner the girls helped my mom prepare — and talked and laughed. Our talks were just chitchat, nothing heavy, and if you didn't know any better, you would have said we were a very happy and emotionally healthy family. During their second visit the next weekend, we had so much fun that I felt worn out from all the practical jokes, horsing around, and gymnastics I tried with the girls and I was quite sore the next day. Their loud laughs and big smiles are genuine, their love and respect obvious

— my girls do love me and I do not fault them for the way they were compelled to behave. When my kids are with just me, with none of the detractors around or involved, they are perfectly happy and free — free to care and love. The challenge will continue to be getting them to act that way when they are anywhere near those negative influences.

The Last Page

To my four children: may you always know how I value our time together and may you always know how much I love you…

Love Always Wins — A Word from Bobbie

These lines are incredibly difficult for me to think of, to know and to write. What is contained in this book has been gut-wrenching to be part of and live through. To know it is real for myself and for people I care so deeply about, is at most times impossible to take in. There is one great tragedy in all of this: it's the reckless programming and endangerment of four young children who are simply fighting to be kids — kids that should be afforded the opportunity to love and appreciate both of their biological parents and have the luxury of MOVING ON from their parents' irreconcilable differences.

After reading Rob's memoire in its entirety, I'd first like to congratulate you; it's not a read for the faint of heart. As such, you might think I have become numb to the severely abnormal — yet 'normal' behavior of a mentally fragmented mother of four kids that I adore. I have been blessed to be part of their lives for more than a year. Still, her careless rages continue to stifle their ability to grow and flourish and, instead of taking in new experiences, they are forced to live in the harsh and arduous past. The mother's actions not only affect, but subject and use children that didn't ask to be part of this — directly putting them in the line of fire and forcing them to choose her side. You may disagree, especially if you haven't seen it with your own eyes, but I believe that blocking your children to do what they are naturally built to do, love their parents — BOTH of their parents — is one of the worst forms of child abuse there is. For now, she continues to get away with this blatant lack of care for the emotional health of her own flesh and blood. It is deeply saddening.

I then think of myself; a woman in her mid-forties who came into the picture just over a year ago. If I'm not equipped to manage these insurmountable painful obstacles and they leave me devastated, time and time again…what is it doing to the children that must live it?

These children, and all children, are not yet equipped with the proper coping mechanisms for this kind of emotional devastation. By nature, those capabilities are to come much later in their adolescence. The sadness is not something you can get past because the children's lives and futures are so precious. While we cannot undo the past, every day is an opportunity to improve their quality of life — each day is a chance to show them love. Rob naturally wants — and needs — a relationship with his children. This is why he relentlessly advocates for them and will never give up on them.

The reality today is that those children are forced, by our court system, to spend the majority of their time with someone who wants them to disown their father. Someone that I initially desired to empathize with, that I strongly encouraged Rob to show compassion to, to reach out to, to try and start over with, to even befriend. After all, we all have broken relationships of some kind. Just because the adults in the relationship can't see eye to eye shouldn't mean the children need to know about, be involved in, or understand those adult differences that cannot be remedied — let alone choose a side. Those children have enough change and transition to work through without feeling they have to choose one parent or the other. The issues that divide couples are rarely about the children, they are about the adults who have made choices in the relationship that they cannot fix. It's a selfish, shameful and disparaging act to use your children to carry out your vengeance, to soothe your own hurt, to spite the other parent, and to compromise them — against someone they naturally love, need and desire to be in relationship with.

Clarity

Being the benefactor in my life of God's grace and knowing that even though it requires significant patience and "letting go," I know that love wins over anger and hate. I continuously made recommendations to Rob about trying to talk with Betty to get her to co-parent in the best interest of their children. Sooner or later, an individual needs compassion — they have to stop hating and embrace what is best for their children. So far, I am completely wrong.

You may recall the day Rob left for work and I was at the house when Betty came by with the kids to get their things. She was ranting about Rob and how abusive he was, saying it is only a matter of time until I get (slapped or hit by) "the hand." I looked at her with wide eyes and said "Betty," and pointed my eyes in the direction of each of the kids, insinuating that it was inappropriate to say what she was saying in front of them. In a subtle way, I suppose, I was trying to get her to stop and just leave. She then said words I never thought I'd hear from any mother: "That's ok, they've heard all of this before, huh Julie? Tell her how dad hit us." Julie just looked at me awkwardly, not knowing what to say and then slightly nodded in agreement with her mother. I looked at the others with blank glazed looks on their faces, almost like this conversation wasn't happening right in front of them. At that moment, I knew nothing was below her and it became painfully obvious that all four kids have been exposed to way more than they ever should have.

Think like me — or else

If you were a child in this situation, how is it that you would survive? If you spent the majority of your time with the vengeful parent, who reminds you at every opportunity how much and why you should hate and ultimately disown the other parent, what would make your life easier? Challenging the vengeful parent, letting them know that you love the other parent and that's all there is to it? Then paying severely for caring, in the form of being ignored, cast out, being told you are never to come back to their house and they never want to see you ever again? As if loving both of your parents after divorce is a sin. Or, would it be easier for a child to make sure the vengeful parent gets what they want so that the majority of your days are smoother, happier and more predictable? Which would you choose? Betty puts them in these extremely unnatural predicaments routinely. Situations that compromise their very existence and confuse them into not knowing how to feel. In the 18 months I have known Rob, I would love nothing more than to tell you that I have seen Betty's loving motherly side — I have yet to witness that.

One of the most attractive qualities I consistently see in Rob, is that of understanding how greatly his kids are already compromised. If Betty is near, they cannot think or speak for themselves, unless it's exactly the way their mother thinks. Nothing less is acceptable on her side, as you have come to read in these pages. Knowing this, Rob does not further complicate the situation for the kids. I can't count the number of times the children have been forced to show their disrespect and disapproval of him. Rob has said, "Christian, it's ok, I know you love me. You don't have to say it." Or "Please do what you'd like to do, but know there's nothing more I want than to spend time with you." He goes so far as to say, "I'd be glad to take you to that party; we'll have a chance to catch up on the way there," or "If you change your mind, I'll be here." He stays strong while he's communicating with them, but make no mistake the pain it causes him. I have seen and felt his brokenness as his children one by one are further alienated from him. While Rob certainly had his part in the problems he and Betty experienced in their marriage – they were just that — MARITAL problems, not their kids' problems. Rob has never once found it appropriate to involved the kids in he and Betty's disagreements and confrontations. He would much sooner remove him-self from the situation to avoid further compromising his kids.

Rob's highest priority will always be his four children, just as my girls are mine. I am confident beyond any words, sooner or later (hopefully sooner) the kids and Rob will have the relationship that was intended from the beginning, because in the end…

…love always wins.

Made in the USA
Columbia, SC
08 September 2017